Community Leadership
in Maryland,
1790–1840

Community Leadership in Maryland, 1790–1840

*A Comparative Analysis
of Power in Society*

by

Whitman H. Ridgway

The University of North Carolina Press
Chapel Hill

Both the initial research and the publication of this work were made possible in part through grants from the National Endowment for the Humanities, a federal agency whose mission is to award grants to support education, scholarship, media programming, libraries, and museums, in order to bring the results of cultural activities to a broad, general public.

© 1979 The University of North Carolina Press

Manufactured in the United States of America

ISBN 0-8078-1355-9

Library of Congress Catalog Card Number 78-23713

Library of Congress Cataloging in Publication Data

Ridgway, Whitman H   1941–
    Community leadership in Maryland, 1790–1840.

    Bibliography: p.
    Includes index.
    1. Community leadership—Maryland—History.
2. Elite (Social sciences)—Maryland—Case studies.
3. Power (Social sciences) I. Title.
HN79.M3R5   301.5'92   78-23713
ISBN 0-8078-1355-9

For Sean and Siobhan

Contents

Tables

Illustrations

Acknowledgments

It is a pleasure to acknowledge the many people whose assistance contributed to the preparation of this book. Were it not for the stimulation from mentors, cooperation and direction from manuscript librarians and their staffs, challenges and insights from fellow researchers, monetary support, and generous assistance from friends who shared their time and skills to rectify my more egregious errors, this book would have fewer virtues and far greater flaws. I, of course, assume the responsibility for any remaining errors.

This project was conceived during my graduate training at the University of Pennsylvania, where I was privileged to study under Lee Benson. Anyone who knows his work will recognize the impact it has had on my own, just as they will discern the differences. Professor Benson was a constant source of help as this book progressed from one stage to another. Two other scholars at Penn, Murray G. Murphey and the late John L. Shover, deepened my appreciation for social science history.

The staffs of several repositories were especially helpful during the research phase. My thanks go to the many people who assisted me at the Maryland Hall of Records, the Maryland Historical Society, the Maryland Room in the University of Maryland's McKeldin Library, the National Archives, and the Manuscript Room of the Library of Congress.

One of the joys of research is finding other people who share an interest in some facet of your topic. I learned a great deal from conversations with David A. Bohmer, Lois Green Carr, Richard Cox, and Bayly E. Marks, all of whom generously shared their research, insights, and writings with me.

A more traumatic joy is the criticism one actually solicits when writing and rewriting a manuscript. Although he begged not to be remembered, the best critic was my colleague, Ronald Hoffman. Paul Kleppner, Richard Jensen, and the many people associated with the Newberry Library's Family and Community History Center challenged me to refine my ideas. Another friend and colleague, Keith Olson, took time from his own work to improve my prose; Sharon Fettus caught most of my idiosyncratic spellings; and Malcolm L. Call exuded the assurance as only an editor can that somehow this manuscript would become a book.

Money, support, and unobligated time are very important commodities for the success of any project. The University of Maryland's Graduate Research Board, Computer Science Center, and Department of History provided unstinting support in many different ways. Special mention ought to go to the History Department's secretarial staff, who typed and retyped drafts with a high level of professionalism. I was also the recipient of a summer stipend and a book subsidy award from the National Endowment for the Humanities. In addition, the Family and Community History Center and the Newberry Library awarded me fellowships at a critical moment in my career. As if a Chicago winter were not inducement enough to stay indoors and write, the Newberry Library provided a stimulating environment within which to spend a creative semester.   •

I have discussed the general themes of this work in several articles appearing in the following publications: "McCulloch vs. the Jacksonians: Patronage and Politics in Maryland," *Maryland Historical Magazine* 70 (Winter 1975): 350–62; "Community Leadership: Baltimore during the First and Second Party Systems," ibid., 71 (Fall 1976): 334–48; and "The Search for Power: Community Leadership in the Jacksonian Era," pages 297–317 in *Law, Society, and Politics in Early Maryland*, eds. Aubrey C. Land, Lois G. Carr, and Edward C. Papenfuse (Baltimore: Johns Hopkins Press, 1977). The copyright holders have graciously allowed me to use material from these articles.

Introduction

Generations of historians fascinated by the evolution of American democracy have generally viewed the important period between the Revolution and the eve of the Civil War from a national perspective. Their interpretations describe the formal government structure, dominant personalities, and events interacting over this period, as well as the subtle mutations associated with the expansion of the franchise or the development of competitive party politics.[1] This literature, however, reveals little of how a democratic society was actually governed. The prevailing national perspective is not, in fact, the most appropriate one from which to analyze this question. Rather than work from the assumption that national events defined local patterns, a more fruitful approach is to determine the structure of democratic leadership on the community level and then to perceive the ways it changed over time, if at all, in response to external pressures.

Before addressing the critical question of leadership, it is necessary to clarify two primary concepts, democracy and egalitarianism, used by historians writing about this period. Democracy refers to a political system, defined by an authoritative legal structure, with broad popular participation and relatively unrestrictive recruitment to formal government offices. Some historians have argued that a measure of American democracy was the relative openness of popular participation levels or recruitment patterns to formal officeholding. Egalitarianism refers to a situation in which barriers inhibiting equal social and economic opportunity were minimal, serving to reduce artificial restraints upon an individual's capacity for self-realization. Historians would argue that such a society was more or less egalitarian in terms of basic inequalities, whether social, legal, or epitomized by an unequal distribution of wealth. Although they have been used as if they were interchangeable, democracy and egalitarianism are not synonymous terms.

Even if democracy and egalitarianism are given distinct meanings, the relationship between an egalitarian society and the distribution of power in a democracy is not well understood. Part of the problem is again conceptual. Intrigued by the rise and fall of party systems and political leaders, historians emphasize the implicit political egalitarianism associated with an expanding franchise, but they generally ignore the difficult question of power itself. The basic paradox inherent in an egalitarian democratic society is nicely stated by Robert A. Dahl: "But if . . . there are great inequalities in the conditions of different citizens, must there not also be great inequalities in the capacities of different citizens to influence the decisions of their various governments? And if, because they are unequal in other conditions, citizens of a democracy are unequal to control their government, then who in fact does govern? How does a "democratic" system work amid inequality of resources?"[2] The question is more easily asked than answered. The difficulty is compounded by a lack of consensus among researchers as to how to conceptualize and solve this problem. Democracy obviously functions as a political system, but how do we structure a systematic approach to the study of power in society for use in a historical context?

The literature developed by contemporary social scientists investigating community power offers several methods for historians to consider. The advantages and disadvantages of these methods are studied in detail in Appendix I. I have adopted the decisional approach, developed by Robert A. Dahl, to study community decision making in a historical context. This method ascribes leadership from an individual's direct participation in decisional situations and then evaluates the quality of democracy by assessing the kinds of people who governed the community. I have gone beyond the original decisional framework in order to evaluate the distribution of power within a community by introducing the concept of strategic elites.[3] I have identified strategic elites in an effort to isolate groups of individuals with a potential power resource, such as great wealth or political position, who have a vested interest in community affairs. A comparison of the overlap between membership in such strategic elites and those who actually made community decisions helps to clarify the distribution of community power.

This study is comparative in place and time so as to maximize the insight it gives into decision making and to reveal the interaction between egalitarianism and democracy. To reduce the risk of systemic variation, I have not selected communities for study randomly, but have purposefully chosen them from a single political culture. The larger political culture is that of one state, Maryland, whose constitution and traditions defined the structure of government and political participation within its boundaries. The four communities selected for comparative analysis are Baltimore City, Frederick, St. Marys, and Talbot counties.

Each of these communities, for which excellent local records survive, provides an example of Maryland's underlying social, economic, and regional variety. Baltimore City was a dynamic urban and commercial oasis in a predominantly agricultural state. St. Marys and Talbot counties were agricultural areas dependent on nonwhite labor. St. Marys County, at the tip of southern Maryland, produced tobacco and became increasingly dependent upon a slave labor force. Talbot County, on Maryland's Eastern Shore, abandoned the cultivation of tobacco for grain before the Revolution and utilized a mixed labor force of slaves and free blacks. Frederick County, on the far reaches of the Chesapeake Bay's Western Shore, epitomized a much more heterogeneous rural area. Settled by diverse social groups, including large numbers of Germans, it produced a wide variety of agricultural goods with a minimal reliance on the slave labor system or its remnants. In addition to comparing decision making in four representative community contexts, this process is examined at two chronological periods—the first and second party eras—to investigate the ways patterns of community leadership may have changed over time.

The major conclusions of this study may be briefly summarized. During the first party era, traditional rural communities were led by groups of wealthy and socially interconnected men who constituted an oligarchy. Despite the generally acknowledged shift in political emphasis from the elite to the voter that occurred between the first and second party eras, members of an oligarchy continued to monopolize positions of community leadership in the second party period in these traditional communities. The iron grip of oligarchical control was relaxed in more heterogeneous communities. In these rural areas, characterized by greater ethnic and economic diversity, different groups competed with the oligarchy for community control. Divisions along urban-rural, ethnic, or property-holding lines undermined any one group's ability to predominate in either time period. In this context, symbols of association, such as ethnicity or ruralness, or a leader's capacity to use the evolving political structures to advantage, created alternative power bases from which new leaders challenged the oligarchy's traditional decision-making role. Different community leadership patterns existed in a nontraditional, rapidly modernizing urban environment. To a greater degree than might be anticipated, a cosmopolitan oligarchy dominated urban decision making in the first party era. By the second party period, however, the remnants of this oligarchy shared power with leaders representing the diversity of the community.

This comparative community analysis demonstrates the contextual significance of party development. Parties have long been defined as if they were extensions of monolithic national or state organizations. Party activity and development, however, are far more subtle and varied when viewed from the community level. In the traditional rural communities, for instance, first-family rivalries monopolized and absorbed major leadership positions in each of the two parties in both periods. In the urban context, the relative disorganization of parties in the first party era facilitated domination by members of the oligarchy; leadership in the second party era slipped from their grasp and into the hands of non-traditional leaders, who served in various authoritative capacities as the parties became institutionalized. This transformation is all the more significant because first party leaders were the primary organizers in the embryonic years of the second party era. Furthermore, important and persisting intraparty competitions affected each party in both periods.

Similarly, a comparison of community decision makers and members of potentially powerful strategic elites leads to a better understanding of the relative distribution of community power. Strategic elites were defined as groups of men sharing a potentially powerful community resource—such as occupying formal government positions, being among the community's most wealthy citizens, or directing local financial institutions. If members in the decisional and strategic elites were drawn from the same socioeconomic pool, then the distribution of power would be highly centralized. If, on the other hand, decisional and strategic elite members were recruited from different pools, then the dynamics of community leadership would be quite different. Oligarchical norms dominated overall elite recruitment in traditional communities during both the first and second party eras. In modernizing and transitional environments, there was far greater elite specialization, which enabled membership in the positional and decisional elites to serve as the vehicle for assimilation into the local leadership structure for individuals who lacked the advantages of wealth or extensive kinship associations.

This comprehensive evaluation of community leadership is important for several reasons. First, it focuses on the area of political life that has long been recognized by social scientists as the primary arena for the analysis of social, cultural, economic, and political rivalries. Drawing on modern community power literature, this study also attempts to analyze the significance and biases inherent in various approaches to the study of community power and to select the one that is most appropriate for identifying who wielded power. Furthermore, my findings suggest that community decision making was far more susceptible to local conditions than the political ramifications of egalitarianism might imply. Despite a widening political base associated with the expansion of the franchise, leaders were recruited primarily from traditional social groups. This pattern, of course, varied with the type of community being considered. In communities undergoing minimal economic or social change, leadership adhered to traditional norms; in those undergoing change, new leaders emerged from the complexity of the larger community, a trend that also indicated a general specialization of leadership. It is important, however, to stress that even in the most modern community, traditional leadership groups competed for community leadership positions and thus continued to participate in community decision making.

Community Leadership
in Maryland,
1790–1840

1

Whose Right to Rule?

An Unresolved Legacy of the Revolution

The era of the Revolution was a time of instability in Maryland. Writing in 1775, the colony's last proprietary governor described the social and political impact of the evolving crisis: "All power is getting fast into the hands of the very lowest people. Those who first encouraged the opposition to government and set these on this licentious behavior will probably be amongs't the first to repent thereof."[1] The lower classes did not gain power, however. Instead, an oligarchy, composed of men of wealth and social standing linked by an extensive kinship network, captured Maryland's government during the revolutionary years and institutionalized itself as the governing class. The lower classes, meanwhile, continued to demand a larger share of political power. This demand, and the efforts of the elite to frustrate it, characterized politics during the revolutionary era and the six decades that followed.

Stress and Continuity: The Revolutionary Settlement

In colonial Maryland, discontent with British authority emanated from two sources: dissatisfaction with government policies under the proprietary system and opposition to parliamentary abuses beginning with the Stamp Act Crisis.[2] Empowered with virtually unrestricted authority by the Charter of 1632, the proprietor vested his power in a governor and various agents who ruled in his absence. In the mid-eighteenth century, colonists appealed in vain to the king for redress from proprietary policies, claiming traditional rights of Englishmen in matters of government and taxation. Because the king was unwilling to interfere and the charter precluded parliamentary involvement, dissatisfaction and opposition surfaced in the lower house of Maryland's General Assembly. Antiproprietary leaders, such as the Carrolls and Dulanys, sought to restrict proprietary privilege and disputed policies regarding taxation, specie, and tobacco; in response, the governor used his powers of patronage and preference to protect the proprietor's interests. Beginning

3

in the 1750s, legislative politics divided the elite into court and country factions. Leaders on both sides of this political debate, however, came from the same social group: men with strong British cultural roots, affiliations primarily with the Anglican church, and membership in the landed slaveholding elite.

The Stamp Act Crisis of 1765 initiated a series of crises that pushed what had been only an upper-class dispute into a broader arena and mobilized a new set of leaders in Maryland. Angered by parliamentary policies, the urban merchants, artisans, and other elements of the population that had not participated openly in the proprietary controversies entered politics to show their support of other colonies against British abuses. When colonial control was challenged in Massachusetts, they formed extralegal associations, such as the Sons of Liberty and Committees of Observation, that grew in importance during the next decade as alternative governing institutions. Despite these developments, large segments of the population did not support the drift toward independence, either remaining apolitical or becoming Tories.

Confronted by a disintegrating political situation, the Patriot elite sought to consolidate their power in the mid-1770s. This faction consisted of a combination of old antiproprietary leaders, former proprietary supporters who had become dissatisfied with the old order, and merchants and others who opposed either parliament's commercial policies or its actions in other colonies. A desire to gain political power and to prevent what began as a political dispute from becoming a social revolution united the Patriot elite. Their policy of authoritative control and the containment of dissent faced a challenge on three fronts: the British, local residents who either were indifferent or covertly opposed to the new government, and the citizens who demanded more radical government changes than the elite would allow.

In 1776, the elite recognized the extent and depth of opposition and made important gestures of apparent concession when they adopted a constitution.[3] They mollified the citizen-soldier to a degree by allowing militia companies to elect their junior officers while the governor continued to appoint senior officers.[4] Voting continued to be limited by freehold and property qualifications, but inflation made a mockery of these limitations during the war. Germans and Catholics were enfranchised under the new constitution, defusing another source of discontent. Although more men may have been able to participate in elections, officeholding was unambiguously restricted to the more affluent through a series of escalating property and personal qualifications. The constitution also adopted a system of direct and indirect election procedures that minimized the impact of the mass electorate. Most men could vote for the annually elected lower house. Fewer men were qualified to vote for the senatorial electors, who were selected every five years to meet as a college to choose a senate. A joint vote of the combined legislature annually elected the governor and a five-member Executive Council. The governor and the council annually appointed all important county officers except the sheriff, who was popularly elected every three years. Voters actually elected only members of the lower house and the sheriff; all other public officers were either elected indirectly or appointed.

Popular participation in government was further limited by the strong sense of localism permeating the Constitution of 1776. The basic unit of representation was the county, not the voter. Each county elected four representatives to the lower house; the cities of Annapolis and Baltimore, despite their unequal size, were each allowed two representatives. Thus, the smallest county was on a parity with the largest, and population change had no effect on representation. The senate consisted of fifteen members, nine from the Western Shore and six from the Eastern Shore, elected on an at-large basis. Each shore had its own state treasurer and meeting of the General Court.

With the adoption of the Maryland Constitution of 1776, the elite legitimized their control of the government. Through stipulations restricting officeholding to men like themselves and by adopting the public viva voce system of voting, which served to intimidate an overly independent voter, they created a system of government that provided large property holders with cumulative advantages. Members of first families, some of whom had served in the proprietary government in the 1770s, filled positions of authority in the new government. This oligarchy of wealth and social standing captured Maryland's government and institutionalized itself as the governing class. Its power lasted far beyond the revolutionary era.

The adoption of the conservative Constitution of 1776 was only a partial victory for the elite; the real test lay in their attempt to expand their authority over a divided and discontented society. They gradually won the allegiance of much of Maryland's population by enacting liberal currency laws and by exerting their political authority with restraint. The liberal currency laws, which allowed debtors to pay specie debts with depreciated paper money and permitted speculators to purchase confiscated property on generous terms, caused consternation and some despair among the elite's more conservative members, but many recognized that a partial loss of property was a small but necessary price to pay for continued political control. The new government also followed an enlightened policy of exercising only nominal authority in disaffected areas where realistically it had no power to enforce greater compliance.

As the British threat diminished, it was able to extend its control of these areas. In the face of wartime passions, policies of caution, concession, restraint, and accommodation encouraged the reassimilation of Tories and nonassociators and ultimately facilitated the reintroduction of government rule.[5]

At the end of the Revolution, the structure of authority in Maryland was in many ways similar to the colonial political system. The proprietor, his agents, and their favorites had been successfully displaced, and much of their property was in the hands of Patriot speculators. But the system had withstood the egalitarian impulses of the Revolution, and the basis for political recruitment and influence remained landed or commercial wealth. The elite, many of whom had resisted or fallen out with the proprietary government before the Revolution, possessed the mandate to rule in the 1780s.

Period of Consolidation

Maryland's revolutionary elite consolidated their power in the years following the Peace of Paris. As a theoretical justification of their control of a nominally republican society, the elite idealized a hierarchical, deferential society. On a practical level, confronted by a socially and economically segmented society that was disorganized politically, they solidified their power through control of the political processes.

The organic society, organized along hierarchical and deferential lines, was glorified in the new nation in the immediate postrevolutionary years. Its components were suggested by Judge Robert Goldsborough's charge to the Grand Jury in 1784: "It is incumbent, by Precept and Example, to instil into the Minds of your Fellow Citizens, a sacred regard for Religion and Piety, Love to our Country, and an inviolable attachment to her Liberty and Laws."[6] To Maryland's revolutionary elite, society formed an organic whole, stratified into a natural hierarchical order, unified by a common value system predicated on an attachment to religion and law, unrent by the spirit of faction, and led from above.[7] Proponents of this consensus ideal became the nucleus of the Federalist party as it emerged in the late 1780s.

The consolidation of power into the hands of the elite was encouraged by Maryland's political system, which favored the monopolization of power by political organizers. Such men tended to define their responsibilities from the perspective of the elite rather than in terms of demands from the diverse elements within the society. As they had for decades before, wealthy and socially prominent men were able to dominate political recruitment because of their central position in community affairs.

The recruitment of public leaders was a significant component of what might be characterized as a cadre political system. Traditionally, prospective candidates, many of whom belonged to the oligarchy or enjoyed its patronage, would solicit support from members of the elite before deciding to enter the canvass.[8] Others were not prevented from taking the field, but the promise of elite support during the election was a distinct advantage. As there was no autonomous agency to make authoritative nominations, aspirants to public office, or their friends, usually published notices in newspapers announcing their candidacy. These announcements emphasized the worth of the individual, his integrity, and his public standing, but rarely specified a particular program. Formal nominations by groups were the exception rather than the rule in these years.

Close to election time, candidates devoted more of their attention to the electorate. They addressed potential voters wherever possible—at militia musters, religious meetings, or civic events—and they often supplied food and liquor for popular enjoyment at the hustings or on polling days.[9] In 1800, Fisher Ames, a New England Federalist, described the special relationship between the oligarchy and the people:

> The character of Maryland is affected by the habits of slave owners. ... The distinction between the rich and poor is too marked not to be felt by both classes. It has been an ancient usage of the aristocrats to pay respect to the sovereign people, by obsequious attentions whenever their suffrages have been requested. The candidates, on both sides, are now travelling through their districts, soliciting the favour of individuals with whom they will associate on no other occasion, and men of the first consideration condescend to collect dissolute and ignorant mobs of hundreds of individuals, to whom they make long speeches in the open air. You are a judge of the eloquence of the bar, and have heard that of the pulpit. That of election meetings allows a wider range for the exercise of genius, it being permitted to affirm anything which will advance the interest of the orator, in any manner likely to impress the imagination of the audience.[10]

The viva voce voting system also promoted elite influence. Citizens voted aloud at a central voting place, in full view of all interested persons.[11] The abuses inherent in this system were suggested by an observer: "There are a few rich federalists here who have tenants and over these they exercise a more despotic sway than ever a Barbary Bashaw could preserve over his piratical subjects."[12] Because voters from the outlying areas had to travel long distances to reach the polling place, elections frequently lasted several days, with the result that political activists scoured their districts to stimulate increased voter participation when an election result was in question.[13]

Political divisions were based on temporary or regional alliances within the elite, and they never challenged the notion of organic political unity. Factionalism was consistent with a political system characterized by an amorphous and often indifferent electorate, the absence of formal party organizational structures, and the preponderance of local cliques of political leaders. During this period, after the Revolution but before the late 1790s when politics polarized into more formal party structures, two major issues dominated political activity. The first, sometimes mistakenly interpreted as a continuation of the debtor-creditor discord of the 1770s and 1780s, revolved around the adoption of the federal Constitution.[14] The second factional division, between the "Potowmack" and the Chesapeake interests, involved competition between two geographical regions, each vying for dominance in the state legislature to protect or advance its economic position. Adherents of the "Potowmack" faction, drawn from the small counties in southern Maryland and on the Eastern Shore, wanted to preserve their status by containing the growing power and influence of Baltimore and the more populous counties and to ensure their own future economic viability by supporting the development of the federal city and a canal on the Potomac River. Members of the Chesapeake faction endorsed the growth of Baltimore. Their plans centered on the improvement of the Susquehanna River to route the rich western Maryland and Pennsylvania wheat trade through Baltimore. They also believed that political representation should be tied to patterns of population growth and not defined by county units. Improvement of the Potomac River, they thought, would reduce Baltimore's prosperity by diverting trade to its commercial rivals: Georgetown, the proposed federal city, or Alexandria, Virginia.[15]

The existence of faction did not preclude general acceptance of a single-party political system as it evolved during the presidency of George Washington.[16] The majesty and nonpartisanship of Washington epitomized consensus to Maryland's elite. As the rejuvenated national government began to function and the economic and political strains of the early 1780s subsided, Maryland's Federalist party emerged as the embodiment of order and prosperity. Not surprisingly, many members of the oligarchy were early and devoted party leaders, and outspoken Anti-Federalists such as Samuel Chase became Federalists. The party was further strengthened by judicious appointments to the new state-level federal offices.[17] Thus, with no effective challenge to the existing political system, the oligarchy consolidated its rule through the institutions created by the Constitution of 1776. The new Federalist party, founded on the principles of the rights and obligations of property and reinforced by a strong religious consciousness, easily secured the allegiance of the elite. Not since the early years of the Revolution had there been such political unanimity as existed during Washington's early presidential years.

Fall from Grace: The Erosion of the Revolutionary Ideal

Political unanimity proved short-lived. Divisions caused by national fiscal and foreign policies in the 1790s polarized members of the cabinet and Congress and overflowed into state politics. Maryland's oligarchy was disturbed by the growing spirit of faction that seemed to jeopardize their ideal of an ordered society, unified by a common ethical purpose and led from above by a harmonious elite. Their sense of foreboding was epitomized in a private prayer offered by Reverend Joseph Jackson in 1796: "The present seems, happily in the general Persuasion, to be a critical moment in the United States. May He who guides the Planets in their Orbits, be pleased still to direct the common Interests of this our happy Nation calmly and evenly, without the Jarring of *discordant Parts*, along the Path of Time! May the cause, the immediate and natural cause, of Harmony and Good to us, be as perceptible and grateful (if possible) to Federal America, as it has been."[18] Although some conservatives ascribed the fall from grace to the forces of the French Revolution, much of the turmoil surfacing in Maryland in the 1790s resulted from the attempt to impose a static mold on a pluralistic and changing society.

The apparently innocuous issue of religion illustrated this problem. Despite a general unwillingness to reinvest the Anglican church as the formally established church at the time of Maryland's Constitutional Convention, mainly because of its recent history of religious abuses, Article 33 of the Declaration of Rights nonetheless pledged state support for religion.[19] This pledge went unredeemed during the war, but for several decades following the peace the question of proper church-state relations disturbed the political consensus. At issue was Reverend William Smith's effort to enlist the aid of the state to build the Episcopal church from the shattered remnants of its Anglican parent. Aided by Samuel Chase, an influential member of the Maryland House of Delegates and an Anglican minister's son, Smith sought to reestablish the special relationship that existed between his church and the state in colonial times and to expand public support for various colleges that educated the children of the elite.[20]

These repeated efforts to create a favored status for the Episcopal church opened fissures of dissent within the ranks of the elite. The most articulate opposition came from the Reverend Patrick Allison, minister of Baltimore's First Presbyterian Church. Writing as "Vindex," Allison questioned the integrity of any established church and the presumption that one faith deserved special treatment.[21] Other elite church leaders, as well as Episcopalians who recalled the earlier abuses associated with the colonial church, adhered to a generalized belief in a religious society but opposed Smith's plans. One reason for the repeated efforts to rejuvenate the Episcopal church was its inability to attract communicants in the postwar period. The church lost members both because of its association with the British cause and because of popular enthusiasm for the new Methodist movement.

Proponents of the organic social ideal considered Methodism a dangerous and pernicious movement. Its evangelical emphasis on personal religious experience, its reliance on an enthusiastic but generally unlettered clergy, and its implied threat to more structured and hierarchical churches were perceived as encouragement to the popular licentiousness that had been effectively contained by existing institutions. The Methodist Episcopal church was not only a threat in itself, but its practices and beliefs were being introduced into Episcopal services by overzealous younger clergy to the chagrin of church leaders.[22] Accompanying the phenomenal growth of Methodism was the more gradual expansion of ethnic faiths in western Maryland.[23] Minority religious leaders demanded recognition of their right to exist and opposed enforced religious conformity through the reestablishment of the Episcopal church.

The gravest danger to the continued health of the conservatives' ideal state was the social chaos and disorganization embodied in the French Revolution. "Regenerated France," exclaimed one conservative Episcopalian, "Pandemonium itself does not contain more fiends, than are now gnawing at the vitals of that unhappy Country."[24] Despite their humane sympathy for the victims of the French Revolution and the succession of European wars, conservatives feared that consensus was being fractured by Jacobinism. Writing at the time of the hotly contested 1800 election, which eventually turned the helm of state over to the Republican party, Charles Carroll of Carrollton observed somberly: "If our country should continue to be the sport of parties, if the mass of the People should be exasperated & roused to pillage the more wealthy, social order will be subverted, anarchy will follow, succeeded by Despotism: these changes have, in that order of succession, taken place in France."[25]

The course of the French Revolution demonstrated to conservatives the excesses of uncontrolled democracy. A people unrestrained by religion or misdirected by worldly philosophers could be excited by any demagogue to the extremes of licentious behaviour.[26] A society without viable political institutions or one where unprincipled men wielded power would assuredly be reduced to anarchy, chaos, and despotism. To some, the spread of Methodism represented nothing less than the contamination of American religion by Jacobin principles.[27] To most, the polarization of national politics into a two-party competition represented the first step in the debasement of the revolutionary settlement.

Conservatives commonly held two men responsible for this degeneration—Thomas Jefferson and Thomas Paine. Jefferson was seen as a misguided philosopher, whose passion for ideas blinded him to the reality of men's baser motivations and whose greatest fault was his inability to control the rivalries and ambitions of his followers.[28] Paine, author of the revolutionary pamphlet *Common Sense* and a member of the French Assembly, was perceived as an unprincipled demagogue who attacked social institutions solely for the pleasure of their destruction and whose religious tirades were a dangerous omen for future events.[29]

In this context of suspicion and fear, Maryland politics, reflecting national divisions, polarized in the mid-1790s. A party coalesced in opposition to the administration's foreign policy, epitomized by the Jay Treaty, and in support of the positions identified with Thomas Jefferson. Known as the Democratic Republicans, the new party was led by former Federalists who advocated a more balanced foreign policy and supported the diverse roots of a pluralist society. The Federalist party, whose leaders saw themselves as the embodiment of a nonpartisan consensus ideal, attacked its opponents as a faction produced by French influence. Federalists viewed advocacy of the Jeffersonian position as an open repudiation of the American revolutionary experiment.

The Federalists' crisis mentality was indicated by their willingness to alter Maryland's electoral procedures and thereby to debase their venerated constitution in an effort to prevent Jefferson's election to the presidency in 1800. Dubbed "Legislative Choice" by its author, Robert Goodloe Harper, the proposal called for the state legislature to change the electoral law, withdrawing the selection of presidential electors from the citizens and reassigning it to the legislature. Maryland's entire electoral strength would thus be thrown behind the Federalist ticket. Party leaders justified the tactic on the grounds that it had been done earlier for political advantage in Virginia and Massachusetts.[30] Writing for the public prints as "Civis" and "Bystander," Harper tried to rally public support for this project.[31]

Harper's sanguine hopes failed for several reasons. The Republicans successfully characterized "Legislative Choice" as a political machination. According to one correspondent, "It is now ascertained that there is in this state a junto of men, who are assiduously meditating the plan of taking from the people the privilege of voting for the election of the President and Vice-President."[32] Once that privilege was abridged, the Republicans predicted that the people would have little influence in their government.[33] Fisher Ames made a more trenchant observation: "The attempt to change the mode of election has therefore created great sensibility . . . it will increase the virulence of party spirit, and finally injure the federal interest in this state."[34] Thus, by threatening to deprive the citizen of his vote, Federalists unintentionally mobilized large numbers of otherwise disinterested citizens into the ranks of the opposition party.

Maryland's Federalist party was further damaged during the election of 1800, when its leadership divided. One group, which disapproved of tampering with government institutions for momentary electoral expediency, ceased to function as leaders.[35] Others were immobilized by their lukewarm support for John Adams.[36] Some favored Alexander Hamilton's thinly veiled plan to replace Adams at the head of the ticket with Charles C. Pinckney, the party's nominal vice-presidential candidate. Unwilling actively to solicit voter support for Adams and equally unenthusiastic about Hamilton's deviousness and Pinckney's candidacy, many Federalist leaders did not bestir themselves for the October election.[37] The result created conflict among Federalists and undermined unanimity within the remnants of the conservative revolutionary elite.

Maryland Republicans exulted in their victory: "The expulsion of Key, of Carroll, of Ridgely, the Thomas's with the whole mass of *fungus*, that too long has corroded our state Legislature, is such a happy omen of the total purification of the body politic of this state from the leprosy of aristocracy, as to give the best hopes that the real sentiments of a large majority of the people of Maryland will never again be the mere play things, the punchinelloes of a set of designing and awkward state jugglers."[38] Federalist James McHenry soon made a more prudent prediction: "Public men, you will observe, are changed and changing. Whether there will be a *total* revolution in measures also, time must discover."[39]

The Past as Prologue:
The Uncertain Future of Party Politics

Permanent parties evolved slowly in Maryland. During the first party era, roughly between the mid-1790s and the War of 1812, competition between Federalists and Republicans was aggressive and vocal.

Yet, serious fissures beneath the veneer of partisan rhetoric and organizational activity precluded the development of a strong party system. Federalists adopted a strategy of selective nonopposition after 1800 in an effort to induce disunity and lethargy among their opponents. Republicans were constantly divided by competition among leaders. The War of 1812 served as the death knell for the national Federalist party, although Maryland Federalists competed for several more years. The demise of two-party competition weakened the Republicans as well, so that by the early 1820s, the Maryland Republicans were a party in name only. The emergence of a strong, persisting party system would have to await the presidency of Andrew Jackson and the political events of the 1830s.[40]

Many important political developments occurred during the first party era. Leaders of both parties sought to mobilize the electorate through a combination of innovative and traditional electoral devices. Besides establishing party presses to disseminate information, each party continued to rely on militia musters, civic societies, and religious meetings as primary organizational vehicles and as opportunities to address large bodies of potential voters. The Federalists continued to preach the virtues of their idealized society, while the Republicans based their appeal on the strengths of a diversified, complex society and the need for new leadership.

The question of political control provided a key to understanding the significance of the first party era. The Federalists, as before, centralized power in small groups of leaders, who often worked in caucuses to reach important community decisions. Despite internal division over the adoption of Republican electoral techniques, the Federalists never wavered from their public view that an elite should govern the society in the interests of the whole. Republicans utilized the convention nomination system and projected a pluralist democratic image, but close examination reveals that the party recruited prominent men as leaders. Notwithstanding differences in attitudes toward voters, both parties were dominated by men of wealth and social standing, whose goal was to consolidate their control of the political system.

Despite their popular appeal and relative sophistication and successes in several counties, Maryland's early parties failed to evolve into a strong voter-based system. The techniques of a voter-based system were introduced in these years—the acceptance of the concept of dynamic party identification and the creation of party presses and conventions—but the elite still heavily influenced all these developments. Popularly based leaders broke some barriers, but not enough to alter significantly the prevailing system of oligarchical dominance. Nonetheless, Federalist jurist Samuel Chase complained in 1803: "Men without *sense* and without *property* are to be our rulers. There can be no union between the heads of the two parties. Confidence is destroyed."[41] Chase's immediate fears were premature, for the new leaders were much the same as the old, but by the middle of the first party era the Federalists' consensus ideal was clearly inappropriate to contain the diverse demands made by Maryland's population.

The transfer of power from one party to the other resulted in several new policy orientations. Once in power, the Republicans, with help from moderate Federalists, attacked the more vulnerable vestiges of the conservative ideal state. The question of state support for religion and public education was laid to rest, the court system was modernized, and the voting base was expanded by eliminating the freehold requirement and by replacing the viva voce system with a ballot.[42] They were unable to modify the nonpopular representation base for the state legislature, nor could they make inroads toward liberalizing the extensive system of indirect elections embodied in the Constitution of 1776. Although revolutionary conservatives might despair for the future of society under a Republican government, their institutional structure remained remarkably intact throughout the period of Republican ascendancy.

The intrusion of national political issues into Maryland politics after 1807 stimulated a Federalist resurgence and undermined Republican hegemony.[43] Responding to popular dissatisfaction with the Embargo, problems with West Indian trade, and the recurring threat of war with Great Britain, Federalists sought to recapture the seats of power. Some new leaders emulated Republican electoral techniques, notably through the creation of the Washington Benevolent Society, as the party unabashedly courted voters. They appeared to be on the threshold of transformation into a mirror image of the Republican party as war broke out.

Despite the heroic defense of Baltimore and Fort McHenry, the war years illuminated the atavistic characteristics of Maryland's first party system. Federalist leadership, already strained by conflicts between old and new leaders over questions of party organization and responsibility, split into hostile factions over which side to support in the war. This division, reflected to a lesser extent by the estrangement between Maryland Republican leaders and the national administration over matters of public policy and defense, encouraged political leaders to adhere to traditional elitist party norms. Voters might be courted by modern electoral techniques, but members of the traditional leadership class successfully perpetuated their right to make policy decisions.

The first party system did not long survive the conclusion of the War of 1812. Maryland Federalists enjoyed a more enduring popular appeal than their partisan brethren did in other states, achieving some notable political successes, but they withered as a political force after 1815.[44] Ironically, the demise of the Federalist party hurt the Republican party grievously. Without the unifying effect of an opposition, Republicans splintered into factions in disagreement over state and national policy. Party labels began to disappear in the early 1820s, self-nomination reappeared, and, after the failure of congressional Republicans to unite behind one presidential candidate in 1823, a politician observed somberly, "I think this is an end of Caucusing in this State, consequently, a death-blow to the Democratic Party."[45] An absence of parties characterized Maryland politics until the presidential contests of 1824 and 1828 reinvigorated partisanship once again. Former Republican and Federalist leaders, realigning into what would have been heretical associations a few years earlier, sought to regain power and influence through boosting the candidacy of the various presidential contenders.

The second party system, which evolved during the decade between 1824 and the formation of the Whig party in 1834, had several significant components.[46] Politicians from the first party era, searching for new bases of political support, tried to recapture positions of leadership by creating new party organizations geared to mobilize a somnolent electorate.[47] One group of Republicans, characterizing themselves the administration party because they held the statehouse and supported John Quincy Adams's presidential aspirations, claimed for themselves the legitimacy of the old party heritage and favored the traditional antiparty consensus ideal articulated earlier by the Federalists and repeated in the early 1820s by a Republican president, James Monroe.[48] But others, disaffected Republicans who broke with those in power or Federalists who found themselves without a viable party, sought to ride presidential coattails into federal and state offices.[49] The role of former first party leaders in the evolution of the second party system has not been generally recognized.

A second component of the new political system was the importance of organizations. Politicians in both parties increasingly recognized and paid deference to the strength of formal nominations.[50] As the individual was subsumed to the political collectivity, party label replaced individual integrity as a basis for voter appeal, party organization was transformed into a regularized democratic procedure, and emerging leaders based their claims for preference on party service. Because the old and new leaders derived their positions from distinctly different sources, internecine competition plagued the evolving Jackson party for most of Andrew Jackson's two terms in office.[51]

The second party system, in contrast to the first, evolved with a primary emphasis on the voter and resulted in a broadening of the base from which leaders were recruited. Political leaders from the former party era played a significant role in reintroducing regularized party competition in the 1820s, but as the institutional innovations were refined and regularized, popularly based leaders challenged elite domination of the political system. In actuality, the oligarchy was not displaced as a leadership pool, but as the second party system matured, it was forced to share power with new men representing different social groups.

Undercurrents for Change: The Ecological Forces

Changes in the distribution of Maryland's population and its productive base strained the institutional structure created by the state constitution in 1776. Besides its conservative bias in favor of property holders, the constitution reflected two other fundamental principles: the county was designed as the primary political unit, and there was to be a regional political balance between the Eastern and the Western Shores. These principles were inconsistent with republican theory and ecological reality. Shifts in the distribution of population, changes in the emphasis of economic production and the type of labor required, and the relative concentration of wealth had major influences on the evolving political system. Between the Revolution and the Civil War, Maryland's population expanded primarily in its western and northern sections, with a heavy concentration in Baltimore City. In response to repeated demands that representation reflect population, constitutional purists, many of whom were from small counties losing population, adhered doggedly to the old system. Similarly, despite Maryland's geographical division by the Chesapeake Bay into Western and Eastern Shores, there were essentially four regions in the state. Distinguished economically and socially, each region fostered the development of an indigenous political culture.

The four regions were the Eastern Shore, southern Maryland, western Maryland, and Baltimore City.[52] Populated predominantly by British stock, the Eastern Shore's religious preferences were Anglican and Methodist, with some Quaker and Presbyterian adherents. Beginning in the early colonial period, farmers cultivated tobacco and relied increasingly on slave labor. By the Revolution, tobacco was being replaced by grain as the region's primary product, and the demand for slaves was decreasing; their numbers declined from 38,591 to 25,997 between 1790 and 1850. Local employers capitalized on an expanding free black population, which increased from 3,907 to 24,770 over the same decades, as a source of agricultural labor.[53] In the early nineteenth century, some local residents, keenly aware that the Eastern Shore was a declining economic region, began to feel more affinity with neighboring Delaware than with the other regions of Maryland, and several proposals were made to form a new state from the Delmarva Peninsula.

In contrast to the Eastern Shore, southern Maryland remained a tobacco-producing region. It was settled by British stock, who tended to be affiliated with either the Anglican or Catholic faiths. While the slave population declined markedly in other regions of the state, it remained stable in southern Maryland (numbering 48,711 in 1790 and 47,785 in 1850) because of the tobacco economy. By 1850, over half of Maryland's slave population lived there.[54] As in the case of the Eastern Shore, however, residents of southern Maryland saw their population decline relatively as the state grew, and most of its politicians clung to the idea of representation by county unit in order to protect regional interests.

Western Maryland was a rapidly growing frontier area in the eighteenth and nineteenth centuries. Producing a wide variety of cereals, grains, and livestock, it was populated by a mixture of British, Scotch-Irish, and Germans, who brought with them a wide religious variety.[55] Although its relative share of Maryland's population hovered around 30 percent between 1790 and 1850, its total population grew from 91,832 to 176,168.[56] Western Maryland lay in the commercial orbits of both Philadelphia and Baltimore, whose merchants competed avidly to monopolize its trade.

Baltimore as an urban center was the most atypical region in Maryland. Economically, at the time of the Revolution it was a focus of the West Indies wheat trade, and it continued to develop as a preindustrial commercial city until the Civil War. Its population expanded from 13,503 in 1790 to 169,054 in 1850. Its labor needs were supplied by its diverse white population, as well as by an ever-increasing free black population.[57]

Regional diversity, combined with an awareness of inequitable representation, produced interregional tension in Maryland and strained the government concept embodied in the Constitution of 1776. The upper Western Shore and Baltimore City saw themselves as the core of a dynamic, commercially oriented area whose success depended on future growth which would be enhanced by state-sponsored internal improvements projects. Since the state legislature was dominated by small counties that often opposed high state expenditures, political and commercial interests in the high-growth regions favored reforming the structure of government to tie representation to population and thereby increase their influence. In general, the smaller counties, especially those counties more dependent on slave labor, were concerned about the transmutation of agricultural labor from slave to free and were apprehensive about future antislavery legislation that might originate from commercial areas. They supported internal improvements projects that would benefit them directly, and their relative population decline made them sensitive about losing their power base in the state legislature.

Throughout the period, the escalating friction of regional rivalries complicated the issues of internal improvements and constitutional reform.[58] Internal improvements initially amounted to building canals along the Potomac and the Susquehanna rivers and later included a crosscut canal between the Chesapeake Bay and the Delaware River. There was also an effort to construct a network of all-weather roads connecting Baltimore City with its hinterland. By the late 1820s, the railroad appeared to be a transportation panacea, and there was intensive interregional rivalry over these projects until the passage of the so-called "Eight Million Dollar Bill" in 1836, which authorized massive state assistance for an ambitious program of canals and railroads throughout the state.

Constitutional reform was another controversial and divisive topic.[59] A bill was introduced in almost every legislative session to reform a portion of the constitution regarding the structure of government or means of election. As the century progressed, reformers were increasingly dissatisfied with the indirectly elected state senate, which opposed almost all reforms and effectively blocked their enactment in the legislature, and with the indirectly elected governor and Executive Council. In 1836, reformers refused to make a quorum in the senate electoral college to elect a new state senate unless a majority of its members pledged to support constitutional reform. Presumably, without a senate no government could be legally elected. The reformers lost the battle, but the system was modified in the next legislative session. Reforms included changing the senate from an at-large organization to one where each county and the city of Baltimore elected one senator; providing for the popular election of the governor; disbanding the Executive Council; and making Baltimore City's representation in the lower house equal to that of the largest county. Similar modifications regarding delegation size were made until the constitution was overhauled in 1851.

Whose Right to Rule? The Problem

This sketch of Maryland's political and economic history between the Revolution and the decade prior to the Civil War suggests the dimensions of the debate over who should rule. Another problem, however, is who did the ruling. This book will present a systematic analysis of the latter question by evaluating decision making in four different community environments during the first and second party eras. The next stage will be to examine decision making in the context of two rural, traditional Maryland communities.

2

The Seamless Web

Oligarchies in Rural Society

Community leadership norms persisted without great change from
the Revolution to the Civil War in many rural areas of Maryland. An
oligarchy of families whose wealth and prominence was tied to extensive
land ownership and control over the labor market provided community
leaders. First families were able to exert substantial influence for generations primarily because of the lack of social and economic momentum
for change. These areas were inhabited by relatively homogeneous social
and cultural groups, which were not in conflict with one another. The
underlying economic base was stable. Committed to the cultivation of
staple crops, such as tobacco or grain, these areas were characterized by
great inequalities of wealth. Over time, the tobacco-producing counties
became increasingly chained to the institution of slavery. Families with
extensive land holdings strove to enhance their economic and social
position through advantageous marriages, either with other rural families
or with urban commercial families, whose lack of tradition was more
than compensated for by their affluence. The lack of both a heterogeneous population and a diversified economy meant that there was no
real alternative base from which others could challenge the existing community leadership structure. Isolated from the modernizing trends that
affected the other parts of Maryland, a rural oligarchy ruled throughout
this period with the constancy of a seamless web.

An analysis of the dimensions of community leadership demonstrates this pattern. Through the accumulation of historical evidence,
both public and private, leaders will be identified and ranked according to their respective roles in making important community decisions.
The decisional situations include political recruitment, internal improvements, and state and federal patronage. If an oligarchy ruled, community
leaders ought to be recruited from the same social strata, sharing common social and economic characteristics, and their power ought to span
both the first and second party eras. My analysis begins with St. Marys
County, on the southern tip of southern Maryland, and then turns to
Talbot County, on the Eastern Shore of the Chesapeake Bay.

20

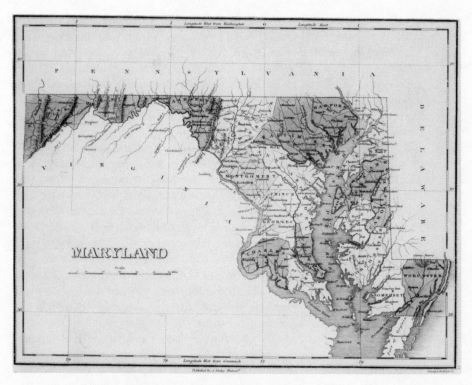

Map of Maryland, 1824
Courtesy of the Maryland Hall of Records, Annapolis

Old Maryland: St. Marys County

St. Marys County was an archetypal tobacco-producing area.[1] As the place of first settlement in 1634, its heritage and traditions were those of Maryland in the transition from colony to state. Yet, as other areas attracted varied social groups or became economically diversified, time appeared to stand still in St. Marys County. On the eve of the Civil War, a homogeneous white population, increasingly dependent upon slave labor, continued to cultivate tobacco as during the colonial era. Economic continuity had important political connotations.

The overwhelmingly homogeneous nature of the population generated few social tensions.[2] The first settlers were English, whose religious preferences were either with the Catholic or Anglican faiths; the county failed to attract new immigrants and remained free of evangelical religion. The county was the site of the colony's first capital, but the promise of future growth was dashed when the legislature moved from St. Marys City to Annapolis in 1694. Thereafter the county settled into the social system characteristic of tobacco-producing areas.

There were few towns in St. Marys County, and the communications system remained primitive. Because machinery was not needed to produce tobacco, there was little demand for the evolution of towns as service centers. Furthermore, the abundance of waterways allowed tobacco factors to deal directly with the producers and, incidentally, to act as merchants by selling goods from ships. Despite the number of individual tobacco warehouses, mills, taverns, general stores, and churches that spread over the county by 1800, there was little impetus for urban growth as a function of economic demand. Indeed, the largest urban place was hardly more than a village. Leonardtown, the county seat, boasted about fifty dwellings, in addition to the courthouse and jail in 1795.[3] Without a strong indigenous mercantile base, there was little justification for local newspapers, so that communication remained informal and erratic.

Men of property and standing rose naturally to positions of community responsibility in this environment. Lacking competition from mercantile groups, they justified their claim to leadership as the right of property owners in a hierarchical society. They were challenged during the Revolution by people who were unhappy with the prevailing conditions and the maldistribution of wealth, but they were not unseated. Local society was sufficiently unified thereafter to enable them to maintain their position of social and political dominance despite the continued unequal distribution of property and wealth.

Political recruitment after the Revolution perpetuated this oligarchical system. Potential candidates solicited backing from first families before declaring themselves publicly; self-nomination was the public vehicle for candidacy; and most political information was exchanged through public letters or private correspondence among members of the elite.[4] As national parties were formed, many prominent local revolutionary leaders became stalwarts of the emerging Federalist party.

The texture of public leadership was exemplified by appointments to the militia when it was reorganized in 1794. Richard Barnes, the wealthiest man in the county, was appointed a brigadier general.[5] He had been a delegate to the state Constitutional Convention in 1775 and a militia colonel during the revolutionary war, while his father served as the chairman of the local Committee of Safety. Not surprisingly, he was a staunch Federalist, whose last formal public office was election in 1788 to the legislature that ratified the federal Constitution. The appointment of Henry Neale and George Plater III as lieutenant colonels is also instructive. Neale, a Catholic, was an active Federalist officeholder, whose property placed him eleventh on the tax rolls.[6] Plater, also an active Federalist officeholder who stood third on the tax rolls, came from a prominent political family.[7] His father had been a congressman, chairman of the ratifying convention in 1788, and was Maryland's governor at the time of his death in 1792. His brother and brothers-in-law were also members of the state and federal government. The first majors to be appointed were equally prominent. William Thomas, Jr., who would become the nucleus of the nascent Jefferson party, was tenth on the tax lists and held county and state offices almost without a break between 1791 and 1813.[8] William Somerville, related to the Plater and Hebb families through marriage, was the second wealthiest man in the county and later served in local government.[9] The values upon which public leadership was based in this oligarchical system were suggested in a letter of recommendation: "we have no gentlemen with us that have seen service, therefore I presume commissions will be given to men in other Respects the best qualified, Men of Education, Manners, and Influence."[10]

As state politics polarized in the 1790s, Republicans in other parts of Maryland pointed to conditions in St. Marys County as epitomizing the aristocratic features of Federalism. "Too long has that county been subjugated to a local aristocracy," wrote the Republican press, because its voters were "reared up in ignorance and cherished by falsehood."[11] The answer was to establish local committees of correspondence and regional newspapers, since "the counties of Allegany, Montgomery, Charles, and St. Marys, on the Western Shore, being unprovided with any press immediately on the spot to refute error and expose federal schemes [voters] are deluded and led away by the desperate wickedness of federalism."[12]

Although the Republicans made an effort to mobilize support to oust their opponents during the Jeffersonian years, the voters were serenely indifferent to their crusade.

Beneath the campaign rhetoric, voters probably recognized that Republican leaders were from the same social group as the Federalists whom they characterized as aristocrats. The Republican party leader, for instance, William Thomas, Jr., owned 1,210 acres and 52 slaves, which placed him tenth on the tax rolls.[13] If the voters would not support the local Republican party, Republicans in other areas did. The Thomas family became the nucleus of the Republican movement in southern Maryland through appointments by state leaders to government positions.

During the first party era, no long-term divisive community decisions arose to mobilize new community leaders.[14] Local support was almost unanimous for the construction of the Potomac Canal, later reorganized as the Chesapeake and Ohio Canal, and for the development of the new federal city on the Potomac because such projects would benefit the county directly; the area's leaders opposed rival enterprises in the legislature, such as the plan to improve navigation of the Susquehanna River, as being to their disadvantage. Many of the affluent planters invested in the Potomac Company. The most disquieting problem facing the county at this time may have been the fear of slave insurrection, but since the oligarchy controlled the militia, the situation appeared to be under control.[15]

The workings of the oligarchy are also illuminated in the patronage correspondence. On the national level, the executive sought the advice of local congressmen or trusted political lieutenants before making appointments; on the state level, the governor and Executive Council expected members of the county delegations to submit entire lists of appointees.[16] Colonel George Plater III revealed the tight-knit structure in St. Mary's County when he wrote the clerk of the Executive Council: "Pray receive the bearer Mr. Sothoron as my particular friend . . . introduce him to the Governor, the Gentlemen of the Council, and such other of our friends as may be in Annapolis." Another time, Colonel Plater and General Barnes observed, in a militia recommendation, that "we have had communications with a number of respectable and influential characters, upon this subject, and . . . they entirely concur in sentiments with [us]."[17] These men of wealth and tradition not only consulted one another within the county, they also formed close personal relationships with other men like themselves from other counties, who served on the highest levels in state government.

Community leadership in St. Marys County was highly centralized in the hands of an oligarchy. Forty-three percent of the holders of political positions were among the fifty wealthiest men in the county. This figure would be greater if all the extended-family interconnections were known. Indeed, when the Maryland legislature selected state directors from the county to sit on the board of the Western Shore Farmer's Bank, its choices were William Thomas, Jr., and William Somerville, members of the local political elite.

Between the first and the second party systems, the political conditions in St. Marys County changed in several subtle ways. The once dominant Federalist party disappeared as a state and national organization, and local politicians, lacking a unifying symbol, were forced to fall back on their own resources. As the second party system evolved, former Federalists often aligned with the rising Jackson party, but it was unable to attract voters in the county. The Republican party, with minimal support among the St. Marys County electorate in the early nineteenth century, formed the backbone of the Administration, or Adams party, in the 1820s and 1830s. Several Republican leaders, notably William Thomas, Jr., and Athanasias Fenwick, were elevated to the Maryland senate through indirect election when Republicans controlled that body; once in office they capitalized on their influence to help other party members rise to power. Indeed, Thomas's two sons, James, who served in the House of Delegates and state senate in the 1820s and as governor in the early 1830s, and Richard, who was elected to both houses of the state legislature in the 1830s and selected as the presiding officer of each, became the major political family in the county. They extended their political influence by occasionally using the democratic organizational devices, such as conventions, to mobilize the electorate, but they refused to yield political control to anyone outside their own set.

Although the broad outlines of political recruitment in St. Marys County conformed to state patterns, they illuminate the ability of first families to exert control in a rural environment. Party nominations for the House of Delegates gradually superseded self-nomination. For some years the Anti-Jackson party fielded a ticket of four persons, which reinforced the notion of party regularity, but the inability of the Jacksonians to establish themselves as an effective opposition party resulted in factionalization among leaders of the dominant party.[18] In an effort to stimulate voter interest, some politicians, to the consternation of local clergy concerned with drunkenness and violence, reintroduced "public treating" in the mid-1820s.[19] Similarly, other politicians tried to establish a political newspaper in neighboring Charles County to serve southern Maryland.[20] The trend toward stronger party identification was stimulated by the presidential contest of 1828, which placed an initial emphasis on the presidential electoral district. The fact that national political boundaries encompassed several counties gave advantages to elite members who had extensive kin networks or friendships rooted in the earlier political system, extending over county lines. For example, two St. Marys County politicians, Congressman Clement Dorsey, who spoke for the administration, and former Federalist Henry G. S. Key, who praised the Jackson cause, addressed a Calvert County administration meeting in May 1827. At the St. Marys County meeting held the following week, officeholders dominated the leadership positions: former Federalist Congressman Raphael Neale called the meeting to order, General James Thomas, member of the state senate, served as chairman, John L. Millard, member of the lower house, acted as secretary, and Congressman Dorsey and Colonel Gerald N. Causin spoke in favor of President Adams.[21] The delegation to the state convention was composed of county notables.[22] In 1831, in a move reminiscent of the defunct legislative caucus favored by the Republicans a decade earlier, Anti-Jackson state legislators convened in Annapolis to call for a presidential convention to nominate an opponent to President Jackson. General Thomas, senator from St. Marys County, chaired that meeting.[23] After parties were firmly established, local meetings fell into disuse and were called only to send delegations to state or national functions. The district even lacked a newspaper and had to be served by those in Annapolis, Baltimore, or Washington, D.C.

First families controlled the emerging political parties in the 1820s as they had in the first party era. Writing in 1826, Nathaniel Fenwick complained bitterly about the influence of Colonel James Forrest: "It is assuredly time for the people to awaken when one man can with a scrape of his pen set aside the public voice and dictate the names of all four of our candidates to the state legislature."[24] A paucity of evidence about Colonel Forrest, who was an extreme Federalist and served as the county register of wills from 1806 to his death in 1826, when new political alignments were just forming, makes it difficult to check the veracity of the charge that one man could wield so much influence. Its plausibility, however, is enhanced because similar charges were leveled against the Thomas family a few years later. Congressman Clement Dorsey, who ran unopposed during the 1820s, believed that the failure of the Thomas brothers to support him at the district convention, as they had promised, cost him the nomination.[25] His frustration increased when he failed to win election to the lower house of the state legislature that year, but his bitterness may have lessened with his appointment to the Maryland judiciary in 1832.[26] Another family found itself isolated from political preference because one of its members offered himself as a senatorial elector candidate in 1831 against the advice and consent "of a certain family."[27] Because one brother served as state senator and later as governor, another as speaker of the House of Delegates, and a third on the Orphans Court, and each one ranked among the twenty-seven wealthiest men in the county, the Thomases had advantages not everyone enjoyed in St. Marys County.

The insignificance of the Jackson party is best summarized in an evaluation by the Anti-Jackson press in 1831: "In St. Marys, the Jackson party is in so small a minority, that no opposition is anticipated."[28] Although it never fielded a ticket for the House of Delegates during this period, nor did it normally choose to run anyone for Congress, the local Jackson party was active in nominating candidates for presidential elector and in sending delegations to state and national Maryland conventions.[29] Its leaders included Henry G. S. Key, son of Federalist Philip Key, himself a former Federalist member of the House of Delegates and the fourth wealthiest man in the county; Richard H. Miles, appointed to the Levy Court in 1830 and twenty-second on the tax rolls; Dr. James W. Roach; and Colonel James Jarboe. Like William Thomas, Jr., who formed the core of the Republican party in a hostile environment in the first party era, these were men of substance and standing.[30] The small Jackson party was sustained by judicious appointments from the federal government, but even these reinforced the elite domination of the party. Of the several Treasury officers in the county when Jackson took office, only Key remained after 1830. William H. Plowden, the collector for St. Marys and the third wealthiest man in the county, did not have his commission renewed after it expired. He was replaced by Thomas R. Johnson, whose political services are unknown, but who stood thirty-eighth on the tax rolls.[31] The remuneration for these positions was not high, less that $300 per year, but it is significant that political largess was awarded to already wealthy men, not to partisans from the ranks of the common man.

Community leadership roles generated in other areas were also dominated by men of affluence, many of whom served as formal officeholders. In the 1820s, there was a flurry of activity among advocates of the Chesapeake and Ohio Canal Company to generate public enthusiasm for greater state support to resuscitate a project stalled by soaring building costs. Of the sixteen men sent as delegates to the various conventions that met between 1825 and 1836, eight were among the county's fifty wealthiest individuals, nine were current or former officeholders, and six held important militia commissions.[32] Some of these men, such as Richard Thomas, Henry G. S. Key, or former political leaders, could be expected to play active roles, as could members of old political families, such as John Rousby Plater.[33] Also included were such community activists as Major Henry Ashton, Colonel Gerald N. Causin, or Colonel Enoch J. Millard, ranking militia officers, or Peter Gough and George S. Leigh. Under other conditions, involvement in internal improvement projects might mobilize different segments of society than were active in political recruitment, but in St. Marys County the same type of men directed community leadership roles in both situations. Rather than serving as a vehicle to expand the base of community leadership, such activities provided the elite another opportunity to extend their control.

The issue of political reform in the 1830s focused on the activities of the nineteen Van Buren senatorial electors who refused to join their colleagues to form the electoral college in Annapolis. They insisted on prior agreement that the new senate would favor constitutional reform; otherwise they threated to boycott the college and prevent a quorum. This plan found almost no support in St. Marys County. Besides the general antipathy of the elite toward the Jackson party, members of both parties did not want their county to lose power in the state legislature. Different men appeared as officers of the meeting,[34] but such familiar faces as Henry G. S. Key, Richard Thomas, Judge Clement Dorsey, and other members of prominent families[35] reaffirmed the county's displeasure with the actions of the recalcitrant electors. As in other cases of community action, leaders were recruited from the oligarchy.

As in the first party era, patronage decisions were highly institutionalized, with the local county representatives and local officeholders advising the executive on patronage matters.[36] For three years from 1833 to 1835, St. Marys' own James Thomas served as governor. The death in 1835 of the register of wills, a much coveted post that required the vote of the state legislature for appointment, illustrated how the system worked.[37]

Five candidates were recommended for the vacancy in 1835. Three were active community leaders, three were also officeholders, two represented wealthy families, and one had been the former register's clerk.[38] The contest narrowed to two men: George S. Leigh and George Coombs. Leigh, whose family had been frustrated by the Thomases in its earlier efforts to obtain political favors, tried to boost his chances of success by capitalizing on kin connections outside the county. Besides the customary St. Marys County endorsements, which included a petition signed by an apolitical member of the Thomas family, he was recommended by his father-in-law, former Congressman John Leeds Kerr of Talbot County, and by Kerr's political ally, Robert H. Goldsborough, soon to be elected to the United States Senate. Both Kerr and Goldsborough were stalwarts in the state Anti-Jackson party.[39] Because George Coombs enjoyed the support of the Thomases and many of the county's positional leaders, he won appointment as register of wills.[40]

A final decisional elite of thirty-four men was aggregated from these decisional situations.[41] Fifty-nine percent of them held political offices during this era, 41 percent were militia officers, and 35 percent were included among the fifty wealthiest citizens of the county. Their average age was forty years, and they were predominantly landed slaveholders. Seventy-one percent held property, with an average value of $4,384, while 62 percent held land, with an average of 723 acres, and 59 percent owned slaves, holding an average of 23. These percentages would be higher if sons without property were credited with holding property they eventually inherited from their fathers.

Decision making and community leadership in St. Marys County changed very little between the first and second party systems. Men of wealth dominated during both periods. They were active in political recruitment and officeholding, and they assumed positions of leadership in alternative community decisions as well. Death and movement to other counties depleted the ranks of families dominant in the first party era, but new leaders emerged whose claim for power was based on the traditional foundations of the planter ideal, property and slaveownership. An oligarchy ruled in the 1830s in St. Marys County as it had in the 1790s.

On the Eastern Shore: Talbot County

Talbot County, on Maryland's Eastern Shore, was, like St. Marys County, populated predominantly by English stock, dependent upon a nonwhite work force, and drew its wealth from the production of agricultural staples.[42] Unlike St. Marys County, it all but abandoned the cultivation of tobacco for the production of grain before the Revolution, and the decline of its slave population was balanced by growth of a free black work force.[43] Talbot County also exhibited greater religious diversity than St. Marys County. Presbyterians and Quakers challenged the Anglican hegemony before the Revolution, and Methodism became increasingly popular beginning in the 1770s. The rejuvenated postrevolutionary Episcopal church tried to reassert its predominance all along the Eastern Shore, but it never captured the allegiance of the people in great numbers. It became identified as a conservative, elite church, and as politics intruded into all facets of life in the 1790s, it avowed the Federalist political faith.[44] Among the evangelical sects, the Presbyterians and Quakers declined numerically in Talbot County after 1800, while the

Methodists continued to expand unabated.[45] The Episcopal church's efforts to reestablish itself as a state-supported church combined with the conservative distrust of social pluralism caused Methodists to align with the Republicans as parties evolved.

Talbot County also served as the government and communications hub for the Eastern Shore. Easton, known as Talbot County Courthouse until after the revolutionary era, was the official meeting place for the Eastern Shore branches of Maryland's colonial and postrevolutionary government and the unofficial second capital of the state. The General Court, the Treasurer of the Eastern Shore, and sundry other offices met there.[46] Easton was an important link in Maryland's news system, boasting two weekly newspapers by 1800; Leonardtown, the county seat for St. Marys County, was scarcely more than a village. Easton was not, however, a large city. In 1795 it was described as having one hundred dwellings, a market house, several dry goods stores, and a courthouse.[47] The abolition of the General Court in 1805 reduced its importance as an administrative center, but because of its central location and competitive press, Easton remained important thereafter as a communications center on the Eastern Shore and as the county seat of Talbot County.

During the first party period, members of the Talbot County oligarchy favored the older preparty consensus ideal in which they saw themselves as the ruling establishment, untarnished by the alleged corruption and depravity of party competition. Many of them later gravitated naturally into the Federalist camp.[48] They were willing to use public meetings and even to tolerate conventions on occasion, but they never abjured their belief that the people should be guided from above. Self-nomination and intraelite negotiations characterized political recruitment before the evolution of party divisions in the 1790s.[49] When the Federalist hegemony was called into question by a series of public meetings criticizing the administration's foreign policy, Federalist leaders correctly perceived these meetings as devices designed to mobilize the electorate behind their traditional rival's candidacy for political office.[50] The Federalists were ambivalent about public meetings and nomination conventions. Several times during this period they used public meetings to elicit community support for the national administration; at these, members of the political and economic elite appeared to overawe the public into accepting the policies they advocated.[51] Once the Federalists actually held a convention to nominate candidates for the House of Delegates. This unusual event occurred in 1800, when they tried to get public support for "Legislative Choice," Robert G. Harper's plan to alter the way presidential electors were to be elected.[52] The normal procedure for Federalist political recruitment was through self-nomination or by an informal caucus decision among party stalwarts.

The hotly disputed congressional election of 1798 illustrated the similarities of both the Federalist and the nascent Republican parties in methods of political recruitment and voter mobilization. Partisans on both sides saw foreign policy as the overriding issue in 1798: a vote for the incumbent, William Hindman, was an endorsement for the administration's handling of foreign affairs, a vote for Jacob Seney of Queen Annes County was a censure of President Adams. Both Hindman and Seney were members of the elite. Hindman, who had served as the chairman of the Talbot County Committee of Safety in 1776 and in both houses of the state legislature and Congress almost continuously thereafter, stood eleventh on the tax rolls.[53] Seney, who had also served in the Continental Congress, in the U.S. House, and as chief judge of Maryland's third district until 1796, contested Hindman's position in 1798. Both were self-nominated. Sensing the importance of the contest, Hindman overcame an initial reluctance to stand for reelection, but his commitment to the campaign was never as ardent as that of his opponent, and his activity was further restricted by injury.[54] Hindman's opponents attacked him as a mediocre congressman, who voted slavishly for such unpopular bills as the Alien and Sedition Acts and whose unthinking actions helped to bring the country to the verge of war with France.[55] The Federalists tried to conjure up the threat of invasion and the need for military preparedness to give substance to their contention that Seney, an alleged Jacobinical pawn of the French, would be a disastrous choice.[56] Seney's supporters went to great lengths during the campaign to dissociate themselves from anything French, and they projected themselves as the peace party.[57] Both sides harangued potential voters at meetings and in the public prints.

Beneath the campaign rhetoric, there was an essential continuity in party leadership and methods of voter mobilization. "A Plebian," writing to defend the Federalist party against the charge of being aristocratic, correctly pointed out that the Jacobin leaders were just as wealthy and well connected as were the Federalists.[58] Despite the fervor of the public campaign, a Federalist privately observed, "Seney is a clever good kind of man in private life, but in politics he is Gallatin the Second."[59] One of Seney's major supporters in Talbot County was Jacob Gibson, a wealthy political activist who was firmly in the elite mold, and it was public knowledge that the wealthiest family, the Lloyds, were Republicans.[60]

Seney won the election, but his unexpected death soon after necessitated another contest.[61] William Hindman declined to stand again, and

Judge Robert Goldsborough, Jr., of Talbot County, announced his candidacy. Judge Goldsborough, who previously had served in both houses of the state legislature, was a wealthy member of a prominent family and an articulate spokesman for the status quo.[62] Joseph Hopper Nicholson of Queen Annes County, who was linked to the Lloyd family by marriage, ran as a Republican. The Federalists continued to tar their opponents as French dupes, and the Republicans rejoined by attacking Judge Goldsborough's earlier advocacy of the establishment of the Episcopal church and the use of state money to support private colleges. Nicholson's victory began a period of Republican ascendancy in the county. Indeed, the situation changed so quickly that a correspondent to the Baltimore Republican paper wrote that "the chain of aristocracy which has for so many years kept this county in a state of bondage, was finally torn asunder; and instead of advocates for a *standing army*, it will now be represented by men who are real friends to their country in the cause of Republicanism."[63]

The Talbot County Republican leaders were much more innovative than their Federalist counterparts in the early years of the first party system. They quickly established a party press, the Easton *Republican Star*, edited by Thomas Perrin Smith, and began to organize politics through meetings and regularized conventions.[64] The convention was a device to counter self-nomination by giving the party's authoritative sanction to a slate of candidates and to prevent factionalization by sending authorized delegations to district and state meetings. Although the system was ostensibly more democratic, evidence for Talbot County, at least, suggests that an elite controlled the important positions during these formative years. Men of wealth, tied firmly by a web of social and political connections that bound the oligarchy together, such as Colonel William Hayward, Jacob Gibson, Colonel Perry Spencer, and sons of first families, such as Edward Lloyd V and Samuel Stevens, Jr., dominated the activities of the early Republican party.[65] Another leader of the old system, Colonel Perry Benson, was present, and new leaders emerged who gained prominence through their organizational activities, such as Thomas Perrin Smith, William Muley, Charles Emory, and James Colston.

Despite the Republicans' electoral success in Talbot County, the convention system proved flawed as a unifying organization. In 1803, an incumbent member of the lower house of the state legislature was not renominated by the party and declared himself as an independent candidate.[66] The following year, Robert H. Golsborough, an aspiring Federalist and son of Judge Robert Goldsborough, Jr., hit upon the strategy of printing handbills in the different districts presenting his name along

with that of a popular local Republican, who was listed as an independent
candidate. This tactic took enough votes away from the fourth member
of the Republican slate to secure Goldsborough's election.[67] With new
emphasis on mobilizing voters, the elite reintroduced "public treating,"
and politicians addressed potential voters assembled at militia musters, at
Methodist meetings, and at civic events.[68]

In terms of community leadership, the polarization of politics into
two competitive parties reflected two different trends. Intraelite disputes
between competing families were now institutionalized under the rubric
of party competition. The Lloyd clan dominated the Republican party
and the Goldsboroughs the Federalist party; in Talbot County, at least,
the evolution of the party system served to keep the elite in power. If the
roots of party leadership were identical, the public image projected by
each was quite different. The Republicans projected an image that con-
doned a pluralistic society. The Federalists, on the other hand, worked to
protect a uniform ideal society and categorized any deviation from this
ideal as the product of foreign machinations. This situation, intensified
by the war hysteria of 1798, mobilized a number of apolitical groups,
including the Methodists, who supported whichever party would accept
them. The Methodists did not seek to elevate members of their own
faith into leadership positions. Consequently, their mobilization did not
involve increased competition for political recruitment; the oligarchy
simply spread its umbrella of protection but continued to perform its
idealized role.[69]

Because ranking militia officers were appointed from among the
very wealthy and because those with distinguished revolutionary records
were still able to serve, control of the rural militia did not rest solely
in the hands of Federalists. Perry Benson, a revolutionary officer, was
appointed as one lieutenant colonel in 1794, and John Hughes was appointed the other. Three of the four majors were among the thirty-three
wealthiest men in the county, and the fourth was the sheriff.[70] When
Colonel Benson was promoted to brigadier general in 1798, William
Hayward, a wealthy Republican, was appointed lieutenant colonel in his
place. In 1807, another prominent Republican, Perry Spencer, was appointed as a lieutenant colonel. The division of officers into Republicans
and Federalists, especially in 1798, dismayed some Federalists concerned
about the efficiency of the militia with the threat of war with France.[71]
Despite this concern about foreign invasion, the militia's primary function was to protect citizens against "internal agitation,"[72] and the most
appropriate leaders for that service remained members of the oligarchy
whatever their political affiliation.

The oligarchy, through its institutional and party leadership, dominated patronage decisions. When President Jefferson took office, there was party pressure to remove Federalists immediately from any position in the gift of the executive. The deputy postmaster for Easton, James Corwan, who also edited the Federalist *Maryland Herald*, resigned in 1801 and was replaced by Thomas Perrin Smith, editor of the Jeffersonian *Republican Star*, who also took over the publication of the federal laws.[73] The appointment was made on the recommendation of the district's Republican congressman, Joseph H. Nicholson.[74] Similarly, the secretary of the treasury asked Nicholson to decide who among the petitioners would be a suitable replacement for Federalist Robert Banning, ousted as the collector for Oxford in 1803, a job he had succeeded to in 1798 upon the death of his father, Colonel Jeremiah Banning, a revolutionary officer and ardent Federalist.[75]

State-level patronage also conformed to established institutional norms. Members of the county delegation to the legislature normally made recommendations for local appointments.[76] Several times persons other than members of the local delegations made recommendations, but they were men like William Hindman, an incumbent congressman with a long and distinguished record of public service from Talbot County, or Jacob Gibson, a prominent Republican leader who served in local and state government throughout this period.[77] Party consideration was a factor when either the Federalist or Republican parties were in power, but they both drew from the same reservoir in the community for appointments.[78]

Talbot County's decisional elite, aggregated from their participation in the foregoing decisional situations, numbered twenty-two men.[79] Many were members of prominent Eastern Shore families and some were important community leaders before, during, and after the Revolution.[80] Several, such as the editors of the competitive presses or new politicians, worked their way into the decisional elite through the expanded organizational activities, but their basis for influence was more tenuous than it would have been had they been related to the first families.[81] Seventy-one percent of the decisional elite owned property, with an average value of $8,179; 67 percent held an average of 1,830 acres; and 76 percent owned an average of fifty slaves. These figures are, however, distorted in two ways: the averages are inflated by the huge wealth of Edward Lloyd IV; and the percentages are less than they should be because sons of prominent men living in their fathers' households did not appear on the tax rolls. Another way of representing their place in Talbot County's society is to observe that 59 percent of the decisional elite were among the county's fifty wealthiest property holders. The average age of the decisional elite was forty years. One-half of them were militia officers; 64 percent were political officeholders between 1795 and 1806. Such an elite clearly constituted an oligarchy. Talbot County, though different in many ways from St. Marys County, was still governed by members of first families who claimed the right to rule on the basis of their traditional service to the community and their extensive property holdings.

Between the 1790s and the 1820s, Talbot County underwent minimal change. Easton's position as Maryland's second capital diminished with the dismemberment of the General Court, but as a small commercial town it grew in importance, and by the end of the 1820s supported the publication of three weekly papers. Farmers and planters continued to cultivate grain, using a mixed labor force of slaves, free blacks, and whites. For several decades the county's population grew modestly, but beginning in 1830 both the slave and white population declined at a rate greater than the state or regional average. By the 1830s, there was an increasing concern about economic stagnation, soil depletion, and ways soil productivity might be increased. Some planters purchased land in the lower South and began to move slaves there to produce cotton. Those who stayed were attentive to contemporary economic and political trends that called for the expenditure of state money to build internal improvement projects to advance the economic interests of the Western Shore or Baltimore City or to reform the constitution to change the basis for representation from the county unit to population, both of which would harm the interests of Talbot County.

The structure of Talbot County's political system in the 1820s was more abreast of state trends than that in St. Marys County. Leaders of both parties in the waning years of the first party system tried to mobilize the electorate through expanded organizational activities to a far greater degree than did leaders in St. Marys County. Led by Robert H. Goldsborough, Talbot County Federalists resuscitated the dormant party press in 1817 and campaigned and organized avidly to attract voter support.[82] By the early 1820s, however, the Federalist party was moribund as a state political organization, and within several years even the Republican party fell prey to factionalization and disunity in Talbot County. The stimulation of the presidential contests in 1824 and 1828 forced the old political leaders to form new and unexpected alignments. Many of the Talbot County Federalist leaders publicly opposed the Republican caucus and supported the election of John Quincy Adams, the nominal leader of the party of Thomas Jefferson, while former Republicans divided among the various other candidates for the presidency.[83] Edward Lloyd V, serving as a United States senator, favored William H. Crawford in 1824 and switched reluctantly to Jackson in 1828. Most Republicans, however, especially those who controlled the state party and saw themselves as the lineal descendants of national republicanism, supported the election of Adams. Consequently, there was an anomalous situation where Republicans were divided among themselves and the Federalists threw their support behind the party they had opposed but a decade earlier. Despite the diversity of their political backgrounds, leaders of the resuscitated political competition were well trained and firmly believed in the art of political organization.

The Anti-Jackson party was highly successful in Talbot County. Between 1827 and 1836, it elected all but five of its candidates to the state legislature, and only in 1829 did the people fail to support its congressional candidate. A key to voter mobilization in Talbot County was its party newspaper, the *Easton Gazette*, the former Federalist party organ. The editor, Alexander Graham, worked to unify Anti-Jacksonians in the other counties that comprised Talbot's presidential and congressional districts and to organize partisans for local elections.[84] The prior Republican paper, Thomas Perrin Smith's *Republican Star*, was published until 1832, but since it was out of step with contemporary political trends and lacked a patron in the late 1820s, it was replaced in 1829 as the administration's publisher of the laws.[85] The pro-Adams Anti-Jackson party leaders were an assortment of first party notables, who justified their right to lead on the grounds of earlier service, and second party activists, who shared local power because of their current service.[86]

The community notables who formed the core of the Anti-Jackson party were members of familiar families who had dominated the first party era. Robert H. Goldsborough, dubbed the "acknowledged leader of the Clay party of this state" by the Jackson press, played an influential role during this era.[87] While other men served as officers of party meetings and conventions, Goldsborough limited his public activity to addressing meetings and guiding the editorial policy of the *Easton Gazette*, which he had helped to found in 1817.[88] He declined all nominations to serve as a presidential elector, as delegate to a party convention, or as a congressional candidate.[89] Goldsborough's ambition was to be reelected to the U.S. Senate, which he realized upon the retirement of Ezekiel F. Chambers in 1835. Another Anti-Jacksonian leader was John Leeds Kerr, son of David Kerr, a Federalist officeholder during the first party era, and nephew of the affluent John Leeds Bozman, who married the daughter of wealthy Samuel Chamberlaine in 1801.[90] Kerr, an attorney and avid Federalist during the first party era, served in the U.S. Congress twice in this period, and frequently addressed party meetings in his district. His son, John Bozman Kerr, who was beginning a legal career and would serve in the House of Delegates in 1836, was far more active in party organizational activities on the county level than his father, as was George S. Leigh, his son-in-law, in St. Marys County. Daniel Martin, a former Republican and an Anti-Jackson leader, was the son of Nicholas Martin, who stood tenth on the tax rolls in 1798. He served on the Executive Council and as governor in this era.[91] He participated in the late 1820s as a party organizer. Members of other first families, such as Colonel John and Tench Tilghman, or Martin and Nicholas Goldsborough, took part in the organizational activities of the Anti-Jackson party as well.[92]

The leadership emerging from the proliferation of partisan activity had varied roots in Talbot's past.[93] General Solomon Dickinson, a moderate landowner who served as a Republican in the House of Delegates in 1806 and again as an Anti-Jacksonian in 1830 and 1831, was the most active party leader between 1827 and 1836. He was frequently chairman of local meetings and delegate to district conventions, and he chaired the district congressional nomination convention in 1833.[94] Edward N. Hambleton, a former Federalist activist, participated in party activities as chairman and delegate between 1828 and 1836, and he was elected to the Maryland senate in 1836. He stood fifth on the county tax rolls in 1832 and earlier had married into the family of Hugh Sherwood of Huntington, a wealthy member of the establishment in the first party era.[95] Alexander Graham, editor of the party press, was a man of modest means, who served as secretary, delegate, or member of the central committee at party meetings. Leaders at the next level of political activity included men of substance, such as Theodore R. Lockerman and Dr. William H. Tilghman, positional leader Joseph Bruff, who was elected to the House of Delegates between 1831 and 1835, and men of limited means, such as Foster Maynard or Thomas C. Nicols.

The Jacksonian paper never tired of exposing the elitist and Federalist roots of the Anti-Jackson party. "A Democrat" observed that "no man who witnessed the movements of the National Republican party in this county, could avoid remarking the absolute control which Robert H. Goldsborough, Edward N. Hambleton, and Colonel William Hughlett have over it. . . . A seat in the House of Representatives or Senate of the U.S., the Gubernatorial Chair, the State Senate and Council to the Governor, were the lowest stations to which this triumvirate would condescend."[96] "A Democrat" was clearly trying to encourage former Republicans to repudiate a party dominated by Federalists or to sow seeds of discord among Anti-Jackson leaders outside this clique, but his assertion ignored the reasons behind their capacity to assume positions of party leadership. These men, as well as John Leeds Kerr, were expected to lead the community because of the rural tradition that men of wealth and position should lead. Furthermore, by scrupulously observing the democratic norm that every section of the county should be represented, both by sending delegates to meetings and by having one of the four candidates for the lower house come from each of the four districts, the pattern of leadership was not at variance with contemporary political philosophy. "A Democrat" also ignored the fact that former Republicans, such as the late Daniel Martin, who served on the Executive Council and later as governor until his death in 1831, also played an important role in the Anti-Jackson party.

The early leaders of the Talbot County Jackson party were Republicans during the 1820s, who had fallen out with their powerful and influential fellow partisans who controlled the state government.[97] Colonel Edward Lloyd V, for example, was a staunch supporter of William H. Crawford before he shifted to Jackson in 1828. First as a Republican officeholder whose career spanned three decades beginning in the first party system, then as the wealthiest man in the county, Lloyd was an important political leader. Lloyd and his brother-in-law, William Hayward, Jr., were instrumental in establishing the county Jacksonian paper, the Easton Eastern Shore Whig and People's Advocate, and indirectly guiding the embryonic party thereafter.[98] Stepping down from the U.S. Senate in 1826, Colonel Lloyd served in the state senate until ill health forced his retirement in 1828. His son, Edward Lloyd VI, assumed the role of primary political organizer in the county as the Jacksonian era began. Two other sons, Daniel and James Murray, worked in lesser capacities and as candidates for local offices.

By far the most publicly active Jacksonian leader was Richard Spencer, a lawyer who stood twenty-second on the tax rolls. Spencer served the party in a wide variety of capacities: foremost as editor of the party press, the Easton Eastern Shore Whig, which was especially important to communicate with other Jacksonians on the Eastern Shore; then as Congressman and as an unsuccessful candidate for reelection to Congress and to the state legislature; and finally as a party organizer.[99] Edward Mulligan, a county native without great wealth, played an important role as Spencer's coeditor between 1830 and 1835. Dr. Samuel S. Dickinson, member of a wealthy local family, chaired several meetings and went as a delegate to conventions between 1832 and 1834.[100] John W. Battee, a cabinetmaker, chaired two meetings and attended a congressional and a presidential convention as a delegate.

Talbot County's Jackson party presented a vocal but electorally ineffectual opposition to the Anti-Jackson party. Generally unsuccessful in electing its candidates to public offices, it was highly successful in disseminating information and organizing party affairs all along the Eastern Shore. Its capabilities were suggested by an admonition to Francis P.

Blair regarding the 1832 presidential campaign: "It would be advisable to say nothing in the *Globe* about the movements in the Eastern Shore District. Our judicious friends there have this thing under their special management, with the fairest prospects of success."[101] Left alone, without undue outside attention, the symbiotic relationship between leader and voter might turn the balance in favor of Jackson.

In much the same pattern as their Anti-Jackson counterparts, the Jacksonians recruited leaders from two sources: the established elite, such as the Lloyd family, and a group of party activists, who worked their way into party leadership positions through organizational activity. Both parties leaned heavily upon their members serving in government to organize and direct party operations. Wealth, family, and election to important public offices all overlapped, and although an occasional man of lesser wealth might hold office, the positions of real influence in each party perpetuated the domination of the oligarchy in Talbot County as in St. Marys County.

The issue of internal improvements tended to highlight Talbot County's Eastern Shore identity. Traditional projects, such as improving the Potomac and Susquehanna rivers or building roads from Baltimore City to its agricultural hinterland, brought little advantage to Talbot County and made it responsible for an increased state debt. The Jacksonians consistently opposed state participation in all internal improvement projects, basing their dissents on the lofty principles articulated by President Jackson in his 1830 Maysville veto.[102] The Anti-Jacksonians, however, were caught in a dilemma: they were philosophically sympathetic to Henry Clay's American System, which advocated government aid for such programs, but they were unsympathetic to purely Western Shore projects. The advent of the railroad resolved this dilemma, and after 1835, they warmed to the prospect of an Eastern Shore railroad. It was initially presented as a Philadelphia-based project, which would have drained trade away from Baltimore, but then it was made part of an ambitious statewide internal improvements project that would incorporate support for railroads and canals, ostensibly benefiting every region.[103]

One public meeting was held in Talbot County to generate support for the comprehensive internal improvements project. The organizers came solely from the ranks of the Anti-Jacksonian party leadership; the Jacksonians boycotted the meeting. Former Congressman John Leeds Kerr and Colonel Edward N. Hambleton, who won election that fall to the state senate, forcefully spoke in favor of the program, while party activists Thomas C. Nicols and N. G. Singleton served as officers.[104] The eventual bill passed the state legislature without help from Talbot

County, but the leaders mobilized by this issue were the very same people who dominated political recruitment. New groups might be mobilized by such an issue in a more diversified political and economic system, but the overlapping leadership pool characteristic of rural Maryland reinforced the domination by an elite firmly rooted by wealth and family in the county's past.

The issue of political reform demonstrated how state parties divided into regional factions. Like their state counterparts, Talbot County Jacksonians favored the principle of popular democracy, but as citizens of a small county losing population, they were loath to implement reform if it meant a diminution of their power and influence in state government. The party paper editorialized in 1832: "But, while we admit the justice of her claim to an increase in representation, we claim also a protection for the small counties. The interests of many of the counties, especially of the Eastern Shore, are so materially different from those of City of Baltimore and the Western counties that . . . great injustice could be done."[105] During the period when many reform conventions were being held, Talbot County failed to send a delegation to any, and the paper was attentive only to those called in other small counties. By 1835 it had formulated the acceptable limits of reform: it favored direct election of the governor and senate, an end to proportional representation for the senate, abandonment of the Executive Council, and increased membership for Baltimore City in the House of Delegates. Such a policy did not endorse popular representation, and it protected the existing powers of the small counties. During the electoral college crisis in 1836, Talbot County Jacksonians favored compromise, and they assembled only once for a desultory meeting after Governor Thomas Veazey made his emergency proclamation.

The reform situation was complicated in 1833 by the rebirth of a movement to form a new state by joining all of the Eastern Shore with Delaware. Coming at the period when large counties were demanding more power in state government and immediately after the challenge of South Carolina's nullification convention in the fall of 1832, it was an especially sensitive issue. Such a realignment did not elicit popular support in Talbot County, and when the matter came before the Maryland legislature it was tabled. Thereafter public interest in the proposal waned.[106]

The Jacksonian reform dilemma was without substance for the Anti-Jacksonians. Party principle and regional goals were uniform: they opposed all reform. As early as 1832, the *Gazette* responded negatively to a series of Baltimore resolutions that "strike at a radical and total revolution in the constitution of the State, and will, if adopted, subjugate the counties and make them mere dependencies of the great commercial city of Baltimore."[107] They quickly organized to protect their position. Anti-Jacksonians were elected as senatorial electors in 1836, and they formed two local meetings to support the government.

The first meeting, held immediately after the electoral college failed to obtain a quorum, was chaired by Colonel Edward N. Hambleton, with Tench Tilghman as secretary. Besides these well-known party leaders, Senator Robert H. Goldsborough and former Congressman John Leeds Kerr addressed the meeting. The second, called to condemn the recalcitrant electors and to support Governor Veazey after his proclamation, was chaired by Colonel William Hughlett, with William W. Huggins as secretary. J. L. Kerr again addressed the meeting and presented resolutions.[108]

On the issues of internal improvements and political reform, it is remarkable that national political leaders, as well as local partisans, assumed leadership roles. In rural Talbot County, the national political leaders preferred to use their influence openly in such situations and delegated official leadership roles to local political leaders. Neither situation served to mobilize new leaders from the community who might challenge the prevailing leadership structure.

Positional leaders played a central role in patronage decisions. On both the state and federal levels, elected representatives were the funnel through which patronage requests flowed.[109] Such requests were almost always honored.[110] National leaders, such as Colonel Edward Lloyd V, Robert H. Goldsborough, and John Leeds Kerr, worked from their positions of prestige to influence patronage directly on both the state and federal levels. The Jacksonians, who could expect few patronage plums from a county delegation dominated in all but one session by the opposition party, had influence only on the federal level. They ousted Alexander Graham, editor of the *Gazette*, as publisher of the laws and as postmaster of Easton and replaced him in both jobs with their own editor. The other important federal patronage position in the county, the collectorship of Oxford, was still held by John Willis, the Republican who had replaced the Federalist incumbent in 1803 and remained undisturbed throughout Jackson's presidency.[111]

Even unusual patronage situations, an appointment to a life tenure office, for instance, did not alter this pattern of deference to local positional and party leaders. Thomas C. Nicols, a lawyer who was an Anti-Jackson activist and acted as chairman for the internal improvements meeting, sought the appointment as clerk of the Eastern Shore Court of Appeals when it fell vacant in 1835. His candidacy was boosted by Robert H. Goldsborough, Edward N. Hambleton, Theodore R. Lockerman, and Tench Tilghman, all major figures in the party or members of the positional elite.[112] Not surprisingly, Nicols got the appointment. The experience of a year earlier, however, when John Leeds Kerr was unable to obtain a judicial appointment, might be construed as an exception to the ability of the oligarchy to exert its will.[113] Kerr had been thwarted not because of opposition from groups within the community but because his claim was less compelling than those of others. When Ezekiel F. Chambers of Kent County was appointed to the vacancy in 1834 instead of Kerr, Chambers resigned from the U.S. Senate; Robert H. Goldsborough was elected to fill his seat during the following legislative session. If two party figures could be satisfied, such as Chambers and Goldsborough, it would be less than expedient to gratify a single former congressman whose claim for preference in terms of service was considerably less than either of the other two leaders.

Aggregating leaders from these various Talbot County community activities resulted in a decisional elite of thirty-one men for the second party era.[114] Members of prominent Eastern Shore families still participated openly in community decision making, while the evolution of a political system more flexible than that found in St. Marys County allowed those without roots in society to participate in such activities as well.[115] Eighty-seven percent of the decisional elite owned property, with an average value of $5,945; 77 percent held an average of 706 acres; and 74 percent owned an average of 14 slaves. Although only one-third were among the county's fifty wealthiest citizens, the community decisional elite contained several sons of wealthy families who reported no taxable property. Inclusion of these sons would increase that figure somewhat, but it would still be less than the 59 percent figure reported for the first party era. The decisional elite's average age was forty-one years. Over one-half were militia officers, and 68 percent served as members of the county's positional elite between 1827 and 1836. They were overwhelmingly affiliated with the Anti-Jackson party (77 percent), but the Jacksonians were recruited from the same social mixture, with an emphasis on wealth and prior public service. Most for whom religious affiliation could be determined belonged to the Episcopal faith (32 percent), yet there was a sizable Methodist presence (23 percent). In contrast to the first party era, however, religion did not serve to radicalize politics in the second party period. The Methodists were overwhelmingly affiliated with the Anti-Jackson party, as were the Episcopalians. Only two men had been active in the first party leadership cadre, while almost one-third (32 percent) were related to members of the decisional elite in the earlier period.

An oligarchy continued to rule in each county during both party eras. Despite their apparent differences, the political culture of each county was influenced by the relative homogeneity of its social and economic infrastructure. There was no substantial social or economic group around which an opposition could assemble. Talbot County's only real minority, its growing free black population, was excluded from the political system by law, and the dominant white population was increasingly concerned about the problem of social control.[116] The Methodists, visibly agitated as a political force during the first party era, were in a period of tranquillity in the early years of the second party system.

A key to the oligarchy's success in maintaining a dominant position was its influence over political recruitment. Prominent and wealthy citizens not only played an active role in the early organization of the second party system, but they adapted to local conditions to maintain their dominance. Without any real party competition in St. Marys County, political recruitment continued in the preparty mold, characterized by alignments along personal or family ties. In Talbot County, the party competition also reflected intraelite competition; two families were the driving force behind political organization. The elite adapted to the proliferation of organizational activities in Talbot County, and the leadership cadre expanded its membership and accommodated some new members, but it never lost control of the evolving system. In both counties the elite monopolized the most prestigious political positions, a pattern Maryland's indirect form of government tended to reinforce. To become governor, U.S. senator, or state senator, one must have peer and political associations beyond county boundaries, and the oligarchy cultivated them through earlier political associations and extensive kin networks. As the system became more open, the advantages of such associations diminished.

In both counties, community leadership roles were heavily influenced by positional and propertied leaders. Rather than mobilizing new leaders representative of untapped subgroups, alternative community decisions demonstrated the rural community's reliance on its institutional leaders. As long as such men were willing to serve, the community apparently expected that they should.

3

Frederick County

The Transitional Area

Frederick County never completely adopted the traditional leadership patterns found in St. Marys and Talbot counties. When this frontier area on Maryland's Western Shore formed into a county in the mid-eighteenth century, local leaders tried to replicate contemporary political forms and practices in use in other counties, but the area's underlying social and economic diversity undermined a successful transplantation. Early community leaders came from the traditional pool of affluent landowners, many of whom were of British-Episcopal extraction, but the community's diversity created potential challenges to this system. Besides the appearance of new leaders, who came from non-British-Episcopal social roots or from nonslaveowning economic bases, solidarity was further rent by an urban-rural conflict. Many of the early leaders lived in and around the county seat, Fredericktown, which served as the nerve center for community affairs. Members of minority ethnic groups widely dispersed throughout the rural sections of the county resented the centralization of power and influence in Fredericktown. This urban-rural rivalry within the county served to complicate political development between the 1780s and 1837, when the legislature created Carroll County from parts of Frederick and Baltimore counties. Because of this fundamental social and economic heterogeneity, it is not surprising to discover that Frederick County's community leadership comprised a complex mosaic during the first and second party eras.

Frederick County's ethnic diversity dated from its first settlement in the 1730s and 1740s. The largest group were English, constituting 72 percent of the county's 1790 population, who migrated from earlier settlements in southern Maryland.[1] The Scots, 5 percent of the population, moved in from the upper sections of Maryland's Western Shore or from Pennsylvania. More than five thousand Germans lived in the county in 1790, comprising 19 percent of its population. Many of them had first migrated into the Monocacy Valley from settlements in Pennsylvania, and this pattern was repeated in the nineteenth century. Their numbers were supplemented by tobacco shippers returning from Europe with

German immigrants who were indentured as servants to pay their passage.[2] The overwhelming majority of Maryland Germans lived in rural areas, among their own kind, demonstrating little interest in assimilating into the dominant English culture.[3] At the end of the eighteenth century they were an untapped political resource.

Such ethnic heterogeneity introduced greater religious variety to Frederick County than existed in other regions of the state. The English tended to affiliate with the Anglican-Episcopal church. Yet the entire county was served by a single parish, All Saints, centered in Fredericktown, which could provide only minimal service. Although members of the elite strove to maintain their adherence to the Episcopal church, existing congregations declined and potential members were lost because the church refused to sponsor new organizations.[4] To the consternation of their clergy, some Frederick County Episcopalians defected to Methodist services for want of activity within their own church.[5] The Methodist church itself, however, was not as popularly supported in Frederick County as in other areas of the upper Western and Eastern Shores. The English population included only a few Baptists and some Quakers.[6] There were also several Catholic churches. The Scots tended to be Presbyterians. The county's religious uniqueness, however, was the result of its German population. The Germans belonged to liturgical faiths, such as the German Reformed or Lutherans, and some adhered to more evangelical churches, such as the Church of the United Brethren, the so-called Dunkers, and the Bethel church.[7] Despite the reported decline among Lutherans in the several decades following the Revolution, the presence of so many German churches, conducting religious services in the German language, was a vital sign of the county's ethnic heterogeneity.

Frederick County was larger and more populous than most Maryland counties. The state intendant of revenue in 1784 gave its acreage as 480,713, at the same time St. Marys County had 206,806 acres, and Talbot County possessed 167,884.[8] Its total population increased from 30,791 in 1790 to 45,789 in 1830.[9] Whereas St. Marys and Talbot counties, indeed southern Maryland and the Eastern Shore in general, fell below Maryland's average white and overall population growth patterns between 1790 and 1840, Frederick County and western Maryland almost always exceeded them. Fredericktown, the county seat, was the third or fourth largest city in the state throughout this era and the most important of the county's twelve towns or villages. Established in 1745, it contained about 2,600 people in 1797. There were about 450 dwellings, seven churches, many shops, and the community supported two or three weekly newspapers during the decade.[10] It served as the adminis-

TO THE POLLS!

Freemen of Frederick County,

The approaching Election is an important one to you. Baltimore

A plan is laid to take all power from the COUNTRY and place all the power of the state in the *City of Baltimore*. The Democrats openly declare that they wish the governor of the state to be elected by a general ticket. In other words they mean

To give the election of Governor to Baltimore.

In Baltimore they can easily assemble together. They can act in concert. They can poll *thousands of illegal votes !* and they are not too good to poll them to carry their point.—How can the people of the *Country* resist them ? We are scattered over a large surface—the counties distant from one another—unable therefore to act in concert and too honest to poll illegal votes if they could find them to poll.

If the democrats succeed the Governor will be elected by a general ticket. Your Governor will then always be chosen from Baltimore. Baltimore will make all appointments to office.

☞ Baltimore will rule the State !

Are you willing to rob yourselves of your birthright and give it to Baltimore ? Do you believe that Baltimore will govern you better than you can govern yourselves ?—NO ! They would rob you of your money as they have robbed the Banks committed to their care. They would plunder your property, as their privateers are now plundering on the ocean the property of the defenceless merchants. The country would be enslaved and made poor to feed the pride and luxury of Baltimore.

The Democrats tell you the treasury of the state is empty. How did it become so ? It was made so by the war brought on us by democrats. It was made so by feeding and clothing and arming the brave militia who turned out to defend our homes and firesides against the enemy. An enemy brought on our defenceless shores by the democratic war. They continually repeat the treasury is poor. Why does it continue poor ? It is because the democrats give to Baltimore the auction tax, which rightfully belongs to the people of the whole state. The democrats give to Baltimore a revenue of at least

☞ Twenty-five Thousand Dollars a year,

Which justly and honestly belongs to the whole state. Read the votes and proceedings of the last session, and you will see this charge against the democrats most fully proved.

FREEMEN OF FREDERICK COUNTY,

Are you in favor of *Baltimore*—or in favor of the *Country ?*

This is the question now to be decided. If you are *in favor of Baltimore*, if you are *against the country*, vote for the democrats. But if you are on the side of the country, then be watchful—be active in the cause—be true to yourselves—and vote like independent men for

Alexander Warfield, Wm. Ross, Robt. G. M'Pherson, & John H. Simmons,

Who are true to the country interest, and free from all suspicion of Baltimore influence, or Baltimore partiality.

TO THE VOTERS OF TALBOT
COUNTY.

MY FELLOW CITIZENS,

MY present engagements, and the necessary attention to my private affairs, will not allow me to appear at every public meeting which is held for the purpose of *Electioneering*. As Free and Independent Men, you are not to be *cajoled* by the show of great *personal respect*, nor caught with the miserable bait of *entertainment*. I have too high a respect for my fellow citizens, to make pretences of the one, or attempt to hold out to them the other. It is enough that the uniform tenor of my conduct is such, as to convince the people, that I hold their good opinion in the highest estimation, and that I am always ready to do them such services as my abilities will enable me to perform.

You have been, for some time past, apprised of my intention to be a Candidate for your suffrages at the next Election for Representatives of the county. If, whilst I was your Representative during several successive years, you thought that I did you *good services*, If you believe that I promoted in some degree the interests of the county, and our *thriving little Capital*, I trust that you will now consider me to be both able and willing to do you like services.

On the score of *Politics*, I would fain avoid the use of those invidious distinctions of Party, by which the country is unhappily divided. It is true that I held WASHINGTON in the highest reverence, and had full confidence in his Administration; and I have not yet been convinced that *Adams* was corrupt; but I solemnly assure you, that if I should be favored with your approbation and elected your Delegate, I will not be, (as I have never been) blindly devoted to any party whatever; but will advocate those measures, and those alone, which I believe to be calculated to advance your interests and preserve your rights. That I will do this, my Fellow Citizens, you have the best security in that common stake which I hold with you all—my *Property*, my *Liberty*, my *Reputation*, and those of my Children.

DAVID KERR.

AUGUST 15, 1803.

Political Broadsides
Courtesy of the Maryland Historical Society, Baltimore

trative center of the county, the communications axis for the region, and
a trading place along the western and eastern commercial routes. Despite
the evolution of strong commercial ties with Baltimore City that pre-
dated the Revolution, when the city had begun to develop as a grain
center, local commercial boosters saw the possibility of Fredericktown's
future autonomous growth. They believed that if roads were improved
to Pennsylvania or if the Monocacy River could be made navigable to the
Potomac River, the lucrative grain trade could be diverted through Fredericktown to exporting facilities in Georgetown or the new federal city.

In the face of such social and economic diversity, a predominantly
British-Episcopalian elite ensconced itself as Frederick County's leadership pool. During the transformation in the late eighteenth century from
a frontier settlement into a stable community, political leaders copied the
prevailing system of political forms and practices in operation throughout the state. Many of these men capitalized on previous experience in
their native counties to assume positions of responsibility, while others
were assimilated into the governing elite through their revolutionary
activity. Most of these community leaders were recruited primarily from
among the English or Scotch, many of whom lived in close proximity to
Fredericktown, thus conforming to the rural oligarchical pattern that
prevailed in Maryland. A disgruntled member of the German community
described the situation prior to 1799: "This County was governed by a
few *Rich* and influential Individuals in and about F[rederick] Towne . . .
altogether forming perhaps the Most *powerful* and *Wealthy* Junto of Feds.
in this or any other state who were enabled from their *Standing, wealth
and talents* to exercise a uncontested influence over a *Similar* set of men
widely distributed over this *County* . . . all [were] inclined to hold in
Sovereign contempt the Germans who form Nearly if not altogether a
Majority of the votes in the County and who with few exceptions had
tamely submitted to this [set] of things."[11]

Between the Revolution and the formation of the first party system
in the 1790s, this elite capitalized upon its natural advantages to monopolize political power. As in other areas, self-nomination, elite interaction, and voter indifference elicited few challenges from the somnolent
mass of society. Elite domination was reinforced by the officer corps of
the reorganized militia, who were recruited from among revolutionary
officers, political leaders, and affluent landowners.[12] The only time this
system appeared to be under attack was during the early stages of the
Whiskey Rebellion in 1794. The Whiskey Boys and local disorganizers
appealed directly to grain producers in Frederick County and found
some sympathy within the ranks of the local militia, but the quick dispatch of militia units from safe areas of the state, combined with prompt

action on the part of local leaders, prevented any lasting erosion of popular support for the existing structure of government.[13]

The polarization of politics into a two-party competition during the 1790s was affected by Frederick County's size, underlying complexity, and a bias against party. Following the statewide pattern, the debate over the Jay Treaty served as a catalyst for the organization of local factions to defend or oppose the national administration. Such polarization violated the existing consensus ideal, and politicians went to great lengths to avoid being stigmatized as members of the opposition.[14] This distrust of parties was stated succinctly by a correspondent writing several years later: "Such are Federals, such Republicans take my word any party would Saddle, Bridle, and Whip us, all Scoundrels, from Adams down to Jefferson."[15]

As political divisions formed simultaneously over national issues in the late 1790s, factions emerged within the new parties along the lines of regional competition within Frederick County itself. During the 1797 state legislative elections, two factions formed over the issue of whether the county should be divided into election districts or remain with one central polling place at the county seat. The reform movement originated in several rural hundreds. They sent delegations to meet in Fredericktown, where the reformers took the unusual step of nominating a slate of four candidates pledged to work for the district system in the state legislature.[16] The Fredericktown faction presented a counterslate, drawn primarily from already self-nominated candidates, in an effort to protect its privileged status.[17] In a series of public letters, the Fredericktown group tried to discredit the reform movement as a sham created by designing men from Taneytown who selfishly sought favorable road legislation or complete autonomy as a new county.[18] The rural faction countered by attacking its opponents as a junto in Fredericktown, composed of "Bankrupt Swindlers! [and] Released Debtors!"[19] The reform slate won the October contest, and two years later the legislature passed a redistricting bill.[20] After its success, the rural coalition disintegrated, while the Fredericktown group still enjoyed the advantages of living in the county seat and having several weekly newspapers at its command.

Many leaders in the preparty system gravitated naturally into the Federalist party. Members of the Johnson family, the Hansons, the Bealls, Colonel John Ross Key, the Potts, the McPhersons, Dr. Philip Thomas, and his son, John Hanson Thomas, to mention only the most active and prominent, were affluent citizens who became party stalwarts, men who concurrently served in political and militia leadership capacities. Talented young men from stagnating areas of the state, notably Roger B. Taney, who married the daughter of Colonel John Ross Key after migrating from Charles County, were selectively assimilated into the elite structure.

Never doubting their right to rule, these leaders had adapted more readily than Federalists in other counties to the changed political conditions as the first party system matured. Appealing to "the friends of religion, order, and government," they enthusiastically organized political meetings and conventions as politics polarized in the late 1790s in an effort to mobilize the electorate to their standard.[21] Frederick County's most prominent citizens chaired meetings to elicit popular support for the Adams administration in 1798 or for "Legislative Choice" in 1800.[22] Federalists were especially attentive to calling regularized conventions for county and district nominations until the electoral tide turned against them.[23] During their active phase, they used militia musters, public celebrations, religious meetings, and barbecues to instruct potential voters in their civic responsibilities.[24] Indeed, one Federalist militia officer, Colonel John Ross Key, was so zealous that he used the ambiguity of the militia law to court-martial common soldiers who differed from his political principles, for "they were Democratic disorganizers and enemies to their country . . . [and] he meant to make use of that law, for the purpose of punishing their political errors."[25] Federalists also recognized the need for a reliable party press. After utilizing the Fredericktown *Rights of Man* for almost a decade, they invited Henry Thompson from Pennsylvania to establish a new party paper, the Fredericktown *Herald*, to act as their principal spokesman.[26]

Between 1802 and 1804 the Federalists were hyperactive in their effort to prevent passage of a suffrage reform bill by the legislature.[27] Armed with a reliable newspaper and led by such dynamic young partisans as Roger B. Taney and John Hanson Thomas, the Federalists took their program to the voters and lost. After 1804 the Federalist party declined as a popular party in the county, but it never tired of informing the people of Republican malfeasance and extolling the virtues of Federalism or of trying to induce factionalism into the opposition camp. In an effort to defeat James Madison's renomination in 1812, for example, Robert G. Harper advised a local leader, "I would suggest for your consideration whether the best method of getting it effected would not be to have an understanding with the Clintonian democrats in your electoral district, and induce them to bring forward Candidates from their own members for whom the federalists will vote, without taking any active or observable part in the election previously."[28] Abandoning public meetings in favor of private caucuses and returning to self-nomination and other preparty forms, the Federalists retained their elitist character. Indeed, considering its transformation from a public to an elitist political orientation, the continuity of its leadership is remarkable. Men of affluence, tradition, and social standing within the community led the party in both its phases.[29]

Unlike the experience in the other rural communities studied thus far, the Republican movement in Frederick County did not develop primarily from a conflict within the ranks of the dominant elite, but evolved when several groups challenged the Federalist hegemony in the last decade of the eighteenth century. The Republican party made a decidedly pluralist appeal to attract rural and ethnic support, and its political goals tended to be more local than national in scope. As in other areas, partisan attention focused on international problems in the 1790s; their real purpose, however, was to change local government and to expand suffrage in an effort to bring new people into the political process. Simultaneously, intraparty rivalry vitiated Republican strength. Like their Federalist counterparts, Fredericktown Republican leaders saw themselves as the proper commanders of party affairs, a view that generated an urban-rural competition. In 1809, even Fredericktown Republicans were involved in a struggle for autonomy, when their Baltimore City brethren tried to centralize party authority by characterizing themselves as the state central committee. Throughout the first party era, local or regional factionalization continuously strained the political stability associated with regularized party procedure.

Republicans saw strength in a pluralist society and appealed to the diverse population for support. They initially projected an antiparty consensus ideal designed to counter the highly partisan Federalist party rhetoric of the late 1790s. As the party gained acceptance, its principles were religious toleration, opposition to entrenched privilege, expansion of suffrage by eliminating freehold requirements, and assimilation of minority ethnic groups into the political process.[30] New leaders emerged from various elements in the county. Characterizing Republican leaders as a "whole clan of inferior demagogues . . . who are no more than candle snuffers in the great play house of democracy" and the impact of their principles on the community as tending "to destroy the regard for every sacred institution, both civil and religious, and to efface from the mind the sense of propriety and decorum," Frederick County Federalists used national stereotypes to pass judgments on their local political opponents.[31] Diversity was a threat to their continued domination and an invitation to social and political disorganization.

To mobilize an apathetic, diverse, and widely distributed population, Frederick County Republicans initiated a policy of aggressive political organization.[32] They proselytized their program to the public at civic and religious meetings, militia musters, and private barbecues. In an attempt to awaken the county's German population, they relied heavily on a few assimilated German families to make partisan appeals in the German language. To facilitate communication in such a large territory, they placed great emphasis on establishing a party press. Initially they used Matthias Bartgis's existing weekly paper, the Fredericktown *Federal Gazette*, which he thoughtfully renamed the *Republican Gazette* in February 1801 to show his support for the new Jefferson administration.[33] Notwithstanding such expediencies, the party's editorial policy was directed by Abraham Shriver, a Fredericktown merchant and activist, who wrote articles and enlisted the aid of his brother, Andrew Shriver, who lived in the rural county, to write German-language pieces.[34] During the campaign season, Bartgis published a second paper, the Fredericktown *Hornet*, primarily as a political sheet, with its last page in German. This combination lasted until the fall of 1802, when Abraham Shriver, alarmed at the possible repercussions that the founding of a new Federalist paper might have on popular support for the delicate suffrage question and dissatisfied with Bartgis because of his "mulish disposition" and his political cowardice, decided on the necessity of creating a truly independent Republican press.[35] By October he had party support to hire a young Baltimore printer, John B. Colvin, who was employed with the Baltimore Republican paper, to edit the Fredericktown *Republican Advocate*.[36] Colvin not only published the *Republican Advocate* but became an active party organizer. The Republicans also published German-language articles in the Hanover, Pennsylvania, *Pennsylvanische Wochenshrift* and used this press to print and distribute political broadsides throughout the county.[37]

Republicans promoted the development of a regularized convention system. Conventions were called to nominate candidates for state and federal offices and to organize support for the official slate.[38] Fredericktown leaders often called for the other districts to send delegations to a convention, but as the system matured, this process became an annual event. By 1806, such Republican organizational activities had produced two different leadership cadres: a nucleus of political insiders, who saw themselves as the core of the party and sought to protect that status; and individuals who assumed irregular district leadership roles and who claimed that the first group was sometimes usurping the right of the whole party from selfish motives.

The political insiders tended to live in Fredericktown and often reflected the British-Episcopalian characteristics of leaders in the preparty system. They included Dr. John Tyler, Roger Nelson, Daniel Clarke, Jr., Abraham Shriver, John Hoffman, and John B. Colvin. Dr. Tyler, a frequent chairman of party events and a candidate as presidential or senatorial elector between 1800 and 1808, moved to Fredericktown in 1786 from neighboring Prince Georges County to practice medicine. A man in his late thirties at the turn of the century, he was an Episcopalian, a Mason, and served in the state senate between 1801 and 1803. Roger Nelson, a native Frederick County attorney, whose wealth placed him forty-third on the 1797 tax rolls, was another Republican leader. He presided at many party meetings and was elected to the House of Delegates, the state senate, and the United States Congress before obtaining a judicial appointment in 1810. He was a captain in a volunteer cavalry unit and belonged to the local Episcopal church and the Masonic society. Daniel Clarke, Jr., another attorney, was a two-term member of the lower house when Nelson served and also a party organizer. Although Tyler, Nelson, and Clarke received all the emoluments of power because they were positional leaders when they were active in party affairs, Abraham Shriver, the connection between the urban Republican party and the widely distributed German community, often believed that it was his work that held the party together. A Fredericktown merchant and militia officer belonging to an important and widely connected local German family affiliated with the Zion Reformed church, he was an indefatigable party worker who thrived on the intrigue and operation of politics. In 1803, he was appointed to the County Court, where he taught himself the law as he served. He remained almost continually on the bench into the 1830s. Another Republican of German descent, John Hoffman, belonged to the Episcopal church and lived in Fredericktown. Between 1800 and 1808 he acted as chairman for several party conventions; in 1805 he was appointed to the Levy Court. John B. Colvin, a native of New York, was an activist between 1802, when he arrived to establish the party press, until the end of 1806, when he left Fredericktown to edit a paper in the national capital. His prominence in the party was due primarily to his position as editor.

The political outsiders were scattered throughout the various rural districts in the county. They included Andrew Shriver, Major Joseph Swearingen, and Ludwig Wampler. Andrew Shriver, Abraham's older brother, operated a family mill in Union Mills and had a large following among the Germans because of his ability to speak and write in their native tongue. An early organizer, he appears to have lost his brother's enthusiasm for the game of politics; although he was appointed to the Levy Court in 1802, he became increasingly dissatisfied with Fredericktown's domination of Republican affairs.[39] Major Joseph Swearingen of Middletown, a Republican party leader of British descent, was a militia officer who became a member of the Levy Court in 1802 along with Andrew Shriver. Ludwig Wampler, a German who belonged to the Evangeli-

cal Reformed church, acted as chairman of the lower house nominating
convention in 1806.

The Shriver family provides a good example of the operations of a
rural ethnic kin network that augmented and solidified local party organization.[40] David Shriver, Sr., a native of Pennsylvania, was a member of
the revolutionary Committee of Observation from 1774 to 1775 and the
Maryland Convention in 1776 and for the next thirty years served almost
continuously in both houses of the state legislature. Two of his other
sons were politically active, as were two sons-in-law, John Schley, who
was beginning a political career that persisted through the second party
system, and Adam Forney of Pennsylvania, who acted as an intermediary
with the German press in Hanover. This German dynasty was the object
of Federalist newspaper attacks, but such barbs often missed their real
significance. During the first party era, ties of kinship acted to cement
people separated by distance and poor communication as mere partisanship never could. The success of the Shrivers was remarkable because
they were not a traditionally wealthy or prominent family, but they were
able to tap the somnolent German population and turn it to political
advantage.

Considering the existence of so many forces inviting disunity among
Republican leaders—personal jealousies, regional competition, and
urban-rural conflict—the evolution of associations within the party designed to promote factional self-interest was almost inevitable. An early
cabal formed around members of the Masonic lodge in Fredericktown,
who were instrumental in choosing lower house candidates in 1808.
Identified with Republicans having roots in the traditional political culture, such as Dr. John Tyler, Congressman Roger Nelson, and Tobias
Butler, the cabal's long-term effect was to polarize Republican leaders
along the lines of old political insiders versus the outsider continuum.[41]
As in the past, the outsiders tended to be members of the German rural constituency. The appearance of an innocuous report soon after the
nomination, announcing the creation of the Republican Library Company
in Fredericktown, hardly suggested the gravity of intraparty factionalization.[42] Originally created to counter the influence and exclusiveness of
Republican Masons, the Library Company, with Abraham Shriver as its
energizing spirit, unexpectedly ran afoul of an effort by urban Republicans to unify the state party under the leadership of Baltimore City's
Congressman Samuel Smith.[43] At issue was the forthcoming congressional election, but beneath the surface a schism developed among Maryland Republicans over who should lead the national party, James Madison
or George Clinton. Samuel Smith's political organization tried to utilize
the Tammany Society to centralize support for Madison and thereby

strengthen Baltimore's control over the state party. From Smith's point of view, Congressman Roger Nelson's application for a local Frederick County Tammany Society charter advanced his plan; in terms of the rivalry among Frederick County Republicans, however, it constituted an immediate threat to the fledgling Republican Library Company and implied its eventual demise because of the hint that future party perquisites would be dispensed only by members of the Tammany Society. The conflict among the Republican Library Company, the Tammany Society, and the Frederick County Republican Masons was solved by compromise and accommodation.[44] Congressman Smith could not force the Tammany Society on the unwilling Frederick County Republicans, nor did he insist that they form a compromise Whig society, but he did encourage them to call a truce and end their mutually destructive feud. Personal battles continued to divide local Republican leadership, but no one was able to construct lasting subparty organizations to perpetuate exclusive control. The Republican Library Company and the ill-fated Tammany Society proved short-term devices.[45]

Thus far I have discussed partisanship in terms of party rhetoric and imagery to suggest that there were fundamental differences between the appeals and assumptions underlying the Federalist and Republican movements in Frederick County. For most communities literary material is the only evidence available to the historian, but for Frederick County the survival of poll books permits analysis based on a unique aspect of political behavior: they reveal the citizens' actual vote. Under the viva voce system a person voted out loud and the clerk entered it into a poll book next to the man's name. By linking individuals through other tax, religious, and social records, and by reaggregating voters into ethnic, economic, or religious groups, the historian may perceive whether the voting patterns correlated with interpretations based on literary sources.[46]

Poll books surviving for Frederick County for the years 1796 to 1802 show that voters fell into two categories. A minority of the electorate divided to form a stable nucleus for both parties. Rather than shifting from one party to another in response to volatile election issues, these individuals rarely changed their voting allegiance. The majority of the potential voting population, however, cast their ballots infrequently, that is, they voted in fewer than three of the eight elections. Most fell into apathy after participating in one election. These infrequent voters, whose numerical strength often held the electoral balance, were the target of the increased voter mobilization efforts by party leaders.

The social basis of electoral behavior can be determined by reaggregating individual voters into party groups.[47] The Federalist party was supported overwhelmingly by British (62.8 percent), Scotch (72 percent), and Irish (59.6 percent), while the Republicans drew strong support from Germans (53.3 percent) and naturalized Germans (66 percent). Members of German religious denominations were ardent Republicans; those of British denominations favored the Federalist party. Such political manifestations of cultural cohesiveness were strongest in homogeneous ethnic enclaves throughout the county, but operated less forcefully as an individual's wealth increased or if he owned slaves. Wealthy or slaveowning Germans, for instance, tended to favor the Federalist party rather than the Republicans. Voter turnout was heaviest in urban places and diminished in rural areas, where access to newspapers and active party recruitment efforts were limited.

Although partisanship and ethnicity were closely interconnected during the first party era, Republican leaders were recruited from the traditional leadership pool. Men such as Roger Nelson, Dr. John Tyler, and Daniel Clarke, Jr., emerged as leaders in the Republican party for reasons independent of the party's cultural appeal. First as residents of Fredericktown, then as young professionals, they were adept at placing themselves at the head of the formerly inarticulate groups who comprised the Republican movement and whose support advanced them into positions of community leadership. Some Germans, such as the Shriver family, also shared political leadership, but the elite norms of the pre-party system held fast in these years.

Community leaders recognized that Frederick County's development was dependent upon internal improvements. Unlike citizens in areas along major waterways, who advocated the construction of canals, local boosters primarily favored road improvements.[48] In the context of the late eighteenth and early nineteenth centuries, this meant resolving two interrelated problems: reforming local government and working to charter private toll roads in the state legislature. Traditionally, the operation of rural local government was entrusted to the county court, which functioned as a combined administrative and judicial unit. This duality was modified for selected counties by passage of a legislative reform act in 1798 that empowered a levy court to oversee local administrative matters and restricted the county court to a judicial role.[49] For Frederick County, this act resulted in the transfer of road maintenance responsibilities from the county court to the levy court.[50] The new overseers, however, were unwilling to expend the money necessary to build an adequate all-weather road system; internal improvement advocates, therefore, soon directed their efforts to establishing private road-building companies incorporated by the state. Such road projects often crossed county borders and became involved in regional internal improvements competition in the state legislature, making the dynamics of local community leadership complex and invariably secretive.

Local boosters worked through the county delegation in the state legislature in their efforts to incorporate private road companies. This involved gathering petitions and memorials attesting to the need for better roads. Often the contending factions on both the county and state levels thwarted their plans.[51] Consequently, despite repeated efforts in Frederick County to charter various projects, only in 1797 and 1805 did the legislature incorporate private road companies during the early national era. In both instances, the key agents were the county delegations to the state legislature. Local notables, many of whom were recruited from the ranks of the positional leadership or from members of the oligarchy, were authorized in the enabling legislation to act as commissioners to sell the stock.[52] Some of these men became managers of the new turnpike companies.[53]

Positional leaders who served in the state legislature also played a dominant role in the political reform and patronage decision-making process. In addition to separating the administrative and judicial functions of the county court and dividing the county into election districts, reformers worked through the legislature to lower suffrage requirements and to expand the electoral base in the state. In Frederick County the question of suffrage reform was highly partisan, and leaders of the Republican party as well as Republican state legislators were popularly identified as securing its passage.

The dispensing of patronage reflected a similar reliance on positional leaders.[54] Local political activists expected their federal representatives to secure and protect preferential mail routes or to obtain federal appointments for them.[55] There were few remunerative federal patronage positions, however, in western Maryland. On the state level, institutional norms funneled patronage decision making through county legislative delegations, and they used their prerogative to best political advantage.[56] For both the federal and state levels, the elected legislative representatives were the most important figures in patronage decision making.

During the first party era, the decisional elite for Frederick County aggregated from various decisional situations numbered fifty-four men.[57] Their average age was forty-seven years; 79 percent owned property, with an average valuation of $3,521, and 70 percent owned an average of 929 acres.[58] Only a minority (21 percent) owned slaves, with an average holding of fourteen. Religious data could be found for just over half (57 percent) of this group. Despite the fact that it was a modestly supported denomination in Frederick County, 67 percent of those for whom re-

ligion could be determined were Episcopalians; the Evangelical German Reformed church had the second most communicants (19 percent)
within the religious group. The ethnicity variable was stronger because
81 percent of the leaders could be categorized. Of this group, almost 70
percent were English (50 percent British, 13 percent English-Welsh,
3 percent Scottish, and 3 percent Scotch-Irish); the remainder were
German.

Community decision makers in Frederick County during the first
party era in some ways mirrored their counterparts in St. Marys and Talbot counties. They were primarily recruited from the ranks of English-
Episcopalian stock and were property owners. There was considerable
continuity for an area characterized by social heterogeneity and economic diversification. Yet, fewer of these leaders held slaves, and the
representation of the German population exceeded their proportion of
the overall population. A large number of the decisional leaders resided
in Fredericktown, and they jealously sought to protect their privileged
status against the encroachments of outlying community leaders.

The Intervening Years

Between the first and second party eras several important developments affected Frederick County. Farmers produced a greater variety of
crops and livestock for local and Baltimore markets, and their interest in
slave labor diminished further. The county continued to attract new
population; by the early 1830s, Fredericktown boasted over five thousand inhabitants.[59] The growth of Fredericktown, however, intensified
the persistent conflict between urban and rural areas. In addition to the
political and government rivalries characteristic of the first party era, new
jealousies arose as Fredericktown residents monopolized county banking operations, especially after the office of the newly created Bank of
Westminster opened in Fredericktown in 1817.[60] Several subtle mutations affected established social patterns. The Germans were plagued by
problems of intergenerational conflict over the issue of assimilation in
the 1820s. In a controversy over the use of English in religious services, German congregations divided between those favoring tradition to
reinforce ethnic identity and second-generation Germans who left the
church in favor of English-language services. Some Lutheran religious
leaders undertook a program to reach German youths in English.[61] The
general trend, however, was a division into German- and English-language
churches and a lessened reliance on religious leaders recruited from
Germany. The basis for ethnic cohesiveness slowly eroded.

Political developments were equally important. The resurgence of Maryland Federalism after 1807 provided a pool of former Federalists who were trained and available to assume leadership positions in both major parties as the second party system evolved. Many of these men, such as Roger B. Taney, Colonel John McPherson, Jr., and Congressman John Lee, stood at the threshold of their careers when the Federalist party disintegrated. The Republicans fared no better. In the early 1820s, local resentment to caucuses and rivalries among supporters of the various presidential contenders culminated in Republican schisms in Frederick County, just as in other areas throughout the state, destroying party unity and strength.[62] Consequently, leading Republicans, notably Dr. William Tyler and John and Madison Nelson, sons of former Congressman Roger Nelson, found themselves in search of a reliable constituency. A curious sidelight to this factionalization was the humiliation visited upon the Shriver family by their own party. Samuel Barnes, the editor of the Republican newspaper who had been recruited enthusiastically by Abraham Shriver in 1813, turned on his former benefactor in the early 1820s by attacking his integrity as a county court judge.[63] Abraham Shriver was too entrenched to be unseated by these aspersions, but his brother Andrew Shriver, a member of the levy court, was removed by the actions of a local Republican state legislator, who adamantly opposed his reappointment on the indefensible grounds that he was "a personal enemy."[64] Both brothers were thus forced to retire from active political service during the early years of the decade. On the eve of the 1824 presidential contest, Andrew Shriver wrote his son: "The old Distinctions of Federal and Republican seem to be lost sight of, and local division {is} starting up on every side, calculated to *loosen* the ties by which we have hitherto held together as *one people*, for the first time we have an approaching Presidential and Gubernatorial Election at hand without any prominent characters being brought forward for either that are calculated {for} the people in a choice."[65]

The Second Party Era

Despite the disturbing political chaos perceived by Andrew Shriver, the emerging community leaders represented an amalgam of families prominent during the first party period and new men who capitalized on their popularity to rise as leaders through the profusion of organizational activities characteristic of the second party period. Visible manifestations of wealth and status, such as membership on church vestries or receipt of militia commissions, were less important in the 1830s and became largely dysfunctional when efforts were made to convert them in actual power relationships. The militia, for instance, a traditional authority symbol in the early national era, was poorly supported by the public, badly disorganized internally, and under attack as being structurally elitist and undemocratic. It ceased to function as a protopolitical organization where potential voters could be assembled and influenced.

The vibrant second party system that evolved in Frederick County between 1824 and 1836 was much more sophisticated in organizational activities than its counterpart in the first party era. Leaders of both parties conscientiously employed an elaborate range of devices to inform and mobilize the electorate. They instituted regular conventions to nominate candidates for county, state, and national elective offices; organized central committees to coordinate and direct party activity; and relied heavily on a Fredericktown press to disseminate party information throughout the county and electoral districts.

The Anti-Jackson party was the lineal descendant of the Republican party in Frederick County, yet its leaders represented a combination of former Republicans and Federalists.[66] Dr. John Tyler and his nephew, Dr. William Bradley Tyler, served on central committees and as officers of conventions. Jacob Shriver, brother of Republican leaders Abraham and Andrew Shriver, won election to the House of Delegates as an Anti-Jacksonian in 1828. William Schley, an attorney who was the Shrivers' nephew and who married into the family of an affluent member of the Washington County political elite, was a member of the central committee before being elected to the Maryland senate in 1836. Descendants of once dominant Federalist families, such as Richard Potts, Jr., or the several sons of Colonel John McPherson, or John Lee, son of former Governor Thomas Sims Lee and an important local political figure in the 1820s in his own right, also rose to prominence in the Anti-Jackson party. Men of less distinctive lineage also became party leaders.[67] Moses Worman, a resident of Fredericktown who belonged to the Levy Court between 1831 and 1836, was the leading Anti-Jackson party activist in this period. A man of moderate wealth but of immoderate activity, he frequently chaired lower house nomination conventions, served as a member of the central committee, and attended other conventions as a delegate.[68]

The editors of the party presses were also important party organizers. William Ogden Niles, son of Hezekiah Niles, publisher of the national *Niles Weekly Register*, edited the Fredericktown *Herald*, which advocated the causes of the Bank of the United States, the American System, internal improvements, and Henry Clay. He also acted as secretary to many party meetings. Samuel Barnes, brother-in-law of Baltimore's Sheppard C. Leakin, who published the Anti-Jackson Baltimore *Commercial Chronicle*, edited the Fredericktown *Political Examiner* from its founding in 1813 until he sold it to George Woodbridge in 1829 and moved to Baltimore to direct the major party newspaper in that city. Besides introducing a purely party campaign paper in 1828, the Fredericktown *Anti-Jacksonian*, he participated in party organizational affairs. Neilson Poe rounded out this politically active editorial phalanx. He purchased the *Examiner* from Woodbridge in 1836 and published it thereafter.[69] During the second party system, party editors were less dependent on backing by members of the local oligarchy and were able to act more autonomously if their paper enjoyed popular support.

Other party leaders included members of distinguished families, Germans, and young professionals.[70] Party delegates to state government, as well as candidates for those offices, acted as party organizers during the campaign season. Some former Republicans, who had fallen out with the dominant Republican faction in the 1820s and had been tepid Jacksonian supporters after 1828, joined the Anti-Jackson party after the Maysville veto in 1830.

The Jackson party coalesced more slowly.[71] Like its political competition, it drew its leadership from the remnants of the earlier political system and from all levels of affluence within the community. Similarly, its Fredericktown members saw themselves as the core of the party and assumed the primary responsibility for directing party operations. The Jacksonians, however, were plagued by an internecine conflict between their former Federalist and Republican leaders, which vitiated the party's effectiveness.

Former Federalists were the dynamic element in the formation of the Frederick County Jackson party. Roger B. Taney, a noted attorney and onetime state senator, was especially active in organizing the party on a statewide basis between 1824 and 1827, although he was more properly a resident of Baltimore City after 1823 than a citizen of Fredericktown. After his departure, his longtime friend, William M. Beall, his former law student, Richard H. Marshall, and his septuagenarian uncle, Joseph Taney, worked in Frederick on behalf of the new party.[72] Francis Thomas, son of the affluent Federalist leader Colonel John Thomas, who ranked as the forty-third wealthiest property holder in 1835, was a primary political organizer as the party took form after 1829. Although he appeared infrequently as a convention officer or delegate, he served in the state legislature and in the federal Congress and used his formal positions to party advantage and to proselytize for reform.[73]

Early Jackson leaders included a number of former Republicans as well. Dr. William Tyler, a prominent Fredericktown physician and wealthy landowner in his forties, was an energetic party leader between 1827 and 1832. As chairman of Fredericktown meetings, member of the central committee, and twice candidate for presidential elector, Dr. Tyler was highly visible. The two sons of Republican Congressman Roger Nelson were also indefatigable party organizers. John Nelson, an attorney elected to the state senate in 1831 and sent as chargé d'affaires to the Kingdom of the Two Sicilies by the Jackson administration in 1832, worked closely with Taney as the party evolved in its early years.[74] Madison Nelson, an attorney in his thirties, acted as a delegate to conventions and was on party central committees about the same time his brother left the county. Most of the Shrivers were publicly neutral to the Jacksonian movement, but one brother, Isaac Shriver, a tavern owner in Westminster, entered party affairs and, to the consternation of his kin, was twice elected to the House of Delegates as a Jacksonian.[75]

The most dynamic party organizers were based in Fredericktown. Besides Dr. Tyler, the Nelson brothers, Roger B. Taney, and William M. Beall, the most active leaders lived in the county seat.[76] Captain George W. Ent, for instance, participated from 1828 to 1836 as chairman of local meetings and of several central committees and as president of the 1833 congressional nomination district convention. In addition, he acted as a delegate to state and national conventions. Ent, whose combined activities made him the highest scoring Jacksonian leader, was a moderate property owner, having three town lots for a total valuation of $580 in 1835. Newspaper editors were also important party organizers. There were three editors of the Jackson paper, the Fredericktown *Independent Citizen*, between 1828 and 1836, and each participated in party affairs during his tenure.[77] Similarly, Matthias E. Bartgis, son of longtime Fredericktown newspaperman Matthias Bartgis who died in 1825, was a local Jackson party activist although his paper, the Fredericktown *Republican Gazette*, was publicly neutral on political matters.

The rivalry within the Jackson party leadership had two sources. Former Republican leaders, especially Dr. William Tyler, who was considered as a potential gubernatorial candidate when the Jacksonians held a legislative majority in Annapolis during the 1829 session, were outraged when the new Jacksonian governor used state patronage to favor Federalist members of the party at the expense of Republicans. That action, followed soon after by President Jackson's famous Maysville veto, convinced Dr. Tyler and his county allies that they should consider abandoning the embryonic Jackson party and attempt to resuscitate a statewide Republican party based firmly on traditional first party principles.[78] As this schism developed, local rivals within the party jockeyed for leadership positions. Francis Thomas, a young attorney elevated to the

House of Delegates in 1829 and selected by his peers as speaker for that session and elected to Congress in 1831, claimed the right to lead the party. By characterizing his opponents within the party as "trimmers" and emphasizing his own unswerving support for President Jackson and the administration's heir apparent, Martin Van Buren, Thomas portrayed himself as a party stalwart. The old Republican wing of the party established its own press in 1833, the Fredericktown *Sentinel*, but they never successfully undermined Thomas's leadership.[79] By 1835 most of his early rivals had been forced from power and his position in the party was enhanced by his aggressive stance on the reform issue. Yet new men continued to vie for Jackson party leadership, and unity was rent by other aspiring leaders seeking to displace Thomas.[80] By the late 1830s, however, Thomas reigned as the recognized leader of the Jackson party in western Maryland.

The socioeconomic characteristics of the Frederick County party activists are presented in Table 3.1. Contrary to party rhetoric and conventional wisdom, the data for leaders of both parties are remarkably alike. Despite the consistently higher wealth figures for the Anti-Jacksonians, the distribution of wealth and the percentage of the party leaders holding it are very similar.

Enthusiasm for internal improvement projects promising to facilitate western trade was substantial in Frederick County. Residents of the Eastern Shore may have been reticent because of their geographical isolation, and those of Baltimore City and southern Maryland may have been divided between canals and railroads as affording the best mode of transport, but both projects benefited western Maryland. Popular fervor was dampened only because of the delay between 1828 and 1832 caused by the dispute over the right-of-way at the strategically placed Point of Rocks between the Chesapeake and Ohio Canal Company and the Baltimore and Ohio Railroad Company which was under adjudication in the courts.

There were two focal points in this effort to bring internal improvements to western Maryland: the state legislature in Annapolis and local popular support for greater state action. In Annapolis, Frederick County delegates persistently pressed for legislative action, and they were aided by intensive lobbying efforts by the companies concerned. The Chesapeake and Ohio Canal Company sent its president, George Corbin Washington, a former Anti-Jackson congressman representing the Montgomery-Frederick County district and a recent member of the Executive Council, to persuade legislators to vote in its interests.[81] In addition to Washington's exertions in Annapolis during the critical 1836 legislative session, the company employed two other lobbyists, James W.

Table 3.1. Frederick County Leaders, 1827–1836

Jackson Party (n = 117)			Anti-Jackson Party (n = 267)		
Variable	n	%	Variable	n	%
Age			*Age*		
60+	2	7	60+	9	16
50–59	8	28	50–59	10	17
40–49	8	28	40–49	12	21
30–39	7	24	30–39	14	24
20–29	4	14	20–29	13	22
n = 29 (25%)			n = 58 (22%)		
mean = 44			mean = 42		
Slaves			*Slaves*		
over 100	0	0	over 100	0	0
20–99	0	0	20–99	3	2
10–19	5	10	10–19	20	17
5–9	16	32	5–9	26	21
1–4	29	58	1–4	70	60
n = 50 (43%)			n = 119 (44%)		
mean = 4			mean = 6		
Lots			*Lots*		
over 10	0	0	over 10	0	0
6–9	1	2	6–9	3	4
2–5	22	54	2–5	30	37
1	18	44	1	48	59
n = 41 (36%)			n = 81 (30%)		
mean = 2.1			mean = 1.8		
Acres			*Acres*		
over 1,000	2	3	over 1,000	7	6
600–999	4	6	600–999	10	8
100–599	39	63	100–599	87	71
10–99	17	28	10–99	18	15
n = 62 (53%)			n = 122 (45%)		
mean = 291			mean = 410		
Wealth			*Wealth*		
over $50,000	0	0	over $50,000	0	0
over $10,000	0	0	over $10,000	3	2
$5,000–$9,999	7	8	$5,000–$9,999	11	5
$1,000–$4,999	39	45	$1,000–$4,999	88	44

Table 3.1. Frederick County Leaders, 1827–1836 *(cont.)*

Jackson Party (n = 117)			Anti-Jackson Party (n = 267)		
Variable	*n*	*%*	*Variable*	*n*	*%*
$600–$999	12	14	$600–$999	31	16
$100–$599	29	33	$100–$599	66	33
$10–$99	—	—	$10–$99	—	—
n = 87 (74%)			*n* = 199 (75%)		
mean = $1,584			mean = $1,706		

McCulloch, a Baltimore County politician and a former speaker of the House of Delegates, and Joseph J. Merrick, an Anti-Jacksonian politician from Washington County who married into the family of Governor James Thomas of St. Marys County.[82] This formidable group did not draw further upon the Frederick County elite for greater lobbying efforts.

Community activists who favored internal improvements organized several meetings to generate public support.[83] The leadership revolved around community notables, bipartisan political leaders, and local officeholders, especially the mayor of Fredericktown. When the railroad link between Baltimore City and Fredericktown opened in November 1831, there was a meeting to celebrate the event and delegations were dispatched to the 1834 canal convention and to the 1836 internal improvements convention, both held in Baltimore City. Only one token delegate was sent to the Brownsville railroad convention in 1836, but such inattention was not surprising since its object would not benefit Frederick County directly. Despite a general enthusiasm for internal improvements, some recognized that Baltimore City would probably be the ultimate benefactor.

Seventy-two persons were involved in community support activities for internal improvements in Frederick County between 1828 and 1836.[84] Thomas Carlton, mayor of Fredericktown and an avid Jacksonian reformer prior to his death in 1835, chaired many of the meetings. Colonel John McPherson, Jr., fourth wealthiest man in the county in 1835 and prominent Anti-Jacksonian political leader, was the second most active internal improvements booster. The remaining supporters included other members of politically important families,[85] members of the community banking establishment,[86] who were overwhelmingly Anti-Jacksonian (72 percent) in their political preferences, and members of the political delegations from both parties who publicly supported this issue.[87] To a far greater degree than was true in Baltimore City, Frederick County community leaders transcended divisive party principle to labor for the benefit of the region. Drawing from the leadership pool of both parties, the banking community, and the positional leaders, internal improvements generated community solidarity.

The reform issue caused an unexpected ambivalence among Frederick County partisans. As in other large and underrepresented populous areas, there was a keen awareness of the basic inequity built into the prevailing system; yet, as in other rural areas, reformers were concerned that Baltimore City's large and growing population should not entitle it to greater representation that might in fact reduce rural areas to the status of mere dependencies.[88] Therefore, they advocated changing the constitution so that population and representation were interrelated, but with restrictions limiting Baltimore City's delegation to the size of that of the largest county.

The party roots of the reform issue were intricately intertwined. Viewed only in the context of the constitutional crisis of 1836, reformers were identified as avid Jacksonians, or, more precisely, as leaders who advocated the succession of Martin Van Buren to the head of the national party. Many of these Van Burenites used reform as a vehicle to assure their dominance of the state party. Over the longer term, however, the bipartisan nature of the reform issue became apparent. Of the 122 persons identified with reform between 1832 and 1836, 60 (49 percent) were Jacksonians and 45 (37 percent) were Anti-Jacksonians.[89] It was with good reason that the Anti-Jackson press of both Fredericktown and Baltimore City strenuously objected to having reform used as a party issue to their exclusion.[90]

The dynamo behind the reform movement was Jacksonian Congressman Francis Thomas.[91] He used the issue of constitutional reform to strengthen his leadership within the local and state Jackson party and to reduce the influence of his county rivals, especially Dr. William Tyler.[92] Beginning in 1832, Dr. Tyler chaired several meetings advocating a bipartisan reform movement.[93] Employing the pages of the Fredericktown *Citizen*, Thomas attacked the principles of bipartisanship through 1833, seeking to compromise Dr. Tyler's credibility as a party leader.[94] By 1835, Dr. Tyler had withdrawn from active politics and Congressman Thomas reinstituted the strategy of local bipartisan reform as his own policy, but the Fredericktown Anti-Jackson press opposed it as being a device solely to achieve Jackson party goals.[95] In 1836, reform was without doubt a Jacksonian issue.

Despite the claims by Jacksonians that reform was their sole possession, their leadership reflected wider community support. Indeed, the leading reformer was Gideon Bantz, the prominent politician who was the Anti-Jacksonian senatorial elector candidate in 1836. A frequent chairman of county meetings, he was called to be vice-chairman of the statewide 1836 Annapolis reform convention. Colonel John McPherson, Jr., an important Anti-Jackson and internal improvements leader, chaired two meetings and belonged to the central reform committee in 1835. Thomas Sappington, an incumbent state senator but not an active party leader, chaired the 1833 reform convention in Baltimore. Other prominent Anti-Jacksonians served in lesser capacities.[96] The Jacksonians, of course, were strongly represented in the reform cause. Besides Congressman Thomas and Dr. Tyler, party leaders, editors, and state legislators were intimately involved with this movement.[97] The bipartisan reform activities by party leaders frustrated Anti-Jackson party purists, one of whom lamented: "I regret *very* much the course that has been taken by some of the members of our party in this *outrageous* and *treasonable* attempt at reform."[98]

As the constitutional reform movement reached its boiling point between 1832 and 1836, there was a concurrent effort to form a new county from parts of Frederick and Baltimore counties in the hope of quelling the long-term rural discontent within Frederick County between the Fredericktown and Westminster cliques. The plan appealed to conservative reformers because it would give western Maryland more representation in the legislature without significantly altering the balance of power built into the existing constitution. The paucity of information regarding this matter in the public press was testimony to the negative power of party leaders to stifle what they did not want broadcast. This fact was recognized by advocates of the new county, who tried unsucessfully to enlist the editor of a politically neutral Fredericktown paper to their cause and were finally forced to establish a new paper in 1833.[99] Furthermore, hidden beneath interparty competition and the reform question was a contest over the new county plan between leaders and candidates within each party. The key political issue before candidates for the state legislature in 1832 and 1833 was not party regularity, but their position on the creation of the new county.[100] Because the formation of a new county could diminish the momentum that was building to challenge the structure of government under the old constitution, reformers treated the new county movement as a conservative trick to divert popular attention from the real need for total constitutional reform.

The creation of Carroll County in 1837 was the product of compromise and conciliation. First proposed as Paca County in 1785, the plan was revived sporadically thereafter and considered in earnest in 1832.[101] A bill authorized the polling of voters in the affected parts of Frederick and Baltimore counties to determine popular support for the creation of the new county. The advocates of the proposed county included Isaac Shriver, Washington Van Bibber, William Cost Johnson, and other political officeholders from both parties.[102] Baltimore County voters and those from Liberty and New Market districts in Frederick County did not ratify the plan with a majority, and it failed in 1833. Proponents of the new county continued to agitate, and they presented a modified plan to the legislature in 1835.[103] Before the legislature acted, the constitutional reform issue intruded itself, and Governor Veazey endorsed the plan as a conciliatory gesture to western Maryland after the abortive senatorial electoral crisis. With its county seat in Westminster, the new Carroll County embodied the principles of minimal change to Maryland's existing institutional structure.

Leadership patterns associated with patronage were similar to those previously experienced in rural areas. The governor and Executive Council dispensed state largess on the advice of the county delegations.[104] Sometimes individuals applied for appointment directly to the governor[105] or were recommended by county party leaders,[106] but political norms were designed to work through the institutional leaders. For instance, General Thomas Contee Worthington, elected to the Executive Council between 1831 and 1833, moderated the conflicting demands of his county delegation. In one instance, he wrote, "I do not concur with the delegates in recommending the foregoing list—It is too proscriptive." In another, he sought balance, observing, "I cannot perceive the policy of turning out one Jackson man, who is moderate and exerts little or no influence against us, and supporting one who is active, bitter and very annoying to our party." If party demands were paramount over political wisdom, the result was inevitable: "We shall lose some votes in this county."[107] General Worthington was not simply responding to the dominant party's normal proclivity to punish its political opponents; he was also asking for restraint to preserve harmony within the Anti-Jacksonian party that had been strained by the new county issue.[108]

On the federal level, in the absence of a Jacksonian congressman representing the district, local party leaders advised the new administration soon after it took office. Initially, Frederick County Jackson leaders advocated shifting the contract to publish the federal laws from the Anti-Jacksonian Fredericktown *Herald* to the new party press, the Fredericktown *Independent Citizen*, but once this was accomplished there was little else of concern.[109] Early state party organizers, such as Dr. William Tyler, John Nelson, and Roger B. Taney, provided contacts for the administration in the county until the election of Francis Thomas to Congress.[110] Following the previously institutionalized norms, the administration thereafter relied increasingly on the Jacksonian congressman for patronage advice.[111] Congressman Thomas's triumph came in 1835 when his nominee was appointed U.S. marshal, defeating the Baltimore City candidate.[112] This appointment probably was designed to distribute federal patronage positions more equitably throughout the state, in deference to widespread rural resentment over the virtual monopoly of such appointments by Baltimore City and to reward Thomas for his unstinting support for Martin Van Buren's presidential aspirations.

The Frederick County Decisional Elite in the Second Party Era

The Frederick County decisional elite in the second party era, aggregated from these activities, numbered seventy-two men.[113] With an average age of forty-seven years, they were primarily property owners of modest affluence in the community. Eight-six percent held an average property valuation of $2,539; 58 percent held a mean 490 acres; and 65 percent owned an average of 6 slaves. Compared to the first party era, the percentage of the decisional elite holding slaves increased from 21 to 65 percent, with the average holding declining from 14 to 6 slaves, while the average acreage also declined from 929 acres to 490 acres. Religion was an elusive variable to ascertain. Compared to the first party era, for which it was discernible for 57 percent of the decisional elite, religion could be identified for only 29 percent of the decisional elite in the second party era. Among those for whom religion was determined, there was far greater variety than demonstrated earlier. The Episcopalians declined from 67 to 33 percent, the German Reformed church membership stayed almost constant (19 versus 14 percent), and there was a greater presence of Methodists (29 percent), in addition to several Presbyterians, Quakers, Catholics, and Lutherans. The number holding militia commissions declined from 30 to 19 percent. In terms of party affiliation, 60 percent were Anti-Jacksonians and 39 percent were Jacksonians.

Compared to the decisional elite of the first party system, this group was rooted less firmly in the oligarchy. Proportionately there were fewer (25 versus 36 percent) among the county's hundred wealthiest citizens, but even in this category leaders in the second party era ranked lower in terms of the wealth they held, as illustrated in Table 3.2.

Frederick County's decisional leaders represented the diversity of the community in contrast to the relative uniformity found in the other

Table 3.2. Decisional Elite: Leaders Who Were among the Hundred Wealthiest

Rank	First Party Era (percent)	Second Party Era (percent)
1–24	50	44
25–50	26	11
51–75	12	17
76–100	12	27
	N = 18	N = 18

rural areas. Members of traditional families, such as Roderick Dorsey, Colonel John McPherson, who married into the family of former Governor Thomas Johnson, Dr. Thomas W. Johnson, Governor Johnson's nephew, Richard Potts, Jr., William M. Beall, Jr., his brother-in-law, Colonel John H. Simmons, Colonel John Thomas's son, Francis Thomas, and Dr. John Tyler and his kin were still prominent in community decision making in the 1820s and 1830s. Members of aspiring families in the first party era, such as Roger Nelson's two sons, John and Madison Nelson, David Shriver, Sr.'s two sons, Jacob and Isaac Shriver, and their kin, such as William Schley, were also part of the establishment during this period. New men became community leaders as the second party system evolved. Some were political functionaries, such as newspaper editors,[114] but others came from inauspicious backgrounds to public leadership through their exertions in the proliferation of party leadership roles. Men such as Captain George W. Ent or Moses Worman, both residents of Fredericktown, entered the leadership cadre through party activities. Similarly, Thomas Carlton, a tavern owner and Jackson party activist who served as mayor of Fredericktown, rose to prominence because of his leadership on behalf of internal improvements.

Several factors account for the existence of greater diversity within Frederick County's decisional elite than that found in St. Marys and Talbot counties. The evolution of a highly organized and regularized competitive party system generated greater demand and opportunity for leaders to rise from the underlying diversity of the community. The former political leaders may have introduced this system in the 1820s with the idea that they would be its dominating force, but it soon passed from their exclusive control. The rivalry within the Jackson party between such old politicians as Dr. Tyler and the Nelsons and Francis Thomas epitomized this conflict. Similarly, the domination of the county by Fredericktown residents by the 1830s served to undermine the viability of oligarchical control in county affairs. Fredericktown was the administrative and commercial center for the county, attracting men of wealth and ambition, who tried to aggrandize as much community power to their control as possible. Lacking the advantages of better information sources and editorial control over the major communication vehicles for the whole county, members of the rural oligarchy were at a distinct disadvantage to assert their traditional role as the natural community leaders. The new county movement reflected the long-term rural-urban conflict within the county.

4

The Dynamics of
Urban Leadership

The community leadership pattern in Baltimore, where a merchant oligarchy dominated community decision making during the early national period, diverged sharply from that in rural areas. Wealth throughout Maryland was an important base for community leadership, but in Baltimore's urban system the rural ideal became increasingly dysfunctional. Whereas a relatively uniform agricultural pattern prevailed in the counties, the city's diversified economic life provided leaders with alternative means to attract political support. Consequently, men with economic and social roots fundamentally different from those of the rural oligarchy competed for leadership positions in the urban community. Leaders possessing the traditional forms of wealth, in land and slaves, also actively participated in politics.

The transformation of Baltimore from a sleepy village to a booming commercial entrepôt was one of the most significant developments accompanying the Revolution in Maryland. In the postwar years trade patterns and commercial relationships begun in the Revolution were expanded, bringing wealth, prosperity, and rapid growth to the city. As a boom town, Baltimore drew immigrants from abroad, from other states, and from rural Maryland. Compared to the rest of the state, it was a polyglot center composed of Scotch-Irish, Germans, some French, and native-born Americans. Its diversity was expressed by the multiplicity of churches serving its population. More significantly, the city as a dynamic urban place generated and released pressures that had an impact on the entire state. Its large and expanding population was an implicit threat to the continued political dominance of state government by small rural counties, just as its commercial base was perceived as a threat to the agrarian standard. The city also served as an information center, boasting several daily newspapers that facilitated the introduction and flow of new ideas.

Historians traditionally portray Baltimore's early leadership as an elite dominated by merchants, who, beginning in the 1770s, helped to bring the backcountry grain trade to the city. One historian asserted that such growth could be attributed to the dynamic role that Scotch-Irish

71

Presbyterians assumed in Baltimore's community affairs.[1] In another interpretation, comparing urban leadership in the four major Atlantic seaboard cities, William B. Wheeler observed: "Whereas the Philadelphia upper class was a composite of old and new individuals, Baltimore's top strata was essentially a new aristocracy in which almost all of its members had risen from middle-class backgrounds after the Revolution."[2] Thus, not only did the urban leaders differ in their religious and social origins from their rural counterparts who were generally Episcopalians, but they were also men of new wealth.[3]

This chapter investigates a variety of important decisional situations in Baltimore, including political nominations, patronage, incorporation, internal improvements, and the establishment of the city's water company. Primary consideration is identification of those who wielded power and influence.

The First Party Era

The urban political structure endured great stress in the first party era. Baltimore City's leaders, like their rural counterparts, expected a general recognition of their right to rule in deference to their economic and social position, and they utilized various private and public organizations to mobilize popular support at the polls. Their control of such organizations resulted from the prevailing system of cumulative inequality. This system permitted a publicly minded man of wealth a better chance to be a militia officer, a church vestryman, or a civic leader on the basis of his station than men without such advantages. Organizational control was easily transformed into community power in the absence of permanent political parties. The rise of a dynamic two-party competition in the mid-1790s suggests the formation of a countervailing force in Baltimore City; yet a closer examination of community decision making undermines this impression. Despite a change in urban political style during the first party era, this transformation did not alter significantly the existing power distribution within the urban political community.

In this period most urban candidates entered the field through self-nomination. By publishing announcements in newspapers, they either presented themselves or were recommended by friends and supporters. Many announced only their intention to stand for office or to establish a poll at the election itself, while others included a short statement of beliefs and goals.[4] Favoring the affluent, this procedure was predicated on the assumption that a candidate was easily recognized by the electorate and that the people could trust his judgment.

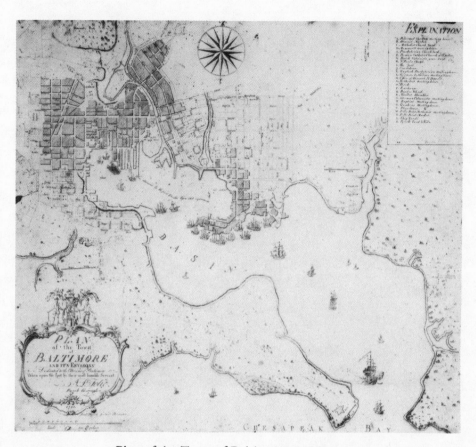

Plan of the Town of Baltimore, 1792
Courtesy of the Maryland Historical Society, Baltimore

"Baltimore from the Northeast," ca. 1800
Courtesy of the Maryland Historical Society, Baltimore

In periods of intense public interest in specific issues, organizational nominations sometimes supplemented self-nomination. In 1794, for example, the debate over the merits of incorporation generated popular opposition from the Mechanical, Republican, and Carpenters' societies; as well as from leaders of the Deptford Hundred, who feared that Fells Point would be placed at a disadvantage if it were incorporated along with Baltimoretown into a new city. They combined to nominate a ticket pledged to oppose the incorporation bill. The nominees took the extreme position of refusing to appear at the hustings to solicit votes because such practices were "anti-republican" and "indecent."[5] Similarly, in 1798 one meeting of "Respectable Citizens" and another called by the Baltimore Mechanics and Manufacturers worked to nominate a ticket representing their specific interests.[6] Before the advent of regularized party nominations, however, such examples of overt organizational support were the exception rather than the rule.

Not until Jefferson's presidency did Baltimore Republicans turn to regular and systematic party nominations, and this development was more a function of intraparty division than a reflection of growing organizational sophistication. The original Republican leaders, headed by General Samuel Smith, were being challenged by aspiring newcomers, especially Thomas McElderry, who sought a greater role in party affairs.[7] This competition resulted in the publication of two Republican tickets in 1803, but within a week the disputing factions met and unified behind a single congressional candidate.[8] When the presidential elections occurred the following year, the editor of the Republican paper, to avoid a repeat of the 1803 schism, proposed a series of ward meetings to send locally elected delegates to district meetings to nominate candidates for local, state, and federal offices. The proposal was important in two respects: it was carefully worded to defend against the charge of constituting a directive; and the need for ward meetings was justified as a means to contend with the problem of voter apathy.[9] After 1804, Baltimore Republicans utilized the party convention as a means to minimize both internal factionalization and voter indifference. Their efforts met with varying degrees of success.[10]

Federalists generally opposed such organizational activities. They favored the preparty system of self-nomination, which was consistent with their belief that members of the elite should rule in the name of the community. Generally the Federalists preferred to organize in caucuses.[11] When Republicans introduced party nominating conventions, Federalists attacked them as undemocratic and manipulative. One correspondent asked, "How could men be *free* and *independent* who would sacrifice their own opinions to become *dupes* and *tools* of party?"[12] Another, writing under the title "More Oppugnation," commented, "The mode of managing matters is admirable. It saves the ignorant swinish multitude the trouble of anything but the *form* of their votes, just as ordered by Bonaparte . . . in his Imperial Republic."[13] Federalists never tired of exposing conventions for being poorly attended, manipulated by Republican leaders, or vehicles for foreign-born control of American interests.[14]

Political nominations were only one facet of the transition from a preparty system to the early stages of party development. An equally important component was the mobilization of the electorate. Voter mobilization depended upon the circulation of information and the proselytization of ideas through semipermanent organizations. If Federalists and Republicans split over the utility of regularized party nominations, both were attentive to the problem of voter mobilization.

Candidates and incumbents traditionally expressed their views through letters published in the commercial press.[15] Public campaign issues were argued in erudite invectives under clever pseudonyms.[16] But as the system expanded to encompass a large political audience, many of whom had scant knowledge of the classical age, leaders of both parties recognized the need for a party press. Using the power of patronage, the Federalists adopted an established commercial paper, the Baltimore *Federal Gazette and Baltimore Daily Advertiser*, as their primary public spokesman.[17] Party leaders were always in search of new editorial talent,[18] and in 1802 they established a rabidly partisan campaign paper, the Baltimore *Republican; or, Anti-Democrat* edited by Charles Prentiss and directed by Robert G. Harper.[19] The early opponents of the Federalists printed notices in the *Federal Gazette* or in the more neutral Baltimore *Telegraphe and Daily Advertiser*. Prior to the creation of a permanent Republican party press, William Pechin's various newspapers served as an anti-Federalist news source.[20] In May 1799, the Republicans established the Baltimore *American and Commercial Advertiser*, edited by Alexander Martin, as a commercial paper and as their regular party press. Not surprisingly, it became the Jefferson administration publisher of the laws, and by 1802 William Pechin was its editor.[21] That same year the Republicans created a more vitriolic campaign newspaper, the *Democratic Republican; Or Anti-Aristocrat*, edited by Cornelius Firebrand (John B. Colvin).[22] By the end of Jefferson's presidency, the Baltimore *Whig* appeared as a second Republican newspaper.

If newspapers served increasingly as sources of popular information, political leaders were always searching for better ways to influence the potential electorate. Besides political meetings, barbecues, Fourth of July celebrations, and religious camp meetings, politicians used militia musters extensively in the 1790s. Many leading political figures held important commissions, and they used musters to make thinly veiled political addresses. As a permanent political institution, however, the militia had a serious drawback: lacking a foreign threat, citizen-soldiers became apathetic and their attendance at musters and civic celebrations fell off.[23] Thus, politicians in search of a guaranteed audience had to seek other political organizations.

In the absence of broad community support for political parties, leaders sought the support of private societies as protopolitical organizations. In the 1780s and 1790s the various fire companies, the Deptford Hundred, and the Republican Society functioned jointly as service and special interest associations. The Mechanical Fire Company for a twenty-year period following the city's incorporation furnished the first six mayors and nearly two-thirds of the councilmen of Baltimore.[24] Such associations, however, were not totally reliable because they often were affected by internal factionalization.

Consequently, politicians formed their own societies. General Samuel Smith and his political lieutenants organized a Tammany Society in 1808 as an urban command center for Maryland's Republican movement. Confronted by considerable division between urban and rural Republican leaders, Smith tried to ensure his own reelection to the United States Senate by working simultaneously for Republican candidates to the state legislature and for Republican electors pledged to James Madison's presidential aspirations.[25] At the same time some Federalists reconsidered their opposition to political organizations and had created the Washington Benevolent Society with Robert G. Harper acting as its president.[26] Both these societies were examples of the transitional state of party development. Each specifically sought to establish control over its political party by creating recognized subgroups tied to charismatic popular leaders.

To appreciate fully the operation of the political system it is useful to focus on an important election. The congressional election of 1798 provides a good example of how leaders, organizations, and voters interacted. In some ways its exceptional qualities might render it unrepresentative, but the tension generated and released that year made relationships explicit that were normally unstated. The central theme of the 1798 election was the perceived breakdown of community unanimity and Federalist hegemony. The dispute over the Jay Treaty, the growing public division within the federal government between French and British partisans, and the worsening foreign relations with France increased popular interest in the election. At issue was whether Samuel Smith, the incumbent congressman, represented the interests of the whole community. General Samuel Smith was a popular politician. As a militia general, an officer who had fought with distinction in the revolutionary war, a Presbyterian lay leader, and a member of a large merchant family that had moved from Pennsylvania to Baltimore before the Revolution, he epitomized the diversity and the recent origins of much of Baltimore.[27] Although he had entered national politics in the early 1790s as a Federalist, by 1798 Smith stood with others who increasingly opposed the policies of President John Adams. His bases of support were the militia, various popular societies, public enthusiasm for France, and wide associations in the mercantile community.[28]

Federalists opposed Smith's reelection because of his political apostasy. His defection from the party of Washington, his pro-French sympathies, and his alleged willingness to pay tribute rather than to stand for national principle in the XYZ affair were added to their displeasure growing from his continued opposition to the Jay Treaty and his refusal to accept instructions.[29] As a studied insult, Smith's opponents staged a public dinner for Senator John Eager Howard, to which Smith was purposefully not invited, where the toasts and sentiments were critical of his behavior.[30] Senator Howard, who embodied the conservative, affluent Episcopal roots of Federalist leadership, led the effort to humble his political rival and to block his reelection.[31]

The contest took place at a time of intense popular interest. The focus of attention was the militia. During the early years of the French Revolution, some Baltimore units took French names, such as the Sans Culottes, and a number of its officers were either openly pro-French or pro-Jefferson in their politics. This led Federalists to attack the urban militia leadership as unpatriotic and potentially unreliable in the event of a French war.[32] Congressman Smith's position as the commanding general of Baltimore's Third Division, which had a number of Federalist officers, caused furious infighting. The symbol of the competition was the black cockade: Federalists favored adopting it generally as a sign of national unity and wanted patriotic officers to wear their uniforms publicly; their opponents continued to don and defend the tricolored national cockade.[33] Such controversy politicized the militia.

No one doubted that Congressman Smith would stand for reelection. Consequently, there was no need for a nomination convention; Smith simply announced his candidacy. During the campaign he used the newspapers to address the public, and he harangued citizen-soldiers at militia musters.[34] The Federalists, on the other hand, did not initially challenge Smith. Two months before the election, James Winchester, a past member of the Republican Society and a former state legislator who had shepherded the Baltimore incorporation bill through the House of

Delegates in 1796, announced his candidacy for Congress. Winchester's Republican past divided Federalist leaders, while his lack of charisma and want of militia association apparently failed to generate enthusiasm within the ranks of the electorate. But as an attorney with wide family connections in Baltimore society, Winchester, like Smith, was a member of the elite, and his candidacy was consistent with the prevailing system.[35]

The election itself was an important event characterized by abuses and violent excesses. Smith won handily by successfully mobilizing his supporters and by aggressively intimidating the opposition whenever possible during the four-day poll. Although defeated, Winchester earned added support from the Federalist establishment, and he was appointed to the federal judiciary in the next year.[36] One of the more interesting aspects of the postelection reaction was the attitude of the Federalist press. The Baltimore *Federal Gazette* wanted to douse smoldering partisanship and even refused to publish the toasts offered at the postelection Winchester dinner.[37] The Philadelphia Federalist paper, *Porcupine's Gazette*, was under no such community injunction, and it continued to attack Smith and to expose the excesses of the recent election.[38]

Urban political recruitment in the first party era remained under the prevailing influence of oligarchical and preparty norms. Despite the volatile nature of politics, where community consensus was polarized by Federalist and Republican party rhetoric and elections were characterized by popular excesses, leaders continued to be recruited according to standard forms and from traditional groups. Men of wealth, extensive social connections, and status enjoyed advantages which most men without them could not overcome.

The patronage situation reveals the nuances of urban community leadership. Not only were state jobs available in Baltimore City, but the new federal government placed most of its better Maryland offices there. The Treasury and Justice departments, as well as the post office, offered positions of power, status, security, and some wealth in this rapidly expanding community. The competition for these jobs displays who was powerful in obtaining appointments and what attributes were desirable in an appointee.

Most of the original federal-level appointees had served in the revolutionary war with distinction. General Otho Holland Williams, the first collector of the port, Robert Ballard, the surveyor, and James McHenry, appointed secretary of war in 1796, all fit into this category. Members of prominent revolutionary families, especially Robert Purviance and his nephew, John H. Purviance, the son of Baltimore's late revolutionary leader Samuel Purviance, and Robert Smith, General Samuel Smith's brother, sought and were rewarded with appointments.[39] Some who applied referred to their revolutionary past, and those who wrote recommendations often justified them on the basis of faithful and selfless service.[40]

Members of the federal patronage establishment were prominent Federalists. Besides General Williams and Secretary of War McHenry, the two district attorneys, Richard Potts and his successor Zebulon Hollingsworth, the U.S. marshal, Reuben Etting, and the district judge, James Winchester, were all active supporters of the new federal government and the administration party. Another prominent Federalist, Colonel John E. Howard, was asked to serve as secretary of war but refused.[41] Increasingly, as the political system polarized into pro- and antiadministration factions, party regularity became a prime consideration.[42] The appointment of Samuel Chase, an anti-Federalist leader in the 1780s, to the federal bench might appear to be a glaring anomaly to this trend, but by 1796 Chase had metamorphosed into an enthusiastic Federalist leader.[43] Some men were recommended in the hope that their appointment would bring wider community support to the party.[44]

The dominance exerted by the revolutionary generation in Baltimore politics and federal patronage during the 1790s continued through the Adams administration and beyond. When Thomas Jefferson took office in 1801 federal officeholders were not swept out; most remained until they resigned or died. As the vacancies occurred, they were filled with deserving Republicans, most of whom boasted a revolutionary heritage.[45] Consequently, a remarkable continuity, with overlapping patterns of political favoritism and nepotism, prevailed in federal patronage practices from the 1790s through the early 1800s. Ostensible political adversaries were linked by family connection. For instance, both General O. H. Williams and Robert Smith, Jefferson's future secretary of the navy, married daughters of William Smith. General Samuel Smith, Robert's brother, was an avid booster of the careers of his family and friends during his entire political career.

A similar continuity existed among those who wrote recommendations. Aspirants to office frequently wrote the president directly, either to solicit an appointment or to enclose supporting materials. President Washington relied heavily on the judgment of James McHenry and O. H. Williams to evaluate Maryland patronage appointments.[46] He also considered the opinion of prominent individuals such as Colonel John E. Howard and Charles Carroll of Carrollton.[47] As a supporter of the national government, Congressman Samuel Smith frequently wrote recommendations, but his influence is difficult to judge since he sometimes recommended several persons for the same position.[48] Clearly, Smith, as

a congressman, like Howard as a United States senator, wielded a respected institutionalized role.

The subtle nuances of influence can best be illustrated by the close
study of the most remunerative job within the gift of the federal executive, the collector of the port of Baltimore. The first appointee, General
O. H. Williams, had held the analogous state job for the previous six
years and won appointment on the strength of his revolutionary career,
his adherence to the federal government, and in consideration of his
declining health.[49] The early death of General Williams in 1794 stimulated a flurry of applications to fill the vacancy.[50] Robert Purviance, a
Baltimore patriot merchant who had suffered numerous reverses in recent years and who enjoyed wide support within the establishment, won
the coveted appointment.[51] Purviance was unhappy with the rate of pay,
to the point of soliciting another appointment, but he, too, served until
his death.[52] The death of the Federalist collector in 1806, almost in the
middle of Jefferson's presidency, kindled statewide interest among partisans.[53] As Purviance lay on his deathbed, Smith wrote recommending
his political lieutenant, James H. McCulloch, for the job; although earlier
he had endorsed the candidacy of Colonel John Stricker, a former revolutionary officer and active militia leader.[54] The president first offered
the collectorship to Joseph H. Nicholson, whose role in Jefferson's election by Congress in 1800 won him popular and administration support,
but he refused to accept it.[55] The position was then given to Gabriel
Christie, a former Republican congressman from Cecil County, who enjoyed merchant associations and ties to Baltimore.[56] Christie, however,
was in failing health, and he died in 1807, thus enabling Senator Smith
finally to secure the job for his favorite.[57] The appointment of James H.
McCulloch as collector, a position he held from 1808 to his death in
1836, signified a subtle but important shift in patronage policy making.
Despite his reputation as a merchant with acknowledged ability, whose
political credentials included service in both houses of the state legislature, McCulloch owed his appointment to the influence of his mentor,
Senator Samuel Smith.

The distribution of state and local patronage followed a similar pattern. The state executive relied on Baltimore City legislators to recommend local appointments.[58] With the exception of several insignificant
controversies that elicited direct correspondence between local politicians and the state executive,[59] the system persisted with its own glacial
majesty.[60] The prevailing norms, characterized by the primacy of elite
consensus over partisanship, may be inferred from an anonymous complaint made to the governor: "Why in the name of Common Sense is Jno.
Moale continued a Justice of the Peace for the City of Baltimore as he

has not Common Sense & I may say Honestly [he is] a Real Federalist at the Same Time Declares war against the true Republican Cause."[61] Despite party labels, the same type of people ran affairs in the confidential realms of patronage decision making.

By far the most important Baltimore community concern in this period was government reform. For years the city had been governed by a patchwork of port wardens and commissioners, augmented by a county system of courts and magistrates, all appointed by the state executive. This institutional structure reflected a dual heritage: dependence upon the county as the basic governing unit, adhering to the principles of Maryland's constitution, and a continuation of the revolutionary formula of government by committee. By the 1780s, however, some Baltimore residents began to criticize this system as being unrepresentative, unresponsive to the particular urban problems retarding the city's future growth, and especially ineffectual to combat fire and urban crime. To resolve these problems, community leaders wanted the state legislature to incorporate Baltimore as an autonomous governing entity.

The first postrevolutionary effort to obtain incorporation from the state was made late in 1784. James Calhoun, Baltimore's first elected mayor thirteen years later, chaired the meeting that called for delegates to be sent from the various districts to form a convention to consider an incorporation bill.[62] The convention's recommendations called for self-government, but did not advocate taking control from the propertied; indeed, the proposed government was even more oligarchical than those of any county.[63] Nevertheless, it allowed most men to participate through voting, divided responsibility between the three branches of government so as to maximize domination by a propertied elite, and diffused the numerical strength of the mass through a system of direct and indirect elections.

The movement for incoporation failed in 1784, but the debate it generated, rekindled by other subsequent bills, signified real community division over the wisdom of such restrictive government. Proponents continued to press for incorporation on the grounds of domestic safety and future economic growth,[64] but critics were unhappy with the high property requirements and the ubiquitous system of indirect elections. "A Citizen," writing in response to an even more elitist bill presented in 1786, called it "a finished system of despotism" and admonished "Our *would be Kings and Nobles*, [who] suppose they can ride better than Britons; let them remember that the Britons have been unhorsed."[65] When a secret petition was presented to the legislature in 1787, "A Watchman" warned, "Will these dignified Gentlemen act for your good without making you pay them? No, No. . . . They are willing to create places of profit, and then fill them themselves, that they may reap the benefits."[66] Again in 1791, "A Baltimorean" cautioned his fellow citizens not to allow the legislature to impose incorporation on them; the impetus for charge should come from the people of the city.[67]

In 1793 an incorporation bill was enacted with the stipulation that it would not go into effect until passed by the next legislature. It called for a municipal government patterned after the state system, abandoning the combined executive-judiciary of the 1784 proposal. Substantial property requirements for officeholding and indirect elections were still required.[68] Opposition to this plan came from several sources. The Baltimore Mechanical Society, an organized group of artisans and merchants, refused to support any bill unless the citizens could vote on it in a referendum.[69] Such opposition articulated the popular fear that laborers and artisans would be excluded by high property requirements and intimidated from voting their choice by the viva voce system; some also objected to white-only voting qualifications.[70] The citizens of Fells Point, then known as the Deptford Hundred, objected to being incorporated into Baltimore City because they did not want to be taxed to improve the harbor facilities of rival Baltimoretown.[71] On the eve of the fall legislative election, committees from the Deptford Hundred, the Mechanical Society, and the Carpenter's Society united in opposition to this bill and called for a popularly elected unicameral city government.[72] Their dissatisfaction, combined with the dispatch in early September of Baltimore's 6th Militia Regiment to help quell the Whiskey Rebellion in the western part of the state, apparently undermined support for the pending bill, and it died for want of passage by the 1794 legislature.

Baltimore was incorporated finally in 1796, but not without further community division. The key figure that year was James Winchester, who was elected to the state general assembly as an incorporation advocate. Winchester represented both sides of the controversy: as a member of the Republican Society, he had popular appeal; as an attorney with wide family connections in the merchant community, he belonged to the establishment. In Annapolis he presented a bill that had been submitted by a public meeting. Members of the urban oligarchy, however, opposed this bill, and they petitioned the legislature to accept instead another bill, reputedly written by Samuel Chase. At first, Winchester sought to postpone legislative consideration of incorporation, but with the endorsement of James Calhoun, a leader of the city's popular movement, he accepted and supported the more conservative bill.[73] Although burdened by property qualifications for voting and officeholding and subject to indirect elections for the second branch of the city council and for the mayor, the new form of government adhered to the principle of separation of powers among the executive, legislative, and judicial branches.[74] Its critics accepted this government on the assumption that it would be more efficient and beneficial than the existing one; conservative elements were pleased to have maintained their influence in its structure and operation.

The creation of the new government in 1797 did not muzzle reformers, who continued their efforts to democratize the charter. There were two primary targets in this assault: to lower property requirements for officeholding and to liberalize voting. In 1806, the mode of election was changed from viva voce to the ballot and the time of election for mayor and city council was moved to October.[75] By 1808 the demand to reduce property requirements for officeholding had become a strict party consideration. The legislature passed a bill calling for citizens of Baltimore to elect delegates to a convention that would either accept or reject a pending bill for charter reform. The Federalist fielded a slate pledged to protect the existing charter; the Republicans favored reform. The reformers won the election, and the convention endorsed the bill reducing property qualifications.[76]

If incorporation provided Baltimore with self-government, the charter itself was a reflection of the prevailing belief in limited government. The combination of property qualifications for officeholding and the complex system of indirect elections gave the people a voice in government, but successfully isolated them from the direct exercise of power. Men in government were to be propertied; and in the city, as in the counties, men of property naturally governed in the interests of the whole community.

If some felt the city's future development was tied to greater self-government, most were certain that Baltimore's prosperity depended upon internal improvements.[77] Baltimore grew during and after the Revolution because of the grain trade. Wheat grown in the western counties of Maryland and Pennsylvania was refined into flour in mills on the several falls flowing near the city; the finished product was then shipped along domestic and foreign trade routes from Baltimore. Baltimore's future, as its recent past, depended upon the city's continued access to its hinterland.[78]

Baltimore was not the only town that coveted the interior grain trade. Boosters of the new federal city, Georgetown, and Alexandria, Virginia, favored completion of a Potomac canal to tap not only the wealth of the western counties, but also the fabled bounty of the Ohio Valley. Citizens of western Maryland's grain-producing counties recognized the potential advantage of a Potomac canal, and some planned an expanded road system and dreamed of improving the Monocacy River to

carry trade to the Potomac. Competition came also from a more dangerous rival, Philadelphia, whose merchants sought to expand their grain
trade by advocating a program of extensive road building. Aware of the
real contest from this quarter and dreading new competition from the
Potomac towns, Baltimore boosters promoted an internal improvements
program that would enhance its opportunities and minimize any accruing
to its rivals.[79]

The interior grain trade could be tapped in two ways: by improving
navigable rivers so that trade could move over natural fall line barriers
and by constructing well-surfaced, all-season roads to the western counties. While the Potomac River region looked to the completion of the
Potomac Company canal for its future prosperity, Baltimore advocates
wanted to improve the Susquehanna River and thus enhance the flow of
grain to the Chesapeake Bay and the city. But a variety of obstacles
confronted such a program. The natural difficulties involved were formidable, and Pennsylvania was certain to oppose any improvements that
placed Philadelphia at a disadvantage. A further source of opposition
came from Maryland's upper counties, which combined with interested
parties in Delaware and Pennsylvania to propose the construction of a
canal from the bay to the Delaware River at the north end of the Delmarva Peninsula. A cross-cut canal would threaten Baltimore's bay trade
hegemony and undermine advantages derived from the Susquehanna
improvement project because that trade would have easier access to
Philadelphia.[80] This multiplicity of factors, further complicated by contemporary norms as to how such improvements should be funded, forced
several strategies on Baltimore boosters.

Internal improvements advocates recognized that success depended
upon obtaining the most advantageous charter. To impress the legislature that their project was the best, they organized meetings and circu-
lated petitions to demonstrate wide local support. Community unanimity
was also necessary if a full stock subscription were to be made. From the
level of community organization, the next step for Baltimore representatives was to lobby for bills in the state legislature. This task required
great finesse. Prior to the division of politicians into Federalists and
Republicans, the legislature divided into sectional interests, known as
the "Potowmack" and Chesapeake factions, each working to maximize
its position and to thwart the plans of its opponents.[81] In this environment, serious competition between regional groups retarded local projects.[82]

The most important battles over internal improvements were fought
in the state legislature. Baltimore's representatives to the House of
Delegates and the senate were expected to boost local projects and to

protect municipal interests against competing programs. Their active role was acknowledged by a grateful press, and their positions on internal improvements were matters of public concern at election time.[83] Regional competition produced more conflict than legislative accomplishment; not until the 1799 session did a compromise omnibus bill pass giving state support for the crosscut canal, the Potomac Company, and the Susquehanna project.[84]

Even with this success, Baltimore's interest groups organized a public meeting to hasten the completion of the Susquehanna project by an innovative if utopian plan. Chaired by the mayor, James Calhoun, the meeting called upon the community to raise a $10,000 fund by contribution to remove rocks from the mouth of the Susquehanna River. A subscription committee was appointed from the political, commercial, and affluent segments of the community; this visionary scheme, however, was not oriented to selling company stock, but instead asked for voluntary contributions to help the community at large. Despite overwhelming endorsements by the press, subscriptions fell short of expectations, and ultimately the project proved inadequate for the task.[85]

The passage of the 1799 bill essentially ended the debate over river and canal improvements, and attention turned to road improvements. Letters in newspapers commented on the deplorable condition of roads radiating out from the city and to the enlightened road-building policy favored by Baltimore's commercial rivals.[86] In the summer of 1803, leaders gathered to organize community support to improve the road to Ellicott's Mill and then on to Frederick County, a second to Reisterstown, and a third to York, Pennsylvania.

The officers and members of the resolutions committee came from the political, commercial, and wealthy elite of the city.[87] Almost all of them later appeared as either officers or directors of the several road companies incorporated during the following years, and those who were not directly involved were associated through family connections.[88] Members of prominent rural families, such as the Ridgelys and Ellicotts of Baltimore County, also participated in both the organizational meetings and the direction of road companies. Even such inveterate political enemies as Samuel Smith and John E. Howard served together as directors of the newly formed Frederick Turnpike Road Company in 1805.

By the end of the first decade of the nineteenth century, Baltimore's future prosperity appeared to be secure because of an aggressive policy of internal improvements. Mobilized by community leaders, guided through a sometimes hostile legislature by city delegates, and sustained by subscriptions, the dual program of improving navigation along the Susquehanna River and building all-weather roads into the grain-producing counties was well under way. These leaders represented the commercial, political, and wealthy segments of Baltimore society and demonstrated once again the vitality of the oligarchy in an urban setting.

A less momentous but equally revealing community concern related to the problem of a healthful water supply. Baltimore's increasing size had overtaxed its natural resources. Concern over epidemics and fire precipitated a public meeting in 1804 to consider the issue. This meeting revealed the elite domination of urban affairs. Chaired by General Samuel Smith, prominent Federalist and Republican leaders and other community activists joined to advocate the creation of a private water company to serve the city. Even before obtaining state incorporation, they successfully solicited pledges for the $250,000 estimated cost to divert water from Jones Falls for city use.[89]

From its creation in 1804 to its ultimate incorporation in 1808, the Baltimore Water Company was directed by seven men. Two were associated with General Smith by family or political ties; three were among the hundred wealthiest real property holders on the city tax rolls; four served as directors or presidents of the city's financial institutions; another represented a wealthy rural merchant milling family.[90] Such complex interaction of holders of great wealth, individuals tied by family or political interconnections, and those active in commerce epitomizes the overlapping style of urban community leadership.

Despite initial enthusiasm, the Baltimore Water Company was not an immediate or resounding success. The project was plagued by conflicts with landowners, mill operators, and construction difficulties; the promised supply of water did not flow until 1807.[91] Then, as in the case of Philadelphia, fresh water was provided for those who could pay for it: the middle and upper classes.

The Urban Decisional Elite in the First Party Era

The decision makers in each of the foregoing situations constituted a final decisional elite of fifty-five men.[92] Like their rural counterparts, they were men of property and standing. Their average age was forty-five; 73 percent had a mean wealth assessment of $4,112; and 56 percent owned slaves.[93] Forty percent were merchants, 26 percent professionals, 16 percent gave only their address or were identified inconspicuously as "Gentleman," 6 percent were skilled laborers, 4 percent worked in a petty clerical capacity, and 6 percent were in white-collar occupations.[94] Twenty-nine percent were also militia officers. The assertion that urban public leaders were men who emigrated to the city only after the Revolution was not sustained by the data: 40 percent lived in Baltimore before the end of the Revolution; 13 percent arrived between 1782 and 1795, 9 percent came between 1796 and 1806, and the arrival date of 38 percent could not be determined. Compared to their rural counterparts they represented a cosmopolitan group. Although birthplace could not be discovered for almost one-third (31 percent) of the urban decisional elite, 22 percent were foreign-born, 27 percent were born in other states, and 20 percent were native-born Marylanders. The notion suggested by earlier scholars that Presbyterians were a vitalizing force in community leadership proved generally correct, but there is an important caveat. Religious data were not found for 29 percent of the group, but 38 percent of the total elite were Presbyterians and 16 percent were Episcopalians. After removing those for whom this variable could not be determined and reaggregating religion into two denominational categories, pietistic and liturgical, 69 percent were pietistic and 31 percent were liturgical. It would be wrong, therefore, to ignore the fact that members of liturgical sects, most of whom were Episcopalians, were also an important component in community leadership.

Decision making in the city, as in the rural areas, was done predominantly by an oligarchy during the first party era. Indeed, 35 percent of the decisional elite were among the city's hundred wealthiest citizens. The urban oligarchy, however, was more diversified than its rural counterparts. Large and minor merchants, from General Samuel Smith to James H. McCulloch, shared power with men of great landed wealth, such as Colonel John E. Howard or Charles Carroll of Carrollton, and both groups adhered to a belief that men of property should rule. Acting like a magnet, the city attracted aspiring merchants and professionals, whose lack of august social connections was compensated for by ambition and ability. These traits were recognized and rewarded in a less deferential, more cosmopolitan and competitive environment. Members of the ruling establishment actively recruited gifted men to Baltimore, such as Luther Martin, Samuel Chase, and Robert Goodloe Harper; others, initially unrecognized, worked their way into the elite.

Because they saw themselves as a vital oligarchy, its members tried to perpetuate their rule by ties of marriage and business association. Charles Carroll of Carrollton, for example, a resident of Anne Arundel County and a Federalist state senator in the 1790s, owned enough property in Baltimore City, Frederick County, and Talbot County to be included among their wealthiest citizens. Carroll was intimately associated with Baltimore City community affairs through the activities of his sons-in-law, Richard Caton and Robert Goodloe Harper, both of whom were members of the decisional elite. Similarly Samuel Smith, the militia general and Republican politician, had wide-ranging family and business connections. Through his father he was connected with the Buchanans and the Sterrets, and he married into the Spear family. Each was a prominent and affluent merchant family. His brother, Robert Smith, married the daughter of a Federalist merchant politician, William Smith, and was thus associated with General Otho H. Williams, the respected Federalist collector, who also owned considerable property in western Maryland. Through his business associations, Samuel Smith was also connected to the family of Mayor James Calhoun.[95]

Many of these men who had been of age saw service in the Revolution. Nine served on revolutionary committees of observation or vigilance, at least five were army or militia officers, and two were descendants of prominent revolutionary families.[96] The associations that extended through kin networks expanded this circle, but it is clear that the major figures of the decisional elite, such as Colonel John E. Howard, General Samuel Smith, and Charles Carroll of Carrollton, were leaders from at least the time of the Revolution.

The bifurcation of politics in the 1790s did not undermine the vitality of the oligarchy to any great degree. The image of aristocratic Federalists and Jacobinical Republicans permeated political exchanges, but its reality would be a simple distortion of fact when measured against Baltimore city leaders. Just as the rich and well connected dominated rural decision making, urban leaders were drawn from the same community pool. This sense of community commonality is suggested by Federalist General John Swann's letter recommending the promotion of Major James Mosher to the command of Baltimore's 39th Regiment at the height of the French crisis: "He is a moderate politician of Democratic principles. Yet being American born and [with] considerable property [I] should not hesitate to appoint him."[97] In other words, Mosher's heretical political association was tolerable because, as a native-born American with property, he could be counted on to defend traditional standards in a changing society.

The Intervening Years

The events of the years between the first and second party systems affected Baltimore City more than any other area in Maryland.[98] As a commercial entrepôt, it was far more susceptible than rural regions to changes in trade patterns and to fluctuations in the monetary system. Economic crises had important ramifications in a system dominated by a merchant oligarchy. At the same time, traditional social relationships

Map of Baltimore, 1838
Courtesy of the Maryland Room, McKeldin Library, University of Maryland

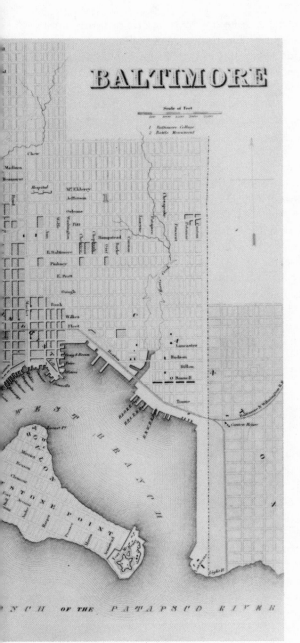

BALTIMORE

were strained by an expanding population and by subtle transformations accompanying the initial stages of the Industrial Revolution. Such economic and social mutations had political implications that introduced important changes to the prevailing political system. Although Baltimore City was Maryland's most dynamic community in the second party era, its dynamism should not obscure the fact that many of these problems had not been fully resolved and that the flux associated with such changes was still in motion.

Lasting through the War of 1812, Baltimore's commercial prosperity was affected by the protracted Napoleonic Wars. These wars had an obvious destabilizing influence on European trade and international credit relations and interfered with Baltimore's highly profitable wheat routes to southern Europe, the West Indies, and South America. Some of the most affluent traders failed during this period; others began to specialize in new endeavors, such as the production of cotton goods.

The national financial crisis of 1819 played havoc with Baltimore's economy and its commercial leadership. In addition to the immediate and persisting curtailment of credit and commerce caused by the depression, the scandal associated with the mismanagement of the Baltimore branch of the Bank of the United States affected many of the city's leading commercial figures. Republican Congressman Samuel Smith, for example, was brought to the brink of financial ruin by the overextensions of his business partner, and many of the city's commercial leaders failed financially in the next few years.[99]

The transformation associated with the early stages of the Industrial Revolution introduced more subtle systemic changes that were not entirely understood at the time they were taking place. The abundance of water power in the immediate Baltimore region, the continued profitability of the wheat trade accompanied by minimal excursions into the production of cotton, the use of large factories, and the adoption of steam power meant that the common catalysts associated with the Industrial Revolution were absent through the 1840s. Yet Baltimore's economic system was influenced by the transportation and communication revolutions in several important ways. The phenomenal success of the Erie Canal caused some merchants to abandon Baltimore for New York City in the 1820s. Others became even more ardent advocates of internal improvements, which they saw as the panacea for the city's recovery and enduring prosperity. Despite a general belief that Baltimore would share the enormous wealth of the Ohio Valley through such projects, some merchants recognized that future profits were linked to expanded European trade and that Baltimore would continue to be at a disadvantage compared to Philadelphia or New York City. These men, notably Alex-

Baltimore View, 1837
Courtesy of the Library of Congress

ander Brown, responded by establishing business branches in those competitive cities with an eye toward developing shipping companies to take advantage of shorter trade routes. Until the evolution of ocean steamers, Baltimore was always at a one- or two-day sailing disadvantage to European ports compared to Philadelphia or New York City.

Improved transportation and communication affected Baltimore's artisans as well. During the late eighteenth century, they geared production for local consumption or regional commerce, but with improved transportation and communication in the early nineteenth century merchants were able to import products from more efficient producers in other areas. Even though factories involved relatively few Baltimore workers, the artisan system was nonetheless being eroded in these years through the evolution of the less skill-demanding "putting-out" production mode. Artisans were still called upon to perform skilled tasks, but the production of goods was being segmented into individual components, some of which could be performed by less skilled workers at a reduced cost.

The erosion of the artisan system was an important component in the general decline of the infrastructure of the merchant oligarchy. Based upon clear status demarcations, from apprentice to journeyman to artisan, and combining the wholesale and retail economic functions, its moribundity suggested the impermanence of status hierarchies in general. As a result, there was labor unrest in Baltimore during the 1820s and 1830s, but it was not the product of factory workers challenging the old system. Rather, it was the discontent of the producing class finding itself increasingly dysfunctional in a changing economic environment.

Baltimore's population growth added to these pressures. The population grew from 26,114 in 1800 to 102,313 in 1840, so that the city's physical size strained existing institutions.[100] This growth was less the product of European immigration, which began with the Irish in the late 1830s augmented by the Germans in the 1840s, than the result of movement from rural Maryland and from other states into Baltimore City. During these years the city also became a haven for free blacks. The free black population grew from 3,771 in 1800 to 17,967 in 1840, while the slave population remained stable at between 2,800 and 3,400 persons. Free blacks remained politically impotent, but they were an important component in the labor market.

Overall, the combination of international war, fiscal contraction, economic change, and population growth undermined the viability of the old merchant oligarchy. Some perished or withdrew to live off their accumulated wealth, others were stunned by one or more of these crises but regained their balance and remained in positions of influence and power, while the overall change introduced the need for specialists where generalists once prevailed.[101] Eschewing the visibly opulent life style of the traditional eighteenth-century merchant class, these new merchants tightly controlled their operations and began to specialize as manufacturers, shippers, or bankers.[102] The demand for professional managers and for business-oriented attorneys accompanied the trend toward specialization.

The growth of specialized leadership roles also manifested itself in the political realm. Concurrent with the decline of the merchant oligarchy and the rise of economic specialization was an enlargement of the political base from which leaders could rise. Members of first families continued to be political leaders and to hold political offices, as did leading merchants, but in the 1820s others who appealed to the increasingly diverse urban constituency rose to positions of power and influence.[103] Rather than one group monopolizing community leadership through a prior claim to legitimacy, more men shared power in the mid-1830s than had a decade earlier. The question would be which men, and why? To find the answer, it is necessary once again to investigate political nominations, internal improvements activities, community action concerning reform, and the more subtle realms of patronage in the second party era.

The Second Party Era

An important difference between the first and second party eras in Baltimore City was the operation and orientation of political recruitment. During the earlier period, urban politics were heavily influenced by an elite whose access to power was enhanced by the loose structure of the formal party. Using the militia and other popular organizations as vehicles to mobilize the electorate, traditional groups were able to optimize their own roles and to modulate entry by nonelite leaders into positions of leadership and power. The demise of competitive parties, accompanied by the reestablishment of single-party domination, reinforced and perpetuated elite domination of the political system. When the presidential contest of 1824 rejuvenated popular interest, elite members who were out of power sought to organize the electorate behind their bid to regain public office by resuscitating the convention system introduced earlier by the Republican party. This nomination device, accompanied by other organizational activities all designed to stimulate popular interest and participation, undermined prolonged elite domination. In the early years of the second party system, members of the

JACKSON TICKET.

Agriculture, Commerce and Manufactures.

FOR THE ASSEMBLY.

GEORGE H. STEUART,
JOHN V. L. McMAHON.

JACKSON TICKET.

AMERICAN SYSTEM.
Speed the plough, the Loom & the Mattock

FOR THE ASSEMBLY
JOHN V. L. McMAHON,
GEORGE H. STEUART.

FOR ASSEMBLY.

Luke Tiernan,
George R. Richardson.

JACKSON TICKE

Internal Improvement by Rail Roads, Canals, &c.

FOR THE ASSEMBLY
JOHN V. L. McMAHON,
GEORGE H. STEUART.

JACKSON TICKET

"The soil, under the influence of whose atmosphere the SHAMROCK became a HICKORY."
Bishop England.

FOR THE ASSEMBLY
JOHN V. L. McMAHON,
GEORGE H. STEUART.

Baltimore Party Tickets, 1828
Courtesy of the Library of Congress

former political elite were elevated to public office, but as the system became routinized and popular leaders worked their way up through the organizational activities to positions of greater influence within the party, new leaders from the diverse urban community challenged the right of the elite to rule in their name. This transformation manifested itself in a variety of ways, two of which may be illustrated here: through an analysis of those who actually led the party; and through an elaboration of two contemporary events—the rise and fall of the Workingmen's party in 1833 and the political response to the Bank of Maryland crisis and the Baltimore Riot of 1835. These examples suggest that, although the urban elite, like their rural counterpart, tried to dominate the political system, the sheer diversity of the community prevented them from doing so.

The Baltimore City Jackson party emerged from the chaos of the 1820s to become a highly successful political organization within a decade.[104] Between 1828 and 1836 all but four members of the House of Delegates were elected from party nominees, and two of the opposition victors were members of the Workingmen's party, which split from the Jacksonian party over a nomination dispute in 1833. Despite repeated efforts by rural Anti-Jacksonians to weaken Baltimore's numerical strength through legislative gerrymandering, many Jacksonians were elected to Congress and as presidential electors throughout this period.

Part of this success was attributable to the Baltimore *Republican and Commercial Advertiser*, the party's central means of communication, both in the city and throughout the state.[105] The paper was established in 1827 by leading anti-Adams urban figures and edited until 1828 by Dabney S. Carr. Carr, the nephew of the United States senator, General Samuel Smith, was appointed as naval officer of the port in 1829 by the Jackson administration. In 1832, after another change in editors, Samuel Harker, who had edited the Delaware *Gazette* since 1820, became editor of the *Republican*, where he remained until 1837. Harker's staunch support of both Jackson and Van Buren was especially important in the presidential succession of 1836. He was also a leading figure in the local party organization.

Jacksonian unity was nonetheless strained by a number of factors. The well-publicized dispute between John C. Calhoun and Martin Van Buren over presidential succession polarized partisans throughout Maryland. Calhoun's defeat and Van Buren's reputed opposition to slavery caused many Jacksonians to reconsider their allegiance to the party.[106] Urban partisans were also divided by the administration's position against federal sponsorship for internal improvements in 1830, but more defected during the protracted financial crisis during the controversy over the recharter of the Second Bank of the United States.

Traditional historical sources portray Jacksonian party leadership as being both continuous with first party norms and influenced by men holding national political positions.[107] Yet a close scrutiny of party leadership over the entire period reveals a totally different picture. Many of these men were active in the initial stages of party development but faded in importance as the party system matured. Roger B. Taney, for instance, was an early party organizer, but his national role in Jackson's cabinet effectively removed him from control over local political operations.[108] Similarly, General Samuel Smith, an eleventh-hour Jacksonian at best, who nonetheless demanded all symbols of preference from the administration as befitting his rank as a United States senator, gave little local public leadership to the party cause.[109] Smith's Republican party political ally dating from the 1790s, Congressman Isaac McKim, also defined his role as a political leader in national terms and saw himself as a representative of the merchant community.[110] Only Congressman Benjamin C. Howard ranked high in local community leadership among the national political officeholders. Historians also have devoted considerable attention to several youthful and aspiring political leaders—such as Reverdy Johnson, John P. Kennedy, and John V. L. McMahon—who were early zealots to the Jackson cause but abjured this allegiance when their ambitions were thwarted.[111]

Overall, the 261 Jackson party organizational leaders represent a much more disparate group when surveyed in depth than has been described by earlier historians.[112] Merchants and skilled laborers, professionals and men of no clear occupation joined together to lead the professed party of the common man against the "monied interests." Table 4.1 compares the Jackson and Anti-Jackson party leadership directly. Broken down into occupation groups, 19 percent of the Jacksonian leaders were professionals, 23 percent came from the ranks of skilled labor, 29 percent were merchants, 7 percent were members of white-collar occupations, and the remaining 22 percent had no occupation listed in the city directory.[113] Their average age was thirty-seven years; 62 percent were below forty years of age. Forty-seven percent held taxable wealth, with an average value of $1,084; only 12 percent owned slaves.[114]

The statistics shown in Table 4.1 reveal the varied backgrounds from which Jackson party leaders were recruited, but they fail to show much about recruitment patterns. In order to understand the dynamics of party leadership and how it was transformed by the maturation of the convention system, party activity was divided into four strata (Table 4.2).

Table 4.1. Baltimore City Leaders, 1827–1836

Jackson Party (n = 261)			Anti-Jackson Party (n = 324)		
Variable	n	%	Variable	n	%
Age			*Age*		
60+	4	3	60+	14	10
50–59	13	10	50–59	17	12
40–49	34	26	40–49	30	22
30–39	45	34	30–39	41	30
20–29	36	27	20–29	36	26
n = 132 (51%)			n = 138 (43%)		
mean = 37			mean = 39		
Slaves			*Slaves*		
over 2	23	77	over 2	38	72
1	7	23	1	15	28
n = 30 (12%)			n = 53 (16%)		
Lots			*Lots*		
over 20	2	2	over 20	3	2
15–19	1	1	15–19	3	2
10–14	7	7	10–14	5	4
5–9	12	11	5–9	19	14
2–4	43	41	2–4	55	41
1	40	38	1	48	37
n = 105 (40%)			n = 133 (41%)		
mean = 3.6			mean = 3.9		
Wealth			*Wealth*		
over $50,000	0	0	over $50,000	0	0
over $10,000	0	0	over $10,000	2	1
$5,000–$9,999	3	2	$5,000–$9,999	9	5
$1,000–$4,999	35	28	$1,000–$4,999	52	31
$500–$999	28	23	$500–$999	39	23
$100–$499	40	33	$100–$499	57	34
$10–$99	17	14	$10–$99	9	5
n = 123 (47%)			n = 168 (52%)		
mean = $1,084			mean = $1,516		

The ability of men to rise from a variety of backgrounds is demonstrated through descriptions of representative cases from each activity stratum.

Table 4.2. Jackson Leadership Patterns

Score	Stratum	Number
Over 51	I	9
26–50	II	35
11–25	III	77
3–10	IV	140

The most active party organizers were men unfamiliar to traditional Baltimore historians. The highest scoring Jackson leader was William Krebs, an attorney in his thirties. A frequent member of both city and state central committees between 1827 and 1836, he chaired local ward meetings, nomination conventions for the lower house, and the 1833 district congressional nomination convention, where he had served as vice-chairman in 1831. He also attended district and state conventions as a delegate. The second and third scoring leaders were both merchants of modest means. Philip Laurenson was an active party organizer and a member of the city and state legislatures. Joshua Turner, a feed store merchant in his fifties, was more involved as a local ward leader and as a delegate to conventions than the other two men, and he also served on central committees in 1833 and 1836.

The remaining members of the upper stratum were predominantly lawyers. McClintock Young and William Frick were close to Roger B. Taney; Young eventually entered the U.S. Treasury Department.[115] William H. Coale and John J. Donaldson also practiced law. Samuel Harker, editor of the Baltimore *Republican*, was active only after his arrival in 1832. In addition to his role as editor and leader, he was often called on to serve as a speaker or member of resolution committees. Colonel Samuel Moore participated between 1827 and 1833, when he was in his early fifties, but his involvement waned after his last service on the central committee in 1830. Taken together, the members of this upper stratum may be best characterized as diligent participants who served over an extended period of time. Some, like Krebs, were leaders in district conventions; others, like Laurenson or Young, functioned primarily as ward leaders, while Harker earned his place through a combination of his leadership and editorial control.

The thirty-five members of the second stratum were a varied group. Benjamin Chew Howard, one of Baltimore's two congressmen, represented the dual pattern of party recruitment in the Jackson era. As the son of the wealthy and politically prominent Federalist leader, Colonel John E. Howard, he owed a portion of his prominence to the family tradition for community leadership.[116] Unlike Congressman Isaac Mc-Kim, who rarely participated in party meetings, Howard was an early supporter of Jackson, serving as delegate, speaker, and officer in many activities. Joshua Vansant, at the other extreme, had no family tradition from which to build. A hatter in his early thirties, he molded his party position from local leadership in the Fifth and Ninth wards and from several attempts to win election to state government.[117] Young professionals, lawyers, such as Frederick J. Dugan, William G. Read, and Thomas L. Murphy, doctors like John J. Graves and Edward J. Alcock, who also edited the reform-oriented *Jeffersonian Reformer* before his death in 1836, similarly worked their way into this stratum through ward-level leadership.[118]

Prominent merchants, such as Hugh McElderry or Beale Randall, allied with merchants of less substantial means, such as William Roney or Jonathan Fitch. Military titles denoted a persisting nostalgia in a city that had positive memories of the War of 1812. General George H. Steuart, who was prominent in the defense of Baltimore, was an active party leader between 1830 and 1835 and had been a member of the House of Delegates in 1828.[119] This group included many members of central committees[120] and some ward officers.[121] Their active years of participation in politics ranged from those with only a few years of experience to some who entered as Jackson activists as early as 1824.

The third stratum contained many leaders who are traditionally identified in secondary accounts: Roger B. Taney, John Nelson, and the Federalist leader, Richard Frisby; Reverdy Johnson and Colonel Nicholas Brewer, two leaders who defected to the Anti-Jackson party, were also included. Although most of the seventy-seven persons in this category did not hold formal positions, they nonetheless participated in a wide variety of political activities. Of those for whom occupations could be determined, twenty-five were merchants, fifteen were skilled workers, thirteen were lawyers, and two were editors of the party papers before 1832. In addition, several of the party's state officeholders fell into this category: Samuel Mass belonged to the Executive Council; Reverdy Johnson and John Nelson were in the senate; Beale H. Richardson and Charles C. Harper were members of the lower house.[122] Johnson, a successful lawyer who became a United States senator as a Whig in the 1840s, was primarily associated with the party's central committee between 1828 and 1829. Harper, son of Federalist leader Robert Goodloe Harper and grandson of Charles Carroll of Carrollton, sought to capitalize on his family connections to build a public career. Other leaders in government did not enjoy similar advantages. Samuel Mass, a cedar cooper and grocer, gained prominence because of his persistence as a Tenth Ward leader between 1831 and 1836; Richardson, a Fifth Ward dry goods merchant, was active between 1830–31 and 1835–36.

The political background of persons in this category varied enormously. Henry Worthington, for example, was a young man in his twenties who frequently acted as secretary in meetings of the Eighth Ward between 1829 and 1831 and again in 1835. Thomas Parkin Scott, a lawyer in his thirties, was first active in 1829, but did not work continuously as a local leader and a delegate to conventions from the Twelfth Ward until 1835 and 1836. Dabney S. Carr, a lawyer-editor and nephew of General Samuel Smith, was a member of the central committee in 1828, but retired from public political activities after his appointment as naval officer in 1829. Robert Armstrong, a soap and candle manufacturer in his late thirties, supported Jackson as early as 1824 and served the Fifth Ward from 1829 to 1836, sometimes as secretary but most frequently as a delegate to conventions. Washington Abrams, a house carpenter in his early thirties, began his political activities in the Workingmen's party in 1833, then gravitated to the Jackson party in 1835–36, where he served on the central committee representing the First Ward. These examples are representative of the variety of experiences of men in this stratum.

The fourth stratum was the largest with 140 members. Individuals who assumed leadership roles for a single year and then either retired or participated infrequently as convention delegates fell into this category. This group included several legislative members from Baltimore. John Spear Nicholas, General Samuel Smith's nephew, represented the city in the lower house for two terms and participated in Seventh Ward affairs between 1829 and 1832. John V. L. McMahon, the noted lawyer and Allegany County legislator, was returned to the House of Delegates to represent Baltimore in 1828. Frustrated in his effort to obtain unanimous party backing for his congressional nomination in 1829, he served on the central committee in 1830 and then drifted into the Anti-Jackson party by 1834. Jesse Hunt, elected to the lower house for three terms, was the mayor of Baltimore from 1832 until the disastrous mob violence of the bank riots of 1835 forced his resignation. As mayor he did not participate in party activities as he had when he was a state legislator from 1827 to 1831.

As Table 4.3 shows, most of the skilled workers and almost half of the merchants who were party leaders fell into the fourth stratum. Included in this stratum were James M. Campbell, Taney's son-in-law; William G. Jones, publisher of the politically neutral *Baltimore Gazette*;

Table 4.3 Jackson Party Leadership
and Occupations (percentages)

Stratum	IV	III	II	I
Merchants	46	35	16	3
Skilled workers	60	23	15	2
Professionals	26	40	22	12

the noted lawyer and author, John Pendleton Kennedy; General John Spear Smith, Senator Samuel Smith's son; and General Tobias E. Stansbury, veteran campaigner from Baltimore County. Most of the persons in this stratum, however, were not well connected, nor were they active for as long as party leaders.

The Jacksonian party leadership of Baltimore was in essence a coalition. Integrating participants from all ranks of society, partisans shared power in an effort to bring the strength of their numbers behind Jackson nominees. Such a coalition was constructed from all strata. Members of traditionally important families, such as Benjamin Chew Howard and Charles Carroll Harper, or eleventh-hour Jacksonians whose political importance was determined by the office they held, such as United States Senator Samuel Smith, were still accorded preferences beyond what their party activities might justify. But the structure of decision making in the second party era also permitted nonelite members to share in party leadership. Professionals, especially lawyers, and skilled artisans were able to convert individual ability or their appeal to a large and relatively inarticulate constituency into party leadership positions. Such a system functioned well as long as leaders recognized that party decision making was a shared responsibility, but if one group demanded too much power, the coalition would disintegrate. This happened in 1833.

The urban Jacksonian coalition came apart with the defection of the Workingmen's party in 1833 over the issue of nomination procedures. The withdrawal of the Workingmen demonstrated the hazards of trying to placate the oligarchy in the face of vocal discontent among a far larger constituency and underscored the interaction necessary for successful coalitional politics. The viability of the coalition system, however, was illustrated by the reintegration of the Workingmen within a year.

During the 1830s, Baltimore workers were restive over economic issues. In an effort to protect the ten-hour day and the prevailing wage structure from encroachments by employers, workers transformed traditional journeymen's associations into purposeful skilled crafts unions.

They also recognized the strength of class action and worked to establish a general trades union organization. With the exception of 1833, this unionization movement in the 1830s was apolitical.[123]

The creation of the Workingmen's party resulted from the breakdown in coalitional bartering in the selection of the Jackson party nominees for the House of Delegates in 1833.[124] At issue was whether the incumbents, with whom the workingmen were dissatisfied, had a right to renomination or whether the workingmen had the right to nominate at least one of the two candidates on the ticket. They objected particularly to the renomination of Charles Carroll Harper, who was as unpopular as he was well connected. In the fashion of earlier elite politics, he was beginning a political career in the lower house of the legislature after earlier federal service abroad as secretary to the American legation in Paris. When the party leaders sustained Harper's renomination, the workingmen defected and nominated their own candidates on the eve of the election.

This action had several important short-term political ramifications. Since the Anti-Jackson party did not make nominations that fall, the division was clearly a factional dispute within the Jackson party despite the repeated claims by the party press that the defection was contrived by the Anti-Jacksonians. It also encouraged an independent Jacksonian to challenge the party congressional nominee. The voters turned out all of the Jackson party candidates in October. Opponents of Martin Van Buren tried to capitalize on this division by calling for a popular meeting to recommend Judge John McLean as Jackson's successor, but the meeting attracted Anti-Jacksonians primarily and did not divide the party further.[125]

Almost as quickly as it had formed, the breach between the workingmen and the Jacksonians was healed, and they rejoined their former party on a firmer political base. Recognizing their mistake, Jackson party leaders apparently convinced the dissidents that they were willing to adhere to the coalitional norms of party leadership.[126]

The Anti-Jackson party was much more active and organized than its marginal electoral success would suggest.[127] Not only did it match the variety of organizational activities used by the Jacksonians between 1827 and 1836, but it actually surpassed them in the organization of young men as a political force. And even when the Anti-Jackson party failed in citywide elections, the local organization belonged to the party that dominated state politics. Consequently, when the contract to publish the federal laws was taken from the *Patriot* and awarded to the *Republican* in 1829, the *Patriot* could still count on some support because it published the state laws. Baltimore's wealth and population gave its leadership respect and prestige, and the press was an important element in their communications network. Similarly, even if Baltimore Anti-Jacksonians could not be elected to state or national office, their party dominated the state legislature which elected the governor, the Executive Council, and other offices for most of the period.

As with the Jackson party, the newspaper was a key organizational tool. The National Republican spokesman of the late 1820s was the Baltimore *Patriot and Mercantile Advertiser*. Isaac Munroe, who founded it as a Madisonian commercial paper in 1812, continued as its editor throughout this period.[128] In 1827 the *Marylander* was established as a weekly campaign paper. Samuel Sands took it over in 1828 and joined it with one of the city's leading commercial papers, the *Commercial Chronicle*, the following year. The *Commercial Chronicle and Daily Marylander*, as the combination was known, was edited by Sands, Sheppard C. Leakin, and Samuel Barnes.[129] Thus, after 1829, the Baltimore Anti-Jackson party was served by two daily papers, each vying for support.[130] Through the presidential campaign of 1832 they were unified by opposition to Jackson, but by 1836 their unanimity broke, when the *Patriot* supported the candidacy of Daniel Webster and the *Chronicle* boosted William Henry Harrison as the Whig candidate.

Despite the dearth of local electoral success, many Anti-Jackson candidates served in public office. Peter Little and John Barney represented the city district in Congress in the late 1820s and stood with the party against Jackson in the initial stages of its development, but both men withdrew from politics during the early years of the new administration.[131] E. L. Finley picked up the congressional standard in 1831; Charles R. Stewart and James P. Heath joined him in 1835, without electoral success. In the state government there were no Baltimore governors, but William R. Steuart, Luke Tiernan, and Nathaniel F. Williams all were appointed to the state Executive Council. Charles F. Mayer was elected to the state senate in 1831; William R. Steuart, E. L. Finley, Luke Tiernan, Thomas Y. Walsh, Joshua Jones, Joseph Cushing, Robert Neilson, and Robert Purviance all ran for the House of Delegates during this period. Many of these individuals were active in party organization, some were recognized by historians, and those who served in state government did so through indirect election in a legislature dominated by the Anti-Jackson party.

With the possible exception of Hezekiah Niles, editor of the *Niles Weekly Register*, and James W. McCulloch, who gained public notoriety for his activities as cashier of the Baltimore branch of the Bank of the United States in 1819 and as the McCulloch of *McCulloch* vs. *Maryland*, few of these Anti-Jackson leaders had national reputations.[132] As a group, they demonstrated as much occupational diversity as the Jacksonians: 34 percent were merchants; 19 percent skilled workers; 17 percent professionals; 7 percent proprietors or clerical; the remaining 23 percent had no occupational listing in the city directory. Their average age was thirty-nine years, and their average wealth was $1,516. Compared to the Jacksonian leaders, more of them owned slaves (16 percent), their average landed property holding was higher (3.9 city lots), and more of them held taxable property (52 percent). The occupational and wealth figures for these two elite party groupings are very similar, as is amply demonstrated by the data in table 4.3.

Table 4.4 divides the party elite into four strata of party activity. Within the first stratum, party editors are much in evidence. Isaac Munroe of the *Patriot* and General Leakin and Samuel Barnes of the *Chronicle* were prominent. Hezekiah Niles, unrecognized by historians for his local party activities,[133] and without scoring the *Register* as a party press, assembled a high score as an indefatigable Seventh Ward party organizer between 1828 and 1834.

Nathaniel F. Williams, second only to Isaac Munroe in party ranking, played a prominent role in the local party from 1827 through 1836. He was a merchant in his thirties from the Tenth Ward, who frequently served on central committees. Although he did not run for public office, Williams was elected by the legislature to the Executive Council from 1835 through 1837. Other lawyers in the first stratum included Colonel Samuel Moale and John M. Steuart. Moale, a Maryland native in his fifties who worked in the Tenth Ward, usually functioned as chairman of ward meetings between 1833 and 1836 and as a member of the central committee. Steuart was primarily active as secretary to various conventions between 1832 and 1836 and in the young men's party movement.

Peter Leary, who was born in 1782 and worked as a hatter, labored in the Anti-Jackson cause from 1824 to 1836. He attended every presidential convention as a delegate, served on the central committee for

Table 4.4. Anti-Jackson
Leadership Patterns

Score	Stratum	Number
Over 51	I	14
26–50	II	26
11–25	III	103
3–10	IV	181

several years, and was involved in the Second Ward organizational activities. General Joshua Medtart, a brewer who was eleven years Leary's junior, also served on the central committee in 1829 and 1836 and was diligent for almost a decade as a leader in the Eleventh and Twelfth wards.

There were also prominent merchants in this first stratum including Luke Tiernan, Robert Purviance, Solomon Etting, and General William McDonald. Purviance was an unsuccessful candidate to the lower house of the legislature. Tiernan was a reluctant but equally unsuccessful candidate for the House of Delegates in 1832 and declined election to the Executive Council in 1836.[134] A native of Ireland, he moved from rural Maryland to Baltimore in 1795, where he built a successful import dry goods business and became the sixth wealthiest Baltimore citizen by 1834. General McDonald ranked twelfth on the city's tax rolls and was an important merchant in his sixties. Solomon Etting was an affluent Jewish merchant who was active between 1824 and 1836. He was on the central committee in 1827 and 1829, and, in addition to local Eleventh Ward activities, he served as a vice-chairman of the 1832 presidential elector convention.[135]

The second stratum with twenty-six members was equally diverse. Among the lawyers of this group, James W. McCulloch is the most fascinating. Momentarily disgraced in the early 1820s because of the Bank of the United States imbroglio, McCulloch served in the House of Delegates from Baltimore County and was elected speaker for the 1826 session.[136] Besides being an active party leader in the county, he was an Adams presidential elector candidate in 1829, the year he was first visible in city politics. The other lawyers, Colonel Samuel Manning and James M. Buchanan, were less colorful. Colonel Manning worked from the Twelfth Ward between 1832 and 1836. Buchanan labored in the Seventh Ward during the same period, holding his most powerful position in 1835, when he chaired the district congressional convention.

Several candidates and officeholders fell into this second stratum. Colonel William R. Steuart had been a candidate for the lower house in 1830. The career of Joshua Jones, a member of the working class, illustrated the cosmopolitan nature of the Anti-Jackson leadership. He was first politically active as the successful House of Delegates candidate for the Workingmen's party in 1833. In 1834 he was returned as an Anti-Jacksonian. Throughout that year of political reorganization when the Whig party formed, and continuing through 1836, Jones participated in many local meetings and attended the congressional, state, and presidential conventions. In 1835 he joined Samuel Barnes as an editor of the *Chronicle*.[137]

A number of Baltimore's leading entrepreneurs accounted for the reputation of the Anti-Jacksonian party as commercially based. Representative figures include: Hugh W. Evans, proprietor of the Levandale cotton factory; James Harwood, a merchant and judge of Baltimore's Orphans Court; John McKim, Jr., a banker and president of the new Merchants Bank in 1836; Colonel Bernard U. Campbell, teller of the Mechanics Bank; and William Meeteer, who owned a paper warehouse.

The prevalent historical emphasis on the commercial elite within the Anti-Jackson hierarchy, however, obscures the presence of skilled craftsmen in the party leadership. Andrew F. Warner, a silversmith with a modest taxable property of $45 in 1834, was a member of several party central committees and participated in Sixth Ward leadership between 1827 and 1835. Edward Needles, a chairmaker in his late thirties with no taxable property noted in 1828 or 1834, was most active between 1833 and 1836 as a local leader or secretary to city conventions. James L. Hawkins was a blacksmith in his fifties, who was active in Sixth Ward politics as early as 1824. James O. Law was a youthful shoemaker in his mid-twenties, who participated between 1834 and 1836. The activity of these men weakens the traditional class emphasis given to the contesting party elites in the Jackson era.

The third stratum of party leaders contains an even greater variety. Some were candidates or served in state government. Colonel E. L. Finley, the congressional candidate in 1831, was a lawyer in his thirties, who was primarily active on the city convention level between 1831 and 1832. Thomas Y. Walsh, a young lawyer in his twenties who twice stood for the legislature, also participated in Fifth Ward meetings and city conventions between 1832 and 1836. Charles F. Mayer, a lawyer who was elected to a five-year term in the state senate in 1831, had been a member of the central committee in 1829 and was active in the events of 1834. David Stewart, an able lawyer of some wealth, was a candidate for presidential elector in 1832 and operated on the ward level between 1832 and 1834. James L. Ridgely, another lawyer, was a candidate for elector to the state senate in 1836. His period of greatest activity was 1835–36, but his first leadership role had been in the presidential campaign of 1828.

Of the 103 persons in this group, 44 were merchants of one sort or another. Alexander Fridge, an affluent merchant in his sixties of the firm Fridge and Morris, chaired the presidential elector convention in 1832 and played a similar role in a local ward meeting in 1836. William P. Dunnington, a merchant in his forties, was primarily involved in party leadership between 1832 and 1836, but he first participated in 1827. A brush manufacturer of modest means, Joseph K. Stapleton participated in party affairs in 1828 and 1834. Asa Needham, a grocer in his mid-forties from the Eighth Ward, chaired a postnomination meeting in 1834 and served as a convention delegate in that year and in 1836. These men are representative of the occupational and wealth variation within the group.[138]

The skilled workmen illustrate the same variation. John Ijams, a carpenter in his late forties, had no taxable property but was prominent in Third Ward meetings between 1834 and 1836. John Tensfield, at the other end of the activity spectrum, served in Seventh Ward party leadership between 1832 and 1835 while he was a successful blacksmith; he owned a slave and property valued at $1,120. Between them were leaders such as Robert D. Millholland, a blockmaker in his forties, who acted primarily as a delegate to conventions between 1828 and 1836, and George Wagner, a native of Virginia in his fifties, who was active in local First Ward meetings during this same period. Wagner, a block and pump maker, owned one lot valued at $40.

Among the others in this group were several Baltimore notables: John B. Morris, president of the Mechanics Bank; Job Smith, Jr., president of the Maryland Savings Institution; and John Glenn, a prominent member of the banking community. The ubiquitous William Gwynn Jones, editor of the *Gazette* from mid-1834 until his conviction for mail theft in 1835, appears in the Anti-Jackson leadership group as well as among the Jacksonians.[139]

The fourth stratum contained the largest number of persons, as shown in Table 4.5 by occupation and score. Within this stratum were several of the remaining candidates for the lower house: William H. Freeman, Dr. L. O'Brien, and George R. Richardson.[140] Neither Colonel Peter Little nor John Barney, the Adams congressmen of 1827, played a role in party affairs other than their unsuccessful candidacy for reelection in 1829.

There were other notables from the city in this group: Mayor Jacob Small played a minor role; James H. McCulloch, the venerable collector

Table 4.5. Anti-Jackson Party Leadership and Occupations (percentages)

Occupation	IV	III	II	I
Merchants	50	41	4	4
Skilled workers	58	27	12	3
Professionals	51	25	10	14

of the port, chaired a meeting in 1828; George H. Calvert, the youthful editor of the Baltimore *American*, and Francis H. Davidge, editor of the Baltimore *Chronicle* until 1829, were Anti-Jacksonian partisans although their papers remained editorially neutral. Several others played minor roles: Solomon Betts, a noted merchant; B. I. Cohen, a banker; the wealthy merchant William Lorman; the sometime Jacksonian John Pendleton Kennedy; and, predictably in 1828, an unpretentious artisan whose name gave him transient notoriety, John Adams.

The Anti-Jacksonians, like their Jacksonian opponents, drew their leaders from many social groups. Close analysis, provided by Table 4.6, demonstrates remarkable uniformity among the competing party elites. Both parties recruited leaders from all segments of society. Table 4.1 presented earlier comparisons of wealth, age, and property-holding characteristics. Overall the party leadership of both competing organizations was similar.

Thus, in terms of occupation, age, and holding property, men of the same socioeconomic background led the two major political parties of Baltimore. The average wealth figure for the Anti-Jacksonians was higher, but the distribution of wealth was almost identical. The reputed political leaders cited in general histories, such as Roger B. Taney or General Samuel Smith, scored lower in the party leadership ranking than their historical reputations might suggest. The men who made decisions and wielded direct leadership in both parties were more obscure nationally than these two. The leaders were active in the realms of artisan, business, and professional affairs on the community level, and they drew on local ties to sustain them politically.

For the city of Baltimore, internal improvements were still synonymous in the 1820s and 1830s with prosperity and modernization.[141] An expanded road system had forged a strong link with its hinterland, but until the development of the railroad only the Chesapeake and Ohio Canal seemed to be a viable way of access to the Ohio Valley. Contemporaries perceived that its completion would almost assure the prosperity of its commercial rivals to Baltimore's disadvantage. The introduction of a steam-powered railroad in the late 1820s was quickly recognized by Baltimore boosters as the way to assure the city of a central position from which to reap the bounty of Ohio trade. To a far greater degree than any other area of the state, members from all segments of Baltimore society organized to boost internal improvements.

The aim of the organizers was to obtain financial support for their project by memorializing both the state and federal governments. Because President Jackson had blocked federal funds with the Maysville veto, the target was local and state support. Until the omnibus 1836

Table 4.6. Occupations of the Leaders

Occupation	Jackson N = 261		Anti-Jackson N = 324	
	Number	Percent	Number	Percent
Merchants	76	29	110	34
Skilled workers	60	23	61	19
Clerical, sales	7	3	10	3
Proprietors	11	4	14	4
Professional	50	19	55	17
Unknown	57	22	74	23

"Eight Million Dollar Act" such requests were on an ad hoc basis. Several important conventions were held: a canal convention met in Baltimore in December 1834 to promote the interests of the stalled Chesapeake and Ohio Canal Company; meetings were held in 1835 to encourage the state senate to enact a lower house aid bill, as well as to organize support for the Brownsville railroad convention at the end of November; and there were meetings in 1836 to support the omnibus internal improvement bill.[142]

Despite an apparently common economic goal, there were seams of division within the community. Even while city papers enthusiastically reported transportation linkages or technological advances,[143] political partisans and advocates of competing modes of transportation fermented dissent. Anti-Jacksonians attacked the national administration at the 1834 canal convention for its failure to support internal improvements, and the convention resisted efforts to aid other internal improvement projects. The great cost of the projects, far in excess of the first estimates in terms of both money and labor, had combined by 1835 with the forced lethargy of the construction delays to produce a state of popular apathy.[144]

Because of the significance of these works, many of the city's leading citizens participated in organizational activities. Table 4.7 ranks leaders in four strata of activity. Since delegates to other conventions were important both because of their participation and public support for the project, they have been scored and counted in the last stratum.

John Pendleton Kennedy, a leading attorney and sometime Jacksonian, ranked first. He was active in the 1834 canal convention, the Brownsville meeting, and the Baltimore convention in May 1836. Jacob

Albert, an apolitical hardware merchant who was president of the Commercial and Farmer's Bank and ranked high among the city's wealthy citizens, was almost as active. Colonel Samuel Moore, an early Jackson party leader, labored primarily in the cause of internal improvements after 1830. He attended conventions in Baltimore, Annapolis, and Brownsville and was vice-president of the 1836 Baltimore internal improvements convention. John Kettlewell, the final member of this group, a grocer in his mid-twenties, was active between 1835 and 1836.

Table 4.7. Baltimore City
Internal Improvement Leaders

Score	Number
Over 30	5
20–29	4
11–19	15
10	86

James W. McCulloch belonged to this stratum because of his reputation for influence in the state legislature. McCulloch publicly worked from both Baltimore City and County for state support of internal improvements. His score would place him in the third stratum, but his role was much greater because he was employed by the Chesapeake and Ohio Canal Company as a lobbyist in Annapolis. The president of the company credited the successful passage of the 1835 internal improvements bill to his efforts.[145] This judgment, in addition to his public role, elevates him to the first stratum.

The next stratum of activity contained two bankers and two of the city's mayors. The mayor of Baltimore played an important role in organizing community meetings and encouraging public support. Both Jesse Hunt and General Samuel Smith ranked in this group. B. I. Cohen, president of his own bank, whose true wealth was clearly understated in the tax record,[146] participated between 1832 and 1834. Samuel Hoffman, who was associated with several banks, also worked for internal improvements.

The third stratum included several important political leaders of both parties. One was Joseph Cushing, who served in the House of Delegates. Members of the banking community were also much in evidence, as well as two who were both bankers and directors of the Baltimore and Ohio Railroad Company.[147]

The last stratum, made up of individuals who participated only once or twice, consisted of commercial, political, and public leaders. Public leaders included Congressman B. C. Howard, former state Senators Heath and Mayer from the city, William H. Marriott and John Nelson, who represented their respective counties before moving to Baltimore, and Roger B. Taney. The president of the Baltimore and Ohio Railroad, Philip E. Thomas, the secretary of the company, George Brown, and several directors publicly organized support for state sponsorship of internal improvements.[148]

These men represented greater personal and business wealth than the party leaders, and their political tone was definitely Anti-Jacksonian. Although 35 percent of this elite were apolitical, 39 percent were associated at one time with the Anti-Jackson party. Five of the party's first-stratum leaders also played active roles in internal improvements.[149] The Jackson press and some of its leaders lent support, public and private,[150] but the tone of the movement, which involved soliciting public support for internal improvements, was more in accord with Clay's American System than with the public policy of the Jackson party.

Just as internal improvements would benefit Baltimore commercially, the frustrated attempts to achieve more equitable representation signified the community's desire for greater influence in state government. With 21.8 percent of the state's total 1840 population and 25.5 percent of the free white population, Baltimore sent only two representatives to the House of Delegates. It is not surprising, therefore, to find bipartisan political support for reform as occurred in Frederick County.

Through 1833, the Anti-Jackson press supported reform and resisted associating the movement with either national party.[151] In the fall of 1832, the Baltimore *Chronicle* advocated abolishing the council, instituting direct election of the governor, reform of the senate, and some form of popular representation in the lower house. It dissented from the January 1833 Baltimore Reform Convention because it was too partisan, but continued to support nonpartisan reform efforts throughout that year.[152] Against strong statewide efforts to identify reform with the Jackson party, the Baltimore political community favored bipartisan cooperation through the spring of 1833.[153] Some of the city's leading Anti-Jacksonian partisans were active in the reform movement.

Not all Jacksonian politicians advocated a bipartisan reform movement. The Baltimore *Republican* consistently identified the "rotten borough" system of representation with the Anti-Jackson party that dominated state government. Although this partisan association was modified in 1832–33 to encourage bipartisan support for reform, the Jackson press, especially in Fredericktown, favored party leadership. From the fall of 1832 through 1837, the Jackson press conscientiously advanced reform as a purely party goal. This was a conscious propaganda device to associate reform and the party to generate popular support for the Jacksonians throughout the state.[154]

The Baltimore reformers were also faced with statewide resistance to the propriety of absolute popular representation. Both small and large counties feared the undiluted representational influence of Baltimore's huge population.[155] In an effort to play down the obvious benefits that would accrue to the city if reform were accomplished, the Baltimore press gave special attention to county reform organizations. Reports were printed from small counties, such as Cecil and Harford, which were also Jackson strongholds, and from larger counties such as Frederick, Washington, and Baltimore. Statewide convention officers were frequently recruited from among the rural reformers as if to diminish Baltimore's role.[156] Early conventions served as an organizational device to generate support for reform throughout the state to memorialize the legislature.

Perhaps the greatest source of frustration to the reformers and the primary reason for the transformation of the movement from a bipartisan to the Jackson cause was the unwillingness of the legislature to consider any reform seriously. Each year new legislation was presented, and just as often the legislative session ended with either outright rejection or inattention to reform bills.[157] When the Jacksonians had the vote in the lower house, the Anti-Jacksonians defeated their bills in the senate.

Despite the fact that the tactics used by the Jackson reformers in the senatorial crisis of 1836 lent credibility to the sensationalist imagery of revolution projected by their opponents,[158] the original goals of reform were achieved in 1837. The organizational efforts of the reformers, combined with the unrestrained reform rhetoric of the Jackson press, convinced the governor and legislature to implement some reform legislation.[159]

Of the 172 persons who publicly identified with Baltimore reform activities, 80 percent had been active in the competing political parties; 47 percent could be identified as Jacksonians, 33 percent as Anti-Jacksonians.[160] Table 4.8 arrays the reformers by activity score.

Four of the five leaders in the first stratum were Jackson party leaders and the other was a party activist. Philip Laurenson, a first-stratum party leader and former member of the House of Delegates, was the highest scoring reform leader. He was a member of central reform committees in 1832–33, when he was also a delegate to conventions. In 1836 he chaired a local meeting and the January state convention, and he went to the June convention as a delegate. General William H. Marriott, who

scored second, was a Jackson leader from the last stratum of activity. He
was a prominent lawyer and had been an Anne Arundel County state
senator before moving to Baltimore around 1832. He was primarily
active in 1832–33 as a chairman, delegate, and member of the central
committee. In 1836 he served only as a delegate to the January convention. Samuel Harker, editor of the *Republican*, and William Krebs, the
highest scoring Jackson leader, also ranked among the most active reform
leaders. James Carroll, a Jackson activist in 1833 and 1835, but not a
leader, participated in reform organization in 1832 and 1836. A man of
great wealth, Carroll was appointed vice-president of the June convention, and he attended the November convention as a delegate in 1836.[161]

Table 4.8. Baltimore City Reformers

Score	Number
Over 30	5
20–29	11
11–19	23
3–10	133

At the second stratum the bipartisan roots of reform leadership are
apparent. Despite the antipathy of the Jackson press, some Anti-Jackson
leaders continued to participate in the movement through 1836, just as
they had between 1832 and 1833. The four highest scoring Anti-Jackson
party leaders fell into this stratum: three party editors, General Sheppard C. Leakin, Isaac Munroe, and Samuel Sands, and the prominent
merchant Nathaniel F. Williams. The editors were primarily members of
early central reform committees; Leakin and Munroe, however, were
among a delegation to memorialize the legislature as late as January
1836. Williams belonged to an early central committee, and he served as
a delegate several times thereafter. William H. Freeman, an attorney in
his forties, and William Patterson, the richest individual on both the
1800 and the 1834 tax rolls, were also Anti-Jackson reformers. Freeman,
who participated in party affairs in the early 1830s, was primarily involved in reform in 1832–33. Patterson, who aligned himself with the
Adams party in 1827 but was not a visible party leader, advocated reform
in 1832.

The five members of the Jackson party in this stratum were also public leaders. William Frick and Colonel Samuel Moore were first-stratum

party leaders; Dr. Graves, General George H. Steuart, and Charles Howard were in the second. Dr. Graves was the secretary for two state conventions in 1836 and a frequent delegate to reform meetings in that year. The others were members of central committees in 1832 and 1833 or delegates to early conventions. Only Charles Howard went as a convention delegate in 1836.

The third stratum consisted of twelve Jacksonians, ten Anti-Jacksonians, and the leader of the trade union movement. Richard Marley, chairman of the Journeymen Cordwainers and the chairman of the 1833 mechanics' convention to form the trade union, chaired a proreform workingmen's meeting to counteract a recent antireform meeting in 1836.[162] Jackson party leaders, delegates to both houses of the state legislature, and members of prominent political families mixed with their counterparts in the Anti-Jackson party in joint efforts to organize support for reform.[163]

The final reform stratum was composed of persons who participated in one activity but rarely more than that. Several of the positional leaders in federal and state offices fell into this category, as did more members of the leadership elite of both parties.[164]

Although Baltimore City residents generally favored reform, the actions of the nineteen senatorial electors favoring Van Buren forced Anti-Jacksonians to oppose them publicly. At a meeting chaired by General William McDonald and addressed by former Jacksonian John V. L. McMahon, many of the city's leading Anti-Jacksonians and merchants went on record against radical reform. Among the officers of this meeting were at least seven men who earlier favored reform, but who renounced the reform strategy in 1836.[165]

The patronage issue illustrated rivalries within the evolving urban political system between the older political elite, many of whom were position holders, and men rising to power through the expanding party organization. Institutional norms favored position holders, who continued to function as conduits through which patronage requests flowed to the executive branch on both the state and federal levels, but the cry for rotation in office rose in intensity from the time President Jackson took office in 1829 until some change was finally made in 1835. Beginning with the federal system, a close examination of the rivalries within the community demonstrates another facet of urban coalition politics in the second party era.

Writing at almost the end of Jackson's second term in office, Samuel Brady, an early party supporter, complained to his congressman, "There is an active thing absolutely necessary before our party will be able to rally with any spirit, that is the fulfilling of the almost unanimous wishes of the party by carrying out the principles of rotation in office."[166] Of all the major federal positions only that of naval officer changed hands, and, despite the common knowledge that other patronage officers or members of their families were openly hostile to the administration, none had been removed. The reason for this anomalous situation was the pre-eminent role played by Senator Samuel Smith, who was in the federal legislature continuously from the 1790s until his retirement in 1833. Because he was chairman of the Senate Finance Committee, the new administration was willing to overlook his being an eleventh-hour Jacksonian and to pay homage to his preferences in matters of Maryland patronage.

During Senator Smith's long public career, members of his family and his political allies received political appointments. His son-in-law, Christopher Hughes, advanced steadily in the diplomatic service and became the chargé d'affaires to Sweden during Jackson's presidency, and his nephew, Dabney S. Carr, the editor of the Baltimore *Republican*, displaced William B. Barney as naval officer in 1829.[167] Carr's appointment underscored several significant aspects of Baltimore politics in the late 1820s. Barney, son of Commodore Joshua Barney, a hero in the ill-fated defense of Washington, D.C., during the War of 1812, replaced his father as naval officer upon the latter's death in 1818 and served thereafter to the satisfaction of the merchant community. His ties to the early party system were enhanced by his marriage to the daughter of Federalist Justice Samuel Chase and by the fact that his brother was a Baltimore congressman in the 1820s. Yet, when he was replaced, admittedly for being a "political adversary," his cries of injustice were ineffectual, and the Senate refused to challenge the new administration's right to make its own appointments.[168] In the context of politics in the 1820s, it is not surprising that the editor of the new party paper, who was also incidentally Senator Smith's nephew, received the appointment instead of someone with ties to Baltimore's Federalist past. If Barney were expendable, the other Baltimore federal officers—the collector of the port, the district attorney, and the marshal—were safe because most of them were longtime friends of the senator and their commissions were always renewed quietly before they expired.[169]

Another signficant early patronage decision showed the primacy of elite over party considerations in the early years of the Jackson period. In this case, there were two Maryland aspirants to the position of secretary to the French legation: James Madison Buchanan and Charles Carroll Harper. Buchanan, a Baltimore County attorney, had impeccable political credentials. An incumbent member of the state legislature in 1827, he voluntarily retired as a candidate for renomination because other members of the party would not withdraw, and his exertions on behalf of the presidential ticket in 1828 drew high praise from the Baltimore County Jacksonian congressman elected in 1829.[170] Harper, whose sole public party activity was membership on the city central committee in 1827, had an advantage party service could not overcome—he was a member of the traditional elite of the city—and in the end he received the appointment.[171]

This situation was no longer tenable by 1835. Reminiscent of Brady's private complaint, the Baltimore *Republican* editorialized: "Many of their friends have been permitted to hold for a long time the best offices in this state which are within the gift of the national executive, and as a just measure of retaliation it is nothing more than right and proper that they should be removed."[172] The first to fall was the marshal, Colonel Thomas Finley, whose commission was allowed to expire in 1835.[173] A minor Jackson party leader was quickly nominated to the position, but he was rejected by the Senate for being too partisan.[174] Thereafter the contest was between two major urban party leaders, John W. Wilmer and Philip Laurenson, and a rural dark horse candidate from Frederick County, Colonel Nicholas Snyder.[175] In the end Colonel Snyder was nominated and confirmed.

The death of James H. McCulloch, the collector of the port from 1808 to 1836, by far the most remunerative and influential federal position in the gift of the government, demonstrated how much conditions had changed since 1829.[176] Among the candidates for the vacancy was Senator Smith's nephew, Dabney S. Carr, and William Frick, a Baltimore attorney, who was also an important party leader. Carr continued to hold his position as naval officer until ousted by the Whigs in 1842, but the retirement of his uncle from the Senate in 1833 invalidated his claim for preferment.[177] Frick, on the other hand, had a firm political base in the urban party, a base that had been frustrated in its demands for better treatment since the beginning of Jackson's presidency. Once in office, Frick appointed other leading party leaders to his staff, notably J. W. Wilmer and Philip Laurenson, and he began to run the collectorship as the archetypal political machine.[178]

Senator Smith's retirement signaled the eclipse of nepotism as a characteristic of Maryland's federal patronage system, epitomized by Carr's inability to obtain the collectorship appointment, and reflected the rise of an awareness within the administration of the need to placate the divergent interests within the state and the community. Congressmen, who were generally ignored if their requests countered the senator's wishes prior to his retirement, could now assert their institutionalized role effectively.[179] Men not connected to the earlier political system or

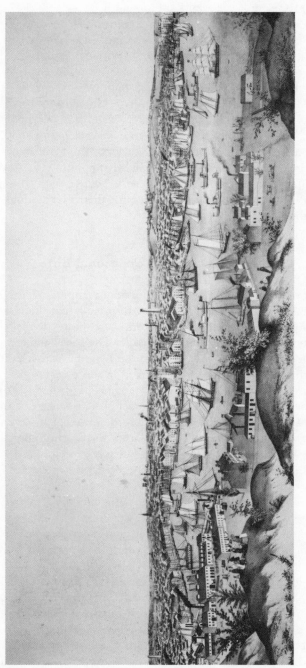

Baltimore View, ca. 1850
Courtesy of the Library of Congress

to dominant political families, but who had ties with the larger community, increasingly received important patronage offices as they fell vacant.

State-level patronage policy was influenced heavily by the fact that the executive branch was decidedly Anti-Jacksonian for all but one term during these years. Because Baltimore City returned Jacksonians to the lower house of the legislature with only two exceptions, the executive tended to rely on the advice of Anti-Jacksonians who were members of the Executive Council and the state senate in making political appointments.[180] When a Jacksonian governor was elected in 1830, the city representatives and members of the Executive Council from the same party were instrumental in making patronage appointments.[181] Therefore, officeholders of the same party as the executive were the most influential in obtaining political preference for their nominations in patronage decisions.

The Urban Decisional Elite

Considering the proliferation of opportunities for men to participate in urban decision making, it is not surprising that the community decisional elite in the second party era were more diversified than their counterpart in the first party period.[182] The social and economic characteristics of these 110 men confirm the hypothesis that as the urban system changed over time, more men from the diversity of the population rose to share community power. The concept of sharing power is important because it acknowledges the fact that remnants of the older elite structure, in this case members of a former merchant oligarchy, were still active and prominent leaders. For the purposes of comparison, Tables 4.9, 4.10, and 4.11 array information for both elites.

Table 4.9 presents economic and wealth information. The decisional elite of the second era averaged almost the same age as those of the first. They continued to be propertied, although their mean wealth figure declined approximately $1,000. Fewer held slaves. These findings are consistent with the hypothesis that men from the lower reaches of the economic spectrum were able to share in community decision making during the second party era.

Table 4.10 compares the occupational characteristics of both elites. Merchants continued as an important component of community decision making, but there were subtle transformations. The old generalist category, gentleman or address only, used by retirees or silent partners, fell into almost total disuse, suggesting that greater emphasis was being placed on one's functional role in the community. At the same time, the

Table 4.9. Wealth Characteristics,
Baltimore City Decisional Leaders

	First Period N = 55	Second Period N = 110
Slaveholding (percent owning)	56	30
Property holding (percent assessed)	73	81
Average property assessment	$4,112	$3,188
Average age	45	46

Table 4.10. Occupations, Baltimore City
Decisional Leaders (percentages)

	First Period N = 55	Second Period N = 110
Merchant	40	38
Artisan	5	16
Petty clerical	4	4
White collar	5	3
Professional	26	34
Gentleman, address only	16	3
None listed	4	2

role of professionals in community decision making increased moderately, while artisans rose from 5.5 to 16.4 percent of the elite. Based on occupational categories alone, a greater variety of people interacted in community decision making in the second party era than had earlier.

Table 4.11 compares birthplace and religion of both elites. For both these variables, at both points in time, reliable data do not exist for a sizable segment of the elite. The available data indicate several suggestive patterns. Fewer Baltimore decisional leaders were either born abroad or in other states, while the percentage who were native-born

Marylanders increased. The proportion of leaders born in Baltimore City or County to those born in rural Maryland remained constant. The increase of the "unknown" category in the religious data could be a result of missing data or it could represent a decline in the overall elite's participation in all facets of community life. In light of the fact that church records were reasonably complete in both periods, the decline of those who were Presbyterians, added to the increase of the unknown category, supports the hypothesis that the older generalist leadership pattern was being supplanted.

If the generalist leadership pattern were in decline, what of the existence of the former merchant oligarchy? Since 68 percent of the decisional elite were born after 1780, only a few were old enough in the first party era to participate in community decision making. Of those that were, General Samuel Smith personified the merchant-politician ideal. William Patterson, the wealthiest man on both the 1800 and the 1834 tax rolls and General Smith's brother-in-law, epitomized how an affluent man could become a community leader without necessarily entering politics.[183] The role of the oligarchy becomes clearer if generational and marital patterns are analyzed. If members of the first party era decisional

Table 4.11. Social Characteristics, Baltimore City
Decisional Leaders (percentages)

	First Period N = 55	Second Period N = 110
Birthplace		
Maryland	20	41
United States	27	13
Foreign	22	6
Unknown	31	40
Religious type		
Liturgical	22	29
Pietistic	49	27
Unknown	29	44
Specific Religions		
Episcopalian	16	19
Presbyterian	38	16
Methodist	4	6
Catholic	2	7

elite perished prior to the second party period, their sons carried on the tradition of family leadership. Eight sons of members of the first party decisional elite were members of the second decisional elite; six more second party leaders married into families prominent in the first.[184] The best example might be the Howard family. Colonel John Eager Howard, General Smith's political nemesis in the first party era, died in 1827. Two sons, Benjamin and Charles, continued as decisional leaders. William George Read, the son of South Carolina's former Congressman Jacob Read, moved to Baltimore in 1822, studied law with Robert Goodloe Harper, married into the Howard family, and became an important community leader. These careers demonstrate that an oligarchy provided an important continuing portion of community leadership in Baltimore.

Community decision making in the second party era engaged a wider variety of men than it had in the first party period. Measured in terms of declining wealth and the percentage of the elite holding slaves, control by the oligarchy was being eroded. Other measures reinforce this interpretation. Fewer members of the decisional elite (16 versus 35 percent) were also among the top hundred wealthiest men on the tax rolls, and fewer (14 versus 29 percent) were militia officers. The fact that more professionals and artisans participated to a greater extent in community decision making can be viewed in two ways. There apparently was a greater opportunity for men without elite connections to share community power, but there also may have been greater specialization in community leadership roles. As society was being diversified, generalists were being supplanted by a proliferation of specialists.

The comparative analysis of community decisional elites in several contexts thus far has ignored an important component of elite recruitment. While it is necessary to justify and elaborate why an individual qualified as a leader, it is equally important to understand the characteristics of potential community leadership pools. Chapter 5 presents the concept of strategic community elites. Membership in strategic elites is compared to that for the various decisional elites to discern patterns of elite recruitment. If social and economic change encouraged the development of specialized leadership roles, community-level comparisons should reveal a variety of patterns indicative of various stages of change.

5

The Distribution of
Community Power

Decision making in Maryland reflected different patterns of elite recruitment. In communities with underlying social or economic homogeneity, decision makers were generally recruited from prominent and wealthy families. In these communities, lacking alternative bases from which challenges to the status quo might be mounted, men with access to wealth or links to first families enjoyed the rewards of cumulative inequality. In more heterogeneous environments with alternative bases from which to enlist community support, namely, commercial as opposed to agricultural wealth, political popularity in contrast to cadre political associations, or ethnic or religious minority groups instead of homogeneous groupings, leaders emerged from the diversity of the more complex community. But, although more men may have participated in decision making in the latter type of community, they shared power with men who enjoyed the traditional advantages derived from wealth and august social lineage. The questions addressed in this chapter are straightforward: given such patterns, what was the distribution of power and how did it change, if at all, during and between the Federalist-Jeffersonian and the Jacksonian eras?

The Strategic Elites

The decisional elite did not represent in itself a measure of the distribution of power within a community. Decisional elite members gained their position from individual activity in the process of reaching community decisions, whereas the distribution of power rested on more subtle distinctions as to who might influence community decision making. Assuming that in every community some individuals possess socially valued resources that give them the potential to effect community outcomes, the problem of power distribution would be solved by comparing membership in various strategic elites to that in the decisional elite. For the purposes of this study, three strategic elites will be identified at the two points in time for each community. They are the positional elite, the propertied elite, and the commercial elite.[1]

Working from the premise that political officeholding constitutes a power resource, rather than uncritically accepting the notion that all officeholders are powerful by definition, I assembled the legislative and executive position holders in the local, state, and federal governments from each community into a positional elite.[2] A comparison of the socio-economic characteristics of the positional elite with those of the decisional elite, as well as an examination of their relative recruitment patterns, helps to improve our understanding of the role that formal political leaders played in community affairs. Public officeholding may have served different purposes in various stages of community development. In a homogeneous environment there may be considerable overlap between decisional and positional leaders, whereas in more complex environments there might be a growing specialization of leadership roles. Indeed, in the latter situation recruitment into the positional elite might serve as a vehicle for political socialization for individuals whose influence rests on personal or collective power resources. Yet, simultaneously, it is important to be sensitive to the role played by the traditional political leaders, men who embody older attributes, as we examine political officeholding.

The second strategic elite is the propertied elite. The assumption that men of wealth are able to influence community affairs to a greater extent than men without its advantages is as old as the study of politics itself. This obvious association between wealth and power has been difficult to delineate fully in historical literature because community decision making has not been studied systematically and because levels of affluence have never been specified or placed in a communitywide context. The identification of a decisional elite answers the question of who held power. Manuscript county-level tax records may be used to isolate and rank affluent men. Tax records, however, are imperfect historical sources.[3] They emphasize real property, land and slaves, and normally ignore other forms of property, such as stocks and shares in mercantile ventures. Even the valuations were less than market value by law.[4] In addition, property held outside the county by a resident went unreported because it was not taxed by the home county. If our goal were to obtain a true valuation of a person's worth, such figures obviously would be inexact and incomplete, but they ought to reflect his relative position within a local wealth hierarchy. Tax records therefore may be used to identify and rank along a continuum those with large amounts of a socially valued resource from those possessing less.[5]

The third strategic elite is the commercial elite. If political office-holding and the possession of large amounts of real property may be construed as potential power resources, then the direction of liquid capital would be of equal importance to community development. Men who controlled the flow of local investment capital in an expanding economy were essential participants in a community's future growth or stagnation. An accurate identification of stockholders in commercial ventures is all but impossible because of the incompleteness of tax records and the paucity of complete business records, but there is evidence to support the contention that major investors served as directors of financial institutions.[6] These men undoubtedly were drawn from two overlapping sources: members of the traditional propertied elite, who were searching for greater return from diversified investments; and others who eschewed conservative reliance on real property investment and were willing to risk larger amounts of their capital in investments than traditional wisdom might dictate. Membership in the commercial elite was awarded to officers and persisting directors of the community's banking and insurance companies.[7]

My evaluation of the distribution of community power is based upon a comparison of the strategic elites and the decisional elite for each community. This process involves several levels of analysis: examination of elite profiles, elite recruitment, and the overlap between elites. An elite's socioeconomic characteristics were compared to discern the social bases from which an elite was drawn and to determine fundamental changes within and between elites over time. The analysis of elite recruitment and overlap reveals the quality and type of a community's leadership pool. Ideally, community power might be polarized into two mutually exclusive categories: traditional and modernizing. The traditional pattern would be characterized by a very restrictive base for elite recruitment, with unequal advantages accruing to those possessing large amounts of valued community resources, and a system of cumulative inequality, whereby those having access to the system monopolize its rewards. A modernizing pattern would demonstrate more flexibility, and leaders would not be restricted to membership in a preordained sect, such as an oligarchy, so that they would be recruited from competing elements in the community. Rather than having a few monopolize the fruits of cumulative inequality, sharing perquisites of power, playing multiple leadership roles, and proscribing others from leadership positions, there would be increased elite specialization. Not only would more people participate in community decision making in a modernizing environment, but access routes to community leadership roles would be varied and not generally proscriptive. Of course, ideal types rarely fit real situations, yet an examination of this dichotomy in terms of the distribution of power reveals the subtle nuances and more blatant differences within and between communities in the first and second party eras.

Homogeneous Agricultural Communities

Following the dual criteria of specifying a homogeneous population and the cultivation of staple products, I selected St. Marys and Talbot counties as representative agricultural communities. Neither county changed significantly between the 1790s and the 1830s. Such persisting conditions suggest that community leaders ought to have been recruited from among large land and slaveowners and that the very affluent may have formed an oligarchy. The term oligarchy, defined as a condition where the power of government is vested in the hands of the few, also acknowledges a condition where "the few"—the so-called upper class—possess cumulative advantages that are the product of wealth and social standing. Such advantages are cumulative because those in power reward men whose backgrounds are similar to their own, and, consequently, recruitment to political positions and any perquisites of office would be restricted to a small group of like-minded men. In more complex environments, where there would be substantial alternative bases of community support, an oligarchy might still attempt to restrict officeholding and its emoluments to its own members, but such efforts might be challenged by leaders whose power base is other than landed wealth or inherited status.

Before examining the characteristics of the decisional and strategic elites, several observations must be made about the basic data. The tables in this chapter have been divided into categories and presented in a standard format to facilitate comparison among communities. This was accomplished without difficulty for such variables as wealth, slaveownership, and age, but one important individual attribute, occupation, was almost impossible to identify in rural areas. Despite efforts to determine formal occupations from rural sources, such as newspaper advertisements and legal documents, the only real occupational division that could be found existed between professionals (doctors, lawyers, and editors) and landowners. Because the ownership of land and slaves, like the distinction between skilled and unskilled labor, has an obvious relationship to status and opportunity, I devised a method to segment rural elite members into five distinct groups. Just as more formal occupations may be collapsed into categories based on their functional equivalency, so individuals can be placed into discrete groups predicated on whether or not they owned slaves, if they fell below or exceeded a threshold of landownership, and whether or not they were professionals.[8] Table 5.1 presents this data for St. Marys County.

The dominant role of slave and large landowners is apparent in all occupational categories for both time periods in St. Marys County. This is evident by comparing the characteristics of the positional elite in the 1790s with their counterpart in the 1830s and by doing the same thing for the propertied elite. Based on this measure, the decisional elite in the Jacksonian era is very similar to the positional elite for the same period. Indeed, the preeminent position of the wealthy is actually understated because some of those who fell into the lowest property-holding category were sons of wealthy families whose patrimony was yet to be divided and because several professionals, mainly doctors, were men with substantial property holdings.

Another way of demonstrating the preeminence of large land and slaveowners as community leaders is to focus on the distribution of wealth and slaves (Tables 5.2 and 5.3). Despite a clustering in the midranges of the wealth tables for each elite, a comparison of the average wealth figures and wealth distribution in the first and second party eras shows that affluent men continued to hold community leadership positions. Indeed, 42 percent of the positional elite also belonged to the propertied elite in the first party era; the comparable figures for the second party period were slightly lower (36 percent). The data for slaveownership reinforces this trend.

Table 5.1. Rural Occupations, St. Marys County

	Decisional Elite		Positional Elite		Propertied Elite	
	1790s	1830s	1790s	1830s	1790s	1830s
N		34	38	36	50	50
Less than 600 acres, no slaves (%)		18	18	17		
Less than 600 acres, with slaves (%)		6	8	11		
More than 600 acres, no slaves (%)		6		3	2	2
More than 600 acres, with slaves (%)		44	55	47	92	86
Professionals (%)		27	18	22	6	12

Table 5.2. Wealth, St. Marys County*

	Decisional Elite		Positional Elite		Propertied Elite	
	1790s	1830s	1790s	1830s	1790s	1830s
N		34	38	36	50	50
$100–999 (%)		15	34	14		
$1,000–2,999 (%)		41	18	41		
$3,000–4,999 (%)		15	18	24	48	44
$5,000–9,999 (%)		18	18	10	34	38
$10,000–29,999 (%)		11	11	10	16	18
$30,000+ (%)					2	
Average ($)		4,422	4,797	3,866	7,963	7,214

*The 1800 tax record lists wealth in pounds; such figures were converted to dollars. For this chapter a minimum wealth of $100 was assigned to individuals not found on the tax rolls for each community.

St. Marys County was ruled by a dynamic oligarchy, whose power base was landed wealth, whose influence was enhanced by a persisting inequality in the distribution of property, and whose dynamic element was a social infrastructure of wide and expanding kinship associations. Many of the propertied elite in the first period, both as individuals and as families, disappeared from the county by the second period. Rather than stimulating a disintegration of the prevailing social structure, this condition allowed men who were only a little less wealthy or men who married advantageously to rise to the top and to prevail as community leaders through kinship and social associations. Because the distribution of property changed little between the 1790s and the 1830s and because the advantages of mass political organization had little impact in a sparsely populated county that lacked even a centralizing newspaper to serve its communications needs, there were few bases from which men of different means could challenge the existing oligarchical rule. Following patterns described in Chapter 2, representatives of affluent families, such as the Platers, the Thomases, or the Somervilles, were found to epitomize the overlap in community decision making between men of property and decisional and positional leaders.

Commercial activity might have been one base from which new men could rise to enter the realm of community decision making. This was not the case in St. Marys County for several reasons. First, trade patterns were such that Baltimore City dominated commercial activities in the county, functioning as its primary market, and diminished the opportunities for the rise of an indigenous merchant class. Leonardtown, the county seat, never assumed the role of a central market. Furthermore, there was no real middle class in the county. People who established general stores or men who entered the professions were generally members of affluent landed families, who were either diversifying or were enjoying the cumulative advantages of wealth by obtaining formal education. Even the appointment of bank directors from the county illustrates how the oligarchy perpetuated itself. The county did not have a bank, but several citizens were appointed by the legislature as directors of the Annapolis branch of the Farmer's Bank. In the Jeffersonian era, it appointed two individuals from St. Marys County: William Somerville and William Thomas, Jr. Both men served in state and local government prior to their appointments, both were commissioned as majors when the militia was reorganized in 1794, and both were affluent and well connected.[9] In the 1830s, the legislature appointed Colonel Joseph Harris, county clerk since 1796 and the second wealthiest man on the tax rolls in 1831, to the same position. In the best tradition of the oligarchy, Colonel Harris's son was a member of the county legislative delegation during this period.

Judged in terms of those who were positional and decisional leaders, how they were recruited to such positions, and the manner in which these elites functioned, an oligarchy governed St. Marys County in the first and second party eras. Despite the spirit of egalitarianism permeating the state in these years, which implied a wide distribution of power, rural community leadership was rooted in a system characterized by great inequalities of wealth and opportunity. Lacking a nonagricultural productive base and functioning without a viable middle class, the county had no cohesive force from which new leaders might challenge the pre-

Table 5.3. Slaveownership, St. Marys County

	Decisional Elite		Positional Elite		Propertied Elite	
	1790s	*1830s*	*1790s*	*1830s*	*1790s*	*1830s*
N		34	38	36	50	50
None (%)		32	26	28	2	2
1–5 (%)		9	13	11	2	2
6–19 (%)		21	26	33	32	30
20+ (%)		38	34	28	64	66

vailing system. The oligarchy adapted to the existence of the various party systems, coopting their potential as a countervailing force, and utilized the strengths of party organization to enhance their own dominant positions.

Talbot County's community leadership patterns were similar to those in St. Marys County, but they embodied several important differences. Community leadership was heavily influenced by a landed, slaveowning, wealthy oligarchy, many of whom were Episcopalians, that recruited leaders from among its own members or assimilated men from less affluent circumstances into responsible positions. The evolution of two competitive party systems, although more pronounced in Talbot County than in St. Marys County, failed to transform the structure of politics because leadership in the Republican and Federalist parties, as well as in the later Jacksonian and Anti-Jacksonian parties, was contained by traditional rivalries among major families. One important difference in the rural experiences of these two counties, however, was the longevity of several prominent families, such as the Lloyds and the Goldsboroughs, whose influence spanned the colonial period through the Civil War. A second difference was the opportunity enjoyed by residents of Easton, the county seat, to be assimilated into community leadership roles. In St. Marys County, Leonardtown persisted as little more than a village over these years, but Easton was the traditional focal point of Eastern Shore politics and commerce. As such, it attracted men with more varied backgrounds, who sometimes became members of the power structure.

The aggregate characteristics of Talbot County's community elites illustrate their compliance with oligarchical patterns. Judged in terms of occupational categories (Table 5.4), community leaders in the various elites were predominantly landed and slaveowning. The continuity of such rural forms is further demonstrated by comparing each elite to itself over the time period.

When property was broken down into wealth and slaveowning categories (Tables 5.5 and 5.6), several suggestive trends emerged. The most obvious trend concerns an increase in average wealth. These figures are unreliable because of the huge fortune of Colonel Edward Lloyd V in the second party era, which skewed average wealth astronomically, but the percentile distribution figures are accurate representations of trends. These data show that wealthy men and their kin were mainstays of community leadership in Talbot County. While there can be no doubt of the role the affluent played in each elite, only the propertied elite continued to invest heavily in the institution of slavery, and even some of its members, following a trend found in other elites, either held fewer slaves or opted not to own any.

Table 5.4. Rural Occupations, Talbot County

	Commercial Elite		Decisional Elite		Positional Elite		Propertied Elite	
	1790s	1830s	1790s	1830s	1790s	1830s	1790s	1830s
N	9	16	22	31	51	42	50	50
Less than 600 acres, no slaves (%)	44	19	14	13	22	24		
Less than 600 acres, with slaves (%)		6	14	7	12	7		2
More than 600 acres, no slaves (%)		13		7	4	7	2	8
More than 600 acres, with slaves (%)	33	38	46	42	49	48	88	80
Professionals (%)	22	25	27	32	14	14	10	10

Table 5.5. Wealth, Talbot County

	Commercial Elite		Decisional Elite		Positional Elite		Propertied Elite	
	1790s	1830s	1790s	1830s	1790s	1830s	1790s	1830s
N	9	16	22	31	51	42	50	50
$100–999 (%)	20	8	13	30	20	26		
$1,000–2,999 (%)	60	8	19	15	43	18	30	30
$3,000–4,999 (%)	20	25	31	19	17	23	38	40
$5,000–9,999 (%)		25	25	22	17	15	22	26
$10,000–29,999 (%)		25	6	15		15	8	
$30,000+ (%)		8	6		3	3	2	4
Average ($)	1,900	10,250	7,869	5,667	4,566	7,912	6,000	10,754

Table 5.6. Slaveownership, Talbot County

	Commercial Elite		Decisional Elite		Positional Elite		Propertied Elite	
	1790s	1830s	1790s	1830s	1790s	1830s	1790s	1830s
N	9	16	22	31	51	42	50	50
None (%)	44	38	23	26	29	33	2	10
1–5 (%)		19	14	29	12	26	12	20
6–19 (%)		6	9	23	35	19	40	16
20+ (%)	56	38	55	23	24	21	46	54

Recruitment patterns of the decisional elite help to explain how the oligarchy maintained its position and power. Wealthy men, some with extensive kinship ties, or their progeny, stood for public office, commanded local militia units, or assumed leading roles in the community decision-making process. Such individuals responded to the organizational demands of both party systems at their embryonic stage of development and fastened themselves securely to the evolving political structure. Often their money helped establish party presses or underwrote party activities. The end result was that, as both party systems matured, affluent men were in controlling situations in each competitive party and strove to maintain their advantage. New men with less wealth or from aspiring families were recruited as community leaders, but rarely were they totally independent of the prevailing system on Maryland's Eastern Shore.

As in St. Marys County, the commercial elite did not represent a threat to such oligarchical control. In the first party era, they numbered nine men who were appointed directors of the Farmer's Bank of the Eastern Shore with its office in Easton. They were political officeholders, men of wealth or first sons of prominent families, attorneys, or men who migrated to Easton from other Eastern Shore counties. In the second party era, the commercial elite numbered sixteen men, but its composition was more local and elitist than that of its earlier counterpart. Easton, considered the second capital of the state during the colonial and early national periods, lost some of its cosmopolitan flavor with the abolition of the General Court, and thereafter it gradually ceased to be the state's administrative center for the Eastern Shore. One-half of the commercial elite belonged to the propertied elite, defined as the fifty wealthiest persons on the tax rolls, and several were members of the positional and decisional elites. Rather than serving as a vehicle to challenge the community leadership structure, the commercial elite buttressed it, and it remained in the hands of the local oligarchy.[10]

In the two rural communities, there was little real change in leadership patterns between the first and second party eras. Each was characterized by an active oligarchy that provided leaders for the emerging political parties, assumed formal political offices, and participated as decisional leaders. The composition of the strategic elites was basically identical, and because there was no viable cultural or economic nucleus around which a challenge could be founded, this oligarchical system persisted relatively intact. In St. Marys County, a structure based on affluence and kinship was the essence of community leadership; in Talbot County this structure was strengthened and enhanced by several families whose wealth, social position, and tradition for leadership entitled them to powerful positions as each generation reached maturity.[11] This is not to suggest that the rhetoric of politics in both periods was unimportant or lacked meaning to its exponents or that a conspiracy existed among the wealthy. On the contrary, the ideological distinctions and the bitter competition over officeholding were undoubtedly of great moment to these men. But, in the final analysis, the structure of politics that resulted as a consequence of the social and economic forces at work within the homogeneous agricultural communities perpetuated the iron grip of oligarchical control.

The Heterogeneous Agricultural Community: Frederick County

Frederick County represented a heterogeneous rural community because of its polyglot social composition and its agricultural diversification. Community leadership often adhered to the oligarchical structure of rural elite recruitment and interaction, but this structure was weakened by competition for leadership predicated on geographical or ethnic rivalries within the community and further strained by the evolution of the first party system in the late 1790s. In both party periods, new leaders emerged as partisans, successful candidates for public office, and decisional leaders, and they were assimilated into an atrophying oligarchical system. An oligarchy existed in the first period, composed of affluent, slaveowning, old families, many of whom were Episcopalians. Yet as the circle of leaders expanded outward, the cohesive force of some of these specific attributes diminished, such as slaveholding or being an Episcopalian, while ties of wealth and kinship continued to cement the whole together. By the second party period, there was no single core element defining the structure of community leadership; rather, there were wedges revealing several paths to power. Some leaders, adhering to traditional rural norms, were members of the rural oligarchy; others, products of the first party era, represented the diversity of the community, who had been assimilated into the establishment within a generation; still others, new leaders in the second party era, unable to make a prior claim based on privileged status, justified their right to rule on contemporary issues and divisions. In contrast to the inherent stability of the homogeneous agricultural communities, characterized by continuity and gradual change over time, patterns in Frederick County appeared to be in a state of flux, adhering to the prevailing structure but never being bound or confined by it, innovating but never reaching the threshold of convulsive changes.

The sheer physical size of the county and its population had an impact on its elite structure. In contrast to St. Marys and Talbot counties, where the number of men who were positional leaders declined, there was a 60 percent increase in Frederick County, and its decisional elite increased by one-third. Not surprisingly for a county where slavery never dominated the labor market, more men without slaves were recruited as leaders in the various elites than in the other rural counties (Table 5.7). What is surprising, however, is a trend affecting all elites between the first and second party eras: larger landowners increasingly owned slaves. This trend countered a general decline in slaveownership in the county, but it may represent a more general Maryland cultural norm, whereby large landownership and slavery went hand in hand.

Several significant characteristics of Frederick County's community elites were masked by a direct comparison with their rural counterparts. Despite the evidence that these elites were less affluent, fewer members held slaves, and those who held slaves fell into the lower categories (Tables 5.8 and 5.9), these were not men of insubstantial means. Like their rural counterparts, the bulk of Frederick County elites were recruited from English stock, many of whom were Episcopalians, yet there was a pronounced German presence. Germans provided almost one-third (32 percent) of the decisional elite, 28 percent of the positional elite, and 21 percent of the propertied elite in the earlier period. Many of these Germans emerged as leaders during the first party era, primarily as Jeffersonian Republicans, and they exemplified the process through which new leaders rose from the diversity of the whole community.

Besides the ethnic dimension, leadership was affected by geographical rivalry within the county. At issue was the dominant and expansive influence of Fredericktown and its citizens in all aspects of community life. Rivalries centered on country versus city factions and were often subsumed in contests between rural Germans and the dominant English power structure, interurban competition among several large towns within the county, especially Westminister and Fredericktown groups, and competition based on family antipathies. Throughout both periods, the citizens of Fredericktown enjoyed distinct advantages as commercial and decisional leaders.

The diversity of Frederick County's community leadership suggests processes that might influence an even less traditional environment, Baltimore City. Just as the prevailing oligarchical system was strained by Frederick County's size and underlying social and agricultural complexity, the real test is in an urban area. Could an oligarchy dominate in a

Table 5.7. Rural Occupations, Frederick County

	Commercial Elite		Decisional Elite		Positional Elite		Propertied Elite	
	1790s	1830s	1790s	1830s	1790s	1830s	1790s	1830s
N		42	54	72	50	80	100	100
Less than 600 acres, no slaves (%)		50	20	14	28	53		
Less than 600 acres, with slaves (%)		7		7		3		2
More than 600 acres, no slaves (%)		5	41	7	46	5	46	20
More than 600 acres, with slaves (%)		19	13	36	10	24	48	63
Professionals (%)		19	26	36	16	16	6	15

Table 5.8. Wealth, Frederick County*

	Commercial Elite		Decisional Elite		Positional Elite		Propertied Elite	
	1790s	1830s	1790s	1830s	1790s	1830s	1790s	1830s
N		42	54	72	50	80	100	100
$100–999 (%)		10	23	31	26	22	27	
$1,000–2,999 (%)		24	40	32	40	28	42	
$3,000–4,999 (%)		33	12	19	13	25	23	57
$5,000–9,999 (%)		24	19	16	16	25	7	39
$10,000–29,999 (%)		10	7	2	5		1	4
$30,000+ (%)								
Average ($)		4,557	3,447	2,636	3,169	3,042	5,610	5,234

*The 1797 Frederick County tax list records wealth in pounds; this information was converted to dollars.

Table 5.9. Slaveownership, Frederick County

	Commercial Elite		Decisional Elite		Positional Elite		Propertied Elite	
	1790s	1830s	1790s	1830s	1790s	1830s	1790s	1830s
N		42	54	72	50	80	100	100
None (%)		55	80	33	82	64	47	21
1–5 (%)		29	2	43		18	13	24
6–19 (%)		14	13	21	12	16	32	47
20+ (%)		2	6	3	6	3	8	8

nontraditional environment; if it were unable to dominate, could it survive so as to wield power in excess of its apparent means?

The Urban Community: Baltimore City

Many components of the dominant rural oligarchical structure were present in Baltimore City's leadership system during the first party era, but in an urban context they could not be fused together to dominate community elites. As in its rural counterparts, urban leadership and wealth were interconnected through the association of prominent merchants with members of the affluent landed families, and this combined oligarchy was rejuvenated and perpetuated through ties of business and kinship. Wealthy men may have seen themselves as a vital oligarchy, but other men without extensive property-holding or close kinship ties to any oligarchy were also recruited as community leaders. Similarly, there was a growing specialization within urban elites. Affluent men became less interested in overseeing all facets of community leadership, preferring instead to focus on matters of business or commerce; at the same time, individuals from the diversity of the community rose through membership in the decisional or positional elites to become community leaders. Unable to proscribe membership in community elites, Baltimore's oligarchy was also incapable of dominating the evolving political party system and resisting the democratic impulse that permeated the first and second party eras. The end result was a far more flexible system, perhaps best described as a polyarchy, in which the remnants of the oligarchy and the more dynamic elements of urban leadership interacted and coexisted.

The sheer size of Baltimore City elites mitigated against control by any one group within the community. With the exception of the propertied elite, which was defined as the one hundred wealthiest men, membership in the other elites was greater than in their rural counterparts. While the number of men filling the unchanging number of political positions in St. Marys and Talbot counties declined between the first and second party systems, the urban positional elite expanded by two-thirds. Baltimore City's decisional elite doubled itself over the same period, and its already large commercial elite grew by 45 percent. Such growth suggests a greater intrinsic demand for leadership within a growing urban system, the expansion of opportunity as political participation became less exclusive, and the difficulty any single group might face meeting this need.

An examination of Baltimore City's community elite occupational structure reveals several distinct recruitment patterns between the 1790s and the 1830s (Table 5.10). The persisting role of merchants as a leadership resource is evident in each elite. Yet, compared by time period, the prominence of merchants diminished as other occupational categories, such as skilled artisans, professionals, or clerical workers, expanded their presence in several elites. Skilled artisans were increasingly engaged as decisional and positional leaders, just as professionals were more active as members of the decisional elite. In the context of urban elite recruitment, men with diversified occupational backgrounds were able to enter the establishment through participation in the positional or decisional elites during the second party system, while merchants continued as an important but contracting element in each elite. If such occupational characteristics reveal a situation where more men with varied backgrounds were able to interact in community decision making in the urban as contrasted to the rural environment, then an analysis of real wealth and slaveholding ought to clarify this trend further.

Judged in terms of property evaluation and slaveholding, Baltimore's community leaders were drawn from a wider spectrum of wealth holders than their rural counterparts (Tables 5.11 and 5.12). If we use slaveholding as an index of an individual's adherence to oligarchical norms, the fact that the percentage of elite members holding slaves in every category shrinks drastically between the 1790s and the 1830s suggests that these norms were in decline among the urban governing class. Only the propertied elite sustained the "peculiar institution." Similarly, in terms of property holding, urban elites recruited more men across a wider wealth spectrum than their rural counterparts, and the pattern between the two time periods may be characterized as the assimilation of more men with less wealth into community leadership positions.

This is not to say that men of wealth were without power or influence. Thirty-five percent of the members of the decisional elite in the first party era were also members of the propertied elite. Furthermore, major landed families, such as the Carrolls and the Howards, and important commercial families, the Smiths, McKims, Olivers, and Pattersons, provided leaders in the commercial, decisional, and positional elites in both eras. Such men were an obvious counterpart to the highly visible and viable rural oligarchies; but in the urban environment they could not monopolize community leadership.

The aggregate data support the hypothesis that a more diversified and complex urban environment would undermine oligarchical patterns and allow more people to assume leadership positions than in its rural counterpart, but the significance of elite participation levels is left unanswered. There may have been an elite within the elites, where the majority of community leaders were active in a single elite role and

Table 5.10. Occupations, Baltimore City

	Commercial Elite		Decisional Elite		Positional Elite		Propertied Elite	
	1790s	1830s	1790s	1830s	1790s	1830s	1790s	1830s
N	102	148	55	110	99	165	100	100
Merchant (%)	73	47	40	38	51	32	56	45
Skilled artisan (%)	4	5	6	16	13	19	3	2
Professional (%)	2	5	26	34	13	9	1	8
Clerical (%)	6	22	9	7	2	25	2	7
Address/Gent. (%)	8	7	16	3	9	7	22	19
None (%)	6	13	4	2	12	8	16	19

Table 5.11. Wealth, Baltimore City*

	Commercial Elite		Decisional Elite		Positional Elite		Propertied Elite	
	1790s	1830s	1790s	1830s	1790s	1830s	1790s	1830s
N	102	148	55	110	99	165	100	100
$100–999 (%)	13	21	17	36	17	53		
$1,000–2,999 (%)	39	37	33	35	48	33		
$3,000–4,999 (%)	29	19	25	12	21	10	51	15
$5,000–9,999 (%)	13	18	17	11	12	3	40	71
$10,000–29,999 (%)	6	4	8	5	2	1	9	13
$30,000+ (%)		1		1		1		1
Average ($)	3,834	3,769	4,112	3,188	2,940	1,673	5,901	8,009

*The earlier tax record gives valuation in pounds; these figures were converted to dollars.

Table 5.12. Slaveownership, Baltimore City*

	Commercial Elite		Decisional Elite		Positional Elite		Propertied Elite	
	1790s	1830s	1790s	1830s	1790s	1830s	1790s	1830s
N	102	148	55	110	99	165	100	100
None (%)	36	70	43	70	39	75	21	58
1 or more (%)	64	30	57	30	61	25	79	42

*Tax records for Baltimore City reported slaveownership as having a "slave or slaves"; therefore, this table discriminates between slaveownership and nonslaveownership only.

a minority of leaders, perhaps with significantly different background characteristics, were able to wield considerably more power because of their actions in multiple roles. The next section compares the characteristics of leaders active in one or more elites to ascertain differences in the leadership of the several communities.

Analysis of Multiple Elite Roles

The analysis of the distribution of community power thus far has focused on the characteristics of the more than eighteen hundred members of the various community elites for both time periods. In this section the elite structure will be discarded, reducing the eighteen hundred community elite membership roles to the analysis of a few more than thirteen hundred individual leaders, shifting the primary emphasis to a leader's participation level in one or more elites. By emphasizing the activity frequency, an effort is made to determine whether there were any meaningful variations in the characteristics of leaders by activity level and therefore whether there might have been an elite operating within a community leadership structure. In an oligarchy, leaders at all levels of activity ought to be recruited from among the dominant landed social elite, so that the overall characteristics of leaders regardless of activity level presumably would be similar, except for fluctuations in average figures. In a polyarchy, characterizing an environment with several alternative bases for community power, there ought to be greater variation among persons participating at different activity levels, although at the same time there is the chance that some men with greater resources might be able to reach the highest elite activity levels. It may well be that a few individuals in a highly heterogeneous environment are able to monopolize the top levels of multiple elite activity in much the same way that the affluent prevailed in a homogeneous environment, but unless it can be demonstrated that they dominated all facets of community decision making, this condition would conform to the situation where several groups have access to community decision making, a basic component of the polyarchical system.

The Rural Homogeneous Agricultural Communities

The pervasiveness of the oligarchical system in rural Maryland, evident at all levels of activity, was especially strong among leaders in two or more elites. Within all leadership categories for both communities there was a basic cultural continuity, judged in terms of nativity and religious information, that augmented and gave cohesion to a system predicated on rule by the affluent. Not only was the rural oligarchical system unchallenged by the structure of community decision making, but leaders belonging to one or more elites increasingly epitomized its association with large property ownership and an underlying social homogeneity.

The similarity of the leadership's cultural patterns for St. Marys and Talbot counties permits a joint analysis for the other variables. Leaders in all categories at both time periods were predominantly native Marylanders in their prime of life.[12] In the first party era, they overwhelmingly belonged to liturgical denominations, the Episcopal or Catholic churches, and in the second party era this pattern was broken only in Talbot County, where an increased percentage of men in one or two elites were Methodists.[13] Those active in three or four elites, however, were almost invariably Episcopalians.

Tables 5.13 and 5.14, presenting rural occupations, similarly demonstrate the positive association between land and slaveownership and multiple elite roles. Professionals, especially in Talbot County, were also visible as leaders in two or more elites. This phenomenon points out a duality in the rural environment. Some professionals, such as editors and attorneys, were young men without remarkable wealth, who served as decisional or positional leaders; others, usually men whose family background provided them with elite educations in medical or law schools, were members of the propertied elite and also participated in other community leadership roles.

The property-owning characteristics of members of one or more elites affirm the interrelationship between owning land and slaves and serving as an active community leader (see Tables 5.15, 5.16, 5.17, and 5.18). As levels of activity increased, so did a leader's affluence and slaveowning category. Such traditional rural patterns were also apparent in Frederick County, where leadership in specific elites revealed a similar but more diversified pattern.

The Heterogeneous Agricultural Community: Frederick County

Individual leadership characteristics in Frederick County displayed the advantages of membership in the oligarchy even in a heterogeneous environment. Members of the diverse elements of the community were more likely to belong to only one or two elites, whereas members of the social groups comprising the oligarchy in other rural areas of the state were more likely to belong to three or four elites. Germans, for instance, formed 31 percent of the membership in the one-elite category, 27 percent in the two-elite group, and only 17 percent in the three-elite

Table 5.13. Rural Occupations, St. Marys County

	1790s				1830s			
	One Elite	Two Elites	Three Elites	Four Elites	One Elite	Two Elites	Three Elites	Four Elites
N	56	16			47	27	7	
Less than 600 acres, no slaves (%)	13				4	22		
Less than 600 acres, with slaves (%)	21				36	26	14	
More than 600 acres, no slaves (%)					2	4		
More than 600 acres, with slaves (%)	50	94			45	30	71	
Professional (%)	16	6			13	19	14	

Table 5.14. Rural Occupations, Talbot County

	1790s				1830s			
	One Elite	Two Elites	Three Elites	Four Elites	One Elite	Two Elites	Three Elites	Four Elites
N	70	14	10	1	57	25	8	2
Less than 600 acres, no slaves (%)	19	29	20		26	16	12	
Less than 600 acres, with slaves (%)	34	7			35	44	25	
More than 600 acres, no slaves (%)					4			
More than 600 acres, with slaves (%)	37	50	50	100	25	28	25	50
Professional (%)	10	14	30		11	12	38	50

Table 5.15. Wealth, St. Marys County*

	1790s				1830s			
	One Elite	Two Elites	Three Elites	Four Elites	One Elite	Two Elites	Three Elites	Four Elites
N	56	14	2		47	27	7	
$100–999 (%)	23				13	30		
$1,000–2,999 (%)	13				19	26		
$3,000–4,999 (%)	38	36			30	26	29	
$5,000–9,999 (%)	20	43	50		30	7	43	
$10,000–29,999 (%)	5	21	50		9	11	29	
$30,000+ (%)	2							
Average ($)	4,753	8,440	19,041		5,233	3,767	7,786	

*The 1800 tax record reported wealth in pounds; such figures were converted to dollars.

Table 5.16. Slaveownership, St. Marys County

	1790s				1830s			
	One Elite	Two Elites	Three Elites	Four Elites	One Elite	Two Elites	Three Elites	Four Elites
N	56	16			47	27	7	
None (%)	20				9	33		
1–5 (%)	11				4	11		
6–19 (%)	32	25			43	22	14	
20+ (%)	38	75			45	33	86	

class in the first party era; the percentage of English-stock leaders correspondingly increased with elite activity. This fact helps to explain why German politicians felt they were being discriminated against in favor of men with roots in the traditional political structure. Similarly, despite a wide variety of religious denominations, membership in the Episcopal church and multiple elite roles went hand in hand during both party periods, and adherents of German denominations were present in the higher elite categories only in the second party era.[14] As was the case in the homogeneous rural areas, individuals who fell into the various elite categories were predominantly native-born and in their forties.[15]

Judged in terms of rural occupations, the dynamics of Frederick County elite participation changed in several ways between the first and second party systems (see Table 5.19). There was a positive relationship between professionals and more active elite participation, but the association between affluence and elite activity in the 1790s is far from clear. One reason is that many of the propertied elite, some of whom were absentee owners, did not belong to more than one elite. Many of those who were associated with two elites were sons of first families, modest property holders from several ethnic groups, or professionals. They were men whose fortunes were yet to be made. Those in three elites were clearly men of wealth, although their adherence to the institution of slavery was ambiguous at best. By the second party era a more pronounced tendency had emerged. Professionals again were prominent as levels of activity increased, and wealth patterns generally rose, but the most interesting trend was the recruitment of slaveowners as leaders, especially at the upper reaches of elite activity in a community where slavery was in general decline.

Table 5.17. Wealth, Talbot County

	1790s				1830s			
	One Elite	Two Elites	Three Elites	Four Elites	One Elite	Two Elites	Three Elites	Four Elites
N	70	14	10	1	57	25	8	2
$100–999 (%)	39	21	20		35	28		
$1,000–2,999 (%)	34	36	10		9	12		
$3,000–4,999 (%)	16	21	30	100	25	28	25	
$5,000–9,999 (%)	7	14	30		19	16	50	
$10,000–29,999 (%)	4	7			12	8	25	100
$30,000+ (%)			10			8		
Average ($)	2,425	3,749	10,139		4,271	4,898*	10,081	20,500

*The great wealth of Colonel Edward Lloyd V was deleted from the average; if it were included the average would be $10,375.

Table 5.18. Slaveownership, Talbot County

	1790s				1830s			
	One Elite	Two Elites	Three Elites	Four Elites	One Elite	Two Elites	Three Elites	Four Elites
N	70	14	10	1	57	25	8	2
None (%)	24	7	20		35	20	12	
1–5 (%)	19	7			19	32	25	
6–19 (%)	40	43		100	21	24		
20+ (%)	17	43	80		25	24	63	100

Table 5.19. Rural Occupations, Frederick County

	1790s				1830s			
	One Elite	Two Elites	Three Elites	Four Elites	One Elite	Two Elites	Three Elites	Four Elites
N	114	27	12		158	44	12	3
Less than 600 acres, no slaves (%)	36	59			47	20		
Less than 600 acres, with slaves (%)	11	7	8		22	34	25	33
More than 600 acres, no slaves (%)	26	7	33		7	2		
More than 600 acres, with slaves (%)	24	7	33		15	16	42	33
Professional (%)	3	19	25		9	27	33	33

The data for wealth and slaveholding, given in Tables 5.20 and 5.21, elaborate these interactions. Compared to the other rural communities, the levels of wealth and slaveownership of men in two or more elites are more modest in Frederick County. For instance, if the ownership of twenty or more slaves is the equivalent of planter status, few elite members achieved that situation, although there was an impressive movement among elite members in the direction of slaveownership at lower levels. These men may not have fit the Maryland mold of planters in the tobacco-producing regions, but they were certainly the most affluent within their immediate community.

The importance of having wealth and traditional social characteristics at the upper reaches of multiple elite participation should not obscure the fact that such leaders could not define the system and that their influence was in decline. In the other rural areas, leadership characteristics at different activity levels tended to reinforce each other. In Frederick County this was not the case. The system's greater demand for leaders and the opportunity for leaders to rise through the competitive party system to powerful positions resulted in the recruitment of individuals with diverse backgrounds and aspirations. If Frederick County traditionalists could control admission into the elite structure, they might have contained this force, but they could not; therefore the oligarchy was doomed to become even more of a minority within the governing structure.

The Urban Community Experience: Baltimore City

Recruitment to one or more elites in Baltimore City's more cosmopolitan environment was far less restricted to the prevailing oligarchical norm than in the rural areas of Maryland. Just as recruitment patterns were more flexible, cultural and economic variation at all levels of individual elite activity in the city was far greater. Concurrently, those men who were the most active as members of three or four elites epitomized both the cosmopolitan and oligarchical ideals. The strength of a polyarchy, where several dynamic groups vie for power, was evident in Baltimore City.

An examination of nativity (see Table 5.22) and religion for urban leaders bears witness to their more diverse origins. Although the samples are small, the evidence for the 1790s shows the representation of native Marylanders, immigrants from other states, and from foreign countries at every level of activity. By the 1830s, the trend was for native Marylanders to predominate, except in the three-elite category, where there were a number of foreign-born. Many of these foreign-born

Table 5.20. Wealth, Frederick County

	1790s*				1830s			
	One Elite	Two Elites	Three Elites	Four Elites	One Elite	Two Elites	Three Elites	Four Elites
N	114	27	12		158	44	12	3
$100–999 (%)	18	41			51	27		
$1,000–2,999 (%)	32	30	17		4	32	8	
$3,000–4,999 (%)	32	11	25		27	25	50	
$5,000–9,999 (%)	12	15	50		17	14	33	
$10,000–29,999 (%)	4	4	8		1	2	8	
$30,000+ (%)	1							100
Average ($)	4,055	2,544	6,538		2,440	2,744	5,318	6,710

*The 1797 Frederick County tax record reported wealth in pounds; this figure was converted to dollars.

Table 5.21. Slaveownership, Frederick County

	1790s				1830s			
	One Elite	Two Elites	Three Elites	Four Elites	One Elite	Two Elites	Three Elites	Four Elites
N	114	27	12		158	44	12	3
None (%)	65	81	33		59	30		
1–5 (%)	10	4			15	41	33	66
6–19 (%)	21	15	42		21	27	66	
20+ (%)	4		25		5	2		33

Table 5.22. Birthplace, Baltimore City

	1790s				1830s			
	One Elite	Two Elites	Three Elites	Four Elites	One Elite	Two Elites	Three Elites	Four Elites
N	30	32	9	7	92	40	13	2
Maryland (%)	33	34	11	29	71	63	53	100
U.S. (%)	30	16	33	43	14	33	15	
Foreign (%)	37	50	56	29	15	5	31	

leaders had been active in community affairs since the first party era, and they do not represent a new wave of immigration. The plethora of urban religious denominations forces the division of the religious variable into liturgical and pietistic categories for analytical purposes. Generally speaking, adherents of the city's two major prestige denominations, the Episcopal and Presbyterian churches, formed the nucleus of the first two elites and predominated in the higher categories. Broken down into liturgical and pietistic groups, they were almost equally divided among the first three categories during both periods; the pietists (Presbyterians) dominated the four-elite category in the 1790s and the liturgicals (Episcopalians) occupied it in the 1830s.[16] In light of the small number of individuals involved and the association of both the Episcopal and Presbyterian churches with the elite, this shift is less significant than the fact that adherents of minor denominations were concentrated in the two lower elite categories. More men from more diversified backgrounds interacted as community leaders in the city, but their levels of participation were at the bottom end of the scale whenever men associated with prestige denominations prevailed at all levels of activity.

The importance of merchants as urban leaders is shown in Table 5.23. They were the single largest element in all leadership categories at both periods of time. Comparing the two periods, professionals and skilled artisans became more involved as leaders, while those whose occupations could not be determined (address/gentleman or none) declined. The activity of the skilled artisan did not extend beyond membership in one or two elites. Professionals became an increasingly more important source of community leaders in all categories.

An examination of wealth and slaveholding tables (5.24 and 5.25) reveals continuity and discontinuity between urban and rural leadership patterns. In both cases, the wealthy, often a greater proportion of whom were slaveowners, were important in multiple elite roles. But in the urban context there was greater variation in the first two categories, accompanied by a decreasing propensity to own slaves.

Community Elites and the Distribution of Power: Summary

The chapter began with a series of questions: what was the distribution of power and how did it change, if at all, during and between the first

Table 5.23. Urban Occupations, Baltimore City

	1790s				1830s			
	One Elite	Two Elites	Three Elites	Four Elites	One Elite	Two Elites	Three Elites	Four Elites
N	134	64	20	8	292	84	17	3
Merchant (%)	43	61	70	38	33	46	71	33
Skilled artisan (%)	13	3			14	11		
Clerical (%)	7	3	10	25	11	10		33
Professional (%)	10	11			12	25	24	33
Address/Gent. (%)	10	14	10	12	12	7	5	
None (%)	17	8	10	25	17	1		

Table 5.24. Wealth, Baltimore City

	1790s				1830s			
	One Elite	Two Elites	Three Elites	Four Elites	One Elite	Two Elites	Three Elites	Four Elites
N	134	65	20	8	292	84	17	3
$100–999 (%)	34	20	10		53	26	18	
$1,000–2,999 (%)	30	32	50		20	31	12	
$3,000–4,999 (%)	19	25	30	63	10	13	18	33
$5,000–9,999 (%)	15	18	10	25	15	26	24	
$10,000–29,999 (%)	2	5		12	2	4	24	66
$30,000+ (%)							5	
Average ($)	2,609	3,592	5,655	6,655	4,476	3,655	8,458	7,283

and second party eras in four Maryland communities? To answer these questions, I first evaluated the characteristics and the recruitment patterns of the previously assembled decisional elites, which were then evaluated and compared with several strategic elites for each community, on the assumption that a comparison of decisional leaders and potential leaders would reveal underlying patterns or discontinuities. The analysis then shifted from the aggregate elite level to an examination of individual elite members to evaluate patterns of elite activity to determine if there were significant variations among individuals according to their level of participation. Several patterns emerged from this analysis.

First, an important contradiction must be noted in the operation of Maryland's political culture during the first and second party systems. In both eras, mass participatory democracy expanded, but this evolution did not fatally weaken the hold exerted by the oligarchy that continued to dominate in areas of political and community leadership. This pattern took several distinct forms. In the relatively stable homogeneous rural communities, St. Marys and Talbot counties, a landed and slaveowning elite, drawn predominantly from English liturgical stock and sustained by kinship ties, served as the primary pool for the recruitment of community leaders in both periods. In a more heterogeneous rural environment, Frederick County, characterized by economic diversification and the existence of several clearly defined social groups, an oligarchy wielded considerable power in the first party period and persisted as a major component in the community's leadership system in the second party era. In the more heterogeneous urban environment of Baltimore City, an oligarchy was formed by the combination of several prominent landed families and affluent merchant families. This urban oligarchy was unable to dominate community leadership as completely as its rural counterpart, and its power and influence underwent a general decline

Table 5.25. Slaveownership, Baltimore City*

	1790s				1830s			
	One Elite	Two Elites	Three Elites	Four Elites	One Elite	Two Elites	Three Elites	Four Elites
N	134	65	20	8	292	84	17	3
None (%)	53	32	20	13	78	65	53	
1 or more (%)	47	68	80	87	22	35	47	100

*Urban tax records give slaveownership in terms of "slave or slaves"; therefore the only meaningful difference is between those who held and those who did not hold slaves.

between the 1790s and the 1830s. Nonetheless, an urban oligarchy persisted in Baltimore City, and its members continued to participate actively in community affairs.

Second, whereas public officeholding remained the key element in affecting the manner by which communities were governed, the configurations of political power were in each instance distinctive and contiguous to the social, cultural, and economic characteristics of the various subcultures. In homogeneous rural areas, the dominance of first families in all aspects of community life helped to perpetuate traditional recruitment patterns. Such men sponsored the development of the competing political parties in both party systems, sought and were rewarded with nominations to the most powerful federal and state political positions, and perpetuated their preeminent role by successfully encouraging their progeny and kin to enter politics as candidates for state and local offices. Individuals who were not as prominent, well connected, or wealthy were also recruited to leadership positions, but in a homogeneous environment there were no alternative power bases and the system continued to be heavily influenced and defined from the top down.

In the more heterogeneous rural context of Frederick County, members of the oligarchy similarly strove to dominate formal and informal recruitment to public leadership positions. But here their efforts were only partially successful. During the first party era, Frederick County's oligarchy enjoyed many of the same advantages as its more traditional rural counterpart. It provided leaders and candidates in the emerging political parties (especially in the Federalist party); its concentration in Fredericktown gave it opportunities to exert political control in excess of its numbers; and it actively sought to rule. Several internal factors, however, undermined these efforts: an urban-rural conflict destroyed solidarity within the oligarchy; representatives of awakening political groups, notably the Germans, were able to thrust themselves forward as leaders at a time when party competition increased and political recruitment became democratized; and, although some of its leaders also belonged to the oligarchy, the Republican party served as the vehicle to challenge the existing political conditions. The end result produced a system at once oligarchical and pluralistic. Traditional leaders, many of whom were concentrated in Fredericktown, increasingly were forced to share community power with representatives from other groups and regions within the county. No balance was struck in the first party era, and the situation remained imbalanced into the second party period.

The political recruitment patterns characteristic of Baltimore's urban community illustrate how difficult it was for an oligarchy to prevail in a diversified and complex environment. The oligarchy formed around an association of merchants and landed families and tried to rule through its influence in the two major parties in both party eras. But despite its efforts, the oligarchy proved unable to monopolize political recruitment as its rural counterparts did. In each instance when the oligarchy attempted to implement restrictive practices, the cries raised by the dissatisfied elements within the community brought defeat. The oligarchy was further weakened by the complex demands of the urban environment. Its members lacked both the numerical strength and the ability to serve in every leadership capacity. The forces of urbanization necessitated a movement toward leadership specialization according to function, thus enabling elements beyond the oligarchy to assimilate themselves. By the time of the second party system, some members of the traditional oligarchy were still prominent community leaders, but they could not dominate either party as they did in the first party era, with the result that the various community elites were much more representative of the community at large.

The examination of community leaders by their membership in one or more elites confirms these patterns. Although there was little diversity between elite activity levels in homogeneous communities, men who embodied traditional leadership characteristics tended to monopolize the higher multiple elite roles. Leaders who represented the community's competing elements tended to cluster at the bottom two activity levels. Two divergent patterns are illustrated: the continued importance of traditional leadership qualities and the increasing size and complexity of the complete elite structure.

An analysis of the distribution of power in these four communities thus suggests several distinct patterns. An oligarchy continued to rule St. Marys and Talbot counties during both party periods. There was no substantive internal challenge to this oligarchical structure, and all external changes, such as the evolution of competing political parties, were assimilated by it. An oligarchy tried to rule in more complex environments, but it met with mixed success in the first party era and declined in the second party period. In both Frederick County and Baltimore City, ecological factors mitigated against any one group's ability to monopolize power, the evolution of political competition exceeded the oligarchy's ability to manipulate it, and the internal demand for specialized leadership resulted in the emergence of new power bases and leaders. Consequently, power was more widely distributed in these more complex environments, and it was shared by a number of competing groups, including important remnants of the oligarchy itself who continued to exercise great influence, but only through a complex of alliances beyond persons of their class and crowd.

6

Paths to Power

Writing in 1834, an anonymous correspondent calling himself "An Observer" made an intriguing comment on prevailing political conditions: "A Union, formed between two families on the Western Shore, and two on the Eastern Shore, now controls the State of Maryland. They have their leaders and active men in each county of the state, and by the agencies of caucuses in the different counties, can always secure such an ascendency in the Legislature to continue all power in their own hands or in those of their immediate friends."[1] Although these remarks were intended primarily to blunt the momentum behind Robert H. Goldsborough's bid for election to the United States Senate, their underlying assumptions highlight the purpose of this chapter. Thus far communities have been studied to determine who governed and how power was distributed. These investigations have revealed clearly delineated paths to power within each environment. As a concept, "paths to power" refers to recruitment patterns where men with certain attributes were able to assume leadership roles with greater ease than men with differing attributes. In this chapter the focus will be on the success or failure of representative men in different community contexts in an effort to understand more fully the dynamics of community power.

Variations among community leadership recruitment patterns occurred partially because of differences between status and achievement societies. In a traditional environment, built upon economic and social homogeneity, an upper-class elite ruled by virtue of its wealth and status. Certain traditional families or families possessing great wealth but lacking an enduring tradition for community leadership acted as a vital oligarchy, recruiting men primarily from their own social network or others dependent upon them as leaders across the spectrum of community activity. New leaders might gain access into this system, qualifying either by the recent accumulation of wealth or by entry into the elite through marriage, but the chances for assimilation without traditional advantages were minimal. In a nontraditional environment, either one in an amorphous developmental stage or one that was clearly being modernized, elite recruitment became more a function of achievement than of status. Leaders with specific abilities and skills, such as professionals or men reflecting the diversity of their constituencies, assumed and relinquished community leadership roles with far greater ease and in far greater numbers in nontraditional than in traditional environments. Members of the oligarchy, representing either traditional landed wealth or the newer forms of merchant wealth, also competed for leadership roles, but the natural advantages accruing to them in an ascriptive status system did not operate in the same way, and they were forced to share power with other members of the society. In contrast to the egalitarian rhetoric associated with the two periods under study, it is important to note the extent to which an ascriptive status society persisted. Yet, as might be expected, achievement norms became increasingly more important in recruitment to leadership positions in nontraditional communities between the Revolution and the Civil War.

The complexity of the status and achievement systems requires elaboration. The following discussion will be divided into two major parts: a discussion of the oligarchical system and how it was able to perpetuate elite recruitment based on status; and a discussion of other leadership groups, clustered around specific types, that owed their success and reputation as community leaders to achievement. Through an understanding of this duality and the competition between them, the concept of community leadership in an age of alleged egalitarianism may be better understood.

The Status Society

The Jacksonian "Observer's" comments were designed to expose how an oligarchy ruled and persisted in an allegedly egalitarian political system. In his efforts to attack a political rival, he ignored the fact that his own party leaders belonged to the same oligarchy. This fact reinforces the trend observable in the last several chapters: in rural areas an oligarchy continued to serve as a primary source of community leaders in both party eras, whereas in an urban environment they competed with other elements in the community for leadership positions. Representative cases in the various community contexts can demonstrate how the oligarchy functioned, prospered, or persisted and how it perpetuated its own society based on ascribed status. Within the oligarchy, three patterns, the continuous, the discontinuous, and the rising oligarchies, existed for at least one hundred years.

The Continuous Oligarchy

Representatives of the first category, the continuous oligarchy, epitomized the cumulative advantages of high social standing and wealth, accompanied by an almost automatic and unquestioned recruitment of successive generations into positions of community leadership. Such families were not only important locally; their extensive intermarriage with families like themselves in other areas resulted in important social networks, providing access to higher social and political circles on the regional, state, and national levels. Besides possessing wealth, status, and offices in the public trust, they continued to dominate because of their persisting presence in the community. This pattern was exemplified by the Lloyds and Goldsboroughs of Talbot County, the Howards of Baltimore, and the McPhersons of Frederick County.

The Lloyds of Wye had been prominent landowners and political figures since the arrival of Edward Lloyd I in 1645. Although they were extensive property holders and held many political offices throughout the proprietary era, lasting through 1768 when Edward Lloyd III was forced out as receiver general because of an intraelite rivalry between colonial political factions, Edward Lloyd IV emerged as an avid Patriot in the early 1770s and served on local and state revolutionary committees and in the new state government almost continuously from 1774 until his death in 1796.[2] His son, Edward Lloyd V, was elected to the House of Delegates when he came of age and served in the United States Congress, as governor of Maryland, as a state senator, and as a United States senator over the next three decades. His son, Edward Lloyd VI, began his career as the second party system formed and emerged as a Jackson party leader and a state legislator in the 1830s. The Lloyds' continued political recruitment to the most prestigious and powerful state and federal positions over several generations indicated their status within the regional and statewide elite. This stature was enhanced through propitious marriages with other distinguished families, such as the Keys of Frederick County, or with aspiring young professionals, such as Joseph Hopper Nicholson, a future Republican congressman and Queen Annes County party leader of considerable ability.[3]

In rural Talbot County men of great wealth who held formal political positions also participated in various other community leadership activities. Besides obtaining militia commissions commensurate with and symbolic of their importance as the wealthiest family in the county, the Lloyds and their kin were instrumental party leaders, both publicly and privately, in every generation from the Revolution through the second party period.[4] Furthermore, as large stockholders in the Farmer's Bank of the Eastern Shore, they served as directors of the Easton branch office. The distribution of community power was thus restricted through the open and varied participation of successive generations of the wealthiest and most eminent families.

Although the political rhetoric conformed to national party divisions during the first and second party eras, competition among major political families was the essence of party rivalry in Talbot County. The Lloyds were a key element in the local Republican and Jacksonian parties at the same time the Goldsboroughs formed the nucleus of the opposing Federalist and Anti-Jacksonian party leadership. Tracing their arrival in Maryland to 1670 and thereafter branching into several family clusters on the Eastern and Western Shores, the Goldsboroughs evolved as affluent landowners and as a source for recruitment to the highest public stations for generations. Two members of that family, Judge Robert Goldsborough IV, and his son, Robert Henry Goldsborough, were especially important.

Judge Robert Goldsborough IV typified the Federalist desideratum of an organic, cohesive, deferential society, led by its most responsible elements. Born into a wealthy and distinguished family, he graduated from Philadelphia College and returned to Talbot County to become a practicing attorney in 1762. During the Revolution he served as a member of the local Committee of Correspondence and thereafter labored as a member of the Maryland senate, as a Federalist to the Constitutional Convention in 1788, and later as a jurist, molding the political structure to conform to his ideal of a balanced organic society. His local prominence was suggested by his ownership of seventeen hundred acres and forty-six slaves in 1800, placing him eighteenth on the tax rolls, and his social station was enhanced by marriage into an old family in neighboring Dorchester County. As a community worthy and political leader he was also especially concerned with the well-being and rejuvenation of the local Episcopal church, for he believed that religion was a vital cohering element within every society, and he bemoaned its diminishing importance to the community at large.[5] Judge Goldsborough passed these assets and responsibilities on to his son.

Robert Henry Goldsborough served his community well in several capacities. As a member of an elite family, he attended St. Johns College, Annapolis, graduating in 1796, and became a gentleman farmer with an interest in improving and modernizing agricultural techniques.[6] Like his father, he served in state government and was a party leader, first as a Federalist and later as an Anti-Jacksonian, acting also as a pillar of the local Episcopal church, and he enhanced his social and economic position by marrying the daughter of Robert Lloyd Nichols, a very wealthy planter-merchant who had been a revolutionary officer.[7] His highest political station was as a United States senator.

The Goldsboroughs, like the Lloyds of Wye, enjoyed a privileged status in the community. They collectively stabilized local society. Their conflicting party rhetoric notwithstanding, the two families shared a mutual self-interest in governing both directly and indirectly to perpetuate their respective hegemonies. And by all measures of continuity and influence, the Goldsboroughs and Lloyds succeeded admirably. To put the matter bluntly, they were the ones who counted because almost all power flowed from them.

But, in contrast to Talbot County, the maintenance of a continuous, stable oligarchy in Frederick County proved impossible. Little more than a thinly populated frontier area in the mid-eighteenth century, divided by the proprietor into large tracts to reward his favorites or to generate revenue, much of this land was redistributed after the Revolution. Even Patriot families holding large tracts, such as the Carrolls who owned the "Manor," were often absentee landowners, thus reducing their direct control of community affairs. The Johnsons illustrated how in this frontier area men of wealth tried to establish themselves in the oligarchical pattern characteristic of the settled areas.

The highly concentrated nature of the frontier oligarchy was symbolized by the Johnson family, which produced Maryland's first state governor and several revolutionary military and political leaders. The Johnsons were also a force behind the region's developing iron industry.[8] Several members of this Episcopal family that originated in southern Maryland were active in proprietary politics from that region before moving in 1774 to build the Catoctin Furnace on a large tract patented a few years earlier by their father. During the Revolution three of the four brothers served in various military and political capacities, while the fourth devoted full time to the family iron business. By the end of the Revolution their claim to power and preference was irresistible: they owned large amounts of land, had amassed great wealth from their iron business, and embodied the socioeconomic attributes of the elite. Added to their identification with the Revolution, all of this assured them an unquestioned place in the frontier oligarchy.

During the early national period, the four Johnson brothers persisted as an important component in Frederick County's leadership structure.[9] Former Governor Thomas Johnson served as a state legislator throughout the 1780s, declining election to the Maryland senate in 1786, before being sent to the constitutional ratifying convention in 1788 and thereafter becoming a member of the state and federal judiciary. Two of his brothers were appointed to the county government in the 1790s.

Besides acting as positional leaders, the Johnsons, all of whom belonged to the propertied elite, were staunch Federalists who were public organizers and leaders in the 1790s as the first party competition took form.

Between the first and second party periods the family's role as community leaders diminished for several reasons. Their interest in running the iron business declined, and their attention shifted outside the county to the development of the new federal city. By 1819, death had claimed the three most dynamic brothers, so that by the second party era several Johnsons could be counted among the propertied and decisional elites, but the family's identification with the dynamic and comprehensive leadership cadre was no longer clearly evident. Belonging to a wealthy and prominent family, however, invited advantageous marriages, and their tradition for leadership persisted through associations with other local and regional political and commercial families.

As in Frederick County, the traditional oligarchy sought to perpetuate its survival in the expansive urban environment in the early nineteenth century. The Howard family of Baltimore epitomized the adaptability of the oligarchy to the urban challenge. In the first party era, consistent with statewide patterns, Colonel John Eager Howard, a revolutionary officer and member of the oligarchy, occupied leadership positions commensurate with his heritage and status. By the maturation of the second party era, despite the changed contextual conditions in urban society, his sons continued to play an important, if different and somewhat diminished, role as community leaders. An analysis of this experience helps explain how the oligarchical structure persisted in both rural and urban environments, while it demonstrates the difficulty the oligarchy faced if it sought to dominate and monopolize power in a more competitive urban environment.

Living at "Belvedere," the family estate on the outskirts of Baltimore City, Colonel Howard was a prime political force in the city and the state during the first party era. His rank as tenth on the 1800 city tax lists understated his real wealth, which was augmented by extensive property holdings in several counties, just as his marriage into the Chew family of Philadelphia failed to convey the significance of his membership in a regional elite structure. But his leadership in the Federalist party, his service as a member of the Continental Congress, as governor, state senator, and United States senator, his role as a member of the Cincinnati Society, on the vestry of the elite St. Paul's Episcopal Church, and his appointment as a major-general in the reorganized militia in 1794 attest to his importance as a community leader in the first party period.[10] A member of all four community elites, Colonel Howard personified the elite ideal of the organic interdependency of wealth, status, public service, and community leadership. Yet Howard and his Federalist associates faced a host of problems. As competitive party politics rose in Baltimore, the Federalist party split into a variety of factions, each promoting separate formulas as to how best to regain power. Other community problems beset the oligarchy, symbolically including the declining membership experienced by the Episcopal church. The consequences of this evolution were well in evidence as Colonel Howard's progeny matured and assumed community leadership positions in the second party era.

Colonel Howard's sons benefited from his affluence and social position.[11] They enjoyed good educations and socially advantageous appointments in civic and militia organizations, and his children married into prominent commercial or rural families. In the context of Baltimore City's 1834 wealth structure, all were members of the propertied elite. Three of his sons did not emerge as dynamic community leaders in their father's image, favoring instead to act as occasional bank directors; the generational mantle for leadership fell on George and Benjamin Chew Howard.

George Howard exemplified the persistence of the rural oligarchical ideal within the family. Although his property holdings placed him among Baltimore's propertied elite, he was more accurately a resident of Anne Arundel County, where he lived as a gentleman farmer after his marriage to the daughter of Governor Charles Carnan Ridgely. Although he was not previously active in politics, his legislative election to the state Executive Council in 1831 resulted in his unexpected elevation to the governor's chair upon the death of the incumbent. Governor Howard, a nominal Anti-Jacksonian, performed his duties to the satisfaction of the legislature, which reelected him as governor to the constitutional limit of three one-year terms.[12]

Benjamin Chew Howard personified the successful oligarchical adaptation to the changed contours of the urban environment between the first and second party eras. Contrary to the traditional recruitment patterns followed by his father and brother, whereby one was elevated to positions of public trust by one's peers, B. C. Howard constantly endeavored to appeal to his urban constituency. First as a Federalist and later as an early and highly visible Jacksonian, he participated frequently in popular political and civic events. During the War of 1812, he was a captain in the popular Mechanical Company and rose to the rank of general in the militia in the 1830s. While he built upon his family heritage and extended his appeal into the higher reaches of urban society through marriage into a leading commercial family, his role as an attorney placed him in contact with other elements in the wider community. Because of his meticulous efforts to reinforce his natural advantages, to reach out and accommodate the very diversity of his community, and to integrate all of these factors for his personal advantage, he rose as a political officeholder in an urban system, first as a city councilman and state legislator in the 1820s and then as a congressman at the turn of the decade. These were the sorts of popular activities his father and brother considered demeaning and refused to do. Yet on occasion his commitment to his diverse constituents was effectively questioned. In 1833 the Workingmen's movement unseated him from Congress. But, ever willing to adapt himself, he won renomination and through a popular campaign regained his seat in 1835. Unlike many of his rural counterparts, Benjamin Chew Howard accepted the changed conditions in the urban political system.[13] Members of the urban oligarchy once had been automatically selected because of popular deference to their elite position, but now had to court and pay deference to their various constituencies if they were to remain in positions of power.

The ability of several families to maintain themselves as community leaders over successive generations should not obscure the fact that other once powerful families faded into the background or disappeared altogether. The next section explains how some families were displaced as community leaders between the first and second party periods.

The Discontinuous Oligarchy

The traditional oligarchy was especially vulnerable to the forces of economic reversal, geographical mobility, mortality, and infecundity. Any of these forces, acting singly or in combination, could have a vitiating effect on community leadership recruitment patterns. The St. Marys County leadership cadre, for example, was devastated by mobility and mortality to a far greater degree than the Talbot County group, resulting in the disappearance of several traditionally powerful families as community decision makers. Several representative cases, Charles Carroll of Carrollton, the Barnes and Plater families of St. Marys County, and the Keys of Frederick County, demonstrate the discontinuous oligarchical pattern.

Charles Carroll of Carrollton belonged to one of Maryland's wealthiest landowning families, whose prosperity and political influence spanned from the proprietary period through the nineteenth century. During the Revolution he developed into an articulate conservative spokesman, advocating moderate reform managed from above, and served in a number of important political capacities, including being a signatory to the Declaration of Independence.[14] Beginning with the war, he belonged to the Maryland senate for over two decades, and he emerged as a strong Federalist in the 1780s. Although he was a resident of Anne Arundel County, his vast property holdings in several regions of the state placed him simultaneously among the propertied elites of Baltimore City, Frederick, and Talbot counties.

A rich and powerful patriarchal figure, Carroll intended to pass intact his legacy of power and influence on to the next generation.[15] His son, Charles Carroll of Homewood, who came to maturity at the time the first party system coalesced and who married into the Philadelphia Chew family and thus became a brother-in-law of Colonel John Eager Howard, did not share his father's capacity for or interest in community leadership. His two daughters married Richard Caton and Robert Goodloe Harper, thus providing him with indirect access to Baltimore's elite. Caton, an English-born businessman who arrived in Baltimore in 1785, was a member of Baltimore's commercial and decisional elites during the first party period and devoted most of his energies thereafter to private entrepreneurial activities. Harper, already a national political figure by the time he settled in Baltimore in 1799, was quickly absorbed into the city's professional and political leadership, becoming a member of the decisional elite and a vital force in the resurgent Federalist party.[16] Unfortunately for dynastic purposes, both the younger Carroll and Harper died in 1825, bequesting the legacy for community leadership to their children.

As the first party era passed into the second, the next generation of Carrolls reached maturity. Most married advantageously, either into titled English families or into politically important and wealthy local or regional American families. Only Charles Carroll Harper, Robert Goodloe Harper's son, aspired to become a community leader in the traditional form. Favored with a good education, entreé to the national political elite, and the experience of being secretary to the French Legation in the early years of the Jackson administration, Charles Carroll Harper returned to Baltimore to claim his right as a member of the oligarchy to initiate his formal political career in the state legislature in the early 1830s. His election as a member of the Jackson party came at a time when other members of the community challenged the right of the elite to rule in their name, and Harper's renomination the next year served as the catalyst for the splintering of the Workingmen's party.[17] His subsequent diplomatic appointment and his untimely death in 1837 obscured the changed circumstances confronting the urban oligarchy that undermined the status system. In any case, his demise and the failure of other Carrolls of his generation to become more than casually involved in all facets of urban or rural community leadership marked the end of the family's active role in the oligarchy. Thereafter they continued to be influential socially and economically, but they no longer commanded the power and respect Charles Carroll of Carrollton had nor did they actively work to shape society to their advantage.

In St. Marys County, the destabilizing impact of mortality and infecundity on the oligarchy was especially evident in the case of the family of Colonel Richard Barnes. As a revolutionary officer, delegate to Maryland's Constitutional Convention in 1775 and to the constitutional ratification convention in 1788, member of the county and state governments in these decades, general in the reorganized militia in 1794, and the county's largest property holder in 1800, Colonel Barnes was an important component of the local ruling elite. He was a leader in the county's Federalist party and acted as a member of the affluent cadre who made community policy. Yet he died childless in 1804, leaving his possessions to distant relatives outside the county, so that just as his property was eventually purchased by other members of the local elite, so, too, his accumulated power was dissipated into the system. His contribution to the perpetuation of the oligarchy ended with his death.

In much the same way, the Plater family of St. Marys County illustrated how mortality and geographic mobility undermined and weakened the oligarchy. Governor George Plater II, member of an old and wealthy southern Maryland family and a political figure during and after the Revolution, died in office in 1792, leaving his three sons an active legacy for community leadership. His sons had married well, establishing a kinship network that included three of the county's wealthiest and politically prominent families, and obtained for themselves positions in local and state government.[18] But their role as agents of an enduring St. Marys County oligarchy soon ended. Governor Plater's namesake, Colonel George Plater III, died in 1802; his other two sons moved to Georgetown, where they focused their political attention. The next generation of Platers showed little interest in continuing their tradition for county leadership, and the family faded from local prominence.[19]

In western Maryland, mortality and geographic mobility also undermined the oligarchical structure. Consider the case of Colonel John Ross Key, a member of an affluent family with British Episcopal roots. His family was among the region's earliest settlers when they moved from Cecil County to occupy a large tract of land in Frederick County purchased from the proprietor in the mid-eighteenth century. The Revolution split family allegiances, but John Ross Key became a militia officer and served several terms in the state legislature during the conflict.[20] In the 1790s, he developed into a staunch Federalist party leader, was again elected to the Maryland General Assembly, and commissioned a militia colonel in 1794; he was a member of the propertied elite. Because he believed literally in the right of the elite to govern and the obligation of the masses to follow, it is not surprising that Colonel Key tried to use his authority as a militia commander, indeed any authority he might obtain, to punish militiamen for their apostasy in favoring the Republican cause.[21]

This tradition for leadership was mandated to the next generation. His son, Francis Scott Key, famous for writing the words to the "Star Spangled Banner" during the War of 1812, attended St. Johns College, studied law under the best jurists in Annapolis, and eventually married a daughter of Colonel Edward Lloyd V.[22] The younger Key, however, soon moved from Fredericktown to the new federal city to practice law, and he would eventually become the United States attorney for the District of Columbia during the Jackson administration. Colonel Key's only daughter married Roger B. Taney, an aspiring young attorney who migrated from southern Maryland to the frontier area in anticipation of building a more lucrative practice. For the first two decades of the nineteenth century, Taney was a driving political force in western Maryland, both as a Federalist party leader and as a state legislator, while at the same time he established his reputation as an able lawyer. By the mid-1820s, however, Taney moved from Fredericktown to Baltimore in an effort to expand his political and professional horizons. Thus the local oligarchy lost two of its promising members because of geographical mobility.

The Rising Oligarchy

The survival of the oligarchical system depended upon its ability to assimilate new members. This was accomplished in several ways. Men of recent wealth married into established families and used the combination of money and status to fulfill immediate ambitions and to anchor new dynasties of community leaders in both settled and developing areas. In other contexts, mortality or geographical mobility created vacancies that were filled by men whose wealth or family tradition were slightly lower than the prevailing threshold for community leadership. The Kerrs of Talbot County, the McPhersons of Frederick County, and the Thomases of St. Marys County illustrate these several trends.

The emergence of the Kerrs as an increasingly important Talbot County family began in the late eighteenth century. David Kerr, a young Scottish merchant, migrated to Annapolis before the Revolution, where he married the granddaughter of the colonial treasurer of the Western

Shore in 1773. Although she died two years later, the marriage brought him property in Anne Arundel County, which was expanded in 1777 when he married a Talbot County widow and moved to Easton. His new wife belonged to the wealthy and prominent Bozman family.[23] Thereafter Kerr emerged as a leading Easton merchant, later entering into partnership with two important local planter families, as a member of local and state government from 1788 through 1802, and as a Federalist party leader. Besides establishing himself as a member of the elite and as a vestryman in the local Episcopal church, his accomplishments boosted the opportunities available to his progeny.

John Leeds Kerr, named after his maternal uncle, who had been the Talbot County clerk from 1738 to 1777, was in the prime of his life during the first and second party eras.[24] As befit a member of an elite family, he attended private preparatory schools and graduated from St. Johns College in 1797, whereupon he studied law in the office of his uncle, John Leeds Bozman. He began his political career as a Federalist, serving in state government, and ended it as an Anti-Jacksonian congressman and party leader. In 1801 he married the daughter of Samuel Chamberlaine, the fifth wealthiest man on the 1800 tax lists, and thus entered a kinship network that included the Lloyds, the Goldsboroughs, and the politically important Gale family in Cecil County.[25] Upon the death of his first wife, he married the daughter of former Governor Charles Goldsborough of Shoal Creek, Dorchester County. During the second party era, John Leeds Kerr belonged to all four Talbot County community elites. As a conscientious member of the oligarchy, he, too, labored on behalf of his progeny.

At the height of his political power, during his service as congressman in the second party system, J. L. Kerr was the patriarch of his own extensive kinship network. His oldest son, John Bozman Kerr, an attorney, initiated a political career as an Anti-Jacksonian member of the state legislature in 1836, a route followed by his third son, David Kerr, some years later; his son-in-law, George S. Leigh, was an aspiring Anti-Jacksonian political figure in St. Marys County.[26]

The career and success of the Kerr family epitomized the rejuvenation of the oligarchy through the assimilation of new blood. Although David Kerr, Sr., never rose higher than membership in local county government, John Leeds Kerr, armed with an education, wealth, and respectability from his maternal connections, not to mention a modicum of ability, found a place in the Talbot County oligarchical structure and was able to pass along such advantages to the following generation.

Frederick County's frontier environment, in which the wealthy were attempting to transplant an oligarchical structure in the absence of an established set of local families whose leadership was enshrined by tradition, encouraged slightly different recruitment patterns. In addition to the Johnsons and the Keys, whose wealth or prominence in their native counties allowed them to enter the leadership structure in Frederick County at the top, other men rose as community leaders through service and advantageous marriages. Colonel John McPherson is an example. As a Presbyterian of Scottish ancestry and a Pennsylvania native who emigrated in 1791, he symbolized the cultural variety of western Maryland, a variety underrepresented in the local governing elite, which was predominantly British and Episcopalian at the time of the Revolution. Aided by a propitious marriage to the only daughter of a very wealthy local merchant, McPherson not only accumulated enough property to belong to Frederick County's propertied elite in 1798, but was also a Federalist political leader, a member of the positional elite, and a militia colonel in 1794.[27] The presence of several McPhersons in the propertied and positional elites during the second party era demonstrates the acceptance of the family as a component in the local ruling elite.

Colonel John McPherson, Jr., followed and expanded upon his father's penchant for community leadership in the new generation. He became an Anti-Jackson party leader, a community advocate of internal improvements, a director of two Fredericktown banks, and a militia colonel in the late 1820s. His status was enhanced by marriage to a granddaughter of former Governor Thomas Johnson, and his prosperity was assured by the purchase of the Catoctin Iron Furnace. Eschewing formal officeholding in the 1830s, he nonetheless belonged to three community elites in this period.

In different community contexts, other leaders rose to prominence in the oligarchy from the ranks of affluent families whose social station was not sufficient to justify automatic membership. The Thomas family of St. Marys County represents this trend. Major William Thomas II, a native of the county, ranked tenth on the local tax records in 1800 and served in various state and local political offices before his election to the Maryland senate in 1803, a position he held until his death in 1813. His role as an outsider in this conservative, traditional community was suggested by the fact that he led the minority Republican party in an overwhelmingly Federalist county, and only his association with the state party secured his indirect election to the local positional elite. Unlike some leaders in St. Marys County, Major Thomas lived long enough to consolidate and expand his wealth and influence, but, more important, to establish a base from which his four sons could initiate their own public careers.

The younger Thomases came of age just as the first party system disintegrated. All four belonged to the propertied elite in 1831, became militia officers, and married well.[28] The family's reputation for community leadership was carried forward by James and Richard Thomas. Like his father two decades earlier, Dr. James Thomas was a Republican party organizer and was elevated to both houses of the state legislature during the 1820s. In 1833 he was elected governor of the state. When the parties reorganized in the late 1820s, Dr. Thomas became an Anti-Jacksonian and a spokesman for the small conservative counties. About the time Dr. Thomas left the legislature, his brother, Richard Thomas, entered it, first in the lower house and after 1836 in the senate. He was also a local Anti-Jackson party leader, and his power was enhanced when he was elected speaker of the House of Delegates and president of the senate. In the context of St. Marys County, where mortality and geographical mobility undercut elite family persistence, the Thomas experience explains how families could be assimilated into the elite and how the structure itself acted as a vehicle for continuity, a functional equivalency to families in other areas. It also reveals how Maryland's system of indirect elections—the election of the state senate or the appointment of local county officials by the state executive—could be used to elevate Republican leaders in predominantly Federalist areas into the positional elite. Because of the family's early Republican identification, it became the core of St. Marys County's Republican-rooted Anti-Jacksonian party, a party that attracted both former Republicans and Federalists on a statewide level.

Such oligarchical patterns epitomize the timelessness of elite recruitment in an agricultural, preindustrial environment. Men with landed wealth who had succeeded in governing their rural communities in the seventeenth and eighteenth centuries continued to do so throughout the first and second party periods. In the face of greater opportunity for individuals without their natural advantages to gain access to leadership positions through the expansion of the electoral base and reduction of officeholding requirements, members of the oligarchy persisted in their domination of community leadership in rural Maryland.

The Achievement Society

The traditional status society ideal characteristic of Maryland prior to the Revolution had gradually eroded in the Confederation and early national periods so that by the time of Andrew Jackson it prevailed only in the most traditional and homogeneous areas of the state. Increasingly in the transforming areas, community leadership became associated with men who did not fit the traditional mold but who reflected society's demand for individual achievement rather than inherited status. This proved especially true among professionals, merchants, skilled artisans, and minorities.

Professionals

As Maryland's economy and society became more complex, opportunities for educated professionals to enter the realm of community leadership increased. The professions were a traditional mixing bowl in the colonial period for talented men, who either enjoyed the fruits of affluence or rose to professional competence from obscure and meager backgrounds, but in the nineteenth century their numerical strength increased dramatically. Some, generally from wealthy families, pursued the study of law or medicine after being educated in preparatory schools and colleges. Others, unable to tap family resources, attached themselves to a professional as a part-time student and clerk, taking longer to master their training. Such initial background differences, which might be insurmountable in a permanently stratified environment, were rendered secondary to ability in the state's transforming communities. Such men, as professionals, were needed in ever-expanding numbers to service an increasingly complex society in which their ability was tested and rewarded individually. The professions—specifically, law, medicine, and newspaper editing—were a vehicle for talented men to rise to positions of community power.

Lawyers have always been called upon to fill community leadership roles. Many lived near the county seat or the state capital, nerve centers for the legal and political systems, and, compared to other occupational groups, a greater proportion of them were involved in civic affairs, often with the expectation of holding a formal government position in the future. Success in law often meant a willingness to be highly mobile. Indeed, a penchant for geographical mobility was characteristic of the profession, from the nature of legal training to the practice of law requiring one to follow the various circuit courts. Established and expanding social and professional connections often served as informal political networks throughout a lawyer's career.[29] Over these years the demand for legal expertise increased because of the growing interaction between the public and private sectors, associated with government support for internal improvements projects and the increased demand for public sanction of private economic activity in the form of state incorporations and charters. For these reasons, men attracted to the practice of law represented a multiplicity of background experiences, and their increasing presence as community leaders reflected an expanding power base. Several individuals illustrate these major trends.

Maryland's most famous nineteenth-century legal figure, Roger B. Taney, personified several of these patterns.[30] Building from his Catholic family's moderate affluence in rural Calvert County, he was able to attend Dickinson College, to study law in the Annapolis office of a prominent jurist, and to gain election to the lower house of the state legislature soon after reaching his majority. In 1801, he moved to Frederick County in anticipation of a more lucrative career before the bar. He made an advantageous marriage into the Key family. Taney's years in Fredericktown established him as an exceptionally able lawyer, an effective Federalist party leader, and a respected member of the state senate. By the mid-1820s he moved to Baltimore City to expand his fortune in the state's leading commercial city. There he emerged as an early and firm supporter of Andrew Jackson's presidential aspirations and worked to unify former Federalists and Republicans behind the new party. Despite his public identification as a leader of the political opposition, he was appointed attorney general of the state in 1827 by the Anti-Jackson administration in recognition of his legal talent and membership in the establishment. By the late 1820s, Taney was a member of the urban elite, a lawyer with wide social and professional connections, but his success would never make him financially independent.[31] Thus in 1831, when he moved from Baltimore to Washington, D.C., to join the federal government, he became a local persona in the Baltimore community elite structure, whose direct power in community affairs diminished by his absence, but whose local symbolic importance grew as he became the object of the Anti-Jacksonian party attacks on the administration's banking policy and in the debate over his own confirmation as secretary of the treasury and later his appointment to the Supreme Court.

There are many other examples of lawyers who moved from rural areas to Maryland's commercial entrepôt to enhance their careers,[32] and who rose quickly in the local power structure because of professional ability or other factors, but no individual career is more instructive than that of John Van Lear McMahon. Born in far western Maryland into an Irish Presbyterian family, he graduated from Princeton College and returned to Cumberland to study law. Soon after being admitted to the bar, he was elected to the lower house of the state legislature, where his father also served for most of this era. McMahon moved to Baltimore in 1826 and was returned by his new constituency to two successive terms in the legislature as a Jacksonian. Although he was thwarted in his ambition to become a congressman, his activities as a Jackson party organizer and orator, combined with his legal talents, brought him wide community support.[33] Following his gradual withdrawal from party affairs after 1829, as he eventually became one of the few public leaders to shift from the Jackson to the Anti-Jackson party, he functioned primarily as an orator at times of political crisis.[34] McMahon's talent ensured his professional success, and his career before the Baltimore bar brought him wide public acclaim.

Members of the oligarchy also became lawyers or used their wealth to sustain legal talent.[35] Colonel John Eager Howard's son, Benjamin Chew Howard, member of four community elites in the second party period, was trained in the law; one of his daughters married William George Read, a youth who came to Baltimore from South Carolina to study law with Robert Goodloe Harper and was soon assimilated into the oligarchy. Roger Nelson, Frederick County's Republican congressman in the first party era, was an able lawyer and belonged to the decisional, positional, and propertied elites. His son, John Nelson, was also an attorney, who, after building a professional and political career in Fredericktown, moved to open a practice in Baltimore City and married into a wealthy merchant family.

Although the symbiotic relationship between wealth and legal talent was a traditional route to power and preference, an important trend in the second party era involved the emergence of lawyers as urban community leaders who did not enjoy close ties to the traditional oligarchy. William Krebs, for instance, a young attorney and Jackson leader who belonged to the commercial, decisional, and positional elites, had few if any ties to the oligarchy. Following a slightly different pattern, William Frick, another lawyer who rose to prominence because of his political activities, was able to draw on family tradition for middle-level community leadership. His father, Peter Frick, a moderately affluent merchant, belonged to three community elites during the first party era, but was not a member of the oligarchy. The younger Frick was admitted to the bar in 1813 and entered the decisional elite because of his labors as a Jackson party organizer—efforts later recognized by his appointment as collector of the port. Both Krebs and Frick demonstrate how men were able to enter community leadership positions from bases other than a close association with the oligarchy.

If the practice of law functioned as a magnet to attract men from diverse social and economic backgrounds into community leadership roles, the interrelationship between medical practitioners and community leadership was less precise. This is partially explained by the fact that in rural areas some doctors were also members of the oligarchy, thus reinforcing their combined social and professional status because they served the community in multiple and highly visible leadership roles.[36]

Freshly trained doctors settled in rural areas, sometimes marrying into a locally prominent family, and were assimilated into the elite structure. Other doctors, dissatisfied with restricting their activities to the practice of medicine, put their general education to use and became editors of limited circulation political presses.[37] Unlike lawyers, whose profession predisposed them to political affairs, leaders who were also doctors seemed motivated less by the influence of tradition-breaking achievement norms than by a close association with the oligarchy. Many doctors were apolitical and remained outside the formal community leadership structure.

As professionals, men whose ability would be measured against achievement, editors were in an anomalous position compared to lawyers or doctors. Those professions generated an independent means for subsistence, whereas control of a small-town newspaper often placed an editor under an obligation to a sponsor. As party presses became self-sustaining, forming an essential part of the community communications network, editors were able to enjoy greater independence. The demand for energetic individuals with newspaper skills offered young educated men, often recruited from outside the community, opportunities to enter the leadership structure at a higher level than their age or prior achievement might otherwise allow. Editors normally fell into one of two patterns: short-term or enduring.

A number of men edited a press for a short time and then took advantage of other opportunities for government employment or geographical mobility. Dabney S. Carr, for instance, trained as an attorney, abandoned the editorship of the Baltimore *Republican and Commercial Advertiser* to accept an appointment as the naval officer of the port.[38] Similarly, Samuel Harker, recruited from Delaware to edit the Baltimore *Republican* in 1832, left six years later to take a position in the post office. John Bond Colvin, trained in the offices of the Baltimore *American and Commercial Advertiser* during the first party era, was brought to edit the Fredericktown *Republican Advocate* in 1802, where he worked for several years prior to taking a job in the federal establishment in the new federal city.[39] Such men were often called upon to participate in party leadership roles and served as an important component in the party's regional communication system.

Some editors formed a stable professional group. Matthias E. Bartgis, father and son, edited various Fredericktown papers for two generations, surviving the vicissitudes of party support and rejection. Hezekiah Niles was succeeded as editor of the *Niles Weekly Register* by his son, William Ogden Niles, who had been groomed as the editor of the *Frederick-Town Herald* in the 1830s. Both men were active political leaders in their respective communities. Like other groups seeking permanence and stability, editors formed kinship groups through advantageous marriages. The editors of the Baltimore *Chronicle*, Samuel Barnes and Sheppard C. Leakin, each married a daughter of Thomas Dobbins, editor of the Baltimore *Telegraphe and Daily Advertiser* in the early nineteenth century. Sometimes editors who had been established at a time of party enthusiasm, such as Isaac Munroe of the Baltimore *Patriot and Mercantile Advertiser* and Thomas Perrin Smith of the Easton *Republican Star*, were cast aside as the official publishers when party leadership changed hands, but they survived independently.

These various examples illustrate how professionals were able to become community leaders. In an achievement society, professionals were successful in defining their own community role; in a status society, professionals frequently discovered that associations and social connections were coequal to ability. In any case, professionals, especially in an urban environment, were an important component in the structure of community leadership, forming a group whose power and influence grew between the first and second party periods.

Merchants

Merchants were a vitalizing element of community leadership in an achievement society. As commercial relationships grew and prospered in colonial America, merchants demanded that their inherent right to govern was coequal to that claimed by landowners, and their struggle for greater power was associated with the rivalry between agricultural areas and the emerging commercial urban areas. This was especially true in Baltimore City, which underwent a phenomenal growth and expansion following the Revolution. It attracted merchants from abroad, other states, and the backcountry, who brought with them a remarkable ethnic, religious, and social variety. Some were content to limit their activities to commerce, perhaps expanding their interest by becoming a bank director; others moved into the political arena as party or positional leaders. Success and affluence among the business elite was often buttressed by a carefully woven infrastructure of social, business, and political connections. Merchants and their children intermarried with other commercial families or with prestigious rural families in the same manner as oligarchical families in an effort to create a more permanent economic and social base. Although this structure was similar to that characterizing an oligarchy, prominent merchants never automatically enjoyed the social and political deference and respect accorded to traditional landed families. Because the system was dynamic, one where a merchant could sustain an economic reversal as unexpectedly as he achieved an economic success, there was an almost fatalistic expectation of change.[40] Various types of merchant leadership patterns prevailed in Baltimore City, and they are best described in several categories: the merchant politician, the traditional merchant, the innovator, and the small merchant.

Samuel Smith of Baltimore personified the merchant politician's career.[41] As a former revolutionary militia officer whose family and business connections allied him with the city's mercantile elite, Smith belonged to all four community elites in the first party era and to the decisional and the positional elites in the second, when he was in his late seventies. Smith used his military reputation and militia command to maintain ties with the voters, just as he used his continuous public career in the federal government from 1793 through 1833 to appeal to the community at large. He was a Republican party leader in the first party era, though as a United States senator whose political position was almost autonomous, he chose to stand in the shadows in the early stages of the second party competition. Other members of his immediate family—such as his brother Robert Smith, his son John Spear Smith, his son-in-law Christopher Hughes—or members of his extended family—such as his nephews Dabney S. Carr and John Spear Nicholas—or his business associate James Calhoun, Jr., owed their public station to his dynamic political force. The family's influence in Baltimore community affairs was well stated in a critical editorial in 1802: "In fine, have you any business, either civil, political, commercial or military, with any of the heads of those institutions, either with the federal, the state, or the municipal government, you will find some branch of this hydra-headed family to have a voice in it."[42] But the influence pointed to by this writer was in fact on the threshold of undergoing a considerable transformation in which family membership would not ensure access to positions of dominance. As Baltimore's society became increasingly segmented, the importance of kin ties, although still valuable, declined as a decisive force.

By the 1830s, the oligarchical underpinnings of the merchant politician's urban power base were not secure enough for him to pass power automatically to the next generation. Dabney S. Carr's inability to secure a better patronage appointment after his uncle's retirement from the Senate suggests this problem, but the career of Senator Smith's son, John Spear Smith, is more instructive. Like his father, John Spear Smith was a prominent merchant, a militia general, and a lay leader in the Presbyterian church, and he became a member of the positional elite with his election to the Maryland senate in 1829.[43] Despite these natural advantages and his repeated efforts to become a leader in the emerging Jackson party, the younger Smith did not establish himself as either a popular party leader or a community figure as had his father. Part of the reason may have been personality differences, but it is important to recognize that his "natural" advantages were dysfunctional in an achievement society and did not assure automatic recruitment into community leadership positions as they might have in a hierarchical status society.

Traditional merchants were men whose primary interest was commercial affairs but whose wealth often cast them in influential roles in the community. Eschewing formal officeholding, they had close contacts with positional leaders and served as a vehicle to collect and disseminate information within the economic elite. Two Baltimore merchant families are examples of this group.[44]

Arriving in Baltimore from Ireland in 1783, Robert Oliver quickly rose in the merchant community as an importer.[45] During the first party era, he belonged to the commercial elite, the decisional elite, and the propertied elite and acted as the local political coordinator for such national figures as Dr. James McHenry.[46] Oliver's influence was enhanced by his two sons-in-law, Roswell L. Colt and Robert M. Gibbes, as well as by his business partners. Colt, a confidant of Nicholas Biddle, was active in Baltimore banking affairs through the 1830s, although his interests increasingly became directed toward New York City.[47] Gibbes, a member of the propertied elite and a director of an insurance company during the 1830s, did not participate openly in community political affairs. Although Oliver was in retirement by the second party period, he stood second on the city's tax rolls in 1834 and was widely recognized as an influential and prominent individual.[48]

William Patterson, a shipping merchant and bank president who immigrated to Baltimore from Ireland during the revolutionary war, was an important community figure until his death in 1835. Standing first on the city tax rolls in 1800, he belonged to the commercial and propertied elites in the first party era and served as a port warden in the preincorporation city government. He generally avoided open partisan identification, but supported the political career of Samuel Smith, his brother-in-law, and was a Presbyterian trustee and a vocal advocate of internal improvements. Even though he was in his late seventies in the second party period, Patterson belonged to the commercial, decisional, and propertied elites and retained his status as the wealthiest person on the city tax ledgers in 1834. His sons were not involved with the political process, following instead mercantile and commercial careers. His daughter's marriage to Jerome Bonaparte may have been a topic of great interest at the time, but it had little impact on the structure of community power in Baltimore.[49]

In a rural environment, such families as the Olivers and the Patter-sons would be the nucleus of a vital oligarchy, whose members would be intimately involved in all facets of community leadership, especially posi-tion holding, but in an urban context these men focused their attention on mercantile and commercial activities. They left the pursuit of politics to others; their careers represented an increasing demand for specialized leadership.

In Baltimore City the small, less prominent merchants were an im-portant component of community leadership in both party eras. John Mackenheimer, for instance, was a small merchant in Old Town at the same time he served in the first branch of the city council. His activities as a militia major, Republican party stalwart, and leader in two fire com-panies were bases for popular community support. Similarly, in the sec-ond party era, Philip Laurenson, a Catholic grocer, served in the city and state legislative branches at the same time he was a conscientious Jackson party organizer and member of the decisional elite.[50] Neither man could tap connections into the social or mercantile elite, yet both were able to establish themselves as community leaders by capitalizing on their associations in the community at large.

The merchant class epitomized the dual legacy of permanence and flux in its contribution to community leadership. Some affluent mer-chants, emulating the rural oligarchical model, enjoyed an enduring privi-leged status and a multiplicity of community responsibilities. Others, less concerned with exerting comprehensive community influence, focused their attention on business and commercial matters. Since this was a dynamic climate, influenced by economic and population fluctuations, access to community leadership was flexible, and merchants from all positions on the economic spectrum utilized various bases of community support to influence the system. In a large urban environment, such as Baltimore City, or in less complex urban places, such as Fredericktown or Easton, merchants were recruited as community leaders, where they acted as a source of innovation in confronting the problems of urban management and economic growth.

Skilled Artisans and Minority Leaders

The following examples of community recruitment patterns cannot be contained in the broad occupational categories utilized thus far. The first category, skilled artisans, represents an urban occupational group; the second, minority leaders, concerns the rise, assimilation, and par-tial disintegration of a rural leadership family who rose to prominence through its ability to mobilize a hitherto somnolent social group into political action.

Skilled artisans formed a vocal pressure group in eighteenth-century urban society. Responding to the disparity between their important economic function and their inconsequential power base in the hierarchical, stratified colonial society, artisans met in informal and formal pressure groups. Informal aggregations of blue-collar workers sought redress of immediate problems through short-term outbursts of mob violence. Artisans increasingly formed into trade associations as the century progressed or joined fire companies and other voluntary organizations, which constituted relatively stable and persisting pressure groups. Despite the high visibility and the apparent influence of such associations in the evolving urban system, especially in the revolutionary era, the weight of artisan power commensurate with their numbers would be realized only several decades later after such structural reforms as the expansion of the franchise and the lowering of property qualifications for officeholding had been effected. This pattern was exemplified in Baltimore City between the first and second party eras, where skilled artisans were recruited into the decisional and positional elites in increasing numbers. Traditionally, artisans formed political alliances with merchant politicians, and during this transitional period members of the ruling elite felt that they could manipulate aspiring artisan politicians.[51] Yet, although skilled artisans rarely were active in more than two community elites, many were able to rise unassisted to positions of power and influence in the urban system during the second party era.

Several examples illuminate the general patterns of community leadership of skilled artisans. James Mosher, an American-born builder by trade, belonged to the decisional and commercial elites in the first party era. His political career was closely tied to that of General Samuel Smith and the Republican party, while his activities as a militia major, as an officer in the Mechanical Fire Company, and as a Presbyterian elder brought him wide contacts both with the elite and with the populace. By the second party era he was comfortably ensconced in the patronage establishment as the surveyor of Baltimore's port, isolated and indifferent to further participation in community leadership. In the 1830s, other types of men who were skilled artisans were recruited as community leaders. Jesse Hunt, a Maryland-born saddler, belonged to the decisional and positional elites, rising first as a popular Jacksonian delegate to the state General Assembly and later as the mayor of the city. Though his community ties were enhanced by marriage into a local publishing family in 1815 and by affiliation with the Episcopal church, he was not a church lay leader or a militia officer. These institutions no longer were necessary perquisites for membership in the community elite. Similarly, Joshua Vansant, a Maryland-born Methodist hatter, belonged to the decisional and positional elites in the 1830s. A man without any direct connections to the city's elite structure, he rose as a popular party leader and was able to use his popularity to claim the right of appointment to the vacant postmastership of the city in 1839.[52] Such men entered the community elite structure and were sustained as leaders through their ties to the populace rather than to the traditional governing class.

Of all the potential ethnic or religious minority groups in the state, only the sizable German population in western Maryland had a discernible political impact. The underlying forces behind their awakening and eventual assimilation into the dominant political culture are still unclear, but the rise of the Shriver family as a manifestation of this process is beyond dispute. As representatives of German culture, belonging to German churches and intermarrying into regional German families, the Shrivers were a link between the political system and the unassimilated Germans who desired more influence in community affairs. Their influence was remarkable because it extended over several generations.[53]

During the first party era, two generations of Shrivers interacted as prominent community leaders in Frederick County. David Shriver, Sr., a Pennsylvania native who fought in the revolutionary war and served in state government during the 1770s and the 1780s, belonged to the decisional and positional elites in the first party era. He represented the institutional strength of the system; his two sons, Abraham and Andrew, labored to win German support behind the evolving Republican party. Abraham, a Fredericktown merchant, was intimately involved with the machinations of the traditional political clique who tried to monopolize party leadership. As a member of the decisional and positional elites and as a militia officer, he was assimilated into the more traditional Frederick County elite structure. Andrew Shriver, whose ability to speak and write in the German language was used extensively in Republican campaigns, retained his rural identification. Although he also belonged to the decisional and positional elites, his role as a flour miller at Union Mills and as one who believed that the Germans were being used by the urban political leaders of both parties restrained his enthusiasm for a total commitment to the existing political structure. Despite such internal variations, the prominence of the Shrivers was recognized externally and perceived by them as devolving from their representation of the German interest in community affairs.

By the second party era, conditions had changed. German participation in community affairs was no longer novel, and the Shrivers were vulnerable to criticism for being part of the establishment. Abraham Shriver, as a long-term member of the county court, continued his interest in politics although his failing eyesight precluded activity as a vital political organizer.[54] Andrew Shriver lost interest in politics and concentrated on business matters with special emphasis on establishing his children advantageously. One son, John S. Shriver, became a Baltimore flour merchant. Both brothers gravitated from the Republican to the Anti-Jackson party in the late 1820s.

Accompanying the formation of the Jackson party was a split within the Shriver family. Two brothers representing the rural portions of the county became Jackson party leaders. Isaac Shriver, a member of the decisional and positional elites, served in the state legislature; Jacob Shriver, a member of the decisional, positional, and propertied elites, belonged to the state and local governments. The careers of both men reflected the mobilization of continued rural discontent with the domination of Fredericktown in community affairs.

The second party era also witnessed a similar division within the extended Shriver family. John Schley, a political ally of the Shrivers and a member of the positional elite in the first party era, married into the Shriver family. By the second party era he was the clerk of the county court and a member of the propertied elite, and several of his sons were entering the political arena as Jacksonians. One became the editor of the Fredericktown *Political Examiner and Public Advertiser* and a member of the House of Delegates; another was a political activist before his election to the state senate in 1836.[55] Within the extended Shriver family, members of the new political generation were competing for community leadership positions held by members of the former political generation.

Afterword

Recruitment into community leadership positions was far more complex than contemporary commentators, such as "An Observer," would have us believe. Rather than being dominated by a single set of first families, it varied by environments according to either a status or an achievement norm. The traditional status norm, whereby members of first families were recruited as community leaders by right of their economic and social position, still operated in many rural areas of Maryland and served to define parts of the political system throughout both party eras. Competing with the traditional status norm was the achievement norm, which replaced dependency on a predefined status group with a demand for men whose leadership qualifications were determined by individual characteristics. In the more traditional areas, the achievement norm could not operate because of the domination of conservative propertied wealth. In transitional and modernizing areas, the achievement norms corresponded with changes in the concentration of wealth and the increased variety in the ways it could be earned.

7

Power in a Changing Society

The search for the answer to the question, who governs, reveals basic relationships underlying a political culture that illuminate larger issues. Community-based histories tell us much about politics at the local level, but far more important is their potential for providing a laboratory where the fundamental characteristics of a period may be examined. For the period under consideration, the community leadership patterns we have been examining highlight the dynamic process of the political system and enable us to draw conclusions about democracy, egalitarianism, elitism, and the distribution of power in the formative years of America's political culture.

Democracy, Egalitarianism, and Elitism

Democracy and egalitarianism are traditional concepts used to characterize the evolution of American political culture between the Revolution and the Civil War. More recently, a counterconcept, elitism, has come into vogue. Its proponents argue that conditions in this period were both unequal and undemocratic. Whatever the interpretative framework, an elaboration of these three concepts is crucial for comprehending each of them.

According to historians and contemporaries alike, the American experience transcended national boundaries and exemplified a process overtaking western Europe in the eighteenth and nineteenth centuries. Recognizing the irresistible forces unleashed by social and economic change, not to mention the destabilizing influence of prolonged warfare, Europeans looked to America for guidance in moderating and controlling the transition from their feudal past to what appeared to be a democratic future. The perceived universality of the American experiment broadened its conceptual significance, but tended to blur some of its contextual variety. Nowhere is this problem more clearly dealt with than in the work of Alexis de Tocqueville.

Tocqueville's *Democracy in America* rests upon several important assumptions. As one who venerated the cultural achievements of traditional European society and feared the tyranny of the majority, Tocqueville was primarily interested in learning from the American experience how popular passions could be moderated and redirected. To Tocqueville the contemporary crisis over legitimacy between the few who by virtue of tradition governed in the name of society and the aspiring spokesmen who demanded greater self-rule on the basis of popular support was the product of a long-term trend toward individualism. As the economic and social barriers inhibiting individualism fell, as traditional and status hierarchies were eroded, the state's ultimate authoritative sanction was transformed from the monarchy to popular opinion.[1] Popular opinion historically was volatile, unstable, and easily perverted by demagogues. Therefore, after accepting the new conditions as a natural development, Tocqueville concluded that the passions of popular opinion could only be contained by popular government. Although he described the institutions and manners of America with this theory in mind, he appreciated the ultimate inappropriateness of transplanting American democracy without modifications into a European context.

The democratic structures and values described by Tocqueville are easily recognized by students of American history. Built upon a framework of law and constitutionalism, they formed a dynamic system that at once represented and restrained the popular will. Frequent elections, relatively unrestricted franchise and officeholding requirements, and an absence of permanent social divisions identified the popular will with government. The inherent danger of concentrated power was minimized by the American tradition of limited and decentralized government. Government was limited functionally by the creation of independent legislative, executive, and judicial branches and decentralized spatially by the formation of local, state, and federal units. The absence of a standing army rendered the whole of government benign. In addition, freedom of the press, the evolution of parties, and the unrestricted opportunity to form voluntary associations all served to inform the individual and to strengthen representative government, while averting the threat of demagoguery.

Tocqueville's search for the essence of democracy and his interest in ascertaining its philosophical and functional roots caused some hasty judgments.[2] Convinced that laws preventing primogeniture restrained landed families from passing their wealth from generation to generation, and hence thinking that many affluent Americans had obtained their riches recently, he seriously underestimated the capacity of some wealthy families to transmit their possessions and status to the next generation almost intact. He was blind, moreover, to their enduring ability to influence economic and political affairs in a democratic environment.[3] Similarly, although his visit coincided with the presidency of Andrew

Jackson, he concluded from his nine-month sojourn that contemporary political parties were noncompetitive. Finally, his emphasis on the philosophical components of government prevented him from appreciating the value of systematic investigation of how government and community decision making in fact functioned. Tocqueville correctly observed the increased reliance of society on lawyers as public leaders, often in place of landowners, but his presentation revealed little about who in fact governed.

Egalitarianism, the second concept used to characterize this period, is often confused with democracy. Tocqueville himself often conflated these terms and even considered using "equality" in the title of his second volume. Unfortunately, it was Tocqueville's almost interchangeable use of the terms "democracy" and "equality" that has fostered much terminological confusion.[4] Rather than confine his definition of democracy to government institutions and functions and apply the concept of equality to social processes in general, he mixed both indiscriminately. More recent scholars have treated egalitarianism with greater care and precision. In the social realm, they have used it to describe the expansion of individualism, accompanied by the relative decline of social and status hierarchies. In the political arena, egalitarianism is seen in the lowering of franchise restrictions to liberalize political participation and the change from indirect to direct election procedures.[5] Egalitarianism has also been identified with the actions of government itself, especially those that had the effect of protecting individual rights, rather than perpetuating vested interests. The many battles over privilege that occurred in this period, such as the debate over the creation of monopolies or matters of social control, essentially involved questions of egalitarianism.[6]

Some historians have suggested that elitism characterizes this period more accurately than the concepts of democracy or egalitarianism.[7] Arguing on the basis of perceived lack of individual upward social mobility and the continued concentration of wealth in the hands of a relatively stable and persisting elite, these historians contend that American society was inelastic and hierarchical and maintain that the political system was undemocratic. Even if a liberalized political system afforded the common man far greater opportunity to influence government than he enjoyed before, government was run by and for the elite. This elite, representing old families and members of the commercially based nouveaux riche, either held positions of power or influenced politics from behind the scenes throughout this period.

Power in Society

The data and conclusions derived from this comparative study of community decision making enable us to test these interpretations. The most useful approach is to address the larger question of power in society with a view toward analyzing sociopolitical relationships over time.

The structure of authority in Maryland's political institutions conformed to Tocqueville's general description of democratic government. The ultimate power behind government rested with the people, while government responsibility was divided through various divisions and balances. Although Tocqueville may have uncritically accepted an informant's assertion in 1831 that "the constitution of Maryland is the most democratic in America,"[8] the fact is that this document was designed to minimize the influence of the propertyless and to ensure the continued political domination of a propertied elite. In response to recurring demands for reform following the Revolution, the constitution was liberalized in several ways: high property requirements for voting and officeholding were dropped, viva voce voting was replaced by the ballot procedure, indirect elections were abandoned, and representation by population was given precedence over the traditional reliance on the county as the basic unit of representation. Nevertheless, wealthy men continued to rule society, a fact that lends credence to the proposition that the political system was undemocratic and elitist. To address this problem in its proper context, however, we must consider not only the structure of power relationships but also the actual operation of power.

Power relationships in society are subtle and complex phenomena. Besides the authoritative power allocations provided by a constitution, which defines who should possess power and how it should be employed, power relationships are influenced by external factors. These factors are traditional usage, either predating or implicit in an authoritative document; competition for formal government positions; and competition in other community affairs.

As we have seen in the context of four Maryland communities in the first and second party eras, wealthy and prominent men enjoyed the fruits of cumulative inequality as they interacted in community matters. During the first party period, an affluent, public-minded man had a better chance to be a militia officer, a church vestryman, or a civic leader than did men without such advantages, and each of these positions could be translated into political power without difficulty. Conditions did not significantly change until the second party system matured. Ironically, the impetus for the perfection of early organizational devices came from leaders of the first party era, who sought to restore or continue themselves in power by mobilizing the somnolent electorate through democratic meetings and conventions in the mid-1820s.

The structure of this democratic system, however, prevented domination by any one group because it invited participation from diverse elements within the community. In areas where there was minimal change between the first and second party eras and almost no competition for leadership, traditional leadership patterns continued unabated. Existing local rivalries successfully absorbed and contained the evolving national party competitions. In more complex communities, new leaders rose to challenge the old order, but their ability to sustain this challenge was undermined in the first party period because of an absence of independent power bases. Lacking a strong and unifying party structure, leaders depended on less reliable protopolitical organizations such as fire companies or militia units to sustain and justify their pretensions for leadership.

The evolution of permanent political parties in the second party period was a more significant development affecting communitywide power relationships than is generally appreciated.[9] Not only did parties institutionalize popularity as a power base; their very strength sustained a leader's claim for greater influence in community affairs. This is not to deny that the original political organizers, many of whom were prominent in the first party era, sought to resuscitate party organizational devices to return themselves to government. Nor is it to deny that they tried to run the early party as their own fiefdom. But their inability to perpetuate their domination, coupled with the rise of new leaders with few ties to the older structure, demonstrate the widening power base characteristic of a more representative system.

Whereas an elite may have dominated political affairs in the first party era, a coalition of leaders representing a community's various constituencies ruled in the second party period. The intensity of coalitional politics was epitomized in urban areas by rivalries for nomination and patronage preferences and in the rural areas by an endemic urban-rural competition and the polarization induced by the reform question. In communities that had very little social or economic diversity, few bases existed upon which a coalition of interests could form. This fact blunted the dynamic force of popularity.

The role of elected position holders in community leadership has been misunderstood. Some scholars conclude that if officials in a democratic system were wealthy, or if their wealth characteristics fluctuated over time, then the system itself was in differing degrees democratic.[10] This conclusion was based on a method that neglected to analyze directly the crucial question of power relationships, namely, who made important community decisions and what role such elected officials played in reaching them. At the same time, this approach failed to confront the more subtle problem of community influence networks. Position holders may well have been the essential ingredient in community decision making, but none of these interpretations has verified this hypothesis. Indeed, the Maryland experience suggests that decision making and position holding varied with regard to the type of community under examination. They overlapped in traditional communities, where they represented the ability of oligarchies to dominate in noncompetitive environments. In urban areas the pattern was less pronounced. In a more complex environment, more leaders were able to participate in the community decision-making process. The effort on the part of some of these studies to denigrate Tocqueville's assertion that America was a real democracy, as opposed to a pseudodemocracy dominated by a persisting elite, diverts attention from a far more important phenomenon: the specialization of leadership.

An examination of decisional situations in several contexts reveals a trend toward leadership specialization in the first and second party periods. This was not just associated with the emergence of lawyers as leaders, a trend noted by Tocqueville. It was also represented by the fact that wealthy and prominent men eschewed direct competition in the political realm in favor of concentrating their energies in other specialized areas. This might also suggest the existence of a sophisticated system of covert influence, where the affluent manipulated public leaders from behind the scenes, but a direct examination of community decision making with such a bias in mind did not reveal the existence of such a pattern.

The trend toward leadership specialization was reinforced by an examination of a community's strategic elites. After hypothetically projecting the idea that men possessing valued community resources might share a common vested interest, we are in a position to aggregate such men into autonomous groups, strategic elites, and to investigate patterns of overlap and interaction. Leadership specialization appears to be a function of a community's underlying social and economic heterogeneity. In complex, competitive environments, there was greater leadership specialization than in relatively undifferentiated and noncompetitive environments. This trend is not readily apparent from data in collective biographies, which emphasize variables such as wealth, occupation, and age, unless some attention is also given to more elusive social and kinship networks. For example, the career of a young, propertyless attorney in either a rural or an urban environment might be evidence of the fact that there were opportunities for lawyers as a class to rise to positions of responsibility in the second party era; but the discovery that he belonged to the local oligarchy places him in a network structure that reveals the more subtle systemic nuances.

Unfortunately, for the breadth of Tocqueville's vision, he did not examine the problem of power in society directly, and he relied on the judgments of others to conclude that a democracy could not be dominated by an elite. Notwithstanding his brilliant understanding and insight into the dynamic relationships affecting political systems, he failed to comprehend that considerable variations in the distribution of power existed in the American democratic experience. It is equally unfortunate that some critics, seeking to refute Tocqueville, adduce general trends from incomplete research designs. Rather than study power relationships directly, they assume that men who hold official political positions or those who lead voluntary associations wield power.[11] This has yet to be proven.

Oligarchy and Polyarchy in a Pluralist Society

The durability of the American experiment is attributable to its capacity to assimilate rivalries. From its inception, various interest groups competed for political dominance, and in the early national years property rights prevailed over democratic political rights. As such restrictions were peeled away through constitutional reform, allowing more citizens to participate in government, new groups and new leaders entered this competition. This was the essence of American pluralism.

It is important to restate the essential differences between elitism and pluralism. Elitist studies often start from the premise that the unequal distribution of property results in the domination of society by the wealthy or their agents. Pluralists posit the existence of a dynamic relationship between the authority structure, tradition, and a society's underlying socioeconomic elements. In this context, leadership patterns represent a community's relative complexity. In relatively homogeneous areas, for instance, competition would be restrained, leadership would be influenced heavily by traditional forms, and an oligarchy might rule. In heterogeneous areas, competition would be far less restrained, loosening the bonds of tradition, and a coalition of leaders forming a polyarchy would interact as decision makers.

The strength of pluralism is associated with the relative openness of the political system. In the first party era, for example, ethnic groups rallied to the Jeffersonian party because it endorsed a heterogeneous society, but few ethnic leaders were able to break into leadership positions because of the prevalence of conservative recruitment norms. By the second party era, although ethnic and religious passions had cooled, the leadership structure had expanded to assimilate a greater variety of men. At the same time it is important to note that oligarchic dominance in a homogeneous community does not represent a repudiation of pluralism. If tradition and wealth were to characterize leadership in both homogeneous and heterogeneous environments, the pluralistic thesis might be invalidated, but for tradition and wealth to dominate primarily in homogeneous communities reflects the absence of competition and the prevalence of tradition. Without competitive interaction among several groups for community dominance, the prevalence of existing norms is almost assured.

American political society was democratic, egalitarian, and pluralistic by the end of the second party era. Freed from the limitations that conservatives had placed on the initial state constitutions and encouraged by the rising opportunities for individual fulfillment, society's diverse elements recognized pluralism as the promise of American political life. Where competition existed, community leadership reflected the clash of competing groups; where competition was minimal, community leadership adhered to its traditional patterns. The strength of a pluralist system was its ability to absorb rivalries and assimilate its competitive elements, while meeting the demands of its constituencies. Between the first and second party eras, American pluralism did all of these things as the United States proceeded on the course of modernization.

Appendix I
Methodological Procedures

Traditional historical scholarship has been challenged by social scientists for being unsystematic, idiosyncratic, and unreliable. Rather than making explicit methodological statements, thus revealing the conceptual underpinnings of their studies, historians generally adopt a graceful literary style that serves to convince the reader of the appropriateness of the interpretation without elaborating the operational components through which it was reached. This study is predicated on the belief that unless the conceptual framework and operational decisions are made explicit, the significance of the overall contribution must be ambiguous at best. Therefore, this appendix addresses the various methodological problems pertaining to the study of power, the aggregation of individuals into elites, the use of collective biography, and the availability and limitations of the primary sources consulted for this study.

The Search for Power

The search for appropriate methods to examine power relationships is fraught with difficulties. Historians may dislike discussing methodological matters openly or tend to favor one approach implicitly; social scientists do not share a unanimous opinion as to which method is superior.[1] Several considerations must influence the selection of a method: its cogency, overall appropriateness, and specific relevance for use with historical materials.

Such conceptual clarification will begin with a working definition of community leadership.[2] It must define and establish the dimensions of the overall system; it must specify criteria used to attribute leadership, specifically by delineating a working definition of power, so as to distinguish leaders from non-leaders; and it must specify ways leaders may be assembled into elites. Finally, some consideration should be given to the question of the distribution of power within a community. Is the distribution of power and the composition of the leadership cadre similar in each community; is there variation among communities; and how can continuity or discontinuity be explained?

To understand the dimensions of community leadership, we must first define what is meant by such primary terms as "community," "political system," and "leadership." The community is defined as a county or incorporated city representing both a political and a geographical unit. These communities may be larger than the underlying social units—such as a settlement area or a religious or ethnic enclave—but they reflect the focal point of political attention because they are the primary units where authoritative community decisions are made. It is on this level that government representatives are recruited and popular efforts are initiated to mobilize support of or opposition to community projects. In this sense, counties and incorporated cities constitute the basic unit of the political system.

The definition of a political system has sharply divided social scientists and left most historians standing mute. The crux of the dispute is definition of the proper boundary separating the political system from the nonpolitical system. Robert Presthus, who favors an expansive definition, would consider a private businessman's decision to locate a company plant as falling within the political system; Robert A. Dahl would exclude any private, economic decision from a political analysis because political analysis deals with power, rule, and authority.[3] Dahl and Lee Benson believe that the study of the political system should center on the authoritative governing agencies of the community. The authoritative agencies are those to which the community has given the ultimate sanction of force to act in the name of the whole. Lee Benson's summary definition of a political system as "the relatively persistent set of patterned interactions that produce authoritative public decisions for a specified body politic or society or community" will serve nicely for this study.[4] This usage differs from his final definition, however, because Benson restricts authoritative power to those agencies having control over the community's coercive forces.[5] In my view, a political system must also incorporate nonauthoritative leadership in political recruitment and the mobilization of public support for community projects, actions designed to influence authoritative policy outputs. The purpose of these activities is to select those who sit in positions of public authority or to influence how they act when they are seated. They differ from private acts of the type Presthus described that never involved authoritative sanction.

The formulation of an adequate working definition of power has not produced unanimity among social scientists. Dahl and his students define power as the relative ability of one person to make another change his mind in a decision-making situation.[6] Robert Presthus is less exacting. First observing that "men are powerful *in relation* to other men," he conceptualizes power "as a system of social relationships."[7] The apparent definitional distance between the specificity of Dahl and the ambiguity of Presthus is explained cogently by Charles Kadushin, who observes: "The basic reason for the multiplicity of definitions . . . is that power, as it is used by social scientists, is a *dispositional* concept."[8] Building from this often rancorous debate, Lee Benson defines political power as "the relative impact that political actors have on the quality of life of the members of a community during some specified time period, to the extent that the quality of life (or well-being) of the members of that community is determined by the authoritative public decisions (positive and negative) made in that community."[9]

Political leaders, then, are those individuals who possess relatively more political power than other individuals in that community.[10] This does not mean that political leadership is limited to those holding formal offices. Leaders who demonstrate power, those who have a higher "relative impact" over policy making, may operate both within and outside of the officeholding system.

Social scientists have developed a number of ingenious ways to identify and to assemble an elite from among the variety of community leaders. These include the positional, reputational, decisional, resources, and sociometric methods. Historians have intuitively emulated several of these methods.

The Positional Method

The positional method has been favored by political scientists and historians alike. Following C. Wright Mills's influential study, *The Power Elite*, scholars seeking to identify powerful men focus on those who occupy government positions.[11] The major underlying assumption of the positional method is that power emanates from the formal positions created to act with the authority of the whole culture. Presumably, positions differ in power according to the allocation of responsibility by an authoritative source, such as a constitution. Thus, in terms of the logical implications of this approach, to understand power, one must identify the source of power, divide government into strata of power allocations, locate those who hold powerful positions, and finally, assess the decisions they make. Rarely, however, is the method extended to make strata differentiations.

In Mills's study, a power elite of the 1950s—comprising the president, the military, and private defense contractors—made the "big-decisions" rendering those in positions of power impotent. Regardless of the accuracy of this interpretation, the approach raises several important methodological questions. The distinction between big and little decisions is inadequate, and the underlying assumption that there was a consensus within the power elite begs the question of influence.[12] Influence can have several meanings. Within a decision it can point to domination by an individual or a group, which, in terms of the positional method, would serve as a test to determine whether officeholders make decisions or act on behalf of others.

A historian favoring the positional approach is Ralph A. Wooster. In two books describing the social characteristics of position holders in the antebellum South, specifically, membership in selected state and county offices, Wooster investigated the question of whether power shifted from one group to another during the volatile 1850s.[13] The problem with this approach is twofold. First, position holding and power are never linked, so that we are forced to accept as an article of faith that such offices were in fact important. Second, the association between changes in the officeholder's social attributes and his political role is also assumed. Despite the usefulness of knowing the aggregate social characteristics of these political elites on the eve of the Civil War, the question of who was making important political decisions is never addressed directly.

The positional approach has the basic attraction of simplicity and directness. Government acts and officials get things done. But the process of getting things done is often explained the least. Officials undoubtedly have power, decisions are made, but the method is inadequate to probe the distribution of power within the system or even within decisions. This basic problem is compounded

when the method is expanded to include nongovernment officials. The mere
identification of economic position holders, or social leaders, does not demonstrate that they exercised political power. This error is extended when the positional elite is presumed to possess operational power, but the assumption is not
tested empirically.[14]

The Reputational Method

The reputational method is widely used by both contemporary sociologists
and political scientists. It was introduced in the work of Floyd Hunter on Regional City in the 1950s.[15] Hunter's basic operation was to interview knowledgeable community informants, who identified the powerful from a preselected
list of leaders. Although the mode of study was not limited to the positional
power holders, Hunter first compiled a list of government, business, civic, and
social position holders from community sources. He then took the four lists of
nominees to a preselected panel, who were instructed to cut this list to the "top
leadership." The final list of forty names represented the top leadership of Regional City.[16] A variation on the selection of leaders is to ask community respondents who they feel would be the most effective leaders to get something
done.[17]

The advantage of the reputational method is its directness and the ease with
which panels of leaders can be selected. Use of positional leadership lists and
interviews with people who know what is going on allows quick identification of
leaders, who can be studied further. Whereas other approaches might ignore
power as an operational concept, the reputational method stresses the leader's
reputation within the community for being powerful. Hunter stated: "To locate
power in Regional City, it is therefore necessary to identify some of the men who
wield power, as well as to describe the physical setting in which they operate."[18]
The emphasis is on the operation of power, the interconnections and relations
among the powerful, not on determining an exact division of power among the
elite. He made this point explicit when he observed: "No pretense is made that
the group to be discussed represents the totality of power leaders of the community, but it is felt that a representative case sample is presented, and that men
described come well within the range of the center of power in the community."[19]
Once Hunter specified this sample of community leaders, he probed stratification
within the group and cohesion within the several strata. Part of the reason for
this probe was to explain business, social, and prestige connections and domination within the community. The practitioners who followed Hunter have modified his procedures.

A major modification has been the use of the reputational method for
comparative community analysis. This has led to refinements in the selection of
knowledgeables and in interview questions and techniques and has also avoided
the problem of deriving misleading conclusions from a single case study.[20] William A. Gamson has suggested a conceptual aspect of "reputation" that significantly alters the meaning of the basic concept. He observes: "Reputation . . . is a
resource; as such, it refers to potential influence rather than influence in use.

Reputation is not simply a manifestation of the possession of large amounts of resources but is, itself, a resource in the same sense that money, wealth, or authority might be."[21] Furthermore, "those who are named as 'reputational leaders' simply comprise a pool of individuals with resources. No claim is made that they form a ruling elite or even a cohesive group of any sort; such claims must rest in demonstration of a number of additional characteristics."[22] By treating reputation as a resource, Gamson tests the question of dominance in actual decisional situations where influence is used to achieve goals. His refinement improves the reputational approach and allows potentially subjective evaluations by respondents to be treated empirically.[23]

Subjectivity and ambiguity have been basic criticisms leveled against Hunter and the advocates of the reputational method. Consider the concept of "power," for example. There is an assumption that the respondent and the interviewer share a similar definition of power; that the respondent is actually a political insider who knows who is powerful; and that the respondent is uniformly knowledgeable across all community issues. It is one thing to ask someone, "who is the 'big man' around here?" or "Who gets things done in the community?" but quite another to identify accurately a person who is responsible for the accomplishment of these goals.[24] There is also the problem of affirming the consequence: to ask "who is the big man?" suggests that there must be a "big man" who gets things done. In fact, several reputational studies show that the reputational leaders are unsuccessful in effecting community decisions.[25] Another issue of dispute is Hunter's numerical cutoff at forty "top leaders." Besides arbitrarily limiting the elite's size, such a cutoff assumes that these forty are the leaders without specifying conditions for inclusion or change.[26] Furthermore, by specifying identification of the community's top leaders, one presupposes that a unified group does in fact exist.[27]

The critics argue convincingly that reputation for power is not analogous to real power.[28] Nelson Polsby observed: "Asking about reputations is asking, at a remove, about behavior. It can be argued that the researcher should make it his business to study behavior directly rather than depend on the opinions of secondhand sources."[29] Since power relations are never studied directly, this method cannot identify who is demonstrably powerful, or, indeed, how the political system operates.[30] The issues Hunter investigated have been criticized as being unrepresentative of larger community issues and limited to verifying his major hypothesis that businessmen dominated community affairs.[31] Raymond Wolfinger pessimistically concluded: "The reputational method for the study of local politics is one of the marvels of contemporary social science: the heavier the weight of evidence against it, the more uses its champions find for it, and the more ambitious are the theories based on its findings."[32]

The advocates of the reputational method acknowledge many of the criticisms and use them to form the basis for conceptual refinements.[33] None, however, accept Wolfinger's plea for a decent burial, which they feel is premature. The vehemence of the attack on the reputational method is partially explained by its widespread use even though an alternative method is available.

The Decisional Method

The decisional method, forcefully advocated by Nelson Polsby and Raymond E. Wolfinger, is identified primarily with the work of Robert A. Dahl. Taken together they form the core of the so-called pluralist movement in the literature of community studies. Pluralism presumes that "nothing categorical can be assumed about power in any community. It rejects the stratification thesis that *some* group necessarily dominates a community."[34] Pluralists advocate operationalizing the concept of power by studying decision making directly in order to determine who actually made important community decisions.

This approach is associated with Robert A. Dahl's influential study of New Haven, *Who Governs?* His primary goal was to explore the democratic implications of governing in contemporary America. Dahl asked the essential question, who governs, in a society where there is open political participation and a pluralist economic and social environment.[35] By who governs, Dahl meant who rules; he sought to identify those who dominated the important community decisions. Given his conceptual framework, Dahl analyzed community power within community decisions. Those who prevailed in these decisions, not those who merely held formal authority positions or those who had a reputation for being powerful, wielded power. Power was a dynamic and testable concept.[36]

Since power is closely linked to ruling in community decisions, a basic question must be, which decisions? Dahl studied urban redevelopment, public education, and political nominations by the two major parties. He selected these issues because of their communitywide implications and because they could be studied over an extended period of time.[37] After specifying these decisions, Dahl reconstructed them through interviews with participants and observers and consulting historical sources such as public documents and newspapers. In addition, one of Dahl's students served in the mayor's office to observe the decision-making process. Dahl gave special attention to leadership roles within each reconstructed decision. The basic criterion was to see who was able "to initiate, modify, veto, or in some visible manner act so as to change outcomes of selected community decisions."[38] Then, after such decisional reconstruction, Dahl tested various hypotheses about the nature of power in New Haven, refuting many conclusions found in earlier community studies.

The decisional approach, like the others, has its critics. Some question the basic assumption that power can be perceived only in the operation of making decisions. They contend that those who set the agenda or who prevent matters from being heard or acted upon exert power.[39] Others question the salience of the preselected decisions to the general community or its leadership and doubt the basic criteria for the selection of decisions.[40] Polsby's defense of Dahl's selection process attempts to answer the latter criticism, but the debate over the other caveats—especially the issue of nondecisions—is far from settled.

The Resources Method

The resources method is based on the premise that those monopolizing scarce resources in a society have a high probability for holding power. Economic and social elites, it is assumed, can convert their socially valued resources into overt political power at will. Recognizing that the boundaries of the political system extend beyond the formal positional method, adherents of the resources approach stress that power can be exercised by direct control of political institutions or by indirect domination through pliable officials. The resources method collapses the political, economic, and social realms and treats the amalgam as a whole. In the same way, positional studies sometimes implicitly combine the positional and resources methods. This overlap is demonstrated by several major works.

Mills in *The Power Elite* found that the military and the corporate executives were able to convert their resources and dominate the decisions of government. Robert and Helen Lynd in their *Middletown* study probed the domination of local affairs by the business community. William Lloyd Warner's Yankee City series showed the control of the status elite in community affairs. E. Digby Baltzell's *Philadelphia Gentlemen* used the social register to show how the cultural elite eschewed direct positional participation but dominated the business and social environs and consequently functioned as the dominant ruling class.[41]

Unfortunately, the resources method assumes more than it can prove. Nelson Polsby convincingly disputed the Lynds' contention that the business elite controlled Middletown in its own interest,[42] and he successfully challenged the conclusions of Warner and Baltzell.[43] The major problem is to demonstrate that any elite dominated community affairs at all. Baltzell, for instance, asserted that the social elite held the prominent business and social positions and that they avoided formal contact with government. He concluded that the real power resided not in formal officeholders but in the business cultural elite.[44] This conclusion was derived from a fundamental tautology. Power was nowhere defined in a testable form. Rather than looking at community outcomes, these studies emphasized the assumed conversion of resources. Actual situations where resources were converted, for instance, where an economic elite acted with some unanimity, were not demonstrated; therefore, the essential assumption was never tested and has not been verified.

The resources approach allows greater conceptual breadth than does a pure positional method. It can treat formal position as but one variable in the conversion of scarce resources. Ideally, one could study decisions in terms of competing or overlapping elites that, if extended over time, could demonstrate changes in the distribution of political power among elites. But to accomplish this, less emphasis must be placed on the purported goals of an elite and on the implications of its dominance on the democratic system and more on understanding the actual distribution of power and its complex operations.

The Sociometric Method

The sociometric method is a recent addition to the literature. It is designed to combine the strengths of both the decisional and reputational approaches and to augment them with an open-ended, or "snowballing," sampling procedure. Originated by Charles Kadushin and elaborated upon by Lee Benson, this approach begins with compilation of lists of allegedly powerful persons followed by exploration of the underlying social network surrounding community leaders. Kadushin views leadership as the product of interaction, where power and influence are similar, so that determination of a leader's social circles will expose patterns of community process. Such a "snowballing" method, following linkages until they end rather than adhering to any arbitrary cutoff, is an improvement on the decisional and reputational approaches. This method has not been utilized in a formal study to date; its promise is as yet unfulfilled.[45]

Several social scientists have begun to question the wisdom of following only one of these approaches. Based on the tentative conclusions of an examination of thirty-three community studies, John Walton made a telling criticism of those using a single methodology: "The type of power structure identified by studies that rely on a single method may well be an artifact of that method."[46] One response to this problem has been the adoption of research strategies employing several methods.

Linton C. Freeman and his associates used four different approaches in their study of Syracuse and compared the results of each. Their conclusion reinforces Walton's disclaimer:

> The various differing approaches to the study of community leadership seem to uncover different types of leaders. The study of reputation, position or organizational participation seems to get at the Institutional Leaders. Studies of participation in decision making, on the other hand, tap the Effectors of community action. And studies of social activity seem to seek out the Activists who gain entry by dint of sheer commitment, time, and energy.[47]

Robert Presthus operationalized this research strategy in his book *Men at the Top*. He studied power in two communities, using a combination of the decisional and the reputational methods. He was consciously responsive to the criticisms of the decisional method, especially on the topics of issue salience and choice of decisions, and one objective was to create an index of power by which members of the decisional elite could be ranked in order of participation in decision making. Presthus asserted that a pure decisional approach identified the second-level leaders, or legmen, so that a reputational panel would be required to redress the imbalance. He felt that the combination of these methods was mutually supportive and demonstrated all aspects of community leadership.[48]

The temper of the argument between the proponents of the reputational and decisional methods has cooled, and contemporary social scientists continue to use these models singly or in conjunction with one another. Dahl's insistence on studying power directly has forced modification of reputational designs, although his own research procedure actually was based on the reputation for leadership within a decisional context. Power and leadership are the key concepts, and in the following section they will be integrated into a research design appropriate to historical sources.

Selection of the Method

The choice of an appropriate method is complicated by two major consider-ations. First, can methods developed for modern analysis be employed in a historical context? Second, does the imperfect nature of historical sources pre-clude their use in a systematic study? Social scientists use historical records, namely, newspapers and public documents, to study leadership roles, and these same works often analyze events in the recent extended past. Social scientists also consult contemporary public records to establish the social characteristics of the resulting elite.[49] They have the advantage, which the historian does not have, of the opportunity to generate new responses through interviews.[50] Noth-ing intrinsic to a past historical context precludes utilization of an appropriate modern method; however, the imperfection of the historical records may influ-ence the question of appropriateness. Obviously, some records were never kept, others are incomplete or have been edited in an effort to protect a public reputa-tion, and some correspondence collections have been destroyed.[51] In addition, newspaper runs are often incomplete and some have not survived at all.

Based upon the type and quality of the surviving Maryland records, and considering the least distorting method to identify individuals as demonstrable community leaders, this study has employed the decisional method. A decisional elite was assembled by examining important community decisions and ascertain-ing leadership roles. In this way, leaders were distinguished from other members of the community. Predicated on my evaluation of the importance of contempo-rary issues and measured against the criteria suggested by Nelson W. Polsby, the following decisions form the core of the analysis: political recruitment to elective office; activity relating to internal improvements; activity relating to political reform; and the allocation of political patronage.[52] Leadership roles in these decisional situations were investigated, scored, and ranked so that a decisional elite could be assembled for each community at two separate points in time.

The specific issues require elaboration. Political recruitment is the central activity of any persisting political system. The ways leaders are recruited to political office reflect the patterns of social and political organization in a com-munity. In the context of the period, the internal improvements issue was impor-tant because it involved concerted community action designed to influence the legislature in its allocation of state resources. There were at least two levels of activity: on the community level, leaders worked to organize local support and to marshal influence; on the legislative level, local representatives and lobbyists worked to protect community interests. Similarly, the issue of political reform generated community action. This issue centered on a more equitable distribu-tion of political power in state and local government. Its major components were the expansion of the franchise and the reallocation of representation in accor-dance with either population or region. The final decisional situation—patronage —is included to test the proposition that there may have been a covert elite. Patronage by its very nature is a system of private influence. Through an exami-nation of patronage on the local, state, and federal levels, we can identify those who made decisions and perceive whether private influentials differed from public leaders.

A decisional leader is defined in this study as one who participated in the decisional process with a demonstrable impact. The role played by the leader may be converted into a quantitative approximation of the power he exerted at whatever level in the decisional process he participated. "Impact" is used to differentiate between political participation and leadership, as well as to structure leadership itself. Leadership may be characterized as direct domination or domination through influence. Influence is a concept relating to extraorganizational impact. That is, someone outside the formal boundaries of the decision-making apparatus may have impact on a decision by appealing to or undercutting the titular leader.

The most reasonable way to differentiate between the various stages of decision making in such issue areas is a simple scoring method. Participation in decisional process should be scored to inflate the position of those who asserted leadership in important decisions over those involved in less important decisions; leadership in the various stages should be scored to differentiate an individual's power within decisions between administrative and authoritative leadership. The combination of scores ought to afford a ranking across all decisions and allow comparison of community decision makers across communities. Such ranking may be subjective and in need of revision, but the basic concept of scoring and scaling leaders in an empirical and logical manner is important to historical research.

Within various community organizational activities, such as political nomination conventions, clear positional leadership hierarchies existed. That is, a chairman of a meeting had more power than a secretary, the secretary more power than a delegate. The possibility that power may have been exerted behind the scenes existed, but public and private evidence was available to make independent evaluations. This system must also weigh the probable impact of the organizational activity. A presidential nomination convention was clearly more important, in the sense that it affected more people, than nominations for the state legislature. Nonetheless, local preconvention meetings called to send delegates to every convention represented the same electoral base and are scored identically. Such gradation between local, county, district, and state meetings should be judged systematically in terms of impact. Table A1.1 presents a rough scoring system that I developed to delineate leadership roles in partisan activities in this study.

Such a scoring method must be considered arbitrary and experimental.[53] The first goal must be to differentiate between leaders and participants in organizational activities. Delegates should be scored to indicate participation, but such scoring must avoid the suggestion that participation in itself represented power. The chairman was scored the highest, then the vice-chairman, followed by the secretary; each of these roles was powerful and they are discussed separately. A second goal in this scoring procedure must be to place stress on the different levels of activity. Some activities were primarily local; others involved conven-

Table A1.1. Scoring

	Ward- District Local	County- City Level	Congressional- Presidential District	State- National
Chairman	5	10	15	20
Vice-chairman	4	8	12	16
Secretary	3	6	9	12
Delegate	1	2	3	4

tions or nominations for Congress or the presidency. To account for the variety of activities, the scoring procedure for these similar roles accounts for the impact of the organizational activity.

Another judgment must be made to discriminate between nomination conventions and local organizational support meetings. Preconvention meetings or postconvention ratification assemblies were important indicators of local leadership, but they ought to be scored to represent local impact regardless of whether they were organized for the lower house of the state assembly or for the presidential elector. Roles in actual conventions are scored to reflect the relative impact of the nomination on the political system.

Among the officers of the meeting, the chairman exhibited the greatest power. He frequently appointed the committees of the meeting, and he often appointed the delegates to the next convention. There are suggestions that some chairmen were selected as unifying symbols of respect or past greatness, which implies that the manipulators had greater power than the chairmen who were appointed. But there are far more examples of chairmen with real operational power, so that such examples do not undermine my confidence in the method.

The power of the vice-chairman was less precise. In many instances, it was a role utilized in multidistrict conventions to acknowledge leadership within delegations. The position lacked clear lines of responsibility and was apparently a tribute to party prestige and regional balance.

The secretary of the meeting was an important component in party organization and communication. Younger men were often brought into the party leadership strata through this role. The chairman and the secretary often acted as local party organizers throughout the entire campaign.

Service as a delegate was not necessarily a mark of power. It did represent, however, continuing political participation, which was important in the transition between political organization and actual nomination. Furthermore, as the conventions became more important, especially state and national conventions, delegates were commonly drawn from a leadership pool of local leaders or members of the positional elite. Therefore, leaders are scored when they were sent as delegates to conventions.

So far this procedure essentially followed in a historical context Dahl's method of emphasizing a decisional situation. Although Dahl maintained that the decisional method was uncontaminated by the positional or reputational methods, and in fact was a corrective for both, his reconstruction procedure borrowed from each. Decisions were emphasized, but specific roles were determined by position and reputation for leadership within decisions. Because there are no adequate sources to evaluate systematically reputation for leadership within decisions, this study emphasizes the demonstrable and potential power of formal positional roles. Besides the organizational roles already specified, the activities of party editors and members of central committees are scored.

Central committees played an important role in the new party system. They oversaw local party organization, sponsored and disseminated party campaign literature, and called for conventions.[54] They also served as correspondents to other party organizers beyond the immediate district. Members of the central committees were active organizers.

Newspaper editors performed an essential function in all party organizational activities. Where there was no central committee, the newspaper frequently called for meetings and conventions. To acknowledge the potential power of editors and central committee members, both are scored as organizational leaders.[55]

This combined decisional-positional method is used to structure leadership roles during the first and second party periods. In addition to ranking political leadership roles, it is applied to individuals working on behalf of internal improvements and political reform. Rather than focus on a single year, this study emphasizes leadership patterns for the whole era.

The problem remains to devise operations to unify these elites into a final community decisional elite for each period. Strata demarcations within the leadership tables are used as a basis for the division between leaders who had a persistent power and those who interacted infrequently. Because all leadership roles were scored and analyzed, individuals who exerted the most power need to be separated from those without persistent power. Leaders who were in the first two strata in the leadership tables and those who had patronage power constitute the core of the final community decisional elite. Leaders who fell into the bottom strata are used for the party comparison, but they have been excluded from the final decisional elite.

Such a procedure has obvious imperfections. Strata demarcations were themselves subjective, and internal stratification levels for the several communities examined were different. Because the selection of strata levels may have been arbitrary, I have combined the first two strata of leaders as the core to assure inclusion of all members of the top elite. Variation occurred among strata levels because all organizational situations were scored impartially. Since there were fewer alternate community decisions over the whole span of time than there were annual political events, the scoring ceiling of the alternate decisions was lower. In an attempt to minimize the possibility that some leaders actually may have been underscored in alternate community decisions, I have added those individuals from the third stratum who participated in more than one activity to the core of community leaders.

A decisional elite, therefore, was assembled for each community from a systematic examination of leadership roles in important decisional contexts. The decisional elite represents an aggregation of individuals with demonstrable community power.

The Concept of Strategic Elites

The identification of a decisional elite represents the isolation of powerful men, but it reveals little about the distribution of power within a community. In deference to criticism of single-method studies and in an effort to identify groups with a high potential for power, several strategic elites were assembled for each community. These strategic elites serve as frames of reference to probe how widely power was shared among different resource groups within each community.[56]

Three strategic elites were isolated for each community. In the period under study, three resources might form the nucleus of interest groups: (1) landed wealth; (2) access to or control over liquid capital; and (3) political position. In the first category, a propertied elite was formed for each community using the manuscript tax records to identify and rank men holding the most real property. For the second category, a commercial elite was assembled from the recurring directors and officers of a community's banking and insurance companies. The creation of a commercial elite was motivated by two considerations: first, directors and officers of such institutions should have been among the community's most dynamic entrepreneurs who would be involved in community development; and second, since tax records emphasize types of landed wealth, but rarely take into account investment or nonlanded capital accumulations, such an elite would probably represent that segment of the community either using or having greater interest in liquid capital. The last category is self-explanatory. A positional elite was gathered from all members of the legislative and executive branches of the local, state, and federal governments. In this context, rather than assuming that they are powerful, men in positions of political authority were treated as a resource group.

An essential difference between the decisional elite and the strategic elites should be emphasized. Members of the decisional elite are leaders with demonstrated power. Members of the strategic elites are men with a resource. It would also be a mistake to assume that any of these elites necessarily represented a cohesive social group. Comparing membership in such elites and looking for social, cultural, or political patterns may indicate that they constituted more than amorphous community associations. Indeed, the emergence of meaningful associations should provide a key to understanding the distribution of power and influence on the community level.

Collective Biography

Once an elite is identified, yet another problem must be confronted: which individual characteristics should be selected for analysis? A historian might an-

swer, with some frustration, "anything you can find." But since social characteristics are perceived as being linked to behavior, the assumptions underlying
collective biography, or prosopography, should be examined.

Historians have long employed collective biography to examine the origins
of political leadership groups, as have social scientists in a modern context, yet
the results have been inconclusive.[57] After reviewing such studies, one political scientist observed, "Their information is frequently left unstructured [and]
the absence of a theoretical framework leaves the reader wondering about the
significance of it all."[58]

Several efforts have been made to structure data collection for collective
biographies in more meaningful ways. Lawrence Stone warns against treating
elite members as if they were "homoeconomicus" and advises researchers to "ask
a set of uniform questions—about birth and death, marriage and family, social
origins and inherited economic position, place of residence, education, amount
and source of personal wealth, occupation, religion, experience in office, and so
on."[59] Some social scientists working with contemporary survey data are trying
to use background variables as predictors of behavior.[60] But to date no formal
model has been proposed attaching specific characteristics to behavior.

Recognizing the limitations inherent in collective biography, we must still
decide which attributes to collect systematically. They fall into three general
categories: social, economic, and political. The social variables are birthplace,
age, marriage, and family patterns. Ethnicity and religious variables were also
collected. The economic variables are the type and quantity of wealth, slaveownership, and occupation. The political variables, determined by available
voting records as well as public and private political activity, identify party
preference, level and type of activity, and patterns of officeholding. Such data
were collected on the individual level, punched into computer cards, and then
aggregated by membership in the various community elites.

The sources used to determine individual biographical information warrant
elucidation. Unfortunately, such information is not always accurate or reliable,
and it must be assembled with caution. This is because linkages are made on the
basis of surname association. Individuals sharing the same name, whether the
same person, kin, or strangers, must be disentangled from one another.

The determination of social characteristics is often the most elusive and the
most prone to error. Birth, marital, family, and death information was gleaned
from printed sources, manuscript religious records, and the Dielman-Hayward
file at the Maryland Historical Society. Ethnicity was based on birth information
or from the categorization of names in the first party era based on the 1790
census.[61] Religion was ascribed with some caution. If a person were a communi-
cant, a church officer, a pew holder, or buried in a denominational cemetery,
his religious identification was considered reliable. If only baptismal or marital references survived, that affiliation was coded but considered less reliable.
Other socially important information, such as militia or government service, was
gleaned from appropriate public records.

Economic information may be found in several sources. Local tax records
provide excellent individual-level economic data. Such manuscript records in-

dicate a person's real and personal property, including slaveholding.[62] Although examination of the tax laws reveals that not everything was taxed and that most items were undervalued, this comprehensive period record reveals an individual's relative position within the community. In some instances, where slaveholding was not indicated, material from the 1800 federal census and the 1798 federal direct tax were used as a surrogate record.[63] City directories indicate occupations for urban dwellers, but there is no comparable source for rural residents. An examination of newspaper advertisements to determine rural occupations yielded only marginal results.

The identification of political preferences came from several sources. Individual roles in all party activities were coded and entered on computer cards.[64] These activities were found in the press, private correspondence, and from broadsides. In addition, poll-book voting records from Baltimore and Frederick counties in the first party era helped to specify a person's party affiliation.

In Retrospect

The basic goal of this project is to ask new questions about old problems and to do so in a reasonable and systematic manner. Historical studies generally suffer from conceptual and methodological imprecision, with the consequence that the resulting analysis is unreliable. This is not to say that historians ask unimportant or meaningless questions. Far from it. The problem is that they ask too many questions without structuring them so that they may be tested and verified. This study is a modest attempt to redirect the ways historians research and interpret their data through the introduction of an explicit research design employing systematic and purposeful data collection and analysis.

Appendix II

Population Tables

Table A2.1. Population Distribution, 1790–1850 (by region*)

	1790	1800	1810	1820	1830	1840	1850
Total							
Eastern Shore	107,639	105,532	117,121	121,709	119,472	117,331	128,504
Southern Maryland	106,754	97,882	106,281	101,328	108,713	103,003	109,308
Western Maryland	91,832	92,062	110,589	121,575	128,276	147,372	176,168
Baltimore City	13,503	26,114	35,583	62,738	80,620	102,313	169,054
Total	319,728	321,530	369,574	407,350	437,081	470,019	583,034
White							
Eastern Shore	65,141	62,675	67,751	70,197	69,589	70,353	77,737
Southern Maryland	55,893	46,201	45,877	46,757	50,337	46,896	50,396
Western Maryland	75,685	74,677	85,377	94,693	100,099	119,808	149,144
Baltimore City	11,925	20,900	27,925	45,602	61,720	81,147	140,666
Total	208,644	204,453	226,930	257,849	281,745	318,204	417,943
Slave							
Eastern Shore	38,591	36,130	35,929	35,312	30,698	25,629	25,997
Southern Maryland	48,711	47,651	50,826	47,016	48,589	44,945	47,785
Western Maryland	14,479	14,616	20,075	20,733	19,201	15,964	13,640
Baltimore City	1,255	2,843	3,714	4,427	4,120	3,199	2,946
Total	103,036	101,240	110,554	107,488	102,608	89,737	90,368
Free Black							
Eastern Shore	3,907	8,777	13,441	15,700	19,185	21,349	24,770
Southern Maryland	2,150	3,970	9,578	7,555	9,787	11,162	11,127

Table A2.1. (cont.)

	1790	1800	1810	1820	1830	1840	1850
Western							
Maryland	1,668	2,751	5,137	6,149	8,976	11,600	13,384
Baltimore City	323	3,771	3,996	10,047	14,790	17,967	25,442
Total	8,048	19,269	32,152	39,451	52,738	62,078	74,723

*Regions: Maryland counties were divided as follows: Eastern Shore: Cecil, Dorchester, Kent, Queen Annes, Somerset, Talbot, and Worcester counties; Southern Maryland: Anne Arundel, Calvert, Charles, Montgomery, Prince Georges, and St. Marys counties; Western Maryland: Allegany, Baltimore, Carroll, Frederick, Harford, and Washington counties; Baltimore City (Baltimore City is a separate unit).

Sources: U.S. Bureau of the Census, *First Census of the U.S., 1790*, p. 47; *Second Census of the U.S., 1800*, n.p.; *Third Census of the U.S., 1810*, p. 53; *Fourth Census of the U.S., 1820*, pp. 20–24; *Fifth Census of the U.S., 1830*, pp. 80–83; *Sixth Census of the U.S., 1840*, pp. 144–45; *Seventh Census of the U.S., 1850*, p. 220.

Table A2.2. Population Distribution and Relative Growth, 1790–1850
(percent by region)

	1790		1800		1810		1820	
	Dist.	Growth	Dist.	Growth	Dist.	Growth	Dist.	Growth
Total								
Eastern Shore	34		33	−2.0	32	11.0	30	3.9
Southern Maryland	33		30	−8.4	29	8.6	25	−4.7
Western Maryland	29		29	.25	30	20.1	30	9.9
Baltimore City	4		8	93.4	10	36.2	15	76.3
Net Increase				.56		14.9		10.2
White								
Eastern Shore	31		31	−3.8	30	8.1	27	4.5
Southern Maryland	27		23	−17.3	20	−.7	18	1.9
Western Maryland	36		37	−1.3	38	14.3	37	10.9
Baltimore City	6		10	75.2	12	33.6	18	63.3
Net Increase				−2.0		11		13.6
Slave								
Eastern Shore	38		36	−6.4	32	−.55	33	−1.7
Southern Maryland	47		47	−2.2	46	6.6	44	−7.5
Western Maryland	14		14	.95	18	37.3	19	3.2
Baltimore City	1		3	127.0	3	30.6	4	19.2
Net Increase				−1.7		9.2		−2.8
Free black								
Eastern Shore	49		46	125	42	53.1	40	16.8
Southern Maryland	27		21	84.6	30	141	19	−21.1
Western Maryland	21		14	64.9	16	36.7	16	19.7
Baltimore City	4		20	1,067	12	6.0	25	151.4
Net Increase				139		66.9		22.7

1830		1840		1850	
Dist.	*Growth*	*Dist.*	*Growth*	*Dist.*	*Growth*
27	−1.8	25	−1.8	22	9.5
25	7.3	22	−5.3	19	6.1
29	5.5	31	14.9	30	19.5
18	28.5	22	26.9	29	65.2
	7.3		7.5		24
25	−1.7	22	1.1	19	10.5
18	7.6	15	−6.8	12	7.5 ·
36	5.7	38	19.7	36	24.5
22	35.3	26	31.5	34	73.5
	9.3		12.9		31.3
30	−13.1	29	−16.5	29	1.4
47	3.3	50	−7.5	53	6.3
19	−7.4	18	−16.9	15	−14.6
4	−6.9	3	−22.4	3	−7.9
	−4.5		−12.5		.70
36	22.2	34	11.3	33	16.0
19	29.5	18	14.0	15	−.31
17	46.0	19	29.2	18	15.4
28	47.2	29	21.5	34	41.6
	33.7		17.7		20.4

Appendix III

Tabular Listing of Maryland Elites,
by County and Elite

Abbreviations:

AJ	Anti-Jackson
CC	County Commissioner
CCt	County Court
CE	Commercial Elite
d.m.	Daughter married
DE	Decisional Elite
DW	Known address in city
EC	Maryland Executive Council
F	Federalist
FB	First Branch, City Council
HD	Maryland House of Delegates
J	Jackson
LC	Levy Court
m	Married
m.d.	Married daughter of
min.	Assigned minimum value for tax record
OCt	Orphans Court
PE	Positional Elite
R	Republican
SB	Second Branch, City Council
TE	Propertied Elite

Table A3.1. Baltimore City, Commercial Elite, First Party Era

Name, Birthplace, Dates, Occupation(s)	Party	Acres	Lots	Slaves	Value (£)	Comments
Baker, William (ca. 1747–1815) Merchant				yes	1,045	Episcopalian; CE
Barry, James						CE, TE; see Table A3.4
Betts, Solomon (d. 1841) Merchant					234	Episcopalian; new resident between 1783 and 1793; d. m. Jacob G. Davies, future mayor; CE
Brown, Aquilla, Jr. Counting house	F				min.	Father member of TE; m.d. consul general for Genoa; CE
Brown, John Potter					876	Presbyterian; militia officer; CE
Brown, Stewart Ireland (1768–1832) Merchant				yes	70	Presbyterian; Hibernian Society; new resident between 1783 and 1793; CE
Buchanan, James A.						CE, TE; see Table A3.4
Calhoun, James						CE, DE, PE, TE; see Table A3.2
Campbell, Archibald						CE, TE; see Table A3.4
Carey, James						CE, PE, TE; see Table A3.3
Carrere, John						CE, TE; see Table A3.4
Carruthers, John Merchant					260	CE
Caton, Richard						CE, DE; see Table A3.2
Chase, Thorndick						CE, PE; see Table A3.3
Clarke, James						CE, TE; see Table A3.4
Cole, William Merchant					660	Episcopalian; CE
Comegys, Benjamin Kent Co. (d. 1809) Merchant				yes	129	Brother of John Comegys; CE
Comegys, John Kent Co. (d. 1814) Merchant					min.	CE
Cooke, William						CE, PE; see Table A3.3
Curson, Richard, Jr. (ca. 1763–1808) Merchant, Counting house				yes	839	Episcopalian; new resident 1778; CE

Table A3.1. Baltimore City, Commercial Elite, First Party Era *(cont.)*

Name, Birthplace, Dates, Occupation(s)	Party	Acres	Lots	Slaves	Value (£)	Comments
Dall, James (ca. 1754–1808) Merchant			yes		1,190	M. as Episcopalian; CE
Diffenderffer, Michael						CE, PE, TE; see Table A3.3
Duguid, William Merchant					min.	CE
Ellicott, Elias						CE, DE; see Table A3.2
Etting, Solomon						CE, DE, TE; see Table A3.2
Fonerden, Adam						CE, DE, PE; see Table A3.2
Frick, Peter						CE, DE, PE; see Table A3.2
Garts, Charles						CE, TE; see Table A3.4
Ghequiere, Charles						CE, TE; see Table A3.4
Gilmore, Robert						CE, PE, TE; see Table A3.3
Gittings, Richard (ca. 1763–1830) DW			yes		1,075	Presbyterian; m. into Sterett family; militia officer; CE
Goldthwait, Samuel (ca. 1733–1806) China and glass store			yes		586	Episcopalian; CE
Grundy, George England (1756–1825) Merchant			yes		914	Episcopalian; business partner, William Gibson (TE); new resident 1783; CE
Hagerty, John Stationer					1,165	Methodist; CE
Hawkins, William						CE, PE, TE; see Table A3.3
Hillen, John						CE, PE; see Table A3.3
Hindman, William Talbot Co. (ca. 1741–1830)	F		yes	min.		Resident of Talbot County; CE
Hoffman, Peter						CE, DE, PE; see Table A3.2
Hollingsworth, Samuel Cecil Co. (ca. 1757–1830) Merchant	F		yes		354	Episcopalian; Rev. service; militia captain; for family, see Table A3.2; CE
Hollins, John						CE, TE; see Table A3.4

Table A3.1. (*cont.*)

Name, Birthplace, Dates, Occupation(s)	Party	Acres	Lots	Slaves	Value (£)	Comments
Howard, John Eager						CE, DE, PE, TE; see Table A3.2
Jessop, William						CE, PE; see Table A3.3
Johnson, Edward						CE, PE; see Table A3.3
Johnston, Christopher Scotland (ca. 1751–1819) Merchant	F			yes	1,070	Presbyterian; Rev. soldier; new resident 1766; CE
Kent, Emanuel						CE, PE; see Table A3.3
Lawson, Richard						CE, PE; see Table A3.3
Lorman, William						CE, PE, TE; see Table A3.3
McCreery, William						CE, PE; see Table A3.3
McCandless, Robert Merchant					184	Presbyterian; CE
McDonald, Alexander (ca. 1773–1836) Merchant					720	Presbyterian; CE
McElderry, Thomas						CE, DE, PE, TE; see Table A3.2
McFadon, John						CE, TE; see Table A3.4
McKim, Alexander						CE, DE; see Table A3.2
McKim, Isaac Balt. (1775–1838) Merchant	R				min.	Episcopalian; son of John McKim, nephew of Alexander McKim, m.d. William Hollins; CE
Matthews, William P. (ca. 1752–1819) Merchant, Counting house	F			yes	1,050	militia captain; CE
Moncrieff, Archibald (d. 1803) DW				yes	136	Episcopalian; CE
Mosher, James						CE, DE; see Table A3.2
Nichols, Henry						CE, PE, TE; see Table A3.3
Norris, William (ca. 1774–1833) Flour merchant				yes	min.	Union Fire Co.; CE
O'Donnell, John						CE, DE, TE see Table A3.2

Table A3.1. Baltimore City, Commercial Elite, First Party Era *(cont.)*

Name, Birthplace, Dates, Occupation(s)	Party	Acres	Lots	Slaves	Value (£)	Comments
Oliver, John Ireland (d. 1823) Merchant					min.	Presbyterian; brother of Robert Oliver (CE, DE, TE); new resident 1790; CE
Oliver, Robert						CE, DE, TE; see Table A3.2
Pascault, Lewis						CE, TE; see Table A3.4
Patterson, William						CE, TE; see Table A3.4
Payson, Henry						CE, PE; see Table A3.3
Pleasants, John Pemberton (ca. 1757–1825) Merchant				yes	285	Episcopalian; new resident between 1783 and 1793; CE
Poultney, Thomas (ca. 1761–1828) Ironmonger, merchant					527	Quaker, linked to Ellicotts; CE
Pringle, Mark						CE, PE; see Table A3.3
Ridgely, Charles of Hampton						CE, PE, TE; see Table A3.3
Salmon, George						CE, DE, TE; see Table A3.2
Schaeffer, Balzer						CE, PE, TE; see Table A3.3
Sears, George						CE, DE, TE; see Table A3.2
Sherlock, John England (d. 1813) Merchant				yes	630	CE
Shields, David (ca. 1737–1811) Hatter	R				374	Presbyterian; CE
Smith, Samuel						CE, DE, PE, TE; see Table A3.2
Smith, Thorowgood						*CE, DE, PE, TE; see Table A3.2*
Somerville, James (ca. 1745–1806) Merchant					976	Presbyterian; CE
Steele, John (ca. 1738–1809) Merchant	R			yes	1,010	Episcopalian; m. Nancy Payson; Republican Society; CE

Table A3.1. (*cont.*)

Name, Birthplace, Dates, Occupation(s)	Party	Acres	Lots	Slaves	Value (£)	Comments
Sterett, Joseph Pa.					1,200	Episcopalian; active in Rev.; militia officer; new resident 1760; CE
Stewart, David						CE, DE, PE, TE; see Table A3.2
Stouffer, Henry						CE, PE; see Table A3.3
Stricker, John						CE, DE, PE, TE; see Table A3.2
Stump, John						CE, TE; see Table A3.4
Swann, John						CE, DE; see Table A3.2
Tenant, Thomas						CE, PE; see Table A3.3
Thompson, Henry England (1774–1837)					min.	Episcopalian; m.d. Daniel Bowley; CE
Thompson, Hugh						CE, TE; see Table A3.4
Thornburgh, Joseph						CE, TE; see Table A3.4
Tiernan, Luke						CE, PE; see Table A3.3
Tyson, Jesse						CE, DE; see Table A3.2
Tyson, Nathan						CE, TE; see Table A3.4
Valck, Adrian						CE, TE; see Table A3.4
Van Wyck, John (ca. 1748–1817)					min.	CE
Weatherburn, John England (1750–1811) Bank president			yes		85	Episcopalian; Rev. soldier; new resident 1772; CE
West, James (ca. 1769–1809) Merchant			yes		680	CE
Williams, Benjamin (d. 1812) Merchant					197	Presbyterian; CE
Williamson, David						CE, TE; see Table A3.4
Willing, Thomas (d. 1821) Bank president					min.	CE
Wilson, William						CE, DE, PE, TE; see Table A3.2

Table A3.1. Baltimore City, Commercial Elite, First Party Era (*cont.*)

Name, Birthplace, Dates, Occupation(s)	Party	Acres	Lots	Slaves	Value (£)	Comments
Winchester, David Frederick Co. (1769–1835) Merchant	F				min.	Episcopalian; brother of James Winchester (DE); militia officer; CE
Winchester, William Frederick Co. (1750–1812) Merchant	F			yes	81	Episcopalian; father of David and James Winchester; active in Frederick Co. during Rev.; CE
Yellott, Jeremiah						CE, TE; see Table A3.4

Table A3.2. Baltimore City, Decisional Elite, First Party Era

Name, Birthplace, Dates, Occupation(s)	Party	Acres	Lots	Slaves	Value (£)	Comments
Aisquith, Edward (1770–1815)	R				min.	DE, PE
Biays, Joseph (ca. 1752–1820) Gent.	F				500	Presbyterian; militia colonel; d.m. Dr. Joseph Allender (PE); DE, PE
Brown, Matthew U.S. (1778–1831) Editor, Balt. *Federal Gazette*	F				min.	Moved to Baltimore 1796, m.d. Peter Frick; captain Balt. Blues; moved to Fred. Co. 1807; DE
Buchanan, Archibald (d. 1800) Attorney	R				min.	Episcopalian; Rev. activity; Republican Society (1793); militia major; HD; DE, PE
Calhoun, James Pa. (1743–1816) Merchant	R			yes	1,400	Presbyterian; to Balt. 1771; m.d. William Gist, d.m. James A. Buchanan; active Rev.; militia officer; CE, DE, PE, TE
Carroll, Charles of Carrollton Annapolis (1737–1832) Gent.	F			yes	1,900	Catholic; Rev. active; m.d. senator; DE, TE

Table A3.2. (*cont.*)

Name, Birthplace Dates, Occupation(s)	Party	Acres	Lots	Slaves	Value (£)	Comments
Caton, Richard England (1763–1845) Merchant				yes	800	Episcopalian; m.d. Charles Carroll of Carrollton, d.m. Robert Patterson; to Baltimore 1785; CE, DE
Chase, Samuel Somerset Co. (1741–1811) Attorney/U.S. judge	F				100	Episcopalian; Rev. active; to Balt. 1786; Federalist leader; DE
Courtenay, Hercules (ca. 1730–1816) Counting house	F			yes	1,228	Episcopalian; active Rev.; DE, PE, TE
Dixon, Thomas Ireland (d. 1810) Hardware merchant	R				200	Presbyterian; Republican leader; Hibernian Society; DE, PE
Dugan, Cumberland Ireland (1747–1836) Ropemaker, tanner, store	R			yes	4,318	Presbyterian; d.m. into Hollins family; member Vigilant Fire Co.; new resident 1769; DE, PE, TE
Ellicott, Andrew (ca. 1775–1823) Flour merchant	F				min.	Quaker; related to Tysons and Poultneys; DE, PE
Ellicott, Elias (ca. 1758–1826) DW	F				492	Quaker; founder of Ellicott's Mills; CE, DE
Etting, Solomon Pa. (1764–1847) Merchant	F			yes	2,000	Jewish; new resident 1780s; brother, Reuben Etting, U.S. marshal; CE, DE, TE
Fonerden, Adam (ca. 1750–1817) Shoe store, wool-cotton card manufacturer	R				925	Methodist; Pres. Md. Abolitionist Society (1796); CE, DE, TE
Frick, Peter Md. (1743–1827) China, glass store	R				928	Zion Lutheran; new resident 1778; member Md. Abolitionist Society; father of William Frick (Table A3.6); CE, DE, PE
Griest, Isaac	R				min.	Presbyterian; pres. Deptford Hundred; active in Rev.; militia officer; DE

Table A3.2. Baltimore City, Decisional Elite, First Party Era *(cont.)*

Name, Birthplace Dates, Occupation(s)	Party	Acres	Lots	Slaves	Value (£)	Comments
Harper, Robert Goodloe Va. (1765–1825) Attorney	F				min.	M.d. Charles Carroll of Carrollton; moved to Balt. 1799; Federalist party leader, former congressman from S.C.; DE
Hoffman, Peter Germany (ca. 1737–1805) Counting house	R			yes	1,200	Evangelical; new resident 1776; vice-pres. Md. Abolitionist Society (1796); CE, DE, PE
Hollingsworth, Jesse Cecil Co. (1731–1810) Merchant	F			yes	2,300	M. as Methodist; m.d. Jeremiah Yellott (CE, TE); brother of Thomas and Zebulon Hollingsworth; family merchant connections in Cecil Co. and Philadelphia; Balt. Co. HD (1786–87); DE, TE
Howard, John Eager Balt. Co. (1752–1827)	F			yes	3,447	Episcopalian; Rev. officer; member of Cincinnati Society; militia officer; Md. sen., gov., U.S. Senate; Federalist leader; m. into Chew family in Philadelphia; CE, DE, PE, TE
Johonnot, George Timber Merchant	R				min.	Member Md. Abolitionist Society; HD; DE, PE
Johnston, Dr. Thomas Balt. Co. (1766–1831) Doctor					min.	MD U. Pa. (1793); Md. senate (1811); DE
McCulloch, James Hugh (1756–1836) McCulloch and Birckhead, merchants	R			yes	300	Presbyterian; Rev. soldier; moved to Baltimore between 1783 and 1793; militia captain; DE, PE
McElderry, Thomas (d. 1810) Builder	R			yes	2,865	Presbyterian; father of Hugh McElderry; militia captain; vice-president Hibernian Society; moved to Baltimore 1793; Republican party leader; CE, DE, PE, TE

Table A3.2. (*cont.*)

Name, Birthplace, Dates, Occupation(s)	Party	Acres	Lots	Slaves	Value (£)	Comments
McHenry, Dr. James Ireland (1753–1816) Doctor, Secretary of War	F		yes		47	Presbyterian; Federalist party leader; to Baltimore ca. 1771; HD, Md. senate; DE, PE
McKim, Alexander Del. (1748–1832) Robert and Alexander McKim, merchants	R		yes		1,000	Episcopalian; pres. Republican Society; vice-pres. Md. Abolitionist Society; to Baltimore before Rev., officer in Rev.; CE, DE
McMechen, David U.S. (ca. 1754–1810) DW			yes		1,800	Episcopalian; Rev. member Whig Club and Balt. Committee; HD (1779–88); militia officer; DE, PE, TE
Martin, Alexander Mass. (ca. 1777–1810) Editor, Baltimore *American*	R				min.	DE
Martin, Luther N.J. (1748–1826) Attorney, attorney general of Md.	F		yes		min.	Former Anti-Federalist leader; Federalist and legal leader; DE
Mosher, James U.S. (1761–1845) DW	R		yes		900	Presbyterian; Mechanical Fire Co.; militia colonel; Republican party leader; CE, DE
O'Donnell, John (1749–1805) pres. insurance co. DW	F		yes		7,800	Presbyterian; militia colonel; Federalist leader; CE, DE, TE
Oliver, Robert Ireland (ca. 1757–1834) Merchant; partner with Hugh Thompson	F		yes		1,900	Presbyterian; Federalist leader; arrived in Baltimore in 1783; CE, DE, TE
Owings, William (ca. 1767–1825) Flour merchant	F				min.	DE

Table A3.2. Baltimore City, Decisional Elite, First Party Era (*cont.*)

Name, Birthplace Dates, Occupation(s)	Party	Acres	Lots	Slaves	Value (£)	Comments
Pechin, William Pa. (1773–1849) Editor, Baltimore *American*	R				min.	Editor several Baltimore papers; Friendship Fire Co.; arrived in city 1796; DE
Poe, David Ireland (1743–1816)				yes	953	Presbyterian; pres. Mechanical Fire Co.; DE, PE
Prentiss, Charles New Eng. Editor, Baltimore *Republican; Or, Anti-Democrat*	F				min.	DE
Purviance, James Baltimore (1772–1836) Merchant	R			yes	100	Presbyterian; son of Robert Purviance, nephew of Rev. leader Samuel Purviance; CE, DE
Ready, John					min.	Secretary of Carpenter's Society; DE
Salmon, George Ireland (1747–1807) Bank president DW				yes	1,300	Presbyterian; Hibernian Society; new resident 1775; port warden, OCt; CE, DE, TE
Scott, John Kent Co. (d. 1813) Attorney	R				300	Presbyterian; new resident before 1800; DE, PE
Sears, George (d. 1800) Merchant	F			yes	1,300	Sec. Republican Society; d.m. James W. McCulloch, Balt. Co.; CE, DE, TE
Shrim, John captain					420	Sec. Mechanical Society; DE, PE
Smith, Robert Pa. (1758–1842) Attorney; sec. of the navy	R			yes	1,100	Presbyterian; new resident prior to Rev.; son of John Smith, brother of Samuel Smith, m.d. of William Smith; DE, PE

Table A3.2. (*cont.*)

Name, Birthplace Dates, Occupation(s)	Party	Acres	Lots	Slaves	Value (£)	Comments
Smith, Samuel Pa. (1752–1839) Merchant, congressman	R			yes	6,400	Presbyterian; for family connections, see above; Rev. officer, militia general; Republican leader; CE, DE, PE, TE
Smith, Thorowgood Va. (1743–1810) Merchant; mayor	F			yes	1,800	Episcopalian; new resident prior to Rev.; CE, DE, PE, TE
Smith, William Pa. (1728–1814) Merchant	F			yes	3,000	Presbyterian; former congressman; daus m. Robert Smith and Gen. Otho H. Williams; active in Rev.; DE, PE, TE
Stephen, John St. Marys Co. (ca. 1780–1814) Attorney					200	DE, PE
Stewart, David Ireland (1746–1817) DW	F			yes	1,300	Presbyterian; Hibernian Society; CE, DE, PE, TE
Stewart, Robert Scotland (ca. 1745–1826) Stonecutter	R			yes	720	New resident 1766; DE, PE
Stricker, John Frederick Co. (1759–1825) navy agent (1801) DW	R			yes	1,400	Presbyterian; son of Col. George Stricker, Fred. Co. Rev. figure; Rev. officer, militia colonel; Republican Society; CE, DE, PE, TE
Swann, John Scotland (1750–1821) Bank president	F			yes	1,065	Presbyterian; Rev. officer; Federalist leader; CE, DE
Tyson, Jesse Merchant				yes	400	Quaker; related to Ellicotts and Poultneys; CE, DE
Wilson, William Ireland (b. 1750) Shipper	R				1,327	Baptist; new resident 1770; treas. Mechanical Society, fire company; CE, DE, PE, TE

Table A3.2. Baltimore City, Decisional Elite, First Party Era (*cont.*)

Name, Birthplace Dates, Occupation(s)	Party	Acres	Lots	Slaves	Value (£)	Comments
Winchester, James Balt. (1772–1806) Attorney, U.S. judge	F				300	Episcopalian; son of William Winchester (CE); owns property in Fred. Co.; member Republican Society; Federalist candidate; DE, PE

Table A3.3. Baltimore City, Positional Elite, First Party Era

Name, Birthplace Dates, Occupation(s)	Party	Acres	Lots	Slaves	Value (£)	Comments
Aisquith, Edward						HD; DE, PE; see Table A3.2
Allender, Dr. Joseph (ca. 1770–1834) Doctor			yes		265	Episcopalian; m.d. Joseph Biays (PE); FB; PE
Beeman, James (ca. 1771–1808) Ship chandler	R				800	M. as Episcopalian; FB; PE
Biays, Joseph						FB; DE, PE; see Table A3.2
Brown, Josiah	R				388	M. as Presbyterian; FB; PE
Buchanan, Archibald (d. 1800) Attorney	R				min.	Episcopalian; Republican Society; militia major; HD; PE
Buchanan, Dr. George Balt. Co. (1763–1808) Doctor	R				700	Episcopalian; MD U. Pa. (1785); new resident 1789; son of Andrew Buchanan, m.d. Judge McLean, moved to Philadelphia 1806; FB, LC; PE
Buchanan, James Merchant, sugar store	R		yes		820	Episcopalian; Republican Society; FB, mayor; PE
Calhoun, James						FB, SB, mayor; CE, DE, PE, TE; see Table A3.2

Table A3.3. (*cont.*)

Name, Birthplace Dates, Occupation(s)	Party	Acres	Lots	Slaves	Value (£)	Comments
Carey, James (d. 1806) Sup. Md. Insurance Co.				yes	1,743	Episcopalian; m. into Ellicott family; FB, SB; CE, PE, TE
Chase, Thorndick (ca. 1754–1838)	R				min.	Presbyterian; Navy in Rev.; SB; PE
Cooke, William (ca. 1746–1817) Gent.				yes	870	Episcopalian; d.m. Robert Gilmor, Jr.; SB; CE, PE
Coulter, Dr. John Doctor	F			yes	562	Presbyterian; active in Rev.; militia major; FB; PE
Courtenay, Hercules						FB; DE, PE, TE; see Table A3.2
Decker, George (1764–1864) Merchant					420	First German Reformed Congregation; son of Frederick Decker; Liberty Fire Co.; FB; PE
Diffenderffer, Michael (ca. 1744–1809) Merchant	R			yes	2,429	German Reformed Congregation; brother of Peter and Zebulon Diffenderffer; new resident 1778; SB; CE, PE, TE
Dixon, Thomas						HD; DE, PE; see Table A3.2
Dugan, Cumberland						SB, HD; DE, PE, TE; see Table A3.2
Edwards, James Dry goods merchant				yes	1,317	Episcopalian; FB; PE, TE
Ellicott, Andrew						HD; DE, PE; see Table A3.2
Fite, Jacob Merchant				yes	441	Liberty Fire Co.; SB; PE
Frick, Peter						FB; CE, DE, PE; see Table A3.2
Gilmor, Robert Scotland (1742–1822) Merchant	F			yes	1,184	Presbyterian; new resident 1778; son m.d. of William Cooke (PE); SB; CE, PE, TE

Table A3.3. Baltimore City, Positional Elite, First Party Era (cont.)

Name, Birthplace Dates, Occupation(s)	Party	Acres	Lots	Slaves	Value (£)	Comments
Goldsmith, William L. Storekeeper					925	SB, LC; PE
Goodwin, William, Sr.				yes	1,598	Episcopalian; SB; PE, TE
Hawkins, William (1754–1818) Merchant tailor				yes	1,807	Methodist; FB; CE, PE, TE
Herring, Ludwig (ca. 1762–1817) Carpenter	R				192	FB; PE
Hewitt, Caleb Tobacconist				yes	955	Methodist; FB; PE
Hillen, John Md. (1761–1840) Grocery and leather store	R				1,125	Catholic; FB; CE, PE
Hillen, Thomas	R				min.	FB; PE
Hoffman, Peter						FB; DE, PE; see Table A3.2
Hollingsworth, Thomas Cecil Co. Counting house	F			yes	1,962	Episcopalian; for family connections see Jesse Hollingsworth, Table A3.2; FB; PE, TE
Hollingsworth, Zebulon Cecil Co. (1761–1824) Attorney, U.S. attorney	F			yes	1,216	Episcopalian; for family see Jesse Hollingsworth, Table A3.2; FB; PE, TE
Howard, John Eager						Gov., Md. senate, U.S. Senate; CE, DE, PE, TE; see Table A3.2
Inloes, Joshua (ca. 1771–1806) Merchant				yes	446	Militia captain; FB; PE
Jackson, William Skilled laborer	R				723	Episcopalian; SB; PE
Jessop, William (ca. 1754–1829) Merchant				yes	774	Episcopalian; identified as one of first settlers; FB; CE, PE

Table A3.3. *(cont.)*

Name, Birthplace Dates, Occupation(s)	Party	Acres	Lots	Slaves	Value (£)	Comments
Johnson, Edward (1767–1829) Brewer				yes	577	Episcopalian; new resident ca. 1767; Republican Society; SB; CE, PE
Johonnot, George						HD; DE, PE; see Table A3.2
Keeports, George Peter (ca. 1753–1817) Insurance broker	R			yes	640	Presbyterian; Rev. soldier; militia major; FB; PE
Kell, Thomas (ca. 1771–1846) Attorney				yes	111	Episcopalian; FB; PE
Kent, Emanuel (ca. 1759–1818) DW	R				393	Methodist; Mechanical Fire Co.; son, Emanuel Kent, Jr., register of Baltimore until 1835; FB; CE, PE
Lawson, Richard (ca. 1749–1803) Merchant					639	Episcopalian; SB; CE, PE·
Lemmon, Joshua Merchant	R			yes	583	FB; PE
Lorman, William (1764–1841) Merchant					1,891	Episcopalian; new resident 1783; militia; FB; CE, PE, TE
Mackenheimer, John John and Peter Mackenheimer, merchants	R			yes	434	Rev. soldier; militia major; FB; PE
McCannon, James Merchant tailor				yes	2,833	Methodist; FB; PE, TE
McCreery, William Ireland (ca. 1750–1814) Merchant	R			yes	789	Republican Society; SB; CE, PE
McCulloch, James Hugh						HD, Md. senate; DE, PE; see Table A3.2
McElderry, Thomas						Md. senate; CE, DE, PE, TE; See Table A3.2

Table A3.3. Baltimore City, Positional Elite, First Party Era *(cont.)*

Name, Birthplace Dates, Occupation(s)	Party	Acres	Lots	Slaves	Value (£)	Comments
McHenry, Dr. James						HD, Md. senate, sec. war; DE, PE; See Table A3.2
McMechen, David						HD, FB; DE, PE, TE; See Table A3.2
Merryman, John Harford Co. (ca. 1736–1814)				yes	2,817	Episcopalian; new resident 1763; active in Rev.; SB; PE, TE
Miles, Aquilla (ca. 1773–1808)					100	Episcopalian; FB; PE
Miller, Jacob Tanner				yes	100	FB; PE
Miller, John Skilled laborer					200	FB; PE
Moore, Philip (d. 1834) Attorney					55	Episcopalian; SB, FB; PE
Mundell, William House carpenter					200	FB; PE
Myers, Jacob Merchant	R				1,070	Methodist; SB; PE
Nichols, Henry Merchant	F			yes	1,275	Episcopalian; SB; CE, PE, TE
Owings, Samuel (1733–1803) Counting house	F				809	Methodist; FB; PE
Payson, Henry Mass. (1762–1815) Merchant: Payson and Smith				yes	545	Presbyterian (later Unitarian); new resident 1778; SB; CE, PE
Pöe, David						FB; DE, PE; See Table A3.2
Presstman, George DW	R			yes	1,890	Episcopalian; FB, SB; PE, TE
Pringle, Mark (ca. 1751–1819) Merchant, counting house	F			yes	604	Episcopalian; moved to Cecil Co. 1819; SB; CE, PE

Table A3.3. (*cont.*)

Name, Birthplace Dates, Occupation(s)	Party	Acres	Lots	Slaves	Value (£)	Comments
Purviance, James						HD; DE, PE; See Table A3.2
Raborg, Christopher (1750–1815) Cooper, tin manufacturer	R			yes	969	Presbyterian; new resident 1778; FB; PE
Reinicker, George Flour merchant				yes	2,205	New resident 1778; FB; PE, TE
Ridgely, Charles of Hampton Md. (1760–1829) Gent.	F			yes	2,530	Rev. officer; militia general; large estate Balt. Co.; d.m. into Chew family of Philadelphia; Md. senate; CE, PE, TE
Robinson, Ephraim				yes	650	Presbyterian; militia paymaster; FB; PE
Rogers, Nicholas (1753–1822) DW	F			yes	1,789	Episcopalian; militia colonel; SB, OCt, LC; PE, TE
Rutter, Thomas (1761–1817) U.S. marshal, counting house	R				40	Otterbein church; active in Rev.; Republican Society; FB; PE
Schaeffer, Balzer (1757–1838) Dry goods merchant	R			yes	1,798	Otterbein church; new resident 1778; FB; CE, PE, TE
Schaeffer, Frederick	R				901	Methodist; FB; PE
Scott, John						HD; DE, PE; see Table A3.2
Shaw, Archibald Wharf builder					400	Associate Reformed church; FB; PE
Shrim, John						FB; DE, PE; see Table A3.2
Simpson, Walter DW					1,182	Methodist; Union Fire Co.; FB; PE
Sloane, James (ca. 1749–1833) Boot and shoe maker	R			yes	741	Presbyterian; FB; PE

Table A3.3. Baltimore City, Positional Elite, First Party Era (*cont.*)

Name, Birthplace Dates, Occupation(s)	Party	Acres	Lots	Slaves	Value (£)	Comments
Small, Jacob, Jr. Balt. (1772–1851) Builder					217	Episcopalian; son of Jacob Small, Sr., builder; militia officer; FB; PE
Smith, Job (ca. 1755–1831) Baker				yes	657	Methodist; militia officer; SB, FB; PE
Smith, Robert						HD, FB, sec. navy; DE, PE; see Table A3.2
Smith, Samuel						U.S. Congress; CE, DE, PE, TE; see Table A3.2
Smith, Thorowgood						Mayor; CE, DE, PE, TE; see Table A3.2
Smith, William						Md. senate; DE, PE, TE; see Table A3.2
Stephen, John						HD, Md. senate (1814), judge (1821); DE, PE; see Table A3.2
Stewart, David						SB; CE, DE, PE, TE; see Table A3.2
Stewart, Richardson Nail manufacturer				yes	505	Episcopalian; FB; PE
Stewart, Robert						FB, HD; DE, PE; see Table A3.2
Stouffer, Henry Pa. (1762–1835) Merchant					min.	New resident 1784; FB; CE, PE
Stricker, John						FB; CE, DE, PE, TE; see Table A3.2
Sutton, Isaac Shipbuilder	R			yes	444	Methodist; FB; PE
Tenant, Thomas (ca. 1767–1836) Merchant				yes	880	Episcopalian; new resident between 1783 and 1793; d.m. John Nelson (Fred. Co.); militia officer; FB; CE, PE
Tiernan, Luke Ireland (1757–1839) Merchant	R			yes	946	Catholic; new resident 1795; Hibernian Society; Union Fire Co.; FB; CE, PE

Table A3.3. *(cont.)*

Name, Birthplace Dates, Occupation(s)	Party	Acres	Lots	Slaves	Value (£)	Comments
Trimble, William Merchant					1,468	Presbyterian; Deptford Fire Co.; FB; PE, TE
Warfield, George F. Flour merchant				yes	300	Episcopalian; FB; PE
Wilson, William						HD; CE, DE, PE, TE; see Table A3.2
Winchester, James						HD; DE, PE; see Table A3.2

Table A3.4. Baltimore City, Propertied Elite, First Party Era

Name, Birthplace Dates, Occupation(s)	Party	Acres	Lots	Slaves	Value (£)	Comments
Barry, James Counting house	F				2,619	Paymaster 6th Regt.; CE, TE (rank no. 022)
Barton, Seth Merchant				yes	2,823	Episcopalian; TE (016)
Bentalou, Paul France (1735–1826) Counting house	R				2,085	Presbyterian; new resident ca. 1765; m.d. Jacob Keeports; militia officer; TE (038)
Brown, Aquila Merchant				yes	2,722	M. as Episcopalian; son, A. Brown, Jr., in CE; TE (020)
Bryden, James (ca. 1770–1820) Innkeeper				yes	1,802	Presbyterian; militia officer; TE (053)
Buchanan, Andrew (d. 1811) Counting house	R			yes	2,021	Episcopalian; son of George Buchanan, see Table A2.3; militia major; Vigilant Fire Co.; TE (041)
Buchanan, James A. Md. (1768–1840) Merchant	R			yes	2,057	Presbyterian; m.d. James Calhoun (see Table A3.2); partnership with Samuel Smith (ibid.); TE (039)
Calhoun, James						CE, DE, PE, TE (080); see Table A3.2

Table A3.4. Baltimore City, Propertied Elite, First Party Era *(cont.)*

Name, Birthplace Dates, Occupation(s)	Party	Acres	Lots	Slaves	Value (£)	Comments
Campbell, Archibald (ca. 1747–1805) Counting house	F			yes	1,700	Episcopalian/Methodist; former navy agent; CE, TE (059)
Carey, James						PE, TE (057); see Table A3.3
Carrere, John France (1759–1841) Merchant, counting house					1,705	Catholic; new resident 1796; m.d. Robert Walsh (TE); CE, TE (058)
Carroll, Charles of Carrollton						DE, TE (049); see Table A3.2
Clarke, James (ca. 1734–1814) Merchant					1,620	Episcopalian; CE, TE (064)
Colvin, Richard (d. 1830) Storekeeper	R			yes	1,348	Methodist; father of John B. Colvin, see Table A3.9; TE (083)
Courtenay, Hercules						DE, PE, TE (098); see Table A3.2
Davey, Alexander W. Merchant				yes	2,011	Episcopalian; TE (042)
Deedy, Daniel					2,205	TE (035)
Diffenderffer, Michael						CE, PE, TE (026); see Table A3.3
Diffenderffer, Peter Hardware merchant	R			yes	1,420	First German Reformed church; brother of Michael and Zebulon Diffenderffer; TE (078)
Ducheran, Francis (ca. 1758–1818) DW					1,430	Catholic; TE (077)
Dugan, Cumberland						DE, PE, TE (006); see Table A3.2
Edwards, James						PE, TE (089); see Table A3.3
Etting, Solomon						CE, DE, TE (040); see Table A3.2

Table A3.4. *(cont.)*

Name, Birthplace Dates, Occupation(s)	Party	Acres	Lots	Slaves	Value (£)	Comments
Evans, William (ca. 1751–1807) Innkeeper	R			yes	2,396	TE (028)
Fonerden, Adam						CE, DE, TE (022); see Table A3.2
Garts, Charles (d. 1811) Merchant, sugar refiner, counting house				yes	1,505	Episcopalian by marriage; CE, TE (071)
Ghequiere, Charles Germany (1758–1818) Merchant				yes	2,180	Catholic; new resident 1782; CE, TE (036)
Gibson, William (ca. 1753–1832) County clerk	F			yes	1,946	Episcopalian; marriage ties to George Grundy (CE) family; TE (044)
Gilmor, Robert						CE, PE, TE (100); see Table A3.3
Goodwin, William, Sr.						PE, TE (026); see Table A3.3
Gough, Henry Dorsey Gent.	F			yes	3,850	Episcopalian; owned "Perry Hall," Balt. Co.; TE (008)
Hackett, John				yes	1,285	TE (092)
Hammond, John				yes	1,624	Episcopalian; TE (063)
Harris, David Pa. (ca. 1753–1809) DW	F			yes	1,585	Presbyterian; militia captain; TE (068)
Hawkins, William						CE, PE, TE (052); see Table A3.3
Heide, George Merchant					1,439	New resident 1778; TE (076)
Hollingsworth, Jesse						DE, TE (030); see Table A3.2
Hollingsworth, Thomas						PE, TE (043); see Table A3.3
Hollingsworth, Zebulon						PE, TE (099); see Table A3.3

Table A3.4. Baltimore City, Propertied Elite, First Party Era (*cont.*)

Name, Birthplace Dates, Occupation(s)	Party	Acres	Lots	Slaves	Value (£)	Comments
Hollins, John England (ca. 1759–1827) Counting house	R			yes	3,962	Presbyterian; daus m. into Cumberland Dugan family; new resident 1783; CE, TE (007)
Howard, John Eager						CE, DE, PE, TE (010); see Table A3.2
Hughes, Christopher DW	R				2,777	Presbyterian; TE (019)
Ireland, Edward Gent.				yes	2,293	Episcopalian; new resident between 1783 and 1793; TE (031)
Keener, Melchor (ca. 1719–1798)					2,440	Identified in obit. as one of oldest settlers of city; TE (025)
Kimmel, Anthony (ca. 1745–1817) Kimmel and Jordon Ironmongers				yes	1,550	TE (070)
Long, James (d. 1807) DW	R			yes	3,762	Episcopalian; new resident 1763; TE (009)
Lorman, William						CE, PE, TE (047); see Table A3.3
McCannon, James						PE, TE (015); see Table A3.3
McCausland, Marcus Merchant, counting house				yes	1,610	Probably Episcopalian; TE (065)
McElderry, Thomas						CE, DE, PE, TE (014); see Table A3.2
McFadon, John Foreign (ca. 1758–1840) Merchant, counting house				yes	1,473	Presbyterian; new resident 1775; CE, TE (072)

Table A3.4. (cont.)

Name, Birthplace Dates, Occupation(s)	Party	Acres	Lots	Slaves	Value (£)	Comments
McKim, John (d. 1817) Merchant	R				1,320	Presbyterian; father of Isaac McKim, brother of Alexander McKim (DE); Republican Society; TE (087)
McMechen, David						DE, PE, TE (051); see Table A3.2
Merryman, John						PE, TE (017); see Table A3.3
Messonier, Henry (ca. 1750–1823)				yes	2,253	Presbyterian; TE (032)
Moale, John Md. (1730–1798)				yes	2,780	Episcopalian; active in Rev.; OCt; TE (018)
Myers, Charles Gent.					1,905	Episcopalian; militia officer; TE (046)
Nichols, Henry						CE, PE, TE (094); see Table A3.3
O'Donnell, John						CE, DE, TE (002); see Table A3.2
Oliver, Robert						CE, DE, TE (045); see Table A3.2
Parnell, John					1,456	Presbyterian; TE (075)
Pascault, Lewis France (ca.1750–1824) Merchant, counting house				yes	4,641	Catholic; d.m. John O'Donnell (CE, DE, TE), d.m. Albert Gallatin; moved to Balt. from Santo Domingo 1780; CE, TE (005)
Patterson, William Ireland (1752–1835) Merchant	R			yes	8,977	Presbyterian; m.d. William Spear, brother-in-law of Samuel Smith, d.m. Jerome Bonaparte; new resident 1778; CE, TE (001)
Presstman, George						PE, TE (048); see Table A3.3
Price, William	F			yes	1,334	Methodist; militia captain; TE (085)

Table A3.4. Baltimore City, Propertied Elite, First Party Era *(cont.)*

Name, Birthplace Dates, Occupation(s)	Party	Acres	Lots	Slaves	Value (£)	Comments
Reinicker, George						PE, TE (034); see Table A3.3
Repold, George Merchant					1,275	TE (093)
Ridgely, Charles						CE, PE, TE (024); see Table A3.3
Rogers, Nicholas						PE, TE (056); see Table A3.3
Salmon, George Ireland (1747–1807) DW				yes	1,323	Presbyterian; new resident 1775; Hibernian Society; OCt; CE, DE, TE (087)
Schaeffer, Balzer						CE, PE, TE (054); see Table A3.3
Sears, George						CE, DE, TE (096); see Table A3.2
Sears, John Innkeeper	R			yes	1,236	TE (097)
Smith, John Ireland (b. 1720) Merchant					4,905	Presbyterian; closely associated with Buchanans, Sterets, and Spears; father of Samuel Smith; new resident 1760; TE (004)
Smith, Samuel						CE, DE, PE, TE (003); see Table A3.2
Smith, Thorowgood						CE, PE, TE (050); see Table A3.3
Smith, William						DE, PE, TE (013); see Table A3.2
Speck, Henry				yes	1,378	TE (082)
Sterling, James Foreign Grocery, dry goods store				yes	3,214	Presbyterian; new resident 1775; TE (012)
Stewart, Archibald (ca. 1757–1833) Merchant, counting house				yes	2,534	Presbyterian; TE (023)

Table A3.4. (*cont.*)

Name, Birthplace Dates, Occupation(s)	Party	Acres	Lots	Slaves	Value (£)	Comments
Stewart, David						CE, DE, PE, TE (091); see Table A3.2
Stiles, George (1760–1819) Merchant	R			yes	2,350	Presbyterian; Mayor (1816–19); TE (029)
Stodder, David Shipbuilder	R			yes	2,409	Presbyterian; Republican Society; militia major; TE (027)
Stricker, John						CE, DE, PE, TE (079); see Table A3.2
Stump, John (1754–1828) Merchant, counting house				yes	1,655	Presbyterian; moved to Cecil Co. 1808; CE, TE (062)
Thompson, Hugh Ireland (1760–1826) Merchant, counting house	F			yes	1,593	Presbyterian; new resident 1784; partnership with Robert Oliver; CE, TE (067)
Thornburgh, Joseph (1760–1820) Merchant					1,462	Quaker; m. into Ellicott family; new resident between 1783 and 1793; CE, TE (074)
Trimble, William						PE, TE (073); see Table A3.3
Tyson, Nathan (1757–1819) Gent.					1,273	Quaker; family connected with Ellicotts; CE, TE (095)
Uhler, Erasmus Tanner, currier	R				1,382	Zion Lutheran church; TE (081)
Usher, Thomas (d. 1800) DW				yes	2,098	TE (037)
Valck, Adrian Tobacco merchant				yes	3,372	German Society; agent for European bankers; new resident 1783; CE, TE (011)

Table A3.4. Baltimore City, Propertied Elite, First Party Era (*cont.*)

Name, Birthplace Dates, Occupation(s)	Party	Acres	Lots	Slaves	Value (£)	Comments
Walsh, Robert Ireland (ca. 1750–1831) Merchant				yes	1,309	Catholic; d.m. John Carrere (TE); TE (090)
Welch, Adam Pa. (1763–1841)				yes	1,340	German Evangelical church; new resident after Rev.; TE (084)
Wells, Cyprian (1749–1814) Grocer	R			yes	1,791	TE (055)
Williamson, David Scotland (1753–1831) Merchant, counting house				yes	1,677	Catholic; son m.d. Luke Tiernan (PE); new resident before 1771; CE, TE (061)
Wilson, William						CE, DE, PE, TE (086); see Table A3.2
Woods, William DW				yes	1,569	Methodist; TE (069)
Yeiser, Englehard DW	F			yes	1,687	TE (060)
Yellott, Jeremiah England (d. 1805) Counting house	F			yes	2,680	Episcopalian; interconnected with Hollingsworth family; new resident 1774; CE, TE (021)
Zollinoffer, Jno. Conrad Merchant					2,245	Otterbein church; German Society; new resident 1783; TE (033)

Table A3.5. Baltimore City, Commercial Elite, Second Party Era

Name, Birthplace, Dates, Occupation(s)	Party	Acres	Lots	Slaves	Value ($)	Comments
Albert, Jacob						CE, DE, TE; see Table A3.6
Allen, Ebenezer					min.	CE
Armstrong, James, Jr.						CE, TE; see Table A3.8
Baker, William Bank president			8		2,548	Episcopalian; CE
Barroll, James Merchant			4	2	3,670	CE
Beatty, James						CE, PE; see Table A3.7
Bennett, Matthew Merchant	J/AJ		1		638	CE
Berry, John (1791–1856) Brick manufacturer	AJ		11		2,521	Militia colonel; CE
Betts, Solomon						CE, TE; see Table A3.8
Bier, Jacob Cashier, bank president					106	CE
Birckhead, Hugh						CE, TE; see Table A3.8
Bohn, Charles Bank president			5		3,041	CE
Bosley, Elijah			3		1,052	CE
Bradford, John (d. 1843) flour merchant	AJ		4		2,389	Presbyterian; m.d. John Stricker, see Table A3.2; CE
Brice, Nicholas Accountant, bank president			6	2	945	Episcopalian; CE
Brown, Alexander Ireland (1764–1834) Shipping merchant			2		3,731	Presbyterian; new resident after 1800; CE
Brown, George Balt. (1787–1859) Treasurer, B&O RR Co.	AJ		2		2,817	Presbyterian; son of Alexander Brown; CE
Brune, Frederick W. (ca. 1776–1860) Shipping merchant			1		1,666	Episcopalian; CE

Table A3.5. Baltimore City, Commercial Elite, Second Party Era *(cont.)*

Name, Birthplace, Dates, Occupation(s)	Party	Acres	Lots	Slaves	Value ($)	Comments
Campbell, James (d. 1846) Dry goods importer			5	1	2,146	Presbyterian; CE
Carman, William DW			2		289	M. as Methodist; CE
Chase, Thorndike (ca. 1754–1838) Sea captain	AJ		2	2	2,497	Presbyterian; CE
Claggett, Elias (ca. 1781–1848) Brewer			2	2	3,838	Episcopalian; CE
Clapp, Aaron Hatter	AJ				43	CE
Clark, John						CE, TE; see Table A3.8
Coale, Abraham G.						CE, PE; see Table A3.7
Cohen, Benjamin I.						CE, DE; see Table A3.6
Cohen, Joshua I.						CE, TE; see Table A3.8
Colt, Roswell L. DW					min.	Presbyterian; m.d. Robert Oliver (TE), brother-in-law Robert M. Gibbes (TE); CE
Conn, Daniel (1776–1836) Architect, builder	J		7	2	1,688	Methodist; CE
Corner, James Merchant	AJ		5	2	3,240	Methodist; CE
Cunningham, John Balt. (b. 1778) Sea captain			3	1	917	Presbyterian; CE
Cushing, Joseph						CE, PE; see Table A3.7
Dallam, Francis J. Collector	AJ				174	Episcopalian; CE
Davies, Jacob G.						CE, DE; see Table A3.6
Davis, Thomas					min.	CE
Decker, George (1764–1864) DW			4		2,150	German Reformed; see Table A3.3; CE

Table A3.5. *(cont.)*

Name, Birthplace, Dates, Occupation(s)	Party	Acres	Lots	Slaves	Value ($)	Comments
Dickinson, William Public appraiser			2		350	CE
Didier, Edmund Merchant			5		2,760	M. as Presbyterian; CE
Donaldson, John Johnston						CE, DE, PE; see Table A3.6
Donaldson, Samuel I. Balt. (b. 1785) Attorney			11		2,980	Presbyterian; brother of John J. Donaldson, see Table A3.6; CE
Donnell, John, Sr.						CE, TE; see Table A3.8
Dorsey, Thomas Beale Md. (1780–1855) Bank president			2		610	Former district attorney; CE
Elder, Basil Spalding (ca. 1774–1869) Grocer and commission merchant	AJ		3		1,842	Catholic; CE
Ellicott, Evan T. Manufacturer of boiler iron			3		335	CE
Ellicott, Thomas Balt. Co. (1777–1859) Bank president			3		3,997	CE
Etting, Solomon						CE, DE; see Table A3.6
Evans, Hugh W.						CE, DE, TE; see Table A3.6
Freeman, William H.						CE, DE, TE; see Table A3.6
Fridge, Alexander						CE, TE; see Table A3.8
George, Archibald						CE, PE; see Table A3.7
Gibson, John Dry goods importer	AJ		6		4,234	Episcopalian; CE
Gittings, John Sterett						CE, TE; see Table A3.8
Gordon, Basil					min.	CE
Gwynn, William Ireland (1775–1854) Bank president					min.	Former editor Balt. *Gazette*; CE

Table A3.5. Baltimore City, Commercial Elite, Second Party Era *(cont.)*

Name, Birthplace, Dates, Occupation(s)	Party	Acres	Lots	Slaves	Value ($)	Comments
Harden, William (ca. 1780–1848) Bank president, dry goods merchant	AJ				54	Episcopalian; CE
Harrison, Thomas Dry goods merchant			2		220	CE
Harryman, George					min.	CE
Harwood, Thomas Grocery and flour merchant			7		2,194	Brother, James Harwood, see Table A3.6; CE
Higdon, Benjamin D.			2		241	CE
Hillen, Thomas			6		1,839	D.m. Louis W. Jenkins (PE); see Table A3.3; CE
Hoffman, Daniel						CE, TE; see Table A3.8
Hoffman, Samuel Owings						CE, DE; see Table A3.6
Hollins, John Smith						CE, DE; see Table A3.6
Howard, Benjamin Chew						CE, DE, PE, TE; see Table A3.6
Howard, Cornelius			1		200	CE
Howard, James						CE, TE; see Table A3.8
Howard, John B. Md. (b. 1801)			28		4,590	Episcopalian; CE
Hubbard, William						CE, DE, PE; see Table A3.6
Hutton, James						CE, TE; see Table A3.8
Jamison, Joseph President, Balt. Shot Tower	AJ		5	2	2,498	Methodist; son-in-law of James L. Ridgely; CE
Jarvis, Leonard Merchant			3		2,958	CE
Jenkins, Felix (ca. 1786–1838) Saddlemaker	J		2		460	Catholic; CE

Table A3.5. *(cont.)*

Name, Birthplace, Dates, Occupation(s)	Party	Acres	Lots	Slaves	Value ($)	Comments
Jenkins, Thomas Courtney (ca. 1765–1834) Hide and leather dealer	AJ				min.	Father of L. W. Jenkins (PE); CE
Johnson, Reverdy						CE, DE, PE; see Table A3.6
Jones, Talbot						CE, TE; see Table A3.8
Karthaus, Charles W.						CE, DE; see Table A3.6
Keener, Christian Chemist, drug store			5	2	2,219	German Reformed; CE
Kelso, Thomas						CE, DE, PE; see Table A3.6
Kennedy, Hugh Grocery, liquor store					min.	CE
Kerr, Archibald						CE, TE; see Table A3.8
King, Joshua T. DW			4		3,544	CE
Krebs, William						CE, DE, PE; see Table A3.6
Leakin, Sheppard C.						CE, DE; see Table A3.6
Littig, Philip (1772–1836) comb and brush manufacturer	AJ		7	2	2,795	Methodist; CE
Lorman, William						CE, TE; see Table A3.8
Lucas, Fielding, Jr.						CE, PE; see Table A3.7
McCauley, Dr. Patrick						CE, PE; see Table A3.7
McConkey, William Balt. (b. 1796) DW					min.	Methodist; CE
McDonald, Alexander (1773–1836) Merchant, McDonald and Ridgely			1		1,112	Presbyterian; CE
McDonald, William						CE, DE, TE; see Table A3.6
McElderry, Hugh						DE, PE; see Table A3.6
McGaw, Richard Balt. Co. (b. 1792)					min.	Episcopalian; CE

Table A3.5. Baltimore City, Commercial Elite, Second Party Era (*cont.*)

Name, Birthplace, Dates, Occupation(s)	Party	Acres	Lots	Slaves	Value ($)	Comments
McKim, John, Jr.						CE, DE, TE; see Table A3.6
McKim, Samuel						CE, TE; see Table A3.8
Martin, John					min.	CE
Mayer, Christian Germany (1763–1842) Merchant, Mayer and Bantz			1		1,472	New resident 1784; father of Charles F. Mayer (DE, PE); CE
Meeteer, William						CE, DE, PE; see Table A3.6
Merryman, Micajah			1		208	CE
Mezick, Baptist (1773–1863) Merchant	AJ		1		2,000	Presbyterian; CE
Mills, William P. Boot and shoemaker	J		4	2	2,580	M. as Methodist; CE
Moore, Philip						CE, PE; see Table A3.7
Morris, John Boucher						CE, DE, PE, TE; see Table A3.6
Myers, Henry						CE, PE; see Table A3.7
Neff, Peter Counting house					225	Probably Evangelical Lutheran; CE
Ogston, John Scotland (ca. 1769–1834)			2		462	CE
Patterson, John Balt. (1783–1857) DW	AJ		9		2,733	Presbyterian; son of William Patterson, brother of Edward, Henry, and Joseph W. Patterson; m. Mrs. Nicholas of Va., tied to Smith family; CE
Patterson, William						CE, DE, TE; see Table A3.6
Pike, Henry (ca. 1794–1856) Hardware merchant			1		700	Catholic; CE
Poppelein, Nicholas Importer			3		1,230	M. as Zion Lutheran; CE

Table A3.5. *(cont.)*

Name, Birthplace, Dates, Occupation(s)	Party	Acres	Lots	Slaves	Value ($)	Comments
Poultney, Evan Bank president DW			2		2,896	Related to Ellicotts and Tysons; CE
Power, John Grocer			4		2,296	CE
Price, Walter (ca. 1794–1840) Bank president	J				min.	CE
Randall, Beale						CE, DE, PE, TE; see Table A3.6
Reese, John						CE, PE; see Table A3.7
Rogers, Jacob						CE, DE; see Table A3.6
Schaeffer, Frederick (1760–1844)	AJ		11		2,242	Methodist; CE
Schroeder, Henry, Jr.					min.	M.d. of Charles Ghequiere, see Table A3.4; CE
Schwartze, Augustus James Bank president DW					min.	M. as Methodist; CE
Smith, Job, Jr.						CE, PE; see Table A3.7
Smith, Robert						CE, TE; see Table A3.8
Spindler, William C. DW			1		910	CE
Stapleton, Joseph K.						CE, DE, PE; see Table A3.6
Stewart, Daniel Bank president	AJ				min.	CE
Stewart, William						CE, PE; see Table A3.7
Sterling, Archibald Balt. (1798–1885) Banker	AJ		12		3,733	Presbyterian; son of James Sterling, see Table A3.4; CE
Taylor, Robert Alexander						CE, TE; see Table A3.8
Taylor, William M. (1769–1832) Bank president			3		2,434	Presbyterian; CE

Table A3.5. Baltimore City, Commercial Elite, Second Party Era (*cont.*)

Name, Birthplace, Dates, Occupation(s)	Party	Acres	Lots	Slaves	Value ($)	Comments
Tenant, Thomas						CE, TE; see Table A3.8
Thomas, Philip Evan						CE, TE; see Table A3.8
Thompson, Henry England (ca. 1774–1837) Commission merchant					min.	Episcopalian; see Table A3.1; former partner to Robert Oliver; CE
Tiernan, Luke						CE, DE, TE; see Table A3.6
Todhunter, Joseph						CE, TE; see Table A3.8
Townsend, Joseph (1756–1841) Glass, oil, paint store			8		2,146	CE
Tucker, William A. Sea captain			1		1,106	CE
Tyson, Isaac, Sr. (1778–1864) Flour merchant					min.	CE
Uhler, Philip (1769–1855) Dry goods merchant	AJ		2		499	Episcopalian; CE
Vickers, Joel						CE, DE; see Table A3.6
Wallace, Joseph A. Insurance co. president			1		663	CE
Warner, Andrew E.						CE, DE; see Table A3.6
Waters, Hezekiah (ca. 1750–1835)			1		3,698	Episcopalian; CE
Wilkins, Henry			1		215	CE
Williams, George Balt. (b. 1768) Commission merchant	AJ				min.	Presbyterian; CE
Williamson, David Scotland (ca. 1753–1831) Insurance co. president	AJ				min.	Catholic; son m.d. Luke Tiernan, see Table A3.6; see also Table A3.4; CE
Wilson, James						CE, TE; see Table A3.8

Table A3.5. (*cont.*)

Name, Birthplace, Dates, Occupation(s)	Party	Acres	Lots	Slaves	Value ($)	Comments
Wilson, Thomas						CE, TE; see Table A3.8
Winchester, David Fred. Co. (1771–1835)					min.	Episcopalian; brother of William Winchester, see Table A3.1, uncle of James (Table A3.2) and George Winchester, see Table A3.1; CE
Worman, Moses (1777–1861)	AJ				min.	Methodist; Fredericktown resident; CE
Worthington, Abraham			3	2	2,239	CE

Table A3.6. Baltimore City, Decisional Elite, Second Party Era

Names, Birthplace, Dates, Occupation(s)	Party	Acres	Lots	Slaves	Value ($)	Comments
Albert, Jacob Pa. (1787–1854) Hardware merchant	AJ		15		9,216	Church of the Ascension; CE, DE, TE
Alcock, Dr. Edward J. Balt. (1802–36) Doctor, Editor, Balt. *Jefferson Reformer*	J		1		555	Episcopalian; Odd Fellow; DE
Bacon, James Ireland (ca.1792–1847) Grocer	J		2		163	Catholic; Irish Emancipation; DE
Barnes, Samuel Kent Co. (1788–1858) Editor, Balt. *Chronicle*	AJ		1		566	Former editor of the Ftwn. *Examiner* (1813–28); brother-in-law of S.C. Leakin; DE, PE
Buchanan, James Madison Balt. Co. (1803–76) Attorney	AJ				180	Associate Reformed Congregation; DE

Table A3.6. Baltimore City, Decisional Elite, Second Party Era (*cont.*)

Name, Birthplace, Dates, Occupation(s)	Party	Acres	Lots	Slaves	Value ($)	Comments
Campbell, Bernard U. (1795–1855) Teller, Mechanics' Bank	AJ		1		512	Hibernian Society; militia colonel; DE
Carroll, James, Jr. Balt. (1791–1873) DW	J		6		16,100	Episcopalian; DE, PE, TE
Cohen, Benjamin I. Va. (1797–1845) Banker	AJ		2		3,485	Jewish; m.d. Solomon Etting; German; CE, DE
Cole, William H. Attorney	J		3		1,208	Methodist; DE, PE
Crawford, William, Jr. Commission merchant	AJ		2	2	1,363	Presbyterian; Hibernian Society; DE
Davies, Jacob G. (1796–1857) Miller	J		3	2	4,047	Former mayor of Baltimore; m.d. Solomon Betts (CE, TE); Hibernian Society; CE, DE
Delcher, John Md. (b. 1804) Brewer	J		1		132	DE
Donaldson, John Johnston Balt. (1788–1866) Attorney	J		2		1,630	Presbyterian; CE, DE, PE
Dugan, Frederick James Md. (1804–58) Attorney	J		3	2	2,104	Presbyterian; DE, PE
Dunnington, William P. (ca. 1787–1850) Tobacco merchant	AJ			2	347	DE
Etting, Solomon Pa. (1764–1847) Merchant	AJ		9		1,749	Jewish; see Table A3.2; Incorp. Jewish Benevolent Society; German Society; d.m. B. I. Cohen; CE, DE

Table A3.6. *(cont.)*

Name, Birthplace, Dates, Occupation(s)	Party	Acres	Lots	Slaves	Value ($)	Comments
Evans, Hugh W. England (1786–1863) Prop. Levandale Cotton Factory	AJ		9	2	6,053	Probably Episcopalian; m.d. Gov. Thomas Johnson, (Fred. Co.); CE, DE, TE
Fitch, Jonathan Bacon merchant	J		5		435	Militia major; DE
Freeman, William H. Md. (1790–1863) Attorney	AJ		13		5,006	CE, DE, TE
Frick, William Md. (1790–1855) Attorney	J		8		3,019	Zion Lutheran; son of Peter Frick (see Table A3.2), Swiss German ancestry; studied law with William H. Winder; DE
Graves, Dr. John James N.Y. (1800–1890) Doctor	J				80	To Balt. ca. 1831; HD (1839–42); DE
Harker, Samuel Del. (1792–1850) Editor, Balt. *Republican*	J				min.	To Balt. ca. 1829 from Del.; DE, PE
Harwood, James (1791–1848) Merchant	AJ		7		2,194	Episcopalian; brother, Thomas Harwood (CE); DE
Hawkins, James L. (1776–1849) Cashier, Franklin Bank	AJ			2	830	DE
Hayman, James R. Clerk	J				min.	DE
Heath, James P. Del. (1777–1854) Congressman DW	J/AJ				min.	DE, PE
Heath, Upton S. Md. (1785–1852) Attorney	J		1		760	Md. senate; DE, PE

Table A3.6. Baltimore City, Decisional Elite, Second Party Era *(cont.)*

Name, Birthplace, Dates, Occupation(s)	Party	Acres	Lots	Slaves	Value ($)	Comments
Hillen, John Md. (1761–1840) Merchant	AJ		4		2,107	Catholic; son of Solomon Hillen; active in earlier period, see Table A3.3; DE
Hoffman, Samuel Owings Md. (b. 1782) Commission merchant	AJ		1		1,407	CE, DE
Hollins, John Smith Md. (1787–1856) DW	J		4		2,896	Presbyterian; related to Smith family, son m.d. Cumberland Dugan (TE); future mayor; CE, DE
Hook, Joseph (1790–1844) Lumber merchant	J		2	2	337	Ship captain; DE
House, Samuel (1778–1848) Lumber merchant	J		5		3,118	DE, PE
Howard, Benjamin Chew Md. (1791–1872) Attorney, congressman	J		24	2	7,822	Episcopalian; son of Colonel John E. Howard, m. into Gilmore family; CE,DE, PE, TE
Howard, Charles Md. (1802–69) Attorney	J		29		9,099	Episcopalian; son of Colonel John E. Howard, brother of Benjamin Chew, George, and J. E. Howard II; DE, TE
Hubbard, William Md. (b. 1805) Grocer	AJ		2	1	536	CE, DE, PE
Hunt, Jesse Balt. Co. (1793–1872) Saddler	J		6		1,500	Episcopalian; m.d. Leonard Yundt, Balt. editor; DE, PE
Johnson, Reverdy Annapolis (1796–1876) Attorney	J/AJ		2		4,365	Md. senate, future U.S. senator; CE, DE, PE

Table A3.6. (*cont.*)

Name, Birthplace, Dates, Occupation(s)	Party	Acres	Lots	Slaves	Value ($)	Comments
Jones, Joshua (d. 1865) Printer	AJ				min.	Methodist; DE, PE
Karthaus, Charles W. Germany (1783–1842) Merchant	AJ	3	1		1,037	German Society; CE, DE
Keerl, Samuel (1788–1853) Tobacco merchant	J				min.	German Society; DE
Kelso, Thomas Ireland (1784–1878) Meat packer, victualer	AJ	14	1		4,147	CE, DE, PE
Kennedy, John Pendleton Balt. (1796–1870) Attorney	J/AJ	3	2		1,517	Presbyterian; father John Kennedy; m.d. of Colonel Thomas Tenant, see Table A3.3; DE
Kettlewell, John Md. (1808–62) Grocer	J	1			30	Future naval officer (1853); DE
Krebs, William (1802–66) Attorney	J	3			1,912	Episcopalian; CE, DE, PE
Lauderman, Henry R. Baker, grocer	J	4			825	DE, PE
Laurenson, Philip (1775–1849) Grocer	J	1			1,298	Catholic; DE, PE
Law, James O. Balt. (1809–47) Boot and shoemaker	AJ				min.	Future mayor; DE
Leakin, Sheppard C. Md. (1790–1867) Editor, Balt. *Chronicle*	AJ	8			2,761	Episcopalian; brother-in-law to Samuel Barnes; future mayor; CE, DE
Leary, Peter (1782–1871) Hatter	AJ				43	DE

Table A3.6. Baltimore City, Decisional Elite, Second Party Era (*cont.*)

Name, Birthplace, Dates, Occupation(s)	Party	Acres	Lots	Slaves	Value ($)	Comments
Lilly, Richard Md. (1805–74) Saddler	J				min.	DE
McClellan, Samuel M. (1787–1858) Agent for People's Steam Navigation Co.	AJ	6	2		1,990	Presbyterian; DE, PE
McCulloch, James William (1788–1861) Attorney	AJ				min.	M. only d. of George Sears, see Table A3.2; DE
McDonald, William (1758–1845) Commission merchant	AJ	18	2		12,093	Presbyterian; militia general; CE, DE, TE
McElderry, Hugh Balt. (1793–1856) Agent, merchant	J	22	2		3,544	Presbyterian; Hibernian Society; son of Thomas McElderry, see Table A3.2; CE, DE, PE
McKim, Isaac Md. (1775–1838) Hardware Merchant, Valona Copper Works, congressman	J	17			15,201	Episcopalian; see Table A3.1; DE, PE, TE
McKim, John, Jr. (ca. 1766–1834) copper warehouse	AJ	13	2		6,830	Presbyterian; d.m. William H. Marriott (DE); CE, DE, TE
McKinnell, Henry Dry goods merchant	J				170	Odd Fellow; DE, PE
Manning, Samuel Mass. (1802–57) Attorney	AJ				min.	M. as Presbyterian; militia colonel; Odd Fellow; DE
Marriott, William Hammond Md. (1789–1851) Attorney, collector (1837–41)	AJ	1	2		2,239	Militia general; DE

Table A3.6. *(cont.)*

Name, Birthplace, Dates, Occupation(s)	Party	Acres	Lots	Slaves	Value ($)	Comments
Mass, Samuel Balt. (b. 1795) Grocer, cedar cooper	J		1		190	Episcopalian; m. d. Rezin Wright; active in Working-men's party; EC; DE, PE
Mayer, Charles F. Balt. (1795–1863) Attorney	AJ		4		2,423	German ancestry, son of Christian Mayer, brother of Bantz Mayer; Md. senate; DE, PE
Medtart, Joshua (1793–1841) Dry goods merchant	AJ		1	1	687	Eng. Lutheran church (founder); militia major; DE
Meeteer, William (1787–1833) Paper warehouse	AJ		1	1	985	CE, DE, PE
Miller, Dr. James Henry Pa. (1788–1853) Doctor	J		1		362	Methodist; new resident 1827; DE
Millington, John N. Md. (b. 1804) Printer	AJ				min.	Episcopalian; active in Workingmen's party; DE
Miltenberger, Anthony (1789–1869) Dry goods merchant	J		4		884	Wife belongs to Eng. Lutheran church; militia general; DE, PE
Moale, Samuel Md. (b. 1780) Attorney	AJ		3		2,473	Catholic; militia colonel; DE, PE
Moore ,Samuel (1777–1845) Bricklayer	J		12	2	3,059	M. as Episcopalian; militia colonel; DE, PE
Morris, John Boucher Md. (1794–1874) Banker	AJ		25	2	8,920	M. into Hollingsworth family; CE, DE, PE, TE
Munroe, Isaac Mass. (1784–1859) Editor, Baltimore *Patriot*	AJ		1	2	1,249	Presbyterian; DE, PE
Murphy, Dr. Thomas L. Md. (b. 1800) Doctor	J				60	English Reformed; Hibernian Society; DE

Table A3.6. Baltimore City, Decisional Elite, Second Party Era (*cont.*)

Name, Birthplace, Dates, Occupation(s)	Party	Acres	Lots	Slaves	Value ($)	Comments
Needles, Edward (1797–1876) Chairmaker	AJ				min.	Quaker; Workingmen's party; DE
Neilson, Robert (1784–1850) Printer	AJ		1	2	498	Episcopalian; DE, PE
Niles, Hezekiah Pa. (1777–1839) Editor, *Niles Weekly Register*	AJ		2		1,075	Son, William Ogden Niles, Fredericktown editor, see Table 3.13; DE
Patterson, William Ireland (1752–1835) Shipping merchant	AJ		34	2	39,883	Presbyterian, see Table A3.4; father of Edward, Henry, Joseph W. Patterson; CE, DE, TE
Peters, Edward Johnson Balt. (1800–1864) Grocery, liquor store	AJ				min.	Episcopalian; DE
Piper, James DW	J		4	2	9,567	Church of the Ascension; DE, TE
Purviance, Robert (1779–1858) Merchant	AJ		1	2	1,051	Presbyterian; son of Samuel Purviance, Rev. leader, nephew of Robert Purviance; DE
Randall, Beale (1782–1853) Lumber merchant	J		15	2	4,800	Militia colonel; CE, DE, PE, TE
Read, William George S.C. (1800–1846) Attorney	J		33	2	6,700	Catholic; youngest son of Congressman Jacob Read, S.C.; m.d. Colonel John E. Howard, see Table A3.2; Hibernian Society; DE, TE
Ready, Samuel Md. (b. 1789) Sailmaker	J		7		2,107	DE, PE
Rogers, Jacob Hatter	AJ		4	2	3,985	Methodist; CE, DE
Roney, William (1782–1844) Grocery, liquor store	J		1		254	Presbyterian; militia captain; DE, PE

Table A3.6. (cont.)

Name, Birthplace, Dates, Occupation(s)	Party	Acres	Lots	Slaves	Value ($)	Comments
Sanders, Benedict I. Grocer	J		3		933	Catholic; DE, PE
Sands, Samuel Md. (b. 1800) Printer, Baltimore Chronicle	AJ		1		175	DE
Slee, Israel	AJ				min.	DE
Smith, Samuel Pa. (1752–1839) Merchant, U.S. Senator	J				min.	See Table A3.2; DE, PE
Southcomb, Carey Plumber	J		3		908	DE, PE
Stansbury, Dr. James B. Md. (1785–1860) Doctor	AJ		4		1,073	DE
Stansbury, John Ensor (1760–1841) Proprietor of coaches	J		12		1,774	M. as Episcopalian; DE, PE
Stapleton, Joseph K. Pa. (1788–1853) Brush manufacturer	AJ		1		360	CE, DE, PE
Steuart, George Hume Annapolis (1790–1867) Attorney	J		1		753	Militia general; DE, PE
Steuart, John M. Attorney	AJ				2,500	Odd Fellow; DE, PE
Steuart, William R.	AJ		6	2	2,496	Md. senate, EC; DE, PE
Stewart, David Md. (1800–1858) Attorney	J/AJ		8		3,213	Presbyterian; DE, PE
Storm, Peter (1762–1842) Tavernkeeper	J				min.	Catholic; German; DE
Taylor, George (1800–1875) Carpenter	AJ				min.	Episcopalian; militia colonel; DE

Table A3.6. Baltimore City, Decisional Elite, Second Party Era (*cont.*)

Name, Birthplace, Dates, Occupation(s)	Party	Acres	Lots	Slaves	Value ($)	Comments
Tiernan, Luke Ireland (1757–1839) Shipping merchant	AJ		34		15,918	Catholic; Hibernian Society; see Table A3.3; CE, DE, TE
Turner, Joshua (1776–1841) Commission merchant, feed store	J		10	1	1,688	Methodist; DE
Vansant, Joshua Md. (1803–84) Hatter	J				min.	Methodist; future congressman; DE, PE
Vickers, Joel Md. (1774–1860) Commission merchant	J		3		2,319	Presbyterian; CE, DE
Warner, Andrew E. Md. (b. 1787) Silversmith	AJ				45	Odd Fellow; CE, DE
Waters, Stephen Carpenter	J		2		236	DE
Watkins, John Wesley (1807–87)	J				min.	Methodist; DE
White, Joseph England (1789–1867) Machinist	J			2	317	DE
Wight, William J. Md. (b. 1786) Lumber merchant	J		5	2	1,462	DE, PE
Williams, Nathaniel F. R.I. (1780–1864) Commission merchant	AJ				630	DE, PE
Wilmer, John W. Md. (1787–1861) Commission merchant	J				242	DE
Winchester, George Md. (1787–1840) Attorney	J		5		5,611	Son of William Winchester (Table A3.1), brother of James Winchester (Table A3.2); DE, TE

Table A3.6. (*cont.*)

Name, Birthplace, Dates, Occupation(s)	Party	Acres	Lots	Slaves	Value ($)	Comments
Young, McClintock Balt. (1801–63) Attorney	J		2		966	Presbyterian; joined Treasury Dept.; DE, PE

Table A3.7. Baltimore City, Positional Elite, Second Party Era

Name, Birthplace Dates, Occupation(s)	Party	Acres	Lots	Slaves	Value ($)	Comments
Alricks, Thomas P. Attorney	J		2		430	FB; PE
Amos, Dr. Corbin Doctor			5	1	3,472	FB; PE
Baer, Dr. Michael S. (1795–1854) Doctor			1	2	1,336	Presbyterian; FB; PE
Ball, Walter Md. (b. ca. 1795) Painter	J		6		1,670	FB; PE
Barnes, Samuel						FB; DE, PE; see Table A3.6
Barney, John Balt. (1785–1857)	AJ				min.	Probably Presbyterian; son of Commodore John Barney, m. into Hindman family; U.S. Congress; PE
Baxley, George Druggist			6		2,203	FB; PE
Beamer, Henry Grocer			2		670	FB; PE
Beatty, James Flour and commission merchant			4		3,210	Presbyterian; SB; CE, PE
Bevan, Richard (ca. 1775–1839) Dry goods merchant	AJ		3		690	FB; PE

Table A3.7. Baltimore City, Positional Elite, Second Party Era *(cont.)*

Name, Birthplace, Dates, Occupation(s)	Party	Acres	Lots	Slaves	Value ($)	Comments
Blair, James (ca. 1777–1849) Justice of the peace	AJ	1			740	Catholic; Odd Fellow; FB; PE
Bosley, Daniel	AJ				min.	Methodist; SB; PE
Boyd, Samuel Carpenter	J		2		342	Methodist; FB; PE
Brady, Samuel Del. (1789–1871) Printer	J		2		340	M. as Methodist; FB; PE
Branson, Joseph Hatter	J		1		130	M. as Presbyterian; FB; PE
Brown, Elias Balt. Co. (1793–1857) Attorney	J				min.	Episcopalian; U.S. Congress; PE
Brown, Stewart						FB; PE, TE; see Table A3.8
Browning, John H. Hardware merchant	J		2		660	FB; PE
Burke, David Balt. (b. 1796) House and sign painter	AJ				min.	Presbyterian; SB; PE
Carroll, James, Jr.						SB; DE, PE, TE; see Table A3.6
Chalmers, William					min.	FB; PE
Childs, Samuel Coachmaker	AJ		2		520	M. as Methodist; Odd Fellow; FB; PE
Clark, James Lumber merchant	AJ		4		655	FB; PE
Coale, Abraham G. (ca. 1799–1853) Lumber merchant	AJ		2	2	470	Odd Fellow; FB; CE, PE
Cohen, Jacob I. Va. (1789–1869) Banker	AJ		2		3,490	Jewish; lottery agent; FB; PE
Cole, William H.						FB; DE, PE; see Table A3.6

Table A3.7. *(cont.)*

Name, Birthplace, Dates, Occupation(s)	Party	Acres	Lots	Slaves	Value ($)	Comments
Cole, William John Balt. (b. 1805) Attorney	J				min.	Episcopalian; FB; PE
Coskery, Bernard (ca. 1764–1837) Nail manufacturer					min.	Catholic; FB; PE
Coulson, John Glue, glass, paper, mattress manufacturer	AJ	7			1,380	FB; PE
Cullum, John					min.	M. as Methodist; FB; PE
Curley, James Carpenter	AJ	3			582	Methodist; FB; PE
Curtain, Thomas (ca. 1767–1839)					min.	Catholic; FB; PE
Cushing, Joseph N.H. (1781–1852) Cushing and Sons, booksellers	J	3			2,020	Associate Reformed Congregation; new resident 1810; HD; CE, PE
Danders, Benedict I.					min.	FB; PE
Danicker, John, Jr.					min.	FB; PE
Davidge, Francis H. (ca. 1796–1861) Attorney, editor	AJ	2	2		932	Episcopalian; SB; PE
Diffenderffer, Charles Grocery and hardware merchant	AJ	5	2		1,750	First German Reformed; FB; PE
Donaldson, John Johnston						FB; CE, DE, PE; see Table A3.6
Dryden, Joshua Worcester Co. (1792–1869) Draper, tailor	AJ	13	2		3,974	Methodist; militia major; FB; PE
Dugan, Frederick James						FB; DE, PE; see Table A3.6
Dushane, Valentine (1788–1850) Carpenter		4			659	FB; PE

Table A3.7. Baltimore City, Positional Elite, Second Party Era (*cont.*)

Name, Birthplace, Dates, Occupation(s)	Party	Acres	Lots	Slaves	Value ($)	Comments
Fenby, Peter England (b. ca. 1787) Grocer	AJ		1		554	Presbyterian; FB, PE
Fields, James (ca. 1781) Grocery, flour store	J		8		1,118	FB, SB; PE
Fosbenner, Daniel Blacksmith			5		1,041	Zion Lutheran; FB; PE
Frazier, James Balt. (b. 1806) Sea captain	AJ		2	2	510	Presbyterian; SB; PE
Gardner, George Shipbuilder	J			2	884	FB; PE
George, Archibald Merchant			3		1,400	Associate Reformed Congregation; FB; CE, PE
Gold, Peter						SB; PE, TE; see Table A3.8
Grafton, Mark Md. (ca. 1795–1854) Boot and shoemaker	J		2		530	FB, SB; PE
Grafton, Nathaniel Skilled artisan	J				min.	FB; PE
Greble, Benjamin Potter					min.	FB; PE
Gross, John, Jr. (ca. 1798–1869)	J		1		163	Catholic; FB; PE
Hanson, William H. DW	AJ		6		925	FB; PE
Harker, Samuel						FB; DE, PE; see Table A3.6
Harper, Charles Carroll Balt. (1802–37)	J		1	2	860	Son of Robert Goodloe Harper, Federalist leader (see Table A3.2), grandson of Charles Carroll of Carrollton, Rev. and Federalist leader. Also owned "Oakland," family estate in Balt. Co., valued at $29,108; HD; PE

Table A3.7. *(cont.)*

Name, Birthplace, Dates, Occupation(s)	Party	Acres	Lots	Slaves	Value ($)	Comments
Heath, James P.						U.S. Congress; DE, PE; see Table A3.6
Heath, Upton S.						Md. senate; DE, PE; see Table A3.6
Hintze, Dr. Frederick E. B. Balt. (1803–65) Doctor	J				min.	First German Reformed; MD U. Md. (1823); FB; PE
House, Samuel						FB; DE, PE; see Table A3.6
Howard, Benjamin Chew						U.S. Congress; CE, DE, PE, TE; see Table A3.6
Hubbard, William						FB, SB; CE, DE, PE; see Table A3.6
Hunt, Jesse						HD, Mayor; DE, PE; see Table A3.6
Inloes, William (1787–1854) Ship joiner	J	7	1		1,180	Methodist; FB, SB; PE
Jenkins, Edward of William (ca. 1773–1833) Saddlery store	J	7			3,677	Catholic; FB; PE
Jenkins, Louis William Balt. (1806–40) Attorney	J		1		460	Catholic; son of Thomas C. Jenkins (CE), m.d. Thomas Hillen (CE), studied law with William Gwynn; HD, FB; PE
Johnson, Reverdy						Md. senate; CE, DE, PE; see Table A3.6
Jones, Joshua						HD; DE, PE; see Table A3.6
Jones, William Gwynn Editor, Baltimore Gazette			1		540	FB; PE
Kelso, Thomas						SB; CE, DE, PE; see Table A3.6

Table A3.7. **Baltimore City, Positional Elite, Second Party Era** (*cont.*)

Name, Birthplace, Dates, Occupation(s)	Party	Acres	Lots	Slaves	Value ($)	Comments
Keyser, George Pa. (1784–1837) China merchant	AJ			2	310	Episcopalian; Mason, Odd Fellow; FB; PE
King, John Paint, oil, and glass store	J		3		310	M. as Methodist; FB; PE
Klinefelter, Michael Innkeeper	J		3		910	SB; PE
Krebs, William						SB; DE, DE, PE; see Table A3.6
Lauderman, Henry R.						FB; DE, PE; see Table A3.6
Laurenson, Philip						SB, HD, FB; DE, PE; see Table A3.6
Lee, James			1		600	Methodist; FB; PE
Legrande, Samuel D. Bacon merchant	J		3		1,067	FB; PE
Lightner, Isaac F. (1795–1836) Gauger	AJ/J		1		650	FB; PE
Little, Peter Pa. (1775–1830)	AJ		2	2	903	Methodist; HD, U.S. Congress; militia colonel; PE
Lucas, Fielding, Jr. (ca. 1781–1854) Bookseller			3	2	2,748	Catholic; SB; CE, PE
Macauley, Dr. Patrick Doctor	J		1	2	2,101	SB, FB; CE, PE
McClellan, Samuel M.						SB; DE, PE; see Table A3.6
McElderry, Hugh						FB, EC; CE, DE, PE; see Table A3.6
McHenry, Dennis J.					min.	FB; PE
McKim, Isaac						U.S. Congress; DE, PE, TE; see Table A3.6
McKinnell, Henry						FB; DE, PE; see Table A3.6
McLean, Cornelius (d. 1861) Attorney	J				min.	HD; PE

Table A3.7. (*cont.*)

Name, Birthplace, Dates, Occupation(s)	Party	Acres	Lots	Slaves	Value ($)	Comments
McMahon, John Van Lear Allegany Co. (1800–1871) Attorney	J/AJ				min.	Son of All. Co. legislator, William McMahon; grad. Princeton College, studied law in Cumberland, sent to state legislature from All. Co.; moved to Balt. 1826; HD, Md. senate; PE
Mallory, John Sea captain			1	1	98	FB; PE
Mass, Samuel						EC; DE, PE; see Table A3.6
Mathiott, August Balt. (1799–1872) Fancy chairmaker	AJ		1		250	Odd Fellow; FB; PE
Mayer, Charles F.						Md. senate; DE, PE; see Table A3.6
Meeteer, William						FB; CE, DE, PE; see Table A3.6
Meredith, Thomas T. (1783–1853)					min.	Catholic; FB; PE
Millholland, Robert E. Pa. (ca. 1788) Blockmaker	AJ		3		840	FB; PE
Miltenberger, Anthony						FB; DE, PE; see Table A3.6
Mitchell, James M. (d. 1836) Dry goods merchant	J		1	2	2,500	FB; PE
Moale, Samuel						FB; DE, PE; see Table A3.6
Monmonier, Dr. John F. Md. (b. 1813) Doctor	J		3		250	Catholic; grad. St. Mary's College, MD U. Md. (1834); FB; PE
Moore, Philip (d.1834) Attorney			1		680	M. as Episcopalian; SB; CE, PE
Moore, Samuel						FB, SB; DE, PE; see Table A3.6
Morris, John Boucher						FB, Md. senate; CE, DE, PE, TE; see Table A3.6

Table A3.7. Baltimore City, Positional Elite, Second Party Era (*cont.*)

Name, Birthplace, Dates, Occupation(s)	Party	Acres	Lots	Slaves	Value ($)	Comments
Morris, Thomas C. (ca. 1784–1862) House carpenter	AJ		2		240	FB; PE
Mosher, James U.S. (1761–1845) Surveyor of the port	J		3	2	1,989	Presbyterian, former Republican, see Table A3.2; SB; PE
Mott, Joshua Lime store			3		740	SB; PE
Munroe, Isaac						FB; DE, PE; see Table A3.6
Myers, Henry (1795–1870) China merchant	J		3		1,939	Militia colonel; FB; CE, PE
Neilson, Robert						FB; DE, PE; see Table A3.6
Nicholas, John Spear Va. (1802–87) Attorney	J				min.	Presbyterian; Samuel Smith's nephew, m. into Gilmor family; new resident 1823; HD; PE
Patterson, Joseph Wilson						SB; PE, TE; see Table A3.8
Peregoy, Charles Balt. (ca. 1804–1900) Carpenter	AJ		2		813	FB, HD; active in Workingmen's party; PE
Peregoy, James (1774–1845) Cooper	J		1		260	M. as Methodist; FB; PE
Perrigo, Daniel			1		272	FB; PE
Randall, Beale						FB; CE, DE, PE, TE; see Table A3.6
Ready, Samuel						FB, SB; DE, PE; see Table A3.6
Reany, William China store	AJ		4		1,010	SB; PE
Reese, John (1800–1858) Flour, grocery merchant	AJ		3		2,227	English Lutheran; FB, SB; CE, PE

Table A3.7. *(cont.)*

Name, Birthplace · Dates, Occupation(s)	Party	Acres	Lots	Slaves	Value ($)	Comments
Richardson, Beale Howard Harford Co. (ca. 1799–1877) Dry goods merchant	J				min.	New resident 1826; HD; PE
Richardson, George R. Worcester Co. (1803–51) Attorney	AJ				min.	EC; PE
Ridgely, James Lot Balt. (1807–81) Attorney	AJ	4			1,410	M. as Methodist; son of Lot Ridgely; FB; PE
Ridgely, Noah (1778–1856) Druggist	AJ	1	2		230	Episcopalian; FB; PE
Roney, William						FB; DE, PE; see Table A3.6
Ross, Benjamin C. Counting room	AJ	9	2		1,730	Presbyterian; FB; PE
Russell, Alexander (1765–1849) Brickmaker	J	4			787	Methodist; FB; PE
Russell, Alexander, Jr. Brickmaker	J	4			787	FB; PE
Sanders, Benedict I.						FB; DE, PE; see Table A3.6
Schaeffer, Baltzer (ca. 1757–1838)					min.	Otterbein; see Table A3.3; SB; PE
Schwartzauer, Daniel (ca. 1777–1847)	J	3			510	FB; PE
Scott, John Grocer	AJ	2			750	FB; PE
Seidenstricker, John Barnhart Balt. (1809–94) Glass, paint, and drug store	J	2			3,590	First German Reformed; German Rhineland family; active as Workingman; FB; PE
Sewell, Thomas Tanner		3			1,235	M. as Methodist; SB; PE

Table A3.7. Baltimore City, Positional Elite, Second Party Era (*cont.*)

Name, Birthplace Dates, Occupation(s)	Party	Acres	Lots	Slaves	Value ($)	Comments
Seyler, Frederick Skilled artisan	AJ				min.	M. in Zion Lutheran church; FB; PE
Sheppard, Thomas S.	AJ		1		362	Odd Fellow; FB, SB; PE
Small, Jacob, Jr. Balt. (ca. 1772–1851) DW	AJ		2	2	730	Episcopalian; see Table A3.3; mayor; PE
Smith, Jacob					min.	SB; PE
Smith, Job, Jr. (d. 1871) Lumber yard, bank president	AJ		3	1	930	M. as Methodist; son of Job Smith, see Table A3.3; FB; CE, PE
Smith, John Spear Balt. (1786–1866)	J				min.	Presbyterian, son of Samuel Smith; militia general; Md. senate; PE
Smith, Samuel						U.S. Senate, mayor; DE, PE; see Tables A3.2, A3.6
Southcomb, Carey						FB; DE, PE; see Table A3.6
Stansbury, Elijah Balt. Co. (1791–1883) Lime merchant	J		2		370	Mason; Odd Fellow; militia major; FB; PE
Stansbury, John Ensor						FB; DE, PE; see Table A3.6
Stapleton, Joseph K.						FB; CE, DE, PE; see Table A3.6
Steuart, George Hume						HD; DE, PE; see Table A3.6
Steuart, John M.						FB; DE, PE; see Table A3.6
Steuart, William R.						Md. senate; DE, PE; see Table A3.6
Stever, George Coachmaker					min.	FB; PE
Stewart, David						SB; DE, PE; see Table A3.6
Stewart, William Balt. (1780–1839) Stonecutter, builder	AJ		6	2	2,470	Methodist; son of Robert Stewart, see Table A3.2; mayor; CE, PE
Stouffer, Henry Pa. (1762–1835) DW	J		3		1,061	New resident 1784; see Table A3.3; SB; PE

Table A3.7. (*cont.*)

Name, Birthplace Dates, Occupation(s)	Party	Acres	Lots	Slaves	Value ($)	Comments
Stran, Thomas P. Mathematical instrument maker			2		570	Methodist; FB; PE
Tensfield, John Blacksmith	AJ		2	1	1,120	FB; PE
Thomas, James H. (1792–1842) Grocer	AJ		5	2	530	FB; PE
Thomas, Lambert (ca. 1782–1835) Cabinetmaker	AJ		7	2	920	Methodist; FB, SB; PE
Tyson, Alexander H.	AJ				min.	M. as Episcopalian; FB; PE
Vansant, Joshua						HD; DE, PE; see Table A3.6
Webb, Charles England (d. 1849) Soap and candle manufacturer	AJ		4		480	New resident 1810; FB; PE
Wight, William J.						SB; DE, PE; see Table A3.6
Williams, Nathaniel F.						Md. senate; DE, PE; see Table A3.6
Williamson, George N. Attorney	AJ		1		210	FB; PE
Wollen, Zackariah					min.	FB; PE
Worthington, John Tolly Hood Balt. Co. (1788–1849)	J		4		1,377	Episcopalian; U.S. Congress; PE
Yates, Dr. John L. Doctor	AJ		5		1,090	Episcopalian; FB; PE
Young, McClintock						FB; DE, PE; see Table A3.6
Zimmerman, Jacob (ca. 1787) Wheelwright	J		3		490	Episcopalian; FB; PE

Table A3.8. Baltimore City, Propertied Elite, Second Party Era

Name, Birthplace, Dates, Occupation(s)	Party	Acres	Lots	Slaves	Value ($)	Comments
Albert, Jacob						CE, DE, TE (rank no. 021); see Table A3.6
Armstrong, James, Jr. (d. 1852) Grocery and commission merchant	J		12	2	10,400	Presbyterian; CE, TE (013)
Armstrong, Robert (1793–1862) Soap and candle manufacturer	J		14		4,620	TE (095)
Bailey, George Druggist	AJ		8		4,800	Episcopalian; TE (088)
Baker, Dr. Samuel Doctor			4	2	5,390	TE (072)
Barnum, David (1770–1844) Hotel proprietor	AJ		4		15,740	Episcopalian; TE (007)
Betts, Solomon (d. 1841) Flour merchant	AJ		5		5,270	See Table A3.1; CE, TE (078)
Birckhead, Hugh (ca. 1788–1853) Commission merchant	AJ		5		5,080	CE, TE (083)
Birckhead, Dr. Solomon Dorchester Co. (1761–1836) Merchant			7		7,170	MD, U. Pa. (1783); TE (040)
Bosley, James Merchant, counting house			12	2	9,910	M. as Episcopalian; TE (015)
Brown, Stewart Ireland (ca. 1768–1832)			15	2	6,530	See Table A3.1; PE, TE (052)
Carey, James, Jr. (ca. 1751–1834)			3		6,140	Episcopalian; TE (056)
Carrere, John France (ca. 1759–1841)			7		5,440	See Table A3.4; TE (071)

Table A3.8. *(cont.)*

Name, Birthplace, Dates, Occupation(s)	Party	Acres	Lots	Slaves	Value ($)	Comments
Carroll, Charles R. DW	J		1		7,520	TE (034)
Carroll, Henry D. G. (b. ca. 1785)	AJ		7		5,900	TE (060)
Carroll, James, Jr.						DE, PE, TE (005); see Table A3.6
Caton, Richard England (1763–1845)			5	2	4,480	See Table A3.2; TE (099)
Clark, John Lottery and exchange office	AJ		2	1	9,410	Episcopalian; CE, TE (020)
Cohen, Joshua I. Va. (1801–70) Banker DW			8	2	5,880	Jewish; CE, TE (061)
Cox, Joseph Importer			12	2	5,700	Presbyterian; TE (064)
Dailey, Daniel			13	1	4,610	TE (096)
Donnell, John, Sr. (ca. 1788–1835) Merchant			11		8,800	CE, TE (025)
Dugan, Cumberland Ireland (1747–1836) DW	J		11	2	7,740	See Table A3.2; TE (032)
Earnest, George China merchant			11		4,520	Methodist; TE (098)
Edmondson, Thomas DW			4		9,960	Episcopalian; TE (014)
Evans, Hugh W.						CE, DE ,TE (059); see Table A3.6
Freeman, William H.						CE, DE, TE (084); see Table A3.6
Fridge, Alexander (ca. 1765–1839) Merchant	AJ		10		6,290	Presbyterian; CE, TE (055)
Frieze, Philip R. J. Window glass manufacturer			11	2	5,560	TE (069)

Table A3.8. Baltimore City, Propertied Elite, Second Party Era (*cont.*)

Name, Birthplace, Dates, Occupation(s)	Party	Acres	Lots	Slaves	Value ($)	Comments
Gibbes, Robert M. DW			5	2	9,670	Presbyterian; m.d. Robert Oliver; brother-in-law of R. L. Colt; TE (016)
Gilmor, Robert, Jr. Balt. (1774–1848) Merchant	AJ		8	2	9,510	Presbyterian; son of Robert Gilmor (see Table A3.3); TE (019)
Gittings, John Sterett Balt. (b. 1798) Stock exchange and commission merchant			20	2	7,510	See Table A3.5; CE, TE (035)
Gold, Peter Sea captain	AJ		7		4,470	PE, TE (100)
Harden, Samuel President Powhattan Manufacturing Co.	AJ		6		5,390	TE (073)
Hoffman, Daniel Pa. (1768–1842) Auctioneer, commission merchant	AJ		7		4,770	CE, TE (094)
Hoffman, George DW			30	2	17,790	Episcopalian; TE (004)
Hoffman, John Balt. (1796–1846) Merchant			6		7,320	TE (037)
Hoffman, Peter, Jr. Balt. (b. ca. 1796) Merchant			20	2	7,350	Zion Lutheran; TE (036)
Hopkins, Johns Anne Arundel Co. (1795–1873) Grocery merchant			8		5,370	TE (074)
Howard, Benjamin Chew						CE, DE, PE, TE (030); see Table A3.6
Howard, Charles						DE, TE (022); see Table A3.6

Table A3.8. (*cont.*)

Name, Birthplace, Dates, Occupation(s)	Party	Acres	Lots	Slaves	Value ($)	Comments
Howard, George Balt. (1789–1846) Governor	AJ		26	2	5,500	Episcopalian; son of Colonel John E. Howard, see entry for B. C. Howard, Table A3.6; TE (070)
Howard, James Md. (1797–1870) Bank president	J		36		8,950	Episcopalian; son of Colonel J. E. Howard; CE, TE (023)
Howard, John Eager, Jr. Md. (b. 1801)			28		4,590	Episcopalian; son of Colonel J. E. Howard; TE (097)
Howard, Dr. William (1793–1834)			29		9,530	Episcopalian; TE (018)
Hutton, James Merchant			5	1	4,990	Presbyterian; CE, TE (085)
Jones, Talbot (ca. 1771–1833) Grocery, commission merchant	AJ		8		6,720	Episcopalian; CE, TE (047)
Karthaus, Peter Arnold			6		5,670	Zion Lutheran church; TE (066)
Keerl, Dr. Henry			9		4,780	German Reformed church; TE (093)
Kelso, John Ireland			10		6,140	Methodist; brother of Thomas Kelso, see Table A3.6; TE (057)
Kerr, Archibald Merchant	J		5	2	5,270	Presbyterian; CE, TE (079)
Keyser, Samuel Keyser and Schaeffer, merchants			7	2	5,770	Episcopalian; TE (062)
Levering, Peter (ca. 1765–1834) DW	AJ		7	2	5,290	TE (076)
Lorman, William (1764–1841) Merchant	AJ		34	2	23,170	Episcopalian; see Table A3.3; CE, TE (003)
Lowe, Henderson P. DW			5		6,640	TE (050)

Table A3.8. Baltimore City, Propertied Elite, Second Party Era (*cont.*)

Name, Birthplace, Dates, Occupation(s)	Party	Acres	Lots	Slaves	Value ($)	Comments
McDonald, William						CE, DE, TE (012); see Table A3.6
McFadon, George			8		5,220	TE (081)
McHenry, James			37		7,220	TE (039)
McKim, Isaac						DE, PE, TE (009); see Table A3.6
McKim, John, Jr.						CE, DE, TE (045); see Table A3.6
McKim, Samuel Del. (1768–1834) Dry goods merchant	AJ		12		6,540	Presbyterian; CE, TE (051)
McKim, William D. Md. Merchant			44		13,560	Brother of I. McKim; TE (010)
Moore, George W.			8		5,660	M. as Methodist; TE (067)
Morris, John Boucher						CE, DE, PE, TE (024); see Table A3.6
Norris, William, Jr. Balt. Dry goods importer			8		4,930	Mason; Odd Fellow; TE (086)
O'Donnell, Columbus Balt. (1792–1873) DW	J		12		7,820	Presbyterian; son of John O'Donnell (see Table A3.2); TE (031)
Oliver, Robert Ireland (ca. 1757–1834) Merchant			25	2	26,120	Presbyterian; daus m. R. L. Colt and R. M. Gibbes; see Table A3.2; TE (002)
Orndorff, John H. Flour merchant			18		5,090	TE (082)
Patterson, Edward Balt. (b. 1789) Iron merchant	AJ		10	2	8,540	Presbyterian; son of William Patterson (TE), brother of Henry (TE) and Joseph W. Patterson (TE); TE (027)
Patterson, George Balt. (b. 1793)			5		6,820	M. as Methodist; for family, see above; TE (046)

Table A3.8. (*cont.*)

Name, Birthplace, Dates, Occupation(s)	Party	Acres	Lots	Slaves	Value ($)	Comments
Patterson, Henry Balt. (b. 1800)		6			8,150	Presbyterian; for family, see above; TE (029)
Patterson, Joseph Wilson Balt. (1786–1866) Iron works		3	2		6,060	Presbyterian; for family, see above; PE, TE (058)
Patterson, William						CE, DE, TE (001); see Table A3.6
Peters, George Balt. (b. 1804) DW	AJ	14	2		5,240	Methodist; TE (080)
Piper, James						DE, TE (017); see Table A3.6
Price, William (ca. 1794–1868) DW	J	9	2		5,280	Episcopalian; TE (077)
Randall, Beale						CE, DE, PE, TE (089); see Table A3.6
Read, William George						DE, TE (048); see Table A3.6
Reinicker, George DW		26	2		15,440	Zion Lutheran; see Table A3.3; TE (008)
Riddle, Robert		3			4,790	Episcopalian; TE (090)
Riddlemosher, Michael		22			4,790	German Catholic; TE (091)
Rogers, Lloyd N.		12			4,900	Episcopalian; TE (087)
Sauervine, Peter Flour dealer and grocer	AJ	8			5,690	TE (065)
Sheppard, Moses Milliner		23			7,000	TE (044)
Smith, Robert Pa. (1758–1842) Attorney		7	2		8,690	Presbyterian; brother of Samuel Smith; see Table A3.2; CE, TE (026)
Smith, Samuel R. (ca. 1741–1831) DW		8	2		7,130	TE (041)

Table A3.8. Baltimore City, Propertied Elite, Second Party Era (cont.)

Name, Birthplace, Dates, Occupation(s)	Party	Acres	Lots	Slaves	Value ($)	Comments
Taylor, Robert Alexander Auctioneer, commission merchant	AJ		10		7,580	Presbyterian; CE, TE (033)
Tenant, Thomas (ca. 1767–1836) Merchant	J		14	2	13,290	Episcopalian; see Table A3.3; CE, TE (011)
Thomas, Philip Evan (1776–1861) Pres. B&O RR Co.			4		4,790	Quaker; CE, TE (092)
Tiernan, Luke						CE, DE, TE (006); see Table A3.6
Todhunter, Joseph (ca. 1781–1848) Dry goods merchant			6		5,935	Episcopalian; CE, TE (075)
Torrance, Charles (b. 1788)			9		7,030	TE (043)
Tyson, Nathaniel (1787–1867) Flour merchant			5		6,340	M. into Ellicott family; TE (053)
Walsh, Adam Pa. (1763–1841) Tanner			10	2	6,310	German Evangelical church; new resident after Rev.; TE (054)
Walsh, John (ca. 1782–1858) Lumber merchant	AJ		20		8,160	Catholic; TE (028)
Wilkins, Joseph DW			9		7,240	TE (038)
Wilkins, William			6		6,988	TE (049)
Wilson, James (b. 1765) Hardware merchant	AJ		9	2	7,100	CE, TE (042)
Wilson, Thomas Harford Co. (b. 1789) DW	AJ		9		5,740	CE, TE (063)
Winchester, George						DE, TE (068); see Table A3.6

Table A3.9. Frederick County, Decisional Elite, First Party Era

Name, Birthplace, Dates, Occupation(s)	Party	Acres	Lots	Slaves	Value (£)	Comments
Baer, George, Jr. Fred. Co. (1763–1834) Merchant	F	2,500	15		920	Ftwn. Evangelical Reform church; German; militia captain; DE, PE, TE
Baltzell, Charles	R	369			655	Militia major; DE
Baltzell, Dr. John Doctor	F	140			75	Lutheran; German; DE
Brengle, Lawrence (1765–1822)	R	500			1,300	Ftwn. Evangelical Reform church; German; militia officer; sheriff; related to Shrivers; DE, TE
Brooke, Basil	F				min.	DE
Brother, Valentine	F				495	Militia officer; British; DE, PE
Bruce, Upton (d. 1829)	R	1,060			1,600	Scot; militia captain; DE, PE, TE
Butler, Tobias (b. 1747)	R	248			530	Episcopalian; British; Mason; DE
Campbell, William Charles Co. (1757–1821)	F	2,030		33	4,900	Episcopalian; Scotch-Irish; moved to Fred. Co. 1797; co-founder Ftwn. *Md. Herald*; DE, PE, TE
Carberry, Henry (b. ca. 1756)	F	380			800	Militia general; DE
Clarke, Daniel, Jr. Attorney	R				min.	English-Welsh; DE, PE
Cockey, Joshua (1755–1827)	R	150			157	British; DE, PE
Colegate, John (d. 1803)	R	400			600	British; identified as Rev. patriot; militia major; DE, PE
Colvin, John Bond Editor, Ftwn. Republican Advocate	R				min.	Formerly of Baltimore City, where worked for Pechin's Balt. *American*; DE
Creager, John	R	557			747	German; DE
Darnall, Henry (d. 1809)	F	2,270			3,200	British; militia major; DE, PE, TE

Table A3.9. Frederick County, Decisional Elite, First Party Era (*cont.*)

Name, Birthplace, Dates, Occupation(s)	Party	Acres	Lots	Slaves	Value (£)	Comments
Dorsey, Joshua	F/R				min.	Episcopalian; British; former member of HD; DE
Duvall, Dr. Grafton Doctor	R				min.	Episcopalian; DE
Duvall, Samuel	R	550			731	Episcopalian; British; former member HD; DE
Emmitt, William (d. 1818)	F	28			161	Presbyterian; British; militia officer; DE, PE
Gist, Joshua (1746–1839)	F	868	10		1,266	British; militia colonel; Rev. officer; DE, PE, TE
Gwinn, John	F	260			590	British; DE, PE
Harbaugh, Jacob, Sr. (1730–1818)	R	2,050			1,300	German; DE, TE
Hawkins, Thomas (1748–1821)	R	2,560		35	2,400	Episcopalian; active in Rev.; militia major; DE, PE, TE
Hoffman, John (1755–1831)	R				500	Episcopalian; German; DE, PE
Johnson, Baker Calvert Co. (1748–1811)	F	2,560		13	3,600	Episcopalian; see entry for Thomas Johnson, below, for family connections; militia colonel; del. to Constitutional Convention (1775); DE, PE, TE
Johnson, James, Sr. Calvert Co. (1736–1809) Attorney	F	2,190		10	2,200	Episcopalian; Eng.-Welsh; militia colonel; see Thomas Johnson for family connections; DE, PE, TE
Johnson, Thomas Calvert Co. (1732–1819) Attorney	F	3,250		5	4,300	Episcopalian; Eng.-Welsh; moved with brothers, Baker and James, to Fred. Co. 1774; member Const. Con. (1774–76), first gov. of Md., HD (1780s), declined election to Md. senate (1786); DE, TE

Table A3.9. (*cont.*)

Name, Birthplace, Dates, Occupation(s)	Party	Acres	Lots	Slaves	Value (£)	Comments
Key, John Ross Cecil Co. (1754–1821)	F	1,800		18	2,500	Episcopalian; son of Francis Key, brother of Philip Barton Key, father of Francis Scott Key; HD, CCt; militia general; DE, TE
Kuhn, Henry Fred. Co. (1760–1834)	R	509			916	Evangelical Reformed church; German; militia officer; DE, PE
McKaleb, Joseph	F	1,410			550	British; DE
McPherson, John Pa. (1760–1829)	F	540		14	1,100	Presbyterian; son married into Johnson family; militia colonel; DE, PE, TE
Myers, Michael	R	120			201	DE
Nelson, Roger Fred. Co. (1762–1815) Attorney	R	890	3	6	1,500	Episcopalian; militia officer; Mason; sons active during second party era; DE, PE, TE
Polk, Charles P.	R				min.	British; DE
Potts, Richard Prince Georges Co. (1753–1808) Attorney, judge	F	1,660	1	25	4,700	Episcopalian; British; DE, PE, TE
Potts, William Md. (1741–1817) merchant	F	840		15	3,700	Episcopalian; British; brother of Richard Potts; OCt (declined); DE, TE
Sappington, Dr. Francis Brown Fred. Co. (1760–1839) Doctor	F		3		100	British; militia officer; DE, PE
Schley, George Jacob	F				425	Ftwn. Evangelical Reform church; militia officer; German; DE
Sheredine, Upton Balt. Co. (1740–1800)	F	1,020	2		2,000	Episcopalian; member Constitutional Convention, HD, CCt; militia officer; DE, PE, TE

Table A3.9. Frederick County, Decisional Elite, First Party Era (*cont.*)

Name, Birthplace, Dates, Occupation(s)	Party	Acres	Lots	Slaves	Value (£)	Comments
Shriver, Abraham (1771–1848) Ftwn. merchant	R				min.	Ftwn. Evangelical Reformed church; German; militia officer; son of David Shriver, Sr. (DE, PE), brother of Andrew Shriver (DE, PE), brother-in-law of John Schley (PE); DE, PE
Shriver, Andrew Md. (1762–1847) Miller, Union Mills	R	52			53	Ftwn. Evangelical Reformed church; German; for social connections, see above; DE, PE
Shriver, David, Sr. Pa. (1735–1826)	R	312			653	German; Rev. soldier, member Constitutional Convention, HD; militia officer, for social connections, see above; DE, PE
Stemple, Frederick	R	470			738	German; DE
Swearingen, Joseph (d. 1825)	R	130			133	British; militia officer; DE, PE
Taney, Roger B. Calvert Co. (1777–1864) Attorney	F				min.	Catholic; British; son of Michael Taney; read law with Jeremiah Townley Chase in Annapolis, bar (1799); HD (Cal. Co.); to Ftwn. (1800); m.d. Colonel John Ross Key (DE, TE); Md. senate; to Balt. City; DE
Thomas, John (1754–1849)	F	153			153	Episcopalian; Eng.-Welsh; militia officer; father of Francis Thomas, see Table A3.13; DE, PE
Thomas, John Hanson Fred. Co. (d. 1815) Attorney	F				min.	Son of Dr. Philip Thomas (DE, TE); DE
Thomas, Dr. Philip Kent Co. (1747–1815) Doctor	F	960			2,000	Episcopalian; Eng.-Welsh; to Fred. Co. 1769, Rev. Comm. of Safety; HD; DE, TE

Table A3.9. (cont.)

Name, Birthplace, Dates, Occupation(s)	Party	Acres	Lots	Slaves	Value (£)	Comments
Thompson, John P. Editor, Ftwn. *Herald*	F				min.	Brought from Pa. to edit Federalist paper 1802; DE
Tyler, Dr. John Prince Georges Co. (1762–1841) Doctor	R				300	Episcopalian; British; Mason; see Table A3.13; DE, PE
Wampler, Ludwig	R	25			405	Ftwn. Evangelical Reformed church; German; DE
Warfield, Henry Ridgely					min.	DE, PE
Waters, Joab	R	700			210	Militia captain; DE, PE

Table A3.10. Frederick County, Positional Elite, First Party Era

Name, Birthplace, Dates, Occupation(s)	Party	Acres	Lots	Slaves	Value (£)	Comments
Baer, George, Jr.						HD, U.S. Cong., OCt; see Table A3.9; DE, PE, TE
Ballinger, William		199			382	Quaker; British; OCt; PE
Beall, William Murdock, Sr. (ca. 1741–1823)	F	5,071			1,245	Episcopalian; British; HD; OCt; PE
Beatty, William (ca. 1739–1803)	F	430	3	13	1,300	Episcopalian; British; militia colonel; HD; PE, TE
Biggs, Benjamin (ca. 1760–1819)	R	165			308	Lutheran; British; HD, LC PE
Brother, Valentine						HD, LC; see Table A3.9; DE, PE
Bruce, Upton						CCt, HD; see Table A3.9; DE, PE, TE
Campbell, William						LC; see Table A3.9; DE, PE, TE
Carlton, John Usher	F				min.	Episcopalian; British; Rev. officer; OCt; PE
Clarke, Daniel, Jr.						HD; see Table A3.9; DE, PE

Table A3.10. Frederick County, Positional Elite, First Party Era *(cont.)*

Name, Birthplace, Dates, Occupation(s)	Party	Acres	Lots	Slaves	Value (£)	Comments
Clemson, John (1758–1846)	F	470			1,000	British; LC; PE, TE
Cockey, Joshua						CCt, HD; see Table A3.9; DE, PE
Colegate, John						CCt; see Table A3.9; DE, PE
Craik, William Charles Co. (1761–1814) Attorney	F				min.	HD (Chas. Co.), Judge, U.S. Congress; PE
Darnall, Henry						OCt; see Table A3.9; DE, PE, TE
Davis, Ignatius (1759–1828)	F	500	12		2,000	Methodist; Eng.-Welsh; LC; PE, TE
Emmitt, William						LC; see Table A3.9; DE, PE
Farquhar, Benjamin	R				min.	Quaker; British; LC; PE
Gist, Joshua						HD; see Table A3.9; DE, PE, TE
Gwinn, John						HD, LC; see Table A3.9; DE, PE
Hawkins, Thomas						HD; see Table A3.9; DE, PE, TE
Hoffman, John						LC; see Table A3.9; DE, PE
Johnson, Baker						OCt; see Table A3.9; DE, PE, TE
Johnson, James, Sr.						LC; see Table A3.9; DE, PE TE
Kemp, Christian	R				min.	Lutheran; German; LC; PE
Kemp, Henry (1763–1833)	R				min.	Lutheran; German; militia officer; HD, OCt; PE
Kemp, Joseph					min.	OCt; PE
Kuhn, Henry						LC, HD, OCt; see Table A3.9; DE, PE
McPherson, John						CCt; see Table A3.9; DE, PE, TE
Magill, Patrick	R				min.	British; OCt; PE

Table A3.10. (*cont.*)

Name, Birthplace, Dates, Occupation(s)	Party	Acres	Lots	Slaves	Value (£)	Comments
Nelson, Roger						HD, Md. senate, U.S. Congress, judge; see Table A3.9; DE, PE, TE
Peters, John	R	100			225	Lutheran; LC; PE
Potts, Richard						Md. senate, U.S. Senate, U.S. attorney; see Table A3.9; DE, PE, TE
Quynn, Allen, Jr.					min.	Irish; HD; PE
Sappington, Francis Brown						OCt, HD, LC; see Table A3.9; DE, PE
Schley, John (1767–1835)	R	324			887	Ftwn. Evangelical Reformed church; German; m. into Shriver family; LC, OCt, HD; PE
Sellman, Leonard					min.	OCt; PE
Sheridine, Upton						CCt, OCt; see Table A3.9; DE, PE, TE
Shriver, Abraham						CCt; see Table A3.9; DE, PE
Shriver, Andrew						LC; see Table A3.9; DE, PE
Shriver, David, Sr.						HD, Md. senate; see Table A3.9; DE, PE
Spalding, Henry (b. ca. 1747)	F	545			865	Catholic; British; LC; PE
Swearingen, Joseph						LC, CCt (refused), HD; see Table A3.9; DE, PE
Thomas, John						HD, LC; see Table A3.9; DE, PE
Tyler, Dr. John						Md. senate; see Table A3.9; DE, PE
Warfield, Alexander of Charles (1764–1835)		662			907	Methodist; LC; PE
Warfield, Henry Ridgely						HD; see Table A3.9; DE, PE
Waters, Joab						HD; see Table A3.9; DE, PE

Table A3.10. Frederick County, Positional Elite, First Party Era (*cont.*)

Name, Birthplace, Dates, Occupation(s)	Party	Acres	Lots	Slaves	Value (£)	Comments
Williams, Henry (1743–1820)	R	281			446	Presbyterian; Eng.-Welsh; LC; PE
Winchester, Richard Fred. Co. (1759–1822)	F	270			1,000	British; militia officer; uncle of James Winchester (Table A3.2, 11); LC; PE, TE

Table A3.11. Frederick County, Propertied Elite, First Party Era

Name, Birthplace, Dates, Occupation(s)	Party	Acres	Lots	Slaves	Value (£)	Comments
Amelung, Frederick M.		800			1,200	German; TE (rank no. 071)
Amelung, Jno. Frederick		1,990			1,500	German; TE (041)
Anderson, Edward		600		14	1,100	British; TE (072)
Baer, George, Jr.						DE, PE, TE (093); see Table A3.9
Bale, Peter	F	670			900	German; TE (094)
Beale, Joseph		1,090			1,300	TE (050)
Beatty, William						PE, TE (051); see Table A3.10
Belt, Jeremiah (ca. 1743–1818)	F	710		26	1,000	Episcopalian; British; TE (092)
Black, Joseph Miller		190			1,000	TE (091)
Brengle, Lawrence						DE, TE (049); see Table A3.9
Browning, Jeremiah	R	620			1,700	British; TE (034)
Bruce, Upton						DE, PE, TE (040); see Table A3.9
Brunner, John (1745–1819)	F	600		2	2,100	Ftwn. Evangelical Reformed; German; TE (020)
Campbell, William						DE, PE, TE (004); see Table A3.9

Table A3.11. (cont.)

Name, Birthplace, Dates, Occupation(s)	Party	Acres	Lots	Slaves	Value (£)	Comments
Carroll, Charles of Carrollton Anne Arundel Co. (1737–1832)	F	12,873		9	35,790	Catholic; active in Rev., Md. senate; res. A. A. Co.; TE (001)
Caton, Richard England (1763–1845)		790		8	1,600	British; son-in-law of C. Carroll of Carrollton, res. Balt. City; see Table A3.2; TE (036)
Clark, James		2,120			1,800	TE (033)
Clemson, John						PE, TE (080); see Table A3.10
Cookerly, John, Sr. (1740–1806)	F	770		16	1,300	Lutheran; TE (058)
Creager, Adam		780		1	1,200	Ftwn. Evangelical Reformed church; German; TE (060)
Creager, Lawrence	R	500			1,000	German; TE (081)
Crum, William, Sr. (1741–1810)	F	480		2	1,500	Episcopalian; British; TE (045)
Darnall, Henry						DE, PE, TE (012); see Table A3.9
Darnall, Thomas (b. 1769)		1,390			1,400	British; militia major; TE (046)
Davis, Ignatius						PE, TE (024); see Table A3.10
Derr, John	R	330		5	1,200	Ftwn. Evangelical Reformed church; TE (059)
Devilbiss, Casper (ca. 1761–1835)	F	630			1,000	Ftwn. Evangelical Reformed church; TE (082)
Dorsey, Basil	F	1,940		14	2,400	British; TE (017)
Dorsey, Daniel	F	520		17	1,200	British; TE (078)
Dorsey, Eli	F	850		19	1,100	British; TE (079)
Dorsey, Evan	F	1,120		13	1,500	British; TE (044)
Duderow, Conrad, Sr.	F	650			1,200	Lutheran; German; TE (061)

Table A3.11. Frederick County, Propertied Elite, First Party Era *(cont.)*

Name, Birthplace, Dates, Occupation(s)	Party	Acres	Lots	Slaves	Value (£)	Comments
Dulany, Benjamin		2,700			5,500	Identified as res. of Charles Co.; TE (003)
Farquhar, Allen	R	1,410			1,900	Quaker; British; TE (029)
Fleming, Robert	F	460		7	900	Presbyterian; British; militia captain; TE (100)
Fout, Battis		470			1,400	TE (047)
Gist, Joshua						DE, PE, TE (057); see Table A3.9
Graham, John (1760–1833)	F	400		19	1,300	Episcopalian; British; m. into Johnson family; militia major; HD (Cal. Co.), CCt (Fred. Co. 1792–95); TE (056)
Hammond, John	F	1,860		11	2,500	British; TE (016)
Harbaugh, Jacob, Sr.						DE, TE (055); see Table A3.9
Harris, Nathan	F	1,710		23	1,100	Eng.-Welsh; TE (074)
Hawkins, Thomas						DE, PE, TE (018); see Table A3.9
Herring, Henry, Sr.	F	430			900	TE (098)
House, William (ca. 1733–1822)	R	1,050		8	1,200	Lutheran; German; to Fred. Co. 1750; TE (065)
Howard, Ephraim	F	1,010		15	2,000	Episcopalian; British; TE (023)
Howard, Joshua	F	710		16	1,900	Presbyterian; British; TE (030)
Hynor, Harbett		840			1,000	TE (084)
James, Daniel (1763–1838)	F	540		13	900	Eng.-Welsh; militia major; TE (099)
Johnson, Baker						DE, PE, TE (010); see Table A3.9
Johnson, Benjamin A.	F	670		17	1,000	Episcopalian; Eng.-Welsh; militia officer; TE (083)
Johnson, James						DE, PE, TE (019); see Table A3.9

Table A3.11. (*cont.*)

Name, Birthplace, Dates, Occupation(s)	Party	Acres	Lots	Slaves	Value (£)	Comments
Johnson, James F.		980			1,100	TE (075)
Johnson, Roger (1749–1831)	F	4,310		33	2,500	Episcopalian; Eng.-Welsh; member of Johnson family (see Table A3.9); TE (015)
Johnson, Thomas						DE, TE (007); see Table A3.9
Johnson, Thomas, Jr.	F	8,250			1,200	Episcopalian; Eng.-Welsh; TE (064)
Kephart, David (1762–1836)	F	350		2	1,800	Lutheran; German; militia officer; TE (032)
Key, John Ross						DE, TE (014); see Table A3.9
Landis, Henry	F	210		4	1,100	German; TE (076)
Lee, Thomas Simms (1745–1819)	F	2,660		109	4,400	Catholic; Eng.-Welsh; politically active in Rev. period, Rev. Constitutional Convention, HD, Gov.; TE (006)
Luckett, William	R	950		2	1,200	Episcopalian; British; militia colonel; TE (063)
McPherson, John						DE, PE, TE (077); see Table A3.9
Mannidier, Henry		1,350			2,100	TE (022)
Marshall, James	F	1,380			3,000	British; TE (013)
Masters, Lehaskins		4,510			4,000	TE (008)
Metcalfe, Thomas		730			1,900	TE (031)
Metzler, Ulrich		540			1,200	TE (062)
Murdock, George (1742–1805) Register of wills	F	440		9	1,400	Episcopalian; Scot; moved to Fred. Co. 1765, active in Rev. Comm. of Safety and Observation; militia colonel; TE (048)
Neill, Thomas (b. ca. 1742)		500			1,200	Presbyterian; Scotch-Irish; TE (070)
Nelson, Roger						DE, PE, TE (043); see Table A3.9

Table A3.11. Frederick County, Propertied Elite, First Party Era (*cont.*)

Name, Birthplace, Dates, Occupation(s)	Party	Acres	Lots	Slaves	Value (£)	Comments
Nichodemus, Henry	R	290			900	German; TE (095)
Ogle, Alexander		260			1,300	Baptist; British; militia officer; TE (053)
Ogle, James (b. 1753)		670			900	Episcopalian; British; TE (096)
Owings, Edward	F	570		19	1,600	British; TE (039)
Patterson, Bennet		560			1,000	TE (090)
Philpot, Barton, Sr.		590		19	1,300	TE (052)
Pool, Henry, Sr. (1764–1822)	F	1,180		12	1,100	British; TE (073)
Potts, Richard						DE, PE, TE (005); see Table A3.9
Potts, William						DE, TE (009); see Table A3.9
Ramsberg, John (ca. 1741–1807)	F	370			2,100	Ftwn. Evangelical Reformed church; German, TE (021)
Randall, Nicholas	F	600		13	1,200	British; militia major; TE (069)
Reynolds, Hugh (ca. 1752–1804)	F	634		9	1,682	Presbyterian; British; TE (038)
Ritchie, John (ca. 1757–1826)	F	600		2	1,532	Presbyterian; Scot; militia colonel; TE (089)
Schnertzell, George	R	840			1,700	TE (035)
Scott, Upton		5,080		9	6,295	TE (002); probably resident of Anne Arundel Co.
Shelmerdine, Stephen	F	920		12	1,300	Methodist; British; TE (054)
Sheridine, Upton						PE, TE (026); see Table A3.9
Shriner, Peter, Sr. (ca. 1747–1838)	F	620			1,900	German; TE (028)
Shriver, Frederick William (1744–1820)	R	620		2	1,200	Lutheran; German; TE (066)

Table A3.11. (*cont.*)

Name, Birthplace, Dates, Occupation(s)	Party	Acres	Lots	Slaves	Value (£)	Comments
Simpson, Richard, Sr.		490			1,000	British; Rev. officer; TE (088)
Smith, Philip	R	930			1,200	Lutheran; Rev. officer; TE (067)
Sprigg, Thomas	F	800			900	Zion Episcopal; British; TE (097)
Thomas, Dr. Philip						DE, TE (025); see Table A3.9
Troxel, John (1747–1830)	F	650		2	1,600	Lutheran; German; TE (037)
Waddington, Joshua		1,780			3,400	Absentee owner living in N.Y.; TE (011)
Weller, John of Jacob (1770–1818)	F	830			1,200	Lutheran; German; TE (068)
Wells, Thomas	R	430		2	1,000	British; TE (085)
Winchester, James Fred. Co. (1772–1806) Attorney	F	270			1,000	British; Balt. City res.; TE (087)
Winchester, Richard						PE, TE (086); see Table A3.10
Wolf, Jacob	F	950		9	1,500	German; TE (042)
Worman, Andrew (ca. 1746–1811)	R	680			1,900	Methodist; TE (027)

Table A3.12. Frederick County, Commercial Elite, Second Party Era

Name, Birthplace, Dates, Occupation(s)	Party	Acres	Lots	Slaves	Value ($)	Comments
Baer, George, Jr. Fred. Co. (1763–1834) Cashier, Fred. Co. Bank	AJ				min.	Former Federalist member of Cong.; see Table A3.9; CE

Table A3.12. Frederick County, Commercial Elite, Second Party Era *(cont.)*

Name, Birthplace, Dates, Occupation(s)	Party	Acres	Lots	Slaves	Value ($)	Comments
Baer, Jacob Pres., Ftwn. Savings Institution					min.	CE
Baltzell, Dr. John						CE, DE; see Table A3.13
Beall, William Murdoch, Jr.						CE, DE; see Table A3.13
Brien, John					min.	CE
Carlton, Thomas						CE, DE; see Table A3.13
Carmack, Samuel					min.	Militia captain; CE
Doyle, Henry Cashier, Fred. Co. Bank					min.	CE
Eichelberger, George M.						CE, DE; see Table A3.13
Englebrecht, George Sec., Ftwn. Savings Institution					min.	CE
Fessler, John					min.	CE
Gaither, Stephen Pres., Ftwn. Savings Institution					min.	CE
Gaither, William					min.	CE
Graham, John Fred. Co. (ca. 1760–1833) Pres., Fred. Co. Bank					min.	Son of Rev. soldier, m.d. Gov. Johnson; HD, OCt, Md. senate; CE
Hammond, Grafton					min.	Militia captain; CE
Hughes, Daniel Montreal (1773–1854)					min.	Militia officer; CE
Jones, Abraham						CE, DE, PE, TE; see Table A3.13
Kemp, Henry, Sr.						CE, DE, PE; see Table A3.13
McPherson, John II						CE, DE, TE; see Table A3.13

Table A3.12. (*cont.*)

Name, Birthplace, Dates, Occupation(s)	Party	Acres	Lots	Slaves	Value ($)	Comments
McPherson, Dr. William S.						CE, DE, PE, TE; see Table A3.13
Mantz, Caspar						CE, TE; see Table A3.15
Mantz, Cyrus						CE, DE; see Table A3.13
Medtart, Lewis Agent					min.	CE
Phillips, Noah					min.	Militia colonel; CE
Potts, Richard II						CE, DE, TE; see Table A3.13
Ross, William						CE, DE; see Table A3.13
Rutherford, Benjamin					min.	CE
Schaeffer, David F.					min.	CE
Schley, Frederick Augustus						CE, TE; see Table A3.15
Schley, Henry						CE,TE; see Table A3.15
Smith, Joseph L.						CE, PE; see Table A3.14
Smith, Joshua						CE, TE; see Table A3.15
Steiner, David Sec., Ftwn. Savings Institution					min.	CE
Stritchie, John C.					min.	CE
Thompson, John P. Pa. Pres., Fred. Co. Bank; bookstore					min.	Former Federalist editor of Ftwn. *Herald*; CE
Torrance, James						CE, TE; see Table A3.15
Turbutt, Nicholas Hotel owner						CE, PE; see Table A3.14
Tyler, Dr. John						CE, DE, TE; see Table A3.13
Tyler, Dr. William						CE, DE, TE; see Table A3.13
Tyler, Dr. William Bradley						CE, DE, TE; see Table A3.13

Table A3.13. **Frederick County, Decisional Elite, Second Party Era** (*cont.*)

Name, Birthplace, Dates, Occupation(s)	Party	Acres	Lots	Slaves	Value ($)	Comments
Hook, Thomas (1792–1869)	AJ	260		3	1,070	Methodist; militia colonel; DE
Johnson, Dr. Thomas W. (1794–1847) Doctor	AJ			3	40	Militia colonel; DE
Johnson, William Cost Fred. Co. (1801–60) Attorney	AJ			2	370	Reformed; son of William Johnson; DE, PE
Jones, Abraham (1777–1854)	AJ	820	7	4	5,360	Methodist; CE, DE, PE, TE
Kemp, David	AJ	800		18	7,900	Militia captain; DE, PE, TE
Kemp, Henry, Sr. (1763–1833)	AJ			18	2,110	Former Republican; member OCt; militia colonel; CE, DE, PE
Kinser, John	J	310		1	1,730	DE, PE
Lambert, Frederick	J				min.	DE
McElfresh, Dr. John Hammond Fred. Co. (1796–1841) Doctor, Attorney	AJ	750	1	2	5,740	M.d. Cyrus Mantz; studied law with Roger Nelson; DE, PE, TE
McKeehan, Dr. Samuel L. (d. 1836) Doctor, editor, Frederick Citizen	J				min.	DE
McKinstry, Evan (1779–1852)	AJ	150			2,070	DE, PE
McPherson, Edward B. Md.	AJ/J	410	4	17	7,700	DE, TE
McPherson, John II Fred. Co. (1796–1874)	AJ	2,420	6	18	10,910	Episcopalian; m. into Thomas Johnson family; father John McPherson; militia colonel; CE, DE, TE

Table A3.13. (*cont.*)

Name, Birthplace, Dates, Occupation(s)	Party	Acres	Lots	Slaves	Value ($)	Comments
McPherson, Dr. William Smith Pa. (1792–1879) Doctor	AJ	460	2	25	8,250	Militia surgeon's mate; to Fred. Co. 1818, to Baltimore 1843; CE, DE, PE, TE
Mantz, Cyrus	AJ			1	130	Lutheran; CE, DE
Markell, Jacob Merchant	J			1	130	DE
Matthias, Jacob (1782–1857)	AJ	260	1	2	1,860	Militia major; DE, PE
Morsell, William	AJ	210	2		810	DE, PE
Nelson, John Fred. Co. (1791–1860) Attorney	J				min.	Son of Congressman Roger Nelson, Republican leader, brother of Madison Nelson; m.d. of Thomas Tenant, Baltimore merchant; DE, PE
Nelson, Madison Fred. Co. (1803–67)	J				min.	For family, see above; DE
Niles, William Ogden Md. (1800–1857) Editor, *Frederick Herald*	AJ				380	Son of Balt. publisher, Hezekiah Niles; became coed. of *Niles Weekly Register* on father's death; DE
Nixdorff, Henry	J	1,400	2		5,170	DE
Palmer, Joseph M. Conn. (d. 1870) Attorney	J		1	1	1,600	Settled Ftwn. 1819; DE, PE
Poe, Neilson (1809–84) Editor, attorney, Ftwn. *Political Examiner*	AJ			3	280	DE
Potts, Richard II Fred. Co. (1786–1865)	AJ	1,140	2	4	7,360	Episcopalian; son Richard Potts, Federalist leader; CE, DE, TE
Price, George (b. 1791) Attorney	AJ	200			500	DE

Table A3.14. Frederick County, Positional Elite, Second Party Era

Name, Birthplace, Dates, Occupation(s)	Party	Acres	Lots	Slaves	Value ($)	Comments
Annan, Robert						HD; DE, PE; see Table A3.13
Baker, Henry					min.	LC; PE
Bowlus, George						HD; DE, PE; see Table A3.13
Brengle, Francis						HD; DE, PE; see Table A3.13
Buhrman, Henry					min.	LC; PE
Cost, John					min.	LC; PE
Crabs, Frederick					min.	LC; PE
Culler, Henry (1786–1861)	AJ	1,180	2	2	6,300	Lutheran; LC; PE, TE
Dorsey, Roderick						HD; DE, PE; see Table A3.13
Dudderar, William					min.	LC; PE
Duvall, Daniel						HD; DE, PE, TE; see Table A3.13
Duvall, Dr. Grafton Md. (1780–1841) Doctor					min.	Former Republican; LC; PE
Eichelberger, Martin					min.	LC; PE
Forrest, Solomon					min.	LC; PE
Foutz, David					min.	LC; PE
Fulton, Robert						LC; DE, PE, TE; see Table A3.13
Getzendanner, Christian					min.	LC; PE
Hammond, Thomas						HD; DE, PE; see Table A3.13
Harbaugh, John					min.	LC; PE
Harding, John L. (1779–1837)	AJ	620	10	10	5,100	OCt; PE, TE
Higgins, James L.		630		18	3,800	LC; PE, TE
Hoffman, George					min.	LC; PE

Table A3.14. *(cont.)*

Name, Birthplace, Dates, Occupation(s)	Party	Acres	Lots	Slaves	Value ($)	Comments
Hoffman, John (ca. 1756–1831) Merchant					min.	Active Republican leader; LC; PE
Johnson, William Cost						HD, U.S. Congress; DE, PE; see Table A3.13
Jones, Abraham						HD, LC; CE, DE, PE, TE; see Table A3.13
Kemp, Christian	AJ	580		11	6,800	Former Republican leader; LC; PE, TE
Kemp, David	AJ	800		18	7,900	Militia captain; HD; DE, PE, TE
Kemp, Henry, Sr.						OCt; CE, DE, PE; see Table A3.13
Kinser, John						HD; DE, PE; see Table A3.13
Kuhn, Henry (1761–1834)					min.	OCt; PE
Kuhn, Zebulon					min.	D.m. Nicholas Snyder; LC; PE
Lorentz, Adam					min.	LC; PE
Lugenbeel, John, Jr.	J				min.	OCt; PE
Lynch, William Fred. Co. (1788–1857)					min.	LC; PE
McCannon, William H.					min.	LC; PE
McElfresh, Dr. John Hammond						HD; DE, PE, TE; see Table A3.13
McKinstry, Evan						LC, HD; DE, PE; see Table A3.13
McPherson, William	AJ				min.	Militia major; HD; PE
McPherson, Dr. William S.						HD; CE, DE, PE, TE; see Table A3.13
Mantz, Peter (1752–1833)					min.	Militia major; OCt; PE
Matthias, Jacob						LC; DE, PE; see Table A3.13

Table A3.15. Frederick County, Propertied Elite, Second Party Era

Name, Birthplace, Dates, Occupation(s)	Party	Acres	Lots	Slaves	Value ($)	Comments
Atlee, Isaac		440			3,600	TE (rank no. 081)
Barger, Singleton		1,850		46	5,200	TE (037)
Bayard, R. H.		940			7,900	TE (010)
Birnie, Clotworthy	J	2,910			3,900	TE (068); absentee owner, attorney in Baltimore
Biser, John		430		10	4,000	TE (066)
Bowlus, John		300	1		3,700	TE (077)
Brengle, Jacob Fred. Co. (1774–1836)	AJ	590	3	10	7,800	TE (013)
Claggett, Henry		140			5,700	TE (030)
Clemson, John S.		910		10	6,200	TE (023)
Coale, James M. Attorney	AJ	480		11	3,300	TE (095)
Coblentz, Dr. John Paul Fred. Co. (1796–1859) Doctor		550		9	3,500	MD, U. Md. (1817); TE (087)
Culler, Henry						PE, TE (022); see Table A3.14
Cunningham, James		1,480		10	11,700	TE (003)
Davis, Thomas, Jr.		530		6	4,700	TE (045)
Derr, John S.		280	1	11	4,200	TE (056)
Devilbiss, Caspar, Sr.		630		2	3,300	TE (096)
Devilbiss, Samuel		1,270		10	4,200	TE (057)
Doub, Jacob S.		630		7	4,100	TE (060)
Doub, Valentine		470			4,100	TE (061)
Dudderar, John						DE, TE (097); see Table A3.13
Duvall, Daniel						DE, PE, TE (074); see Table A3.13
Erb, Peter	AJ	1,540		6	3,600	TE (082)
Fout, Balzer	AJ	470		3	4,800	TE (044)

Table A3.15. (cont.)

Name, Birthplace, Dates, Occupation(s)	Party	Acres	Lots	Slaves	Value ($)	Comments
Fulton, Robert						DE, PE, TE (069); see Table A3.13
Goldsborough, Dr. Edward G. Fred. Co. (1797–1850) Doctor		270	1	12	5,100	Son of William Goldsborough; TE (040)
Grabill, John	AJ	840		6	3,500	TE (088)
Haines, Uriah		800			3,500	TE (089)
Hammond, Nathan	AJ	600		16	3,400	TE (090)
Harding, John L.						PE, TE (041); see Table A3.14
Hawkins, James S.		580		16	5,900	TE (028)
Higgins, James L.						PE, TE (075); see Table A3.14
Holtz, Nicholas						DE, TE (016); see Table A3.13
Horsey, Outerbridge Somerset Co. (1777–1842)	AJ	430		39	5,200	Former U.S. senator from Delaware; son-in-law of Gov. Thomas Simms Lee, brother-in-law of former Congressman John Lee (TE); to Frederick Co. 1828; TE (038)
Hosselback, John	AJ	410		25	6,500	TE (020)
Houck, George	J	310	3		3,600	TE (083)
Howard, Dennis D.		1,030	2	13	7,900	TE (011)
Jackson, Bolton		340			3,700	TE (078)
Jackson, John R.		800			6,000	TE (025)
James, Daniel		1,320		15	4,300	Militia major; TE (053)
Jarboe, William	AJ	820		10	3,300	TE (098)
Johnson, Richard		830			3,400	Militia captain; member of Johnson family; TE (091)
Johnson, Thomas of William	AJ	520		7	4,700	Militia colonel; former Federalist; TE (046)

Table A3.15. Frederick County, Propertied Elite, Second Party Era *(cont.)*

Name, Birthplace, Dates, Occupation(s)	Party	Acres	Lots	Slaves	Value ($)	Comments
Shriver, Abraham Fred. Co. (1771–1848) Judge, CCt	AJ	190	5	3	4,100	Former Republican leader, see Table A3.9; TE (063)
Shriver, Jacob						Brother of Abraham Shriver; DE, PE, TE (072); see Table A3.13
Simmons, John H.						DE, PE, TE (094); see Table A3.13
Slingluff, Jesse						PE, TE (073); see Table A3.14
Smith, Joshua	AJ	370		5	3,700	CE, TE (080)
Sourer, Peter		350	5	3	5,400	TE (035)
Stokes, Robert Y.		480		10	5,600	TE (032)
Stoner, John S. Clover Seed Mill	J	610			5,300	TE (036)
Taylor, Griffin		660		25	8,400	TE (007)
Thomas, John (1754–1849)	J	730		16	5,100	Father of Francis Thomas; former Federalist leader; militia colonel; see Table A3.9; TE (043)
Thomas, Michael	J	860		5	6,600	TE (019)
Torrance, James		670	3	7	4,400	CE, TE (052)
Tyler, Dr. John						CE, DE, TE (100); see Table A3.13
Tyler, Dr. William						CE, DE, TE (009); see Table A3.13
Tyler, Dr. William Bradley						CE, DE, TE (099); see Table A3.13
VanBibber, Washington	AJ	750		19	5,600	TE (033)
Waesche, George H.		590		3	6,000	TE (027)
Warring, Henry		760			4,100	TE (064)
Wells, Thomas		440		8	4,100	Former Republican; TE (065)

Table A3.15. (*cont.*)

Name, Birthplace, Dates, Occupation(s)	Party	Acres	Lots	Slaves	Value ($)	Comments
Wilson, Dr. William M. Doctor, merchant		310	5	8	4,300	TE (055)
Worman, Moses						CE, DE, PE, TE (021); see Table A3.13

Table A3.16. St. Marys County, Positional Elite, First Party Era

Name, Birthplace, Dates, Occupation(s)	Party	Acres	Lots	Slaves	Value (£)	Comments
Barber, Luke White (d. 1830)		848		39	2,517	Episcopalian; d.m. Baltimore merchant; HD; PE, TE
Barber, Thomas (1766–1826)	R				min.	LC, OCt; PE
Blackistone, Thomas St. Marys Co. (1773–1837) Attorney					min.	Son of Nehemiah H. Blackistone (TE); HD; PE
Bond, Richard (d. 1808)		720		18	1,562	Episcopalian; LC; PE, TE
Brown, William H. Attorney					min.	HD; PE
Clarke, Matthias		283		8	858	LC; PE
Clements, Henry Mariner	R	202		13	709	LC; PE
DeButts, John (d. 1796)					min.	Episcopalian; CCt; PE
Egerton, James (d. 1810) Merchant in wheat trade	R	985		14	2,360	OCt; PE, TE
Fenwick, Athanasias (d. 1824) Attorney					min.	Catholic; militia officer; OCt; PE

Table A3.16. St. Marys County, Positional Elite, First Party Era (*cont.*)

Name, Birthplace, Dates, Occupation(s)	Party	Acres	Lots	Slaves	Value (£)	Comments
Thomas, William II St. Marys Co. (1758–1813)	R	1,210		52	3,530	Sons, James, George, Richard, active in second party era; militia major; HD, OCt, LC, CCt; Md. senate; PE, TE
Thompson, James Tavernkeeper		31		2	203	LC; PE

Table A3.17. St. Marys County, Propertied Elite, First Party Era

Name, Birthplace, Dates, Occupation(s)	Party	Acres	Lots	Slaves	Value (£)	Comments
Ashcom, John C.		670		7	1,730	TE (rank no. 31)
Barber, Luke White						PE, TE (16); see Table A3.16
Barber, W. Barnet		600		22	1,490	TE (44)
Barnes, Richard (d. 1804)	F	4,410		238	15,500	Rev. officer; militia general; del. Const. Convention (1788); OCt, HD; TE (01)
Biscoe, George Naval officer		880		32	2,500	Episcopalian; son of Thomas Biscoe; TE (17)
Biscoe, James		940		13	1,420	Episcopalian; TE (50)
Blackistone, Nehemiah Herbert St. Marys Co. (d. 1816)		850		21	2,660	Episcopalian; m. into Hebb family; father of Thomas Blackistone (PE); TE (14)
Bond, John of Thomas (d. 1814)		600		10	1,420	Episcopalian; TE (49)
Bond, Richard						PE, TE (38); see Table A3.16
Briscoe, John L. (d. 1822) Merchant		950		24	2,300	Mill; TE (20)

Table A3.17. *(cont.)*

Name, Birthplace, Dates, Occupation(s)	Party	Acres	Lots	Slaves	Value (£)	Comments
Briscoe, McBride *(minor)*		720		19	1,920	TE (24)
Brook, Francis (d. 1803)		700		26	1,910	TE (25)
Brown, Dr. Gustavus Scotland (1744–1801)		1,350		20	1,900	Episcopalian; TE (26)
Carpenter, George (d. 1802)		1,010		17	1,480	TE (45)
Egerton, James						PE, TE (19); see Table A3.16
Fenwick, James						PE, TE (15); see Table A3.16
Ford, Philip						PE, TE (21); see Table A3.16
Grindall, Josiah Barton (d. 1809)		800		14	1,560	TE (39)
Hall, Dr. Joseph Doctor		650		18	2,420	TE (18)
Hebb, William						PE, TE (09); see Table A3.16
Hill, Henry		630		17	1,670	TE (33)
Holton, William (d. ca. 1812)		1,160		26	2,030	TE (22); mill
Hopewell, James						PE, TE (27); see Table A3.16
Jones, Mordecai						PE, TE (30); see Table A3.16
Key, Philip						PE, TE (08); see Table A3.16
Kilgour, William						PE, TE (48); see Table A3.16
Landsdale, Dr. William						PE, TE (42); see Table A3.16
Locke, Jesse (d. 1816)		840		26	1,540	M. niece of T. A. Reeder (TE); TE (40)

Table A3.18. St. Marys County, Decisional Elite, Second Party Era (cont.)

Name, Birthplace, Dates, Occupation(s)	Party	Acres	Lots	Slaves	Value ($)	Comments
Ford, William	AJ				min.	DE, PE
Forrest, James (d. 1826) Register of wills	AJ	2,090		26	9,900	Son of Colonel Zachariah Forrest, earlier register of wills; militia general; DE, TE
Fowler, Henry	AJ	296		4	1,410	DE, PE
Gough, Peter (b. 1778)	AJ			26	2,188	Catholic; active in internal improvements; DE
Gough, Stephen H.	AJ				min.	DE, PE
Harris, Benjamin Gwinn St. Marys Co. (1806–95) Attorney	AJ				min.	Son of Joseph Harris; ed. Yale and Harvard; m.d. John Harris, Balt. City; DE, PE
Hawkins, John T. (ca. 1798–1835)	AJ	1,090		34	8,400	DE, PE, TE
Heard, Benedict I.	AJ				min.	DE, PE
Heard, Benedict J.	AJ	700		23	4,000	Militia colonel; DE, PE, TE
Hopewell, James Robert W.	AJ	935			2,496	M.d. Thomas Culbreth, Clerk EC; member Const. Conv. (1850); DE, PE
Jarboe, James	J	422		15	2,743	Lieutenant colonel 12th Regt.; DE
Key, Henry Greenfield Sothoron Collector of Llewellensburg	J	1,590		59	15,200	Son of Philip Key; brother-in-law of John Barnes, reg. wills, Charles Co.; DE, TE
Leigh, George S.	AJ	330			738	Son of John Leigh (DE, TE), son-in-law of John Leeds Kerr (T. Co.), Table A3.26; DE
Leigh, John (ca. 1776–1832)	AJ	1,420		4	4,300	Father of George S. Leigh (DE); DE, TE
Miles, Richard H.	J	840		15	5,600	DE, PE, TE
Millard, Enoch J. (ca. 1772–1835) Register of wills	J	37			610	Lieutenant colonel 12th Regt.; active for internal improvements; DE

Table A3.18. (*cont.*)

Name, Birthplace, Dates, Occupation(s)	Party	Acres	Lots	Slaves	Value ($)	Comments
Millard, John L. (1789–1836)	AJ	1,000		35	7,100	Militia captain; DE, TE
Neale, Raphael, Jr. St. Marys Co. (d. 1833)	AJ	450		21	3,900	Fed. member of Congress (1819–25); internal improvements advocate; DE, TE
Roach, Dr. James W. Doctor	J	160		11	1,420	DE
Shaw, Dr. Joseph F. Doctor	AJ		1		156	MD U. Pa. (1827); internal improvements advocate; DE, PE
Sothoron, John H. St. Marys Co. (1808–93)	AJ				min.	DE, PE
Stone, Dr. Joseph (1784–1836) Doctor	AJ	900		29	4,900	M.d. Dr. Barton Tabbs; internal improvements advocate; former Republican; DE, PE, TE
Thomas, James St. Marys Co. (1785–1836) Doctor	AJ	1,760		48	13,800	Son of William Thomas II, Table A3.16, brother Richard Thomas (DE, PE, TE); militia general; former Republican; DE, PE, TE
Thomas, Richard St. Marys Co. (d. 1849)	AJ	400		23	5,300	For family, see above; militia; DE, PE, TE

Table A3.19. St. Marys County, Positional Elite, Second Party Era

Name, Birthplace, Dates, Occupation(s)	Party	Acres	Lots	Slaves	Value ($)	Comments
Barber, Luke W.						OCt; DE, PE, TE; see Table A3.18
Blackistone, William J.						HD; DE, PE; see Table A3.18

Table A3.19. St. Marys County, Positional Elite, Second Party Era (*cont.*)

Name, Birthplace, Dates, Occupation(s)	Party	Acres	Lots	Slaves	Value ($)	Comments
Thomas, Richard						HD (speaker), OCt, Md. senate (president); DE, PE, TE; see Table A3.18

Table A3.20. St. Marys County, Propertied Elite, Second Party Era

Name, Birthplace, Dates, Occupation(s)	Party	Acres	Lots	Slaves	Value ($)	Comments
Avery, Jeremiah		1,850		18	9,500	TE (rank no. 12)
Barber, Luke, Jr.		390		25	4,400	TE (40)
Barber, Luke W.						DE, PE, TE (06); see Table A3.18
Billingsley, Chapman	J	600		17	5,400	TE (26)
Binny, Archibald		820		8	4,100	TE (46)
Briscoe, Dr. Walter H. S.						PE, TE (36); see Table A3.19
Carberry, Rev. Joseph		2,647		90	26,500	TE (01)
Carroll, Michael B.		520		43	5,700	TE (21)
Edelen, Dr. Richard Prince Georges Co. (1764–1835) Doctor		1,660		23	10,600	TE (07)
Forrest, James						DE, TE (10); see Table A3.18
Gough, Bennett		420		13	4,100	Militia officer; TE (44)
Gough, Joseph						PE, TE (43); see Table A3.19
Gough, Stephen						PE, TE (50); see Table A3.19
Gough, Thomas		660		18	4,800	TE (33)
Harris, Joseph Md. (1773–1855) Clerk CCt		2,650		48	15,400	Militia colonel; director Farmer's Bank, Annapolis branch; father of Benjamin G. Harris (PE); TE (02)

Table A3.20. (*cont.*)

Name, Birthplace, Dates, Occupation(s)	Party	Acres	Lots	Slaves	Value ($)	Comments
Hawkins, John T.						DE, PE, TE (15); see Table A3.18
Hayden, Peregrine		1,070		12	4,000	TE (48)
Heard, Benedict J.						DE, PE, TE (47); see Table A3.18
Heard, Edward J.	AJ	380		23	4,600	Moved to La. before 1838; TE (37)
Hebb, James (1783–1847)		560		25	4,900	TE (32)
Johnson, Thomas R. Collector for St. Marys Co.		670		8	4,500	TE (38)
Jones, Benjamin		2,370			8,600	Identified as resident of Philadelphia; TE (14)
Jones, Dr. Mordecai Caleb St. Marys Co. (1788–1869) Doctor	AJ	490		24	4,900	MD U. Pa. (1813); Surgeon's mate militia; HD (1817); TE (31)
Key, Henry Greenfield Sothoron						DE, TE (04); see Table A3.18
Kirk, James		990		38	5,900	TE (20)
Leigh, John						DE, TE (42); see Table A3.18
Loker, Thomas						PE, TE (41); see Table A3.19
Manning, Cornelius		680		22	5,600	TE (23)
Miles, Richard H.						DE, PE, TE (22); see Table A3.18
Millard, John L.						DE, TE (17); see Table A3.18
Morgan, Raphael		1,180		23	5,500	TE (24)
Neale, Raphael, Jr.						DE, TE (49); see Table A3.18
Neill, Rev. J. A.		740		47	9,900	TE (11)

Table A3.22. Talbot County, Decisional Elite, First Party Era (*cont.*)

Name, Birthplace, Dates, Occupation(s)	Party	Acres	Lots	Slaves	Value ($)	Comments
Dickinson, John Talbot Co. (1732–1808)	F	1,124		23	2,960	M. in Episcopal church; militia captain; DE, PE, TE
Emory, Charles	R			3	min.	DE
Gibson, Jacob Talbot Co. (1759–1818)	R	1,230		47	6,500	DE, PE, TE
Goldsborough, Robert IV Talbot Co. (1740–98) Judge	F	1,718		46	4,657	Episcopalian; active in Rev.; father of Robert H. Goldsborough; DE, PE, TE
Goldsborough, Robert Henry Talbot Co. (1779–1836)	F			28	min.	Episcopalian; militia captain; DE, PE
Hayward, William (1759–1834) Attorney	R	1,242		47	4,973	Episcopalian; lieutenant colonel militia; m. into Lloyd family; DE, PE, TE
Hemsley, William	F	1,959		49	10,678	Episcopalian; son of Colonel William Hemsley, QA Co; m.d. James Lloyd, QA Co.; DE, TE
Hindman, William Dorchester Co. (1743–1822) Attorney	F	1,330		86	7,550	Episcopalian; family ties to William Perry (TE, PE); chr. T. Co. Comm. of Safety, 1776; DE, PE, TE
Kerr, David Scotland (1749–1814) Merchant	F	180		46	800	Episcopalian; Mason; m. into Bozman family, father of John Leeds Kerr; David Kerr, Jr., m. into William Perry (TE) family; DE, PE
Lloyd, Edward IV Talbot Co. (1744–96)	F	11,400		304	60,300	Active in rev. and postrev. governments; militia; many social connections; father of Edward Lloyd V; DE, PE, TE

Table A3.22. (*cont.*)

Name, Birthplace, Dates, Occupation(s)	Party	Acres	Lots	Slaves	Value ($)	Comments
Lloyd, Edward V Md. (1779–1834)	R				min.	Son of Edward Lloyd IV; CE, DE, PE
Martin, Dr. Ennalls Talbot Co. (1758–1834) Doctor	F	712		3	2,637	Episcopalian; militia; DE TE
Muley, William (d. 1815)	R				975	CE, DE, PE
Perry, William Caroline Co. (1746–99)	F	1,880		71	9,200	Episcopalian; brother-in-law of William Hindman (DE, PE, TE); d.m. David Kerr, Jr. (PE); DE, PE, TE
Roberts, John (d. 1810)	F	1,370		21	4,200	M. as Episcopalian; DE, PE, TE
Smith, Thomas Perrin Va. (1776–1832) Editor, Easton Republican Star	R				min.	Paymaster 4th Regt.; postmaster, Easton (1812 and later); DE
Spencer, Perry	R	1,083		6	4,564	Shipbuilder; lieutenant colonel militia; m. as Methodist; CE, DE, PE, TE
Stevens, Samuel, Jr. Talbot Co. (1778–1860)	R				min.	Episcopalian; militia officer; DE

Table A3.23. Talbot County, Positional Elite, First Party Era

Name, Birthplace, Dates, Occupation(s)	Party	Acres	Lots	Slaves	Value ($)	Comments
Benson, Perry Talbot Co. (1757–1827)	R	357		11	1,921	Episcopalian; militia general; HD, OCt; DE, PE
Blake, John (ca. 1759–1807)		80 perches		4	775	M. as Methodist; LC; PE

Table A3.23. Talbot County, Positional Elite, First Party Era *(cont.)*

Name, Birthplace, Dates, Occupation(s)	Party	Acres	Lots	Slaves	Value ($)	Comments
Chambers, James			1		min.	LC; PE
Cox, Daniel Powell (d. 1800)	F	377		16	1,327	Militia major; sheriff; LC; PE
Dawson, William (d. 1805)		320		15	1,600	Episcopalian; OCt, LC; PE
Denny, Peter		260		3	1,179	LC; PE
Denny, Thomas Skinner (d. 1810)	R	751		11	1,948	HD, LC; PE
Dickinson, John						LC; DE, PE, TE; see Table A3.22
Dickinson, Samuel, Jr.					min.	Episcopalian; LC; PE
Dickinson, Dr. Samuel S. Talbot Co. (1771–1840) Doctor	R				min.	Episcopalian; son of Samuel Dickinson; CCt; PE
Dickinson, Solomon (d. 1836)	R				min.	Episcopalian; militia major; HD; PE
Earle, Richard Tilghman Talbot Co. (b. 1767) Attorney	R				min.	Episcopalian; militia adjutant; EC; PE
Edmondson, John (d. 1841)	F	536		8	2,670	Episcopalian; HD, PE, TE
Garey, Obediah (d. 1812)		307		5	1,260	Militia captain, lieutenant colonel; LC; PE
Gibson, Jacob						CCt, Md. senate; DE, PE, TE; see Table A3.22
Goldsborough, Howes (d. 1797)	F				min.	D.m. son of Nicholas Hammond (PE, CE); active during Rev.; HD, CCt; PE
Goldsborough, James Talbot Co. (1763–1825)		310		15	1,900	Episcopalian; militia captain; LC; PE
Goldsborough, Robert IV						CCt, chief judge, General Ct; DE, PE, TE; see Table A3.22

Table A3.23. (*cont.*)

Name, Birthplace, Dates, Occupation(s)	Party	Acres	Lots	Slaves	Value ($)	Comments
Goldsborough, Robert Henry						HD; DE, PE; see Table A3.22
Hammond, Nicholas Isle of Jersey (1758–1830) Attorney	F	14		8	388	Episcopalian; settled in Easton 1789; Mason; Md. senate; CE, PE
Harwood, John (d. 1813)				8	min.	Episcopalian; m. Mary Brewer of Annapolis (1798); militia lieutenant; cashier, Easton Br. Farmer's Bank (1813); HD; PE
Hayward, William						HD, CCt, Md. senate; DE, PE, TE; see Table A3.22
Hindman, William						U.S. Cong., U.S. Senate; DE, PE, TE; see Table A3.22
Johns, Richard (d. 1796)		567			1,786	HD, OCt; PE
Johnson, Henry (d. 1809)	F	220		18	900	General Perry Benson (PE) father-in-law; militia captain; HD; PE
Kerr, David						HD, OCt, LC, CCt; DE, PE; see Table A3.22
Kerr, David, Jr. Talbot Co. (ca. 1782–1814) Dry goods, grocery store	F				min.	Episcopalian; son of David Kerr; m.d. William Perry (TE); HD, LC; PE
Kersey, John (1755–1808)	F	500		9	2,520	Methodist; LC; PE, TE
Lambdin, Wrightson		320		15	1,000	HD; PE
Lloyd, Edward IV						Md. senate; DE, PE, TE; see Table A3.22
Lloyd, Edward V						HD, U.S. Cong., Md. gov.; CE, DE, PE; see Table A3.22

Table A3.23. Talbot County, Positional Elite, First Party Era (*cont.*)

Name, Birthplace, Dates, Occupation(s)	Party	Acres	Lots	Slaves	Value ($)	Comments
Martin, Edward Talbot Co. (1767–1848)					min.	Episcopalian; son of Thomas Martin (TE); HD; PE
Martin, Nicholas, Sr. (d. 1808)	R	1,607		17	8,370	Episcopalian; militia captain; HD; PE, TE
Martin, Thomas Oldham					min.	Militia captain; HD; PE
Muley, William						HD; CE, DE, PE; see Table A3.22
Nabb, James (d. 1823)	R			8	min.	Militia captain; HD, LC, EC, Md. senate; PE
Nabb, John (d. 1810)	R	130		7	432	M. as Episcopalian; LC; PE
Perry, William						Md. senate; DE, PE, TE; see Table A3.22
Roberts, John						HD, CCt; DE, PE, TE; see Table A3.22
Rose, William (ca. 1750–1808)	R	320		15	1,600	M. as Episcopalian; militia captain; HD; PE
Seth, Dr. William Ebert (d. 1813) Doctor		320		15	1,300	M. as Episcopalian; Surgeon 26th Regt.; OCt; PE
Sherwood, Hugh of Huntington Bay Talbot Co. (1753–1807)	F	1,060		22	3,800	Episcopalian; militia major; HD, OCt; PE, TE
Sherwood, Philemon (d. 1813)		39		2	189	HD; PE
Skinner, Richard					min.	M. as Episcopalian; OCt; PE
Spencer, Perry						LC, HD; CE, DE, PE, TE; see Table A3.22
Thomas, William of Oxford Neck		939		10	2,802	M. as Episcopalian; LC, OCt; PE, TE
Tilghman, James, Jr. Talbot Co. (1748–96)	F				min.	HD, CCt; PE

Table A3.23. *(cont.)*

Name, Birthplace, Dates, Occupation(s)	Party	Acres	Lots	Slaves	Value ($)	Comments
Tilghman, Peregrine Talbot Co. (1741–1807)	F	1,940		74	8,800	Episcopalian; Rev. officer; Md. senate; PE, TE
Webb, Peter (d. 1800)		1,044			3,982	Militia major; LC; PE, TE
Wheeler, Bennett (d. 1809) Merchant	R			5	min.	M. as Episcopalian; LC; PE
Yarnall, Samuel Del. (d. 1807)		60 perches			470	Quaker; LC; PE

Table A3.24. Talbot County, Propertied Elite, First Party Era

Name, Birthplace, Dates, Occupation(s)	Party	Acres	Lots	Slaves	Value ($)	Comments
Akers, William		568		2	2,475	TE (rank no. 49))
Banning, Jeremiah						DE, TE (31); see Table A3.22
Barwick, William		663		2	2,641	TE (43)
Bowie, Rev. John Prince Georges Co. (1744–1801)		3,095		21	2,443	Episcopal minister; TE (48)
Bozman, John Leeds Talbot Co. (1755–1823) Attorney	F	1,788		19	6,921	Grad. U. Pa. (1783), studied law in Middle Temple; brother-in-law of David Kerr (PE); uncle of John Leeds Kerr; TE (12)
Bryan, Arthur		1,477		25	5,661	TE (15)
Bush, John		1,098		1	2,919	TE (37)
Carroll, Charles of Carrollton Annapolis (1737–1832)	F	799		38	3,816	Catholic; member state senate from Anne Arundel Co.; TE (25)
Catrop, William M.		800		18	3,946	TE (23)

Table A3.24. Talbot County, Propertied Elite, First Party Era (cont.)

Name, Birthplace, Dates, Occupation(s)	Party	Acres	Lots	Slaves	Value ($)	Comments
Chamberlaine, Robins Talbot Co.		736		9	9,346	Brigade major; TE (06)
Chamberlaine, Samuel Talbot Co. (1742–1811)	F	4,725		64	10,174	Episcopalian; d.m. John Leeds Kerr, d.m. John Goldsborough; HD (1788); TE (05)
Dawson, George		698		19	3,204	TE (28)
Dickinson, John						DE, PE, TE (35); see Table A3.22
Dickinson, Samuel (d. 1804)	R	1,314		17	4,824	Episcopalian; TE (17)
Edmondson, Horatio		1,298		15	6,435	Militia; TE (14)
Edmondson, John						PE, TE (42); see Table A3.23
Fisher, John	F	854		24	3,375	TE (27)
Gibson, Jacob						DE, PE, TE (13); see Table A3.22
Goldsborough, John	F	783		15	3,082	Episcopalian; m.d. Samuel Chamberlaine (TE); TE (30)
Goldsborough, Robert IV						DE, PE, TE (18); see Table A3.22
Goldsborough, William (d. 1801)		820		18	3,000	Militia major; Rev. officer; HD (1770s); TE (33)
Greentree, Matthew		536		1	3,118	TE (29)
Harrison, John W.		1,035		10	3,015	TE (32)
Hayward, George Robins Somerset Co. (1767–1811)	F	471		36	2,934	Episcopalian; TE (36)
Hayward, William						DE, PE, TE (16); see Table A3.22
Hemsley, William						DE, TE (04); see Table A3.22
Hindman, William						DE, PE, TE (11); see Table A3.22

Table A3.24. (*cont.*)

Name, Birthplace, Dates, Occupation(s)	Party	Acres	Lots	Slaves	Value ($)	Comments
Kersey, John						PE, TE (47); see Table A3.23
Lloyd, Edward IV						DE, PE, TE (01); see Table A3.22
Lloyd, Captain James Talbot Co. (d. 1815)		1,012		14	2,812	Episcopalian; Rev. officer; d.m. John Dickinson (PE, TE); TE (40)
Martin, Dr. Ennalls						DE, TE (44); see Table A3.22
Martin, Nicholas, Sr.						PE, TE (10); see Table A3.23
Martin, Thomas		475		15	2,542	Episcopalian; d.m. Capt. James Lloyd (TE); TE (46)
Nichols, Henry, Jr.	F	1,589		35	8,626	Episcopalian; TE (09)
Nichols, Robert Lloyd Planter-merchant		2,940		22	12,990	Episcopalian; Rev. officer; militia major; partner with David Kerr, Sr., and Thomas Chamberlaine in Easton store; father-in-law of Robert H. Goldsborough (DE, PE); TE (03)
Perry, William						DE, PE, TE (07); see Table A3.22
Roberts, Edward		1,031		10	2,992	M. as Episcopalian; militia captain; TE (34)
Roberts, John						DE, PE, TE (20); see Table A3.22
Sherwood, Hugh of Huntington Bay						PE, TE (26); see Table A3.23
Singleton, John		864		20	4,050	Episcopalian; Rev. officer; TE (21)
Spencer, Perry						CE, DE, PE, TE (19); see Table A3.22
Stevens, William		514		7	2,385	TE (50)
Thomas, John Wye		862		20	2,835	TE (39)
Thomas, Philemon		700		15	2,867	Episcopalian; TE (38)

Table A3.24. Talbot County, Propertied Elite, First Party Era *(cont.)*

Name, Birthplace, Dates, Occupation(s)	Party	Acres	Lots	Slaves	Value ($)	Comments
Thomas, William of Oxford Neck						PE, TE (41); see Table A3.23
Tilghman, Lloyd Talbot Co. (1747–1811)		3,852	103		13,873	Related to Carrolls, William Tilghman, William Hemsley, James Lloyd, Tench Tilghman; father active in Rev.; TE (02)
Tilghman, Peregrine						PE, TE (08); see Table A3.23
Tilghman, Richard IV Queen Annes Co. (1739–1810)		638		57	3,825	Active in Rev. Comm. of Safety; m. cousin, d. of Edward Tilghman; TE (24)
Vickers, John C.		756		3	2,565	TE (45)
Webb, Peter						PE, TE (22); see Table A3.23

Table A3.25. Talbot County, Commercial Elite, Second Party Era

Name, Birthplace, Dates, Occupation(s)	Party	Acres	Lots	Slaves	Value ($)	Comments
Bullitt, Thomas James Attorney				min.		Episcopalian; former Federalist; CE
Clark, William						CE, TE; see Table A3.28
Edmondson, John						CE, PE, TE; see Table A3.27
Emory, John M. G.						CE, TE; see Table A3.28
Groome, Samuel						CE, TE; see Table A3.28
Groome, William H.				min.		Episcopalian; militia officer; CE
Harrison, Samuel						CE, TE; see Table A3.28
Hayward, William, Jr.						CE, TE; see Table A3.28
Holliday, Henry II						CE, TE; see Table A3.28
Hughlett, William						CE, DE, PE, TE; see Table A3.26

Table A3.25. (*cont.*)

Name, Birthplace, Dates, Occupation(s)	Party	Acres	Lots	Slaves	Value ($)	Comments
Kennard, Samuel T.	AJ	340			2,600	M. as Episcopalian; militia officer; CE
Kerr, John Leeds						CE, DE, PE, TE; see Table A3.26
Lockerman, Theodore Richard						CE, DE; see Table A3.26
Moore, William W.					min.	CE
Price, James					min.	CE
Spencer, Dr. Lambert W.						CE, PE; see Table A3.27

Table A3.26. Talbot County, Decisional Elite, Second Party Era

Name, Birthplace, Dates, Occupation(s)	Party	Acres	Lots	Slaves	Value ($)	Comments
Banning, Robert Talbot Co. (1776–1845)	AJ	658		32	6,295	Son of Jeremiah Banning, Federalist collector; Federalist member HD; m. as Episcopalian; DE, TE
Battee, John W. Md. (ca. 1776–1844)	J	20		5	756	DE
Boyle, John (b. ca. 1795)	AJ			5	557	M. as Methodist; DE, PE
Bruff, Joseph Md. (b. 1775) House carpenter	AJ	130			618	Methodist; militia officer; DE, PE
Denny, Spry (1782–1845)	AJ	350		10	3,212	M. as Methodist; DE, PE
Dickinson, Dr. Samuel S. Talbot Co. (1771–1840) Doctor	J	500		8	3,693	Episcopalian; son of Samuel Dickinson (see Table A3.24); DE

Table A3.26. Talbot County, Decisional Elite, Second Party Era (*cont.*)

Name, Birthplace, Dates, Occupation(s)	Party	Acres	Lots	Slaves	Value ($)	Comments
Dickinson, Solomon (d. 1836)	AJ	590		23	6,285	Episcopalian; militia general; Rep. member PE in first party era, see Table A3.23; DE, PE, TE
Dudley, George (ca. 1795–1849)	AJ	210		2	1,020	M. as Methodist; militia officer; DE, PE
Goldsborough, Robert Henry Talbot Co. (1779–1836)	AJ	2,382		62	24,196	Episcopalian; son of Judge Robert Goldsborough IV (see Table A3.22); former Federalist leader in first party era (see Tables A3.22, 23); militia officer; DE, PE, TE
Graham, Alexander (ca. 1785–1845) Editor, Easton *Gazette*	AJ	30		3	398	DE
Hambleton, Edward Needles Md. (b. 1775)	AJ	1,850		35	18,500	Former Federalist; m. into Hugh Sherwood family (see Tables A3.23, 24); militia officer; Md. senate; DE, PE, TE
Hambleton, Samuel Jr. Talbot Co. (1812–86) Attorney	AJ	480		3	4,883	M. as Episcopalian; son of Edward N. Hambleton (above); DE, PE, TE
Hughlett, William (1769–1845)	AJ	3,300		29	23,800	Militia colonel; HD, Md. senate; member Baltimore City CE; CE, DE, PE, TE
Kerr, John Bozman Talbot Co. (1809–78) Attorney	AJ				min.	Episcopalian; son of John Leeds Kerr; DE, PE
Kerr, John Leeds Md. (1780–1844) Attorney	AJ	1,930		34	17,200	Episcopalian; son of David Kerr (see Table A3.23); m.d. Samuel Chamberlaine (see Table A3.24); militia captain; Federalist leader; CE, DE, PE, TE

Table A3.26. (cont.)

Name, Birthplace, Dates, Occupation(s)	Party	Acres	Lots	Slaves	Value ($)	Comments
Lloyd, Edward VI Talbot Co. (1798–1861)	J				min.	Son of Edward Lloyd V (PE, TE), Table A3.27; DE, PE
Lockerman, Theodore Richard Talbot Co. (1798–1851) Attorney	AJ	20		3	736	Son of Jacob Lockerman (TE); militia officer; CE, DE
Martin, Daniel Talbot Co. (1780–1831)	AJ	400			4,986	Episcopalian; son of Nicholas Martin, Sr. (see Table A3.23); militia officer; gov.; DE, PE, TE
Martin, Nicholas, Jr. Talbot Co. (1784–1858)	J	940		9	7,900	Son of Nicholas Martin, brother of Gov. Daniel Martin; militia officer; DE, TE
Martin, Thomas Oldham Md. (b. 1801)	AJ	380		10	1,836	M. as Episcopalian; DE, PE
Maynard, Foster (b. ca. 1785)	AJ	170		14	2,234	Methodist; DE
Millis, Levin	AJ				150	DE, PE
Mullikin, Edward C. Talbot Co. (1797–1835) Editor, Easton *Eastern Shore Whig*	J				90	Methodist; postmaster; DE
Mullikin, Solomon Md. (ca. 1787–1855)	AJ	100		3	842	M. as Methodist; militia officer; DE, PE
Nicols, Thomas C. Md. (b. 1792) Attorney, Clerk, Dist. Court	AJ				min.	Militia captain; DE
Sherwood, George W. Talbot Co. (b. 1813) Editor, Easton *Eastern Shore Whig*	J				min.	DE

Table A3.26. Talbot County, Decisional Elite, Second Party Era *(cont.)*

Name, Birthplace, Dates, Occupation(s)	Party	Acres	Lots	Slaves	Value ($)	Comments
Spencer, Henry (d. 1837)	AJ	460		11	3,821	M. as Methodist; DE, PE
Spencer, Richard Talbot Co. (1796–1868) Attorney, Editor, Easton *Eastern Shore Whig*	J	690		20	7,800	Militia captain; DE, PE, TE
Stevens, John	AJ	650		3	6,700	M. as Episcopalian; Lieutenant colonel militia; DE, PE, TE
Tilghman, Dr. William H. (d. 1858) Doctor	AJ	500		10	3,049	Militia officer; DE, PE
Townsend, William Md. (b. 1800)	AJ	200		1	1,375	Methodist; militia officer; DE, PE

Table A3.27. Talbot County, Positional Elite, Second Party Era

Name, Birthplace, Dates, Occupation(s)	Party	Acres	Lots	Slaves	Value ($)	Comments
Benny, William	AJ				500	M. as Episcopalian; CC; PE
Boyle, John						HD; DE, PE; see Table A3.26
Bracco, Bennett	AJ	290		6	3,034	M. as Episcopalian; LC; PE
Bruff, Joseph						LC, HD; DE, PE; see Table A3.26
Chambers, James	AJ				min.	LC; PE
Denny, Spry						HD, CC; DE, PE; see Table A3.26
Dickinson, Solomon						OCt, HD; DE, PE, TE; see Table A3.26

Table A3.27. (*cont.*)

Name, Birthplace, Dates, Occupation(s)	Party	Acres	Lots	Slaves	Value ($)	Comments
Dudley, George						HD; DE, PE; see Table A3.26
Edmondson, John (d. 1841)	AJ	538		32	7,295	Episcopalian; PE, TE first party era; Table A3.23; former Federalist; LC, CC; CE, PE, TE
Goldsborough, Robert Henry						U.S. Senate; DE, PE, TE; see Table A3.26
Hambleton, Edward Needles						OCt, Md. senate; DE, PE, TE; see Table A3.26
Hambleton, Samuel, Jr.						HD; DE, PE, TE; see Table A3.26
Harrison, Joseph of Joseph	J	160		15	1,900	LC; PE
Hayward, James C.					min.	LC; militia major; PE
Henrix, Thomas	J	310		4	3,400	Methodist; militia captain; PE
Horney, Philip	J				200	HD; PE
Hughlett, William						HD, Md. senate; CE, DE, PE, TE; see Table A3.26
Jenkins, William					min.	OCt; PE
Kerr, John Bozman						HD; DE, PE; see Table A3.26
Kerr, John Leeds						U.S. Congress; CE, DE, PE, TE; see Table A3.26
Leonard, Robert	AJ				min.	M. as Methodist; CC; PE
Lloyd, Edward V Talbot Co. (1779–1834)	J	12,005		577	141,812	Son of Edward Lloyd IV; see Table A3.22; father of Edward Lloyd VI; Rep. DE in first party era; militia colonel; U.S. Senate, Md. senate; PE, TE
Lloyd, Edward VI						LC; DE, PE; see Table A3.26
Martin, Daniel						EC, gov.; DE, PE, TE; see Table A3.26

Table A3.27. Talbot County, Positional Elite, Second Party Era (*cont.*)

Name, Birthplace, Dates, Occupation(s)	Party	Acres	Lots	Slaves	Value ($)	Comments
Martin, Thomas Oldham						CC, HD; DE, PE; see Table A3.26
Millis, Levin						HD; DE, PE; see Table A3.26
Mullikin, Solomon						HD; DE, PE; see Table A3.26
Neal, James					min.	Probably Quaker; LC; PE
Reardon, Lambert	J	259		4	2,155	OCt; PE
Reyner, Stephen					min.	OCt; PE
Robinson, Perry	J			2	100	LC; PE
Spencer, Henry						HD, CC; DE, PE; see Table A3.26
Spencer, Dr. Lambert Wickes	J	315		10	3,173	M. as Methodist; m.d. Colonel Perry Spencer; postmaster of Easton; OCt; CE, PE
Spencer, Richard						U.S. Congress, HD; DE, PE, TE; see Table A3.26
Stevens, George	AJ	180		6	1,300	M. as Episcopalian; LC, CC; PE
Stevens, John						HD; DE, PE, TE; see Table A3.26
Stevens, Samuel, Jr. Talbot Co. (1778–1860)	J	700		26	10,000	Episcopalian; lieutenant colonel militia; former Republican; DE first party era; Table A3.22; gov.; PE, TE
Thomas, Henry	J	180			200	M. as Episcopalian; LC; PE
Tilghman, Dr. William H.						LC, CC; DE, PE; see Table A3.26
Townsend, William						HD; DE, PE; see Table A3.26
Valiant, Jeremiah	AJ			2	500	LC, CC; PE
Webb, Peter	J	600		5	4,500	LC; PE, TE

Table A3.28. Talbot County, Propertied Elite, Second Party Era

Name, Birthplace, Dates, Occupation(s)	Party	Acres	Lots	Slaves	Value ($)	Comments
Banning, Robert						DE, TE (rank. no. 30); see Table A3.26
Barnett, Dr. John Doctor		701		27	6,679	M. as Episcopalian to Sally Goldsborough; TE (25)
Bordley, John W.		1,701		3	4,501	TE (40)
Chamberlaine, James H. Talbot Co. (1785–1844)		730		25	9,249	Episcopalian; son of Samuel Chamberlaine (see Table A3.24); ed. Princeton; TE (17)
Clark, William	AJ	300			5,722	Mgr. Md. Colonization Society (1831); CE, TE (33)
Denny, Theodore		230		6	4,599	M. as Methodist; TE (39)
Dickinson, Solomon						DE, PE, TE (31); see Table A3.26
Dickinson, William		905		4	4,119	M. as Methodist; TE (44)
Edmondson, John						CE, PE, TE (23); see Table A3.27
Emory, John M. G.		495		2	4,107	M. as Methodist; militia officer; CE, TE (45)
Gibson, Fayette	AJ	532		33	8,290	Son of Jacob Gibson (see Table A3.22); TE (20)
Goldsborough, John		1,370		21	10,409	Episcopalian; m.d. Samuel Chamberlaine (see Table A3.24); former Federalist; member TE first party era (see Table A3.24); TE (14)
Goldsborough, Martin	AJ	320		4	4,817	TE (37)
Goldsborough, Nicholas VI Talbot Co. (b. 1787)	AJ	1,097		49	11,842	Episcopalian; son of Nicholas Goldsborough V, grandfather member T. Co. Comm. of Safety; m.d. Colonel Tench Tilghman; militia captain; TE (11)
Goldsborough, Robert Henry						DE, PE, TE (03); see Table A3.26

Table A3.28. Talbot County, Propertied Elite, Second Party Era (*cont.*)

Name, Birthplace, Dates, Occupation(s)	Party	Acres	Lots	Slaves	Value ($)	Comments
Groome, Samuel	AJ	370		3	6,563	CE, TE (27)
Hambleton, Edward Needles						DE, PE, TE (05); see Table A3.26
Hambleton, Samuel, Jr.						DE, PE, TE (36); see Table A3.26
Harrison, Alexander Bradford	J	270		5	6,200	Militia captain; TE (32)
Harrison, Samuel	J	4,313		59	33,709	Militia officer; CE, TE (02)
Hayward, Thomas		890		24	9,118	M. as Episcopalian; TE (18)
Hayward, William, Jr. Talbot Co. (1787–1836)		400		21	4,484	Episcopalian; son of William Hayward (see Table A3.22); related to Lloyd family; CE, TE (42)
Hayward, William, Sr. Md. (1759–1834) Attorney	J	580			5,700	Episcopalian; former Republican leader (see Table A3.22); militia officer; m. into Lloyd Family; TE (34)
Hemsley, Alexander		307		8	3,805	M. as Episcopalian; TE (48)
Hindman, Jacob		1,106			6,381	TE (29)
Holliday, Henry II Talbot Co. (1771–1850)		1,269		58	13,563	M. as Episcopalian; CE, TE (09)
Hughlett, William						CE, DE, PE, TE (04); see Table A3.26
Kennard, Robert W.		628			4,316	TE (43)
Kerr, John Leeds						CE, DE, PE, TE (07); see Table A3.26
Lloyd, Edward V						PE, TE (01); see Table A3.27
Lockerman, Jacob Talbot Co. (1759–1839) Clerk, CCt		1,210		22	11,694	Episcopalian; father of T. R. Lockerman (see Table A3.26); TE (12)
Martin, Daniel						DE, PE, TE (35); see Table A3.26

Table A3.28. *(cont.)*

Name, Birthplace, Dates, Occupation(s)	Party	Acres	Lots	Slaves	Value ($)	Comments
Martin, Edward Talbot Co. (ca. 1767–1848)		595		30	8,482	M. as Episcopalian; member PE first party era (see Table A3.23); TE (19)
Martin, Joseph		1,162		33	9,346	TE (16)
Martin, Nicholas, Jr.						DE, TE (21); see Table A3.26
Rhodes, Ignatius		336		10	3,956	TE (47)
Ridgaway, James		1,556		17	6,651	M. as Methodist; TE (26)
Rogers, John		1,491		38	15,505	Episcopalian; m. into Kerr family; TE (08)
Sears, William		538		9	3,761	TE (50)
Skinner, Andrew		778		46	11,307	M. as Episcopalian; TE (13)
Spencer, Richard						DE, PE, TE (22); see Table A3.26
Stevens, John						DE, PE, TE (24); see Table A3.26
Stevens, Samuel, Jr.						PE, TE (15); see Table A3.27
Thomas, Nicholas	AJ	483		9	6,443	Episcopalian; militia captain; TE (28)
Tilghman, John Queen Annes Co. (b. 1785)	AJ	1,716		44	12,165	Episcopalian; son of James Tilghman, Rev. leader; militia colonel; TE (10)
Tilghman, Tench Talbot Co. (1810–74)	AJ	550		27	4,000	Episcopalian; m. into Kerr family (see Table A3.26); TE (46)
Tilghman, William Hemsley Talbot Co. (1784–1863)		1,101		70	17,408	Son of Peregrine Tilghman (see Table A3.23); militia officer; TE (06)
Webb, Peter						PE, TE (41); see Table A3.27
Willis, Noah		409		4	3,787	TE (49)
Wilson, James		343		10	4,680	TE (38)

Notes

Abbreviations

DU   Perkins Library, Duke University, Durham, N.C.

HSPa   Historical Society of Pennsylvania, Philadelphia, Pa.

LC   Manuscripts Division, Library of Congress, Washington, D.C.

MdDA   Maryland Diocesan Archives of the Protestant Episcopal Church, on deposit at the Maryland Historical Society, Baltimore, Md.

MdHR   Maryland Hall of Records, Annapolis, Md.

MdHS   Maryland Historical Society, Baltimore, Md.

MsHS   Massachusetts Historical Society, Boston, Mass.

NA   National Archives, Washington, D.C.

NYHS   New York Historical Society, New York, N.Y.

NYPL   New York Public Library, New York, N.Y.

PU   Firestone Library, Princeton University, Princeton, N.J.

UNC   Southern Historical Collection, University of North Carolina, Chapel Hill, N.C.

Introduction

1. For a historiographical overview, see Ronald P. Formisano's two articles: "Deferential-Participant Politics," and "Toward a Reorientation of Jacksonian Politics."

2. Robert A. Dahl, *Who Governs?* p. 3.

3. For a discussion of the concept of strategic elites, see Suzanne I. Keller, *Beyond the Ruling Class*. See also my methodological Appendix I.

Chapter 1

1. Cited in Ronald Hoffman, *A Spirit of Dissension*, p. 150.

2. My interpretation of the Revolution draws heavily on the argument developed by Hoffman, ibid. An older and still useful interpretation is Charles A. Barker, *The Background of the Revolution in Maryland*; see also David C. Skaggs, *Roots of Maryland Democracy, 1753–1776*, and James Haw, "Politics in Revolutionary Maryland, 1753–1788," Ph.D. dissertation, University of Virginia, 1972.

3. Hoffman summarizes: "What they actually wanted was an orderly society whose direction would remain in the hands of the rich and the well born. Those popular leaders who had guided the colony haltingly toward independence now worked to establish a highly conservative constitution. During the Constitutional Convention, the aristocratic characteristics of the popular party came to the surface. The party leaders were determined to shape the institutions of the new government in a fashion that would insure their future control" (*Spirit of Dissension*, p. 169; see also p. 222). For a description of the Constitution of 1776 see ibid., p. 179; Barker, *Background of the Revolution*, pp. 371–72; Skaggs, *Roots of Maryland Democracy*, pp. 174–99; and Haw, "Politics in Revolutionary Maryland," pp. 169–241.

4. The role of the militia is thoughtfully developed by Skaggs, *Roots of Maryland Democracy*, pp. 156–73, 184.

5. Hoffman, *Spirit of Dissension*, pp. 169–241.

6. Judge Robert Goldsborough's Charges to the Grand Jury, 13 Sept. 1784; see also 12 Sept. 1786 and April 1791, MdDA. Consider also the remarks of "A Calvinist," writing at the time of the religious establishment controversy: "The two greatest foundations of order and happiness among mankind evidently are religion and government. . . . The

wisest legislators of old, through the whole process of their systems of government, considered Religion as essential to civil polity" (Baltimore *Maryland Journal and the Baltimore Advertiser*, 7 Dec. 1784).

7. See especially Gordon Wood, *The Creation of the American Republic, 1776–1787*, chap. 12.

8. As examples of intraelite organizational activities, see the following correspondence: Nathaniel Ramsey to Otho H. Williams, 29 Dec. 1788, Otho Holland Williams Papers, MdHS; also letters to William Tilghman from George Gale, 1 Jan. 1789, Hy. Hollingsworth, 5 Jan. 1789, George Dent, 13 Aug. 1790, William Tilghman Papers, and Tobias Rudulph to Levi Hollingsworth & Sons, 20 July 1798, Hollingsworth Papers, HSPa.

9. Thomas B. Adams described a canvass as follows: "These are always held, in different parts of the State of Maryland, and generally in the Southern States, as I am told, where there is known to be a great concourse of people—at a horse race—a cock-fight—or a Methodist quarterly meeting. Here, the candidates for political honors or preferent, assemble with their partizans—they mount the Rostrum, made out of an empty barrel or hogshead, Harrangue the Sovereign people—praise & recommend themselves at the expense of their adversary's character & pretentions" (Adams to William S. Shaw, 8 Aug. 1800, Charles G. Washburn, ed., "Letters of Thomas Boylston Adams," p. 121). Not all Federalists followed this ritual: "But I would not stoop to the little artifices of low, local Politics for all the gratifications that can be found in the noisey applause of the capricious multitude" (O. H. Williams to [P. Thomas], 16 Oct. 1790, Williams Papers).

10. Ames to Oliver Wolcott, 10 Aug. 1800, George Gibbs, *Memoirs of the Administrations of George Washington and John Adams edited from the Papers of Oliver Wolcott*, 2:404.

11. The only study of Maryland poll-book voting is David A. Bohmer's excellent "Voting Behavior during the First American Party System: Maryland, 1796–1816," Ph.D. dissertation, University of Michigan, 1974. For a contemporary description, see "A Baltimorean," Baltimore *Maryland Journal*, 24 Oct. 1788.

12. "Washington County," Fredericktown *Republican Advocate*, 1 June 1804. Less sensational, but equally compelling, were Charles Carroll of Carrollton's remarks to Horatio Ridout, 22 Aug. 1806: "I will speak to my manager and to my clerk and prevail upon them to vote for you and Col. Mercer, and to obtain as many votes for you both as electors of the Senate in this neighborhood as their influence and exertions can procure" ("Two Letters of Charles Carroll of Carrollton," pp. 216–17).

13. See especially, John Stull to O. H. Williams, 11 Jan. 1789, Williams Papers.

14. See especially Edward C. Papenfuse, "An Undelivered Defense of a Winning Cause," pp. 220–51. For a more extensive treatment of Maryland politics in this transitional period, see Philip A. Crowl, *Maryland during and after the Revolution*; L. Marx Renzulli, Jr., *Maryland*; Dorothy Brown, "Party Battles and Beginnings in Maryland," Ph.D. dissertation, Georgetown University, 1962; and Lee L. Verstandig, "The Emergence of the Two-Party System in Maryland, 1787–1796," Ph.D. dissertation, Brown University, 1970.

15. Renzulli, *Maryland*, pp. 148–59.

16. Shaw Livermore stated the essence of Federalism succinctly: "Federalism was the political expression of those who sought security and self-fulfillment in an ordered, structured social system" (*The Twilight of Federalism*, p. 4).

17. Lisle A. Rose develops an interesting argument that Washington used the Cincinnati Society as a protopolitical organization and that the state-level political appointments were made to men who would support the federal government. Rose misses an interesting facet of this process: of all the members of the society, only Nathaniel Ramsey was considered for an active command when the army was reorganized in 1798. Was the society seen as a military reserve for officers or just as a political pressure group? See Lisle A. Rose, *Prologue to Democracy*, pp. 19–20, 83–84; Carl E. Prince, *The Federalists and the Origins of the U.S. Civil Service*, pp. 94–104.

18. Rev. Joseph Jackson to Bp. Thomas J. Claggett, 26 Oct. 1796, MdDA.

19. See Barker, *Background of the Revolution*, pp. 47–51, 361–66; Hoffman, *Spirit of Dissension*, pp. 118–20; and Skaggs, *Roots of Maryland Democracy*, pp. 123–39, 192, 194.

20. For Smith's petition see his *An Address to the Members of the Protestant Episcopal Church of Maryland* . . . , and the following supportive essays published in the Baltimore *Maryland Journal*: "Democritus," 31 Oct. 1783; "Extracts of a letter from a Gentleman," 26 Oct. 1784; "An Address of the House of Delegates of Maryland to their Constituents," 18 Jan., "Agricola," 8 March, "Philander," 22 March, 19 April 1785. See also Nelson W. Rightmeyer, *Maryland's Established Church*, pp. 124–29.

21. See [Patrick Allison] "Vindex," *Candid Animadversions* . . . For an example of the varied opposition from other quarters to Smith's plan, see in the Baltimore *Maryland Journal*: "Theophillis," 19 Sept., "English School Master," 28 Oct. 1783; "Probus," 5 Nov., "Loelius," 26 Nov., 3, 14 Dec., "Verus," 28 Dec. 1784; "Civis," 11, 21 Jan., "Philo," 4, 25 Feb., "Octavianus," 25 Feb., and "A Christian," 17 May 1785.

22. Rev. Joseph J. G. Bend to Rev. James Kemp, 29 April 1802, MdDA.

23. A useful contemporary analysis of religion is provided by [William Duke], *Observations of the Present State of Religion in Maryland*; John Asplund, *The Universal Annual Register of the Baptist Denomination in North America for the Year, 1794 and 1795*, shows that there were few Baptists in the state; Jesse Lee, *A Short History of the Methodists in the U.S.A., 1776 . . . 1809*, and the *Minutes of the Methodist Conferences, 1773 to 1813* demonstrate the growing number of Methodists.

24. Rev. Bend to Rev. Kemp, 9 April 1798, MdDA. Bend wrote Rev. William Duke, 8 July 1799, "The Disasters, which have lately befallen the French, are healing to the soul of every Federalist" (ibid.); see also Rev. Colin Ferguson, "On the Approaching War with France," 9 May 1798, ibid.

25. Charles Carroll of Carrollton to James McHenry, 4 Nov. 1800, Bernard C. Steiner, *Life and Correspondence of James McHenry*, p. 473. See also Carroll to Alexander Hamilton, 27 Aug. 1800, Kate Mason Rowland, *The Life of Charles Carroll of Carrollton, 1737–1832, His Correspondence and Public Papers*, 2:239; also Carroll's son-in-law, Robert Goodloe Harper, to H. G. Otis, 27 May 1806, Harper-Pennington Papers, MdHS.

26. For an admittedly extreme antirepublican assessment, see Rev. Bend to Rev. Duke, 27 March 1801, MdDA.

27. Rev. Bend to Rev. Duke, 3 Nov. 1798, ibid.

28. See Bp. Claggett to Rev. Kemp, 11 Feb. 1801, regarding Jefferson's attitude toward religion, ibid.; also "Juvenis Americanus," 28 May 1800, Baltimore *Federal Gazette and Baltimore Daily Advertiser*. See Charles Carroll of Carrollton's disparaging remarks on Jefferson's leadership qualities, Carroll to Alexander Hamilton, 18 April 1800, Rowland, *Life of Charles Carroll*, 2:235–36.

29. For a sense of the federalist reaction to Paine's visit, see "A Federalist," 8 Jan., and "Observer," 23 Feb. 1803, *Frederick-Town Herald*; Charles Carroll of Carrollton to Robert G. Harper, 14 Dec. 1802, Harper-Pennington Papers; and the more judicious James McHenry to Rufus King, 12 Nov. 1802, Rufus King Papers, NYHS. The Fredericktown Republican paper commented: "Tom Paine, by the way, is of more service to the federalists than the republicans. If he had not come to America, federalism would have been a bankrupt before now. He serves the federalists as a bank for calumny, upon which they draw when their credit is gone elsewhere" (*Republican Advocate*, 10 June 1803). Roger Nelson, a Republican congressman, was less charitable: "How do the Federalists seem to stand it, are they as bitter as ever? I suppose Tom Paine is a fine subject for them to discant upon, I wish myself he had went to Hell rather than to have come to this Country in the Present State of the Public Mind" (Nelson to Andrew Shriver, 5 Dec. 1802 [MS 2085], Shriver Papers, MdHS).

30. The background of the 1800 presidential campaign is best described by the participants: James McHenry to Oliver Wolcott, 22 July 1800, Gibbs, *Memoirs*, 2:384–86; R. G. Harper to H. G. Otis, 22 Aug. 1800, Samuel E. Morison, *Life and Letters of Harrison Gray Otis, 1765–1848*, 1:194; and Charles Carroll of Carrollton to Alexander Hamilton, 22 Aug. 1800, Rowland, *Life of Charles Carroll*, 2:238–41.

31. [Robert Goodloe Harper], *Bystander*. See also, "A Marylander," 14 June 1800, "Cauius," 21 June 1800, and "Fair Play," 8 Aug. 1800, all in the Baltimore *Federal Gazette*;

Harper's optimistic evaluation of "Legislative Choice," Harper to Theodore Sedgwick, 11 Aug. 1800, Miscellaneous Manuscripts, NYHS.

32. "A Voter," Baltimore *Federal Gazette*, 18 July 1800.

33. With heavy irony, "The Times" anticipated the future should the Federalists win on the issue of "Legislative Choice": "For, as the people of Maryland of all things pride themselves the most upon the privilege of voting for the electors . . . they will soon be brought to give up the right of voting for representatives to congress—for electors of senators—for sheriffs—and finally for assembly men. And then the people will be justly placed exactly where they ought to remain. Then, as they will have nothing to do with the means of government, they will be more properly employed . . . than in reading newspapers and talking about their superiors" (ibid., 24 June 1800). In a second article, "The Times" facetiously suggested that "two or three thousand republicans" should be hung to do away with political opposition altogether (Baltimore *American and Commercial Advertiser*, 7 Aug. 1800).

34. Ames to Wolcott, 10 Aug. 1800, Gibbs, *Memoirs*, 2:404.

35. One election description pinpointed Federalist discontent: "The Democrats, or Republicans as they term themselves, have carried their Election with us. . . . Not that there is a general change of politicks with the people. But many federalists were alarmed at the Idea of the Legislature taking the Rights the people have heretofore enjoyed of choosing the Electors from them. A majority of the people are still federalists but will not go through thick and thin with their federalism" (Wallace and Whann to Levi Hollingsworth and Sons, 11 Oct. 1800, Hollingsworth Papers).

36. See James McHenry to Oliver Wolcott, 24 Aug. 1800, 2:408–9, 23 Sept. 1800, 2:419–20, 9 Nov. 1800, 2:445, in Gibbs, *Memoirs*. See also Rev. Bend to Rev. Duke, 3 April 1799, and Rev. Bend to Rev. Kemp, 29 Aug. 1800, MdDA. Charles Carroll of Carrollton stated: "If Mr. Adams should be reelected, I fear our constitution would be more injured by his unruly passions, antipathies, & jealousy, than by the whimsies of Jefferson" (Carroll to James McHenry, 4 Nov. 1800, Steiner, *Life of James McHenry*, p. 473).

37. James McHenry wrote to Oliver Wolcott, 12 Oct. 1800: "There is every symptom of languour, and inactivity, with some exceptions, among the well informed federalists, which every new recurrence to the conduct and character of the chief, seems rather to increase, than diminish. Mr. Charles Carroll, of Carrollton, did not go down to Annapolis, from his country residence, to aid in the election of members for our legislature" (Gibbs, *Memoirs*, 2:433).

38. Baltimore *American and Commercial Advertiser*, 20 Oct. 1800.

39. McHenry to Rufus King, 18 Dec. 1800, King Papers; for a more pessimistic evaluation, see Gen. James Lloyd to William Tilghman, 17 Jan. 1801, Tilghman Papers; and Jesse Hollingsworth to L. Hollingsworth & Sons, 18 Oct. 1800, Hollingsworth Papers.

40. The best analytical description of party development is Ronald P. Formisano, "Deferential-Participant Politics," pp. 473–87.

41. Chase to Gouverneur Morris, 6 March 1803, Society Collection, HSPa.

42. For the Republican viewpoint, see the Fredericktown *Republican Advocate*: "Abolition of the General Court" series, April–June 1805; "Plain Truth," 13 Sept. 1805; two untitled editorials, 8, 15 Nov. 1805; and articles regarding suffrage reform, 20, 23 May, 3, 10 June 1803.

43. For the resurgence of the Federalist party, see Victor Sapio, "Maryland's Federalist Revival, 1808–1812," pp. 1–17; and Renzulli, *Maryland*, pp. 238–321.

44. There is no satisfactory history of political events between 1815 and 1823. Renzulli uses some good material in his interpretation, especially the papers of A. C. Hanson and Robert G. Harper, but he did not utilize the insightful correspondence of Robert H. Goldsborough in the Bozman-Kerr Papers, LC.

45. Solomon Dickinson to Edward Lloyd, 1 Dec. 1823; see also William R. Steuart to Lloyd, 21 Nov. 1824, Edward Lloyd Papers, MdHS. For further correspondence regarding the breakdown of the Republican party in the early 1820s, see letters to Virgil Maxcy from Ezekiel F. Chambers, 4 Jan., 27 April 1824; Frisby Tilghman, 15 Oct. 1824; Daniel Jenifer,

15 Feb. 1824; and Charles S. Ridgely, (?) March 1825, in Virgil Maxcy Correspondence, Galloway-Maxcy-Markoe Papers, LC.

46. For a general history of the politics of the 1820s, see Mark H. Haller, "The Rise of the Jackson Party in Maryland, 1820–1830," Master's thesis, University of Maryland, 1953. His main points may be found in his article, "The Rise of the Jackson Party in Maryland, 1820–29," pp. 307–27. See also Richard P. McCormick, *The Second Party System*, pp. 154–66; and Wilbur Wayne Smith, "The Whig Party in Maryland, 1826–1856," Ph.D. dissertation, University of Maryland, 1967. Smith has published two articles on this material: "Jacksonian Democracy on the Chesapeake: Political Institutions," pp. 381–93; "Jacksonian Democracy on the Chesapeake: Class, Kinship, and Politics," pp. 55–67. See also my "A Social Analysis of Maryland Community Elites, 1827–1836: A Study of the Distribution of Power in Baltimore City, Frederick County, and Talbot County," Ph.D. dissertation, University of Pennsylvania, 1973, esp. pp. 96–212.

47. Men such as Roger B. Taney, Richard Frisby, or Virgil Maxcy, to mention a few, worked hard to mobilize the electorate between 1826 and 1829. See reports in the Baltimore *Patriot and Mercantile Advertiser*, 28 April 1827; Baltimore *Republican and Commercial Advertiser*, 23 May 1827; Annapolis *Maryland Republican*, 29 April, 3 June 1828. The editor of *Niles Weekly Register* commented disdainfully on such activities, "There has been a considerable excitement, and many night meetings have been held and long speeches made to gatherings of the people, by all the candidates—a practice which has too long prevailed in Baltimore and became a public nuisance" (*Niles Weekly Register* 31 [30 Sept. 1826]: 66–67). See also Duff Green to Virgil Maxcy, 21 Aug. 1826, Maxcy-Markoe Letterbook, Galloway-Maxcy-Markoe Papers.

48. Hezekiah Niles, editor of the *Niles Weekly Register*, observed wistfully when reporting the election returns of 1828: "For the sake of brevity and clearness, we have adopted the terms 'Adams' and 'Jackson,' as applied to parties—but, as old republicans, we enter our protest against such practices. In times past, parties were guided by principle" (ibid., 35 [11 Oct. 1828]: 97). For more examples of his distaste, see his letters to William Darlington, 9 Nov. 1827, 10 June 1829, 10 Sept. 1830, and 23 Sept. 1834, William Darlington Papers, LC. For an extended treatment of antipartyism see Ronald P. Formisano, "Political Character, Antipartyism, and the Second Party System," pp. 683–709; and Richard Hofstader, *The Idea of a Party System*.

49. Virgil Maxcy insightfully commented on the transformation in a letter to John C. Calhoun, 7 May 1829: "That the talent and respectability of what was once the federal Party in Maryland is with Jackson and friendly to you; the majority of that party however, went with Adams. . . . That directly the reverse of this is true, with respect to the Democratic Party, almost all the political managers of this party having gone with the late Administration [Adams], while a majority of the Democratic voters, are with Jackson" (J. Franklin Jameson, ed., *Correspondence of John C. Calhoun*, p. 801).

50. The editor of the Baltimore Jacksonian paper remarked on the subject of political nominations: "This will prevent our ranks being broken, and our strength fettered away by indulging in personal preferences, at a danger of a sacrifice of principle" (Baltimore *Republican*, "As It Should Be," 1 June 1833). See also, in the same paper, "Baltimore County," 9 April 1829, 6 Oct. 1830, 3 Oct. 1831; 6 March, 23 April 1832; 3, 13 June 1833. In 1834, an anti-Jacksonian paper observed without regret that everyone elected to the House of Delegates had been nominated (*Cambridge Chronicle*, 25 Oct. 1834). For examples of politicians accepting the notion that party unity should supersede personal ambition, see the case of Virgil Maxcy: John C. Calhoun to Maxcy, 6 June, 11 Oct. 1826, 2 Nov. 1829; I. D. Ingham to Maxcy, 19 Nov. 1829, Maxcy-Markoe Letterbook, Galloway-Maxcy-Markoe Papers; and the case of James M. Buchanan: letters of recommendation in 1829 to various officers in the administration from Maryland Jacksonian leaders, reel 3/frames 635–78, Letters of Application and Recommendation during the Administration of Andrew Jackson, NA. Some politicians challenged this system and sometimes won; note James P. Heath's experience: Baltimore *Commercial Chronicle and Daily Marylander*, 8 July 1833; Baltimore *Republican*, 13 July, 22 Sept., 2 Oct. 1835.

51. I have developed this theme in greater detail in an article, "McCulloch vs. the Jacksonians," pp. 350–62.

52. See Appendix II, Table A2.1.

53. Ibid.

54. See Appendix II, Table A2.2.

55. For a county-by-county breakdown of ethnicity, based on the 1790 federal census, see Bohmer, "Voting Behavior," p. 96. Essentially every county ranged between 60 and over 90 percent English, with the Germans concentrating in Frederick and Washington counties.

56. See Appendix II, Table A2.1.

57. Ibid.

58. For general treatments of internal improvements, see Walter S. Sanderlin, *The Great National Project*, esp. chaps. 4 and 5; George W. Ward, *Early Development of the Chesapeake and Ohio Canal Project*, esp. chaps. 9–11; Milton Reizenstein, *The Economic History of the Baltimore and Ohio Railroad, 1827–1853*; Hugh S. Hanna, *A Financial History of Maryland*, esp. chap. 4; and J. Thomas Scharf, *History of Baltimore City and County*, pp. 312–27.

59. The basic secondary interpretations regarding constitutional reform are Bernard C. Steiner, "The Electoral College for the Senate of Maryland and the Nineteen Van Buren Electors," pp. 129–67; A. Clarke Hagensick, "Revolution or Reform in 1836," pp. 346–66. A contemporary but essentially antireform view is provided by the pamphlet, *Brief Outline of the Rise, Progress, and Failure of the Nineteen Van Buren Electors of the Senate of Maryland*. After it appeared, the proreform Baltimore *Republican* queried rhetorically if the pamphlet had been written by Governor Veazey, who opposed reform (6 Jan. 1837). For the background and substance of the constitutional changes made in 1851, see James W. Harry, *The Maryland Constitution of 1851*.

Chapter 2

1. No adequate history of St. Marys County yet exists, but the St. Marys City Commission, under the direction of Lois Green Carr, is doing excellent work on its colonial phase. A representative sample of their innovative findings may be found in the *Maryland Historical Magazine*, 69 (Summer 1974): 123–227. Bayly E. Marks, at the University of Maryland, is writing a dissertation entitled "Response to Change in a Mono-Crop Plantation System: St. Marys County, 1780–1840."

2. Based on the 1790 census, St. Marys County was 93.5 percent English and 4.8 percent Scottish stock; David A. Bohmer, "Voting Behavior during the First American Party System: Maryland, 1796–1816," Ph.D. dissertation, University of Michigan, 1974, p. 96.

3. Joseph Scott, *United States Gazeteer*, divided the population by a factor of six, which he considered to be the average household size, to determine the number of dwellings in a town.

4. See John F. Mercer to William Thomas, Jr., 20 Dec. 1788; Dr. E. J. Parkham to Thomas, 16 July 1792; Thomas to the Free and Independent Voters of St. Marys County, 1793; Walter Dorsey to Thomas, 22 Aug. 1794, Gift Collection, James Thomas Papers, MdHR. Because of the lack of convenient local vehicles to disseminate political information, such news was often communicated through letters and broadsides; see George Dent to Thomas, 20 Jan., Feb. 1794; and P. Briscoe to Thomas, Sept. 1809, ibid.

5. For Barnes's career, see the *Archives of Maryland*, 11:3; 12:100; J. Thomas Scharf, *History of Maryland*, 2:194; Baltimore *Maryland Journal and the Baltimore Advertiser*, 15 April 1788. He owned 4,410 acres, 238 slaves, valued at £15,500 in 1800, and served in the lower house and the state senate for most of the 1770s and 1780s. Wealth figures are from St. Marys County Commissioners, Tax Ledger, 1800, MdHR.

6. Henry Neale served on the County Court (1798–1802) and in the House of Delegates. He owned 1,503 acres, 44 slaves, and a mill, valued at £3,523 in 1800.

7. George Plater III owned 3,700 acres, 51 slaves, valued at £8,150. For his father,

George Plater II, see Frank White, Jr., *The Governors of Maryland, 1777–1970*, pp. 28–31; Philip A. Crowl, *Maryland during and after the Revolution*, p. 149. His brother, John Rousby Plater, served on the County Court and in the House of Delegates. One brother-in-law, Uriah Forrest, served in the Revolution, then moved to Montgomery County, where he was elected to the House of Delegates, the U.S. Congress, and eventually to the state senate; see J. Thomas Scharf, *History of Western Maryland*, 1:682. A second brother-in-law, Philip Barton Key, was another prominent political figure. See also "The Plater Family," pp. 370–72.

8. Thomas was elected to the House of Delegates (1791–93, 1795–97), appointed to the Orphans Court (1802–3), and then the state senate (1803–13), where he was elected president of that body.

9. William Somerville owned 5,143 acres, 125 slaves, valued at £10,733. He married the daughter of Vernon Hebb, a member of the Committee of Safety in 1776, and his daughter married George Plater. He served in the House of Delegates in 1783 and 1785, and he was appointed to the Levy Court between 1799 and 1801, but he refused to accept appointment to the Orphans Court in 1802.

10. J. A. Thomas to John Davidson, 24 Aug. 1795, Adjutant Generals Papers, MdHR (hereafter cited as AG Papers).

11. Fredericktown *Republican Advocate*, 31 Aug. 1804. Later on in the election, the Baltimore Republican paper exulted: "Last year but 113 men could be found in the *whole county*, who were sufficiently independent in principle to advocate the cause of republicanism—this year, however, one election district has given 127 votes to the republican cause" (Baltimore *American and Commercial Advertiser*, 4 Oct. 1804). Actually, voter turnout was about 65 percent in 1804, against a normal turnout of below 40 percent in previous years, but the Republican share was only 29 percent of the voters.

12. Fredericktown *Republican Advocate*, 14 Oct. 1803. "An Old Man," recommended . forming local political committees in southern Maryland because "they could disseminate true information among the people relative to political affairs, and remove the veil of error which is so very thick in Calvert, St. Marys, Dorchester, and Worcester" (ibid., 13 April 1804). The *Republican Advocate*'s interest in the election so angered local Federalists that William Hebb, a candidate for the legislature, attacked it for meddling in county politics. With an indelicacy common to such partisan exchanges, the paper disparaged Hebb's qualifications for office, observing "in truth [he] is much better calculated to preside in a brothel" (ibid., 21 Sept. 1804).

13. Philip Ford, who stood twenty-first on the tax rolls, was also on the Republican ticket, as were two other members of prominent local families.

14. When a meeting was called for the congressional district regarding foreign affairs, the county was not represented (Baltimore *Maryland Journal and the Baltimore Advertiser*, 21 April 1794). According to the Methodist records, there were only forty-nine whites and twenty-five black communicants in the county in 1808 (*Minutes of the Methodist Conferences, 1773 to 1813*, pp. 422–23). The Episcopal clergy felt that the greatest problem was not revivalism but apathy: "Never were a people more astray . . . they are . . . as sheep without a Shepherd—Sabbath breaking, drinking, and idleness have been the bane of everything good here" (Rev. Joseph Jackson to Rev. James Kemp, 21 March 1812, MdDA). See also Jackson to Kemp, 12 Feb. 1812, 2 Jan. 1814; Clement Dorsey to Bp. Kemp, 18 Feb. 1819; Rev. R. Kearney to Bp. Kemp, 10 Jan. 1826, ibid.

15. Writing that local blacks were troublesome and had been overheard making such remarks as, "in a short time the whites will see [that] the Blacks are as good as they are," or "the whites will *soon* pay for selling negroes to Georgia men," several prominent citizens wrote the governor asking him to arm the militia; see Joseph Harris, E. J. Millard, and Peter Gough to the Governor and Council, 11 July 1802, AG Papers.

16. See Ninian Pinckney to William Thomas, Jr., 24 Nov. 1797, Thomas Papers; Governor to Speaker of House of Delegates, 1 Dec. 1795, Joseph Harris to John Davidson, 16 Nov. 1800, James Hopewell to Davidson, 27 April, 7 May 1801, Raphael Neale and Wilfred Neale to Governor and Council, 24 Dec. 1802, 3, 5, 6 Jan. 1803, R. Neale et al. to

Governor and Council, 26 Dec. 1804, State Papers, MdHR. On the national level, local members of Congress or members of the elite wrote recommendations. See the following letters to George Washington from Richard Barnes, 28 April 1789, reel 119, George Plater, 30 April 1789, reel 119, M. J. Stone, 22 July 1789, reel 123, George Washington Papers, LC.

17. Col. Plater to John Davidson, 2 April 1794; Col. Plater and Gen. Richard Barnes to Governor and Council, 20 April 1794, AG Papers.

18. See the election reports in the Annapolis *Maryland Republican* for 25 Sept. 1824; 30 Aug., 20 Sept. 1825; 19 Sept. 1826; 8 Oct. 1831; 3 Sept. 1833; and 12 Sept. 1835.

19. Rev. Kearney to Gen. James Forrest, June 1825, "The James Forrest Papers," p. 296.

20. See the prospectuses for a southern Maryland paper in the following papers: Washington, D.C., *National Journal*, 25 Aug. 1830; Annapolis *Maryland Republican*, 19 Feb. 1833, 6 Aug. 1839. See also Bell and Norwood to Secretary of State, 15 Jan. 1831, and Clement Dorsey to Secretary of State, 13 Feb. 1831, Miscellaneous Letters Received Regarding Publishers of the Laws, NA (hereafter cited as Publishers of the Laws).

21. See Baltimore *Patriot and Mercantile Advertiser*, 21 May, 9 June 1827; Washington, D.C., *National Journal*, 12 June 1827.

22. The delegation included two of William Thomas's sons, William and Richard, who were also among the fifty wealthiest persons in the county; several representatives to the state and federal government (Congressman Clement Dorsey, former Congressman Raphael Neale, members of the House of Delegates Stephen H. Gough, John T. Hawkins, and former member Dr. Caleb Jones); several high-ranking militia officers from the county (Cornelius Coombs, Gerald N. Causin, and Benedict J. Heard); and, in addition to those above who qualify, wealthy citizens of the county (John Simms, who ranked eighteenth on the tax rolls, and Luke W. Barber, who ranked sixth).

23. Annapolis *Maryland Republican*, 19 Feb. 1831.

24. Nathaniel Fenwick to Col. James Thomas, 12 April ca. 1826, Thomas Papers.

25. See George Brent to James Thomas, 27 Aug. 1831 (ibid.). Dorsey, who lost the election, was among six candidates for the House of Delegates that year (Annapolis *Maryland Republican*, 8 Oct. 1831); see also the derisive remark in the Jacksonian Baltimore *Republican and Commerical Advertiser*, 8 Oct. 1831.

26. Annapolis *Maryland Republican*, 27 Aug. 1833, listed all the Maryland judicial districts and incumbents. The correspondence in the State Papers regarding judicial appointments is scarce, but with Richard Thomas as speaker of the House of Delegates, it is difficult to imagine that Dorsey would be appointed against the Thomas family's wishes.

27. John Leigh deposition (ca. 1831), John Leigh Papers, MdHS.

28. Baltimore *Freeman's Banner*, 23 July 1831. A Jacksonian leader wrote a Talbot County partisan: "We cannot present an opposition for the Legislature, we have not the men, who can afford to enter into politics—and whatever strength we have, should be reserved for the senatorial election" (Henry G. S. Key to Edward Lloyd, 4 Aug. 1835, Edward Lloyd Papers, MdHS).

29. See the Annapolis *Maryland Republican*, 26 June 1824, 7 June 1828; Washington, D.C., *National Journal*, 28 May 1827; Baltimore *Republican*, 12 Aug. 1832, 21 May 1835; Washington, D.C., *Globe*, 18 Sept. 1832; and *Hagerstown Mail*, 3 April 1835.

30. Key owned 1,590 acres, 59 slaves, valued at $15,200; Miles owned 840 acres, 15 slaves, valued at $5,600; Dr. Roach owned 160 acres, 11 slaves, valued at $1,420; and Col. Jarboe owned 422 acres, 15 slaves, valued at $2,743 (St. Marys County, County Commissioners, Tax Ledgers, 1831, MdHR. All information concerning wealth for the elite in the second party era is from this source).

31. See U.S. Department of State, *Register of All Officers and Agents, Civil, Military, and Naval in the Service of the U.S.*, 1827, p. 51; 1829, p. 57; 1833, p. 65; and U.S. Senate, *Journal of Executive Proceedings, 1829–1869*, 4:47, 93, 529. William D. Harrison, the surveyor of Nanjemoy, served until his commission expired in 1830, when he was replaced by Robert Digges. The position held by Henry G. S. Key, surveyor of Llewellensburg, was earlier held by Edmund Key (Easton *Republican Star*, 16 Oct. 1804).

32. For identification of these sixteen men see the Annapolis *Maryland Republican*, 17 Dec. 1825, 2, 12 Dec. 1826; Baltimore *Republican*, 3 May 1836. Their social, wealth, and political characteristics are discussed in Chapter 5.

33. Former Congressman Raphael Neale, Col. James Forrest, and state Senator Athanasias Fenwick.

34. Peter Gough, who went to several internal improvements conventions and was a member of the Adams committee of correspondence in 1827, acted as chairman. For an autobiographical statement of his earlier, nonpolitical career, see Peter Gough, *A Refutation . . .* William Coad, a cavalry officer and an Anti-Jackson activist, was secretary. For a full report, see the Annapolis *Maryland Republican*, 15 Nov. 1836.

35. Benedict J. Heard, senatorial elector, militia colonel, former member of the House of Delegates, and forty-seventh wealthiest man on the tax rolls; John M. C. Causin, an Anti-Jackson attorney who was brother of Gerald N. Causin; George S. Leigh, son of John Leigh and son-in-law of Congressman John Leeds Kerr from Talbot County; and William J. Blackistone, son of Col. Thomas Blackistone, a leader in the first party era and himself a former member of the House of Delegates (speaker, 1834), militia officer and Anti-Jackson partisan. All are examples of the county's dependence on the elite for its community leadership.

36. See, for instance, William J. Blackistone, Jno. H. Sothoron, and Henry Fowler (House of Delegates members) to Governor and Council, 10 March 1835, State Papers. Sometimes a member of the organization that had a vacancy made a recommendation: see Dr. Charles L. Gardiner to Governor, 10, 20 May 1835; and Thomas Loker, an Orphans Court judge, who wrote Gov. James Thomas, 11 May 1835, "Enclosed I send you a recommendation of your Brother, as a Judge of the Orphans Court, presuming you may feel some delicacy in advancing the appointment yourself, I shall be pleased that you lay the petition or recommendation, before the Council, as coming from the people" (ibid.).

37. The incumbent, Col. Enoch J. Millard, was appointed register of wills in 1827 after the death of Gen. James Forrest. He was one of three candidates for the position. See the *Journal and Proceedings of the House of Delegates, 1826*, pp. 26, 59; and the Annapolis *Maryland Republican*, 6 Jan. 1827, for his appointment; and the Washington, D.C. *National Intelligencer*, 24 March 1835, for an announcement of his death.

38. The candidates were Luke W. Barber, the sixth wealthiest man on the tax rolls and a member of the Orphans Court (1827–29, 1831); Levy Court (1834–35) member George Coombs; House of Delegates (1824–30) member Stephen H. Gough; George S. Leigh, son of John Leigh, who was the forty-sixth wealthiest man on the tax ledgers and an active community leader; and Forrest's clerk, Joseph Spalding.

39. See the following letters to the Governor and Council from John Leeds Kerr, 24 March 1835; Robert H. Goldsborough, 7 April 1835; Dr. William Thomas et al., 6 May 1835; John Delany et al., 5 May 1835; Chapman Billingslea et al., 10 May 1835; George Crane et al., 11 May 1835, State Papers. See also John Leigh to George S. Leigh, 11 April 1824, as an example of how the family tried to mobilize its connections earlier for patronage advantage, Leigh Papers.

40. See the following letters to the Governor and Council from Richard Thomas, 23 March 1833; William D. Merrick, his brother-in-law and a Charles County legislator, 14 May 1835; Henry Fowler (HD member), 11 May 1835; B. J. Heard (HD member), 12 May 1835; John H. Sothoron, 12 May 1835; Joseph Harris (clerk of the County Court), second wealthiest man in the county, 28 March 1835; Cornelius Coombs, an Orphans Court judge and relative, 21 March 1835; and from N. Williams, an important Baltimore politician, 18 May 1835, State Papers.

41. The names and attributes of the decisional elite are listed individually in the Appendix III, Table A3.18.

42. According to the 1790 census, Talbot County contained 90.3 percent English, 6.4 percent Scottish, and .8 percent German stock; Bohmer, "Voting Behavior," p. 96.

43. The best discussion of the Eastern Shore's transformation from a tobacco to a grain economy is provided by Paul Clemens, "From Tobacco to Grain: Economic Development

on Maryland's Eastern Shore, 1660–1774," Ph.D. dissertation, University of Wisconsin, 1974.

44. As testament to the flagging interest in the Episcopal church in the county and on the Eastern Shore in general, see "Viator," 5 Oct. 1790, Easton *Maryland Herald and Eastern Shore Intelligencer*; St. Peter's Parish Report, 5 June 1797, Rev. James Jackson to Bp. Claggett, 7 May 1811, and John Singleton to Rev. Jackson, 17 June 1814, MdDA.

45. For the Quakers, see Kenneth Carroll, *Quakerism on the Eastern Shore*, pp. 155–69. A short history of Methodism is provided by Easton District. *History of the Methodist Episcopal Church*; and for a statistical breakdown of white and black membership, showing that white membership grew from 504 in 1801 to 1,139 in 1802, where it stayed between 1,413 (1803) and 1,019 (1810) for the next eight years, see *Minutes of the Methodist Conferences*, passim.

46. As a center for social and political communication, consider the following description: "The General Court for the eastern shore of this State, were lately convened at Easton. At this court were a great collection of very respectable men from the eight counties of the E[astern] S[hore] as well as some from the Western Shore. The [Jay] treaty occasionally became the topic. I do assure you that by nine-tenths of the gentlemen collected from all the counties the treaty was approved" (William Vans Murray to Oliver Wolcott, 2 Oct. 1795, George Gibbs, *Memoirs of the Administrations of George Washington and John Adams Edited from the Papers of Oliver Wolcott*, 1:249).

47. Scott, *United States Gazetteer*.

48. In 1792, "No Party" observed: "Settled in the peaceful scenes of a country life— and exalting my views whenever I spend a thought of public affairs, it is with contempt and indignation that I stumble forever on this dispute. When I take up a Philadelphia paper. . . I behold the miserable attempt to decoy the passions of the whole country into sides and party by an uncandid display of the weakness of the two secretaries" (Easton *Maryland Herald*, 16 Oct. 1792). In 1800, "Cato" observed, "A faction then being made-up of only a part of the people, it breaths nought but the *spirit of opposition*. It opposes with violence and obstinacy whatever others approve of. It hates order and loves confusion. It is restless and turbulent" (ibid., 9 Sept. 1800). See also, in the same paper, "A Friend of Peace," 1 Sept. 1801; and Robert H. Goldsborough's justification for his self-nomination: "I venerate the voice of the people when freely and fairly expressed, as the most commanding feature of Republican government, but when it comes forth polluted by passion or party spirit, its beauties are all faded, its commanding power is lost, because it ceases to be the generous offering of Independent Free Will" (7 June 1803).

49. As examples of self-nomination, see the following announcements to the voters of Talbot County in the Easton *Maryland Herald* by: John Goldsborough, Jr., 30 Sept. 1794, 20 Nov. 1798; David Kerr, 10 Sept. 1793; Hugh Sherwood of Huntington, 17 Sept. 1793; and William Hindman, 19 Aug. 1794. John Goldsborough, Jr., stated the purpose behind this exercise: "I, thus, previously to the Election, apprise you of my intention, that you may have an opportunity of making the necessary inquiries, and thereby determining whether I justly merit your suffrages or not" (ibid., 3 Sept. 1793).

50. Following the announcement of a meeting to be held over the issue of the Jay Treaty, William Hemsley, a wealthy Federalist with extensive property in Talbot and Queen Annes counties, wrote William Tilghman, 10 Aug. 1795: "We can't find out who put up the notice but it is generally conjectured that Mr. Robert Wright has done it, and I suppose he means to clamor against Government and offer himself for Congress" (William Tilghman Papers, HSPa). Consider also the advice to the electorate found in the Federalist paper, the Easton *Maryland Herald*, from "Common Sense": "The best rule to be recommended at present is the following: In acting upon this petition, Reject the advice of him who may offer it for your signature: You may be persuaded he is a Jacobin, or the Dupe of a Jacobin" (27 Oct. 1795); or "Hortensius": "The ease, with which ambitious men,—ever the most dangerous sort to a state—, procure seats in our National Councils, may be attributed, not only to their own increasing activity and exertions, but to our own negligence and inattention" (3 May 1796); see also "A Farmer," 26 July 1796.

51. For the reports of the proadministration foreign policy meetings, see ibid., 10

Sept. 1793; 26 April 1795; 10 May 1796. The latter meeting, chaired by Judge Robert Goldsborough, Jr., displayed many county notables who defended the administration: there were two revolutionary colonels (Jeremiah Banning and Peregrine Tilghman), a colonel and a major in the reorganized militia (Col. Perry Benson and Maj. Daniel P. Cox), a number of former members of the House of Delegates (J. Banning, Samuel Chamberlaine, D. P. Cox, Howes Goldsborough, R. Goldsborough, Jr., William Hayward, John Roberts, and James Tilghman), a chief judge of the General Court (R. Goldsborough, Jr.), and two members of the County Court (H. Goldsborough and W. Hayward). Of the fourteen men, seven were among the thirty-one wealthiest men in the county and most were affiliated with the Episcopal church.

52. Ibid., 10, 24 June 1800.

53. Hindman, an Episcopalian, owned 1,330 acres, 86 slaves, valued at $7,550. For a sketch of his career and that of his widely connected family, see Samuel A. Harrison, ed., "Memoirs of the Hon. William Hindman," pp. 5–59.

54. Writing a year before the election, William Hemsley described the political tone of Hindman's district: "If we are to judge from the Election . . . it would seem as if French principles and Democracy were gaining ground, but I don't think those Elections are the proper criterion to form an opinion on. I am well satisfied when the Election for a member of Congress comes on that Mr. Hindman will be elected by a great majority—and on any great national question you would see all the wealth and respectability on the side of Government—I have no fears but that Mr. Hindman's declining to serve, and I have endeavoured to press on him the necessity of continuing his Services until some Federal man of respectability can be prevailed on to take his place" (Hemsley to James McHenry, 13 Nov. 1797, James McHenry Papers, LC).

55. See Jacob Gibson to William Hindman, 4 Sept.; "Brutus" to Jacob Gibson, 11 Sept.; Gibson to my Fellow Citizens, 18 Sept.; "A Federalist," 2 Oct.; Easton *Maryland Herald*; William Hindman to James McHenry, 8 Sept., S. Sitgreaves to McHenry, 16 Sept. 1798, McHenry Papers, LC.

56. For a sense of the military crisis, see in the Easton *Maryland Herald*: "Many," "A Subscriber," 22 May; the report of the public meeting at the county courthouse, 5 June; "Juvenis," who observed, "A war with France is inevitable" (26 June); and for attacks on Seney himself, see "A Federal Whig," 21 Aug.; "X," 4 Sept.; "A Native American," 11 Sept. 1798. Of the ten participants at the French crisis meeting, reported on 5 June 1798, six were either current or former members of the state legislature, three were ranking militia officers, and six ranked among the top twenty-five property holders in the county.

57. Hindman to McHenry, ca. 1797, McHenry Papers, LC. See also his later assessment of the French question, Hindman to McHenry, 1 April, 7 May 1797, ibid.

58. Easton *Maryland Herald*, 25 Sept. 1798.

59. George Salmon to James McHenry, 25 Sept. 1798, McHenry Papers, LC.

60. Jacob Gibson, who led Seney's campaign in Talbot County, was thirteenth on the tax rolls with 1,230 acres, 47 slaves, valued at $6,500. He was an outspoken French enthusiast, who had been elected captain of a militia company in 1775; his brother Jonathan served as a major in the Revolution. See also Oswald Tilghman, comp., *History of Talbot County, Maryland, 1661–1861*, 1:231–56.

61. For the election results, see the Easton *Maryland Herald*, 9 Oct. 1798; for Hindman's reaction to defeat and Seney's death, see Hindman to Rufus King, 8 April 1799, Charles R. King, ed., *Life and Correspondence of Rufus King*, 2:593; reflecting the passion of the day, a Federalist signing himself "Monitor" eulogized Seney's death; "Of the dead we must say nothing, but what is good, and all must agree that a Jacobin in the grave is not without merit; for there, and there only, will he cease to defame the best of governments and foment sedition and discord among the people" (Easton *Maryland Herald*, 20 Nov. 1798).

62. Judge Goldsborough owned 1,718 acres, 46 slaves, valued at $4,657. He was an attorney, an Episcopalian vestryman, and had been appointed chief judge of the General Court in 1796. See his announcement, 20 Nov. 1798, ibid.

63. Baltimore *American and Commercial Advertiser*, 18 Oct. 1799.

64. The most ambitious effort to organize through conventions was suggested by "Demophilus," 30 July 1805, Easton *Republican Star*. For the Republicans' use of meetings, see the various reports in the same paper: 14 Sept. 1802; 31 May, 7, 14, 21 June 1803; 13 March, 15, 22 May, 26 June , 24 July, 28 Aug. 1804; 16 July, 20 Aug., 1 Oct. 1805. See also Baltimore *American*, 28 June 1800.

65. The oligarchical roots of the Republican party are epitomized by the Lloyd family. Edward Lloyd IV, who served in the Council of Safety between 1775 and 1777, the Maryland Convention, the House of Delegates, and the state senate, was the wealthiest man in the county. His son Edward V was an active Republican, who began his public career at this time. William Hayward, another member of the affluent elite (standing sixteenth on the county tax lists with 1,242 acres, 47 slaves, valued at $4,973), was related to the Lloyds by his son's marriage to one of Edward IV's daughters. Joseph H. Nicholson, future congressman from Queen Annes County, also married into the Lloyd family.

66. See Nicholas Martin's public announcement: "Presuming that nomination is not the vox populi, I do, at the request of a number of my fellow citizens . . . offer myself as a candidate" (Easton *Republican Star*, 5 July 1803). See also "A Mechanic of Easton," 26 July 1803; and the election results, 4, 11 Oct. 1803, ibid.; "Mentor," 11 Sept. 1804, Easton *Maryland Herald*.

67. See the Easton *Maryland Herald*, 11, 18 Sept. 1804; Easton *Republican Star*, 25 Sept., 2, 9, 23, 25 Oct. 1804; 15 Oct. 1805. See also the Federalist satire on a Republican convention meeting, Easton *Maryland Herald*, 31 Aug., 14, 21 Sept. 1802.

68. Federalists usually objected to "public treating" as being pernicious and creating a false camaraderie between the voter and candidates; see "Independent Farmer," 7 Aug. 1792, 5 Nov. 1799; "One of the People," 27 May 1800, Easton *Maryland Herald*. Regarding the practice of addressing the people wherever they congregated and the sensational charge that Goldsborough dispensed liquor at a Methodist quarterly meeting, see the Easton *Republican Star*, 30 Aug., 6 Sept. 1803.

69. The Federalist-Episcopal position was nicely stated by "Monitor," who believed "that good government, religion and morality, were blessings of mankind; but regenerated France happily got rid of them all" (18 Dec. 1798, Easton *Maryland Herald*); see also, in the same paper, "Juvenis," 8 May 1798; "A Layman," 17 May, 26 July 1803. Writing about the election of 1800, a Methodist historian observed: "This year was marked by great political controversy, in which the Methodists, being mostly Republicans . . . , were warmly assailed and ridiculed by the clergy of the Episcopal Church, who charged that the Methodist preachers were 'unlearned' and unable to stand in equal combat with the deism of the age, and that if the infidelity of Jefferson and Paine should sweep the land, the Episcopal clergy were the only ones to whom we could look for a refutation of their blasphemies" (*History of the Methodist Episcopal Church*, p. 9). For a contemporary association between the Methodists and a more pluralistic Republican party, see Jacob Gibson, "For the Herald," 11 Dec. 1798; "Nestor," 22, 29 Jan. 1799; "Isaac Bickerstaff," 12, 19 Feb. 1799, all in Easton *Maryland Herald*.

70. The majors were Hugh Sherwood of Huntington, an Episcopalian, who ranked twenty-sixth on the tax rolls with 1,060 acres, 22 slaves, valued at $3,800; William Goldsborough, who had been a lieutenant in the Revolution and stood thirty-third on the tax list with 820 acres, 18 slaves, valued at $3,000; Robert Lloyd Nichols, who served as a major in 1775, was an Easton merchant in the 1790s in partnership with David Kerr and Thomas Chamberlaine, and was the father-in-law of Robert H. Goldsborough. Nichols held 2,940 acres, 22 slaves, worth $12,990, and was third on the tax lists. Daniel P. Cox, the sheriff, owned 377 acres, 16 slaves, valued at $1,327. For the initial appointments, see Annapolis *Maryland Gazette*, 12 June 1794.

71. William Hindman remarked to James McHenry, 12 Aug. 1798: "There have been some late Jacobinical Promotions in the Militia here, Col. Benson is made a General, who recently before publicly said at Easton, that if Mr. Jefferson had been President, we should not now be at War or at the eve of War with France—meaning no Doubt thereby that the War is ascribable to Mr. Adams. Mr William Hayward is made a Colonel, who has long been deemed jacobinical (he is changing and will vote for me). Col. James Wright com-

mands another Regiment in this District (A most bitter French Jacobin)— You see what Reliance may be placed upon the Militia here" (James McHenry Papers, MdHS).

72. Gov. Henry wrote Capt. Jno. Coats of Talbot County, 9 Aug. 1798, asking him to hold his company in readiness because "I have received information that some danger is to be apprehended from the riotous disposition of the negroes in and about Cambridge" (State Papers). See also Ninian Pinckney to John Coats, 30 Nov. 1807, ibid. The reality of this perceived danger is difficult to judge because few references were made in the public prints about race relations.

73. See the Easton *Maryland Herald*, 9 Nov. 1802. William C. Spencer to Secretary of State, 16 Oct. 1826, alluded to the fact that the *Republican Star* had been publishing the laws for the last twenty or twenty-five years (Publishers of the Laws, NA). For a list of Talbot County officeholders when Jefferson took office, see U.S. Department of the Treasury, *Message from the President of the U.S., Transmitting a Roll of Persons Having Office or Employment under the U.S.*, p. 35.

74. See Joseph Habersham to Joseph H. Nicholson, 15 June 1801, and Gideon Granger to Nicholson, 21 Dec. 1801, Joseph H. Nicholson Papers, LC.

75. See Albert Gallatin to Nicholson, 15 March, 4 April 1803, ibid. For the petitions and counterpetitions, see the following letters to various officers of the administration from Philemon Willis, 7 March 1803; Petition from Citizens of Oxford, 22 March 1803; Robert Wright and Joseph H. Nicholson, 9 April 1803; Robert Banning, 22 March, 17 May 1804, reel 1/frames 527–40, Letters of Application and Recommendation during the Administration of Thomas Jefferson, NA.

76. See the following letters to the Governor and Council from David Kerr and William Dawson, 14 April 1796; P. Sherwood et al., 14 Dec. 1797; David Kerr et al., 22 Dec. 1797; William Dawson et al., 5 March 1798, P. Sherwood et al., 1799; John Edmondson, 26 Dec. 1800; Edward Lloyd V et al., April 1802, State Papers.

77. Consider the following letters to the Governor and Council from William Hindman, 13 July, 26 Nov. 1796; John Roberts, 26 Nov. 1796; and Jacob Gibson, 18 Feb. 1805, ibid.

78. For an articulation of party considerations, see the following letters: Lt. Col. John Hughes to Capt. James Thomas, 29 Aug. 1799, AG Papers; Jacob Gibson to Governor and Council, 9 May 1805, James Nabb to Governor and Council, 21 Jan. 1808, State Papers.

79. For a list of the decisional elite, see Appendix III, Table A3.22.

80. Col. Jeremiah Banning; Gen. Perry Benson; John Dickinson; Jacob Gibson; Judge Robert Goldsborough, Jr.; his son, Robert H. Goldsborough; Col. William Hayward, whose son married into the Lloyd family, the wealthiest in the county; William Hemsley of Queen Annes and Talbot counties, who married into the family of Gen. James Lloyd of Kent County and was thus related to William Tilghman; William Hindman, whose sister married William Perry of Talbot County, who stood seventh on the tax rolls and served as a state senator until his death, when Hindman was elected to replace him; David Kerr, whose brother-in-law was John Leeds Bozman, the twelfth wealthiest person on the tax rolls; Edward Lloyd IV; his son Edward V, members of the wealthiest family in the county; Dr. Ennals Martin, who stood forty-fourth on the tax rolls; John Roberts, who served in the lower house throughout the 1780s and was the twentieth wealthiest person; and Perry Spencer, the nineteenth wealthiest person.

81. Notably Thomas Perrin Smith, editor of the *Republican Star*, and James Corwan, who sold the *Maryland Herald* and left Easton in 1804; and James Colston, Charles Emory, William Muley, a member of the House of Delegates, who were Republican party organizers.

82. See Robert H. Goldsborough to John Leeds Kerr, 21 July 1815, Bozman-Kerr Papers, LC, as well as many other letters exchanged between them in the same collection between 1814 and 1817, as examples of Federalist acceptance of the necessity of active campaigning. The *Easton Gazette* was established in 1817, with the financial support of R. H. Goldsborough, under the editorship of Alexander Graham. By the late 1820s it was the Anti-Jacksonian paper for the county; see the Easton *Eastern Shore Whig and People's Advocate*, 7 Sept. 1830.

83. For a description of the disintegration of the Republican party in the early 1820s and the rivalry generated, see Robert H. Goldsborough to Levin R. Key, 24 Dec. 1824, Edward Lloyd Papers, MdHS; and letters addressed to Edward Lloyd from Samuel Ringgold, 2 May 1823; John S. Skinner, 7 Oct. 1823, 23 April 1824; William Dickinson, 21 Nov. 1823; Thomas H. Carroll, 9 Feb. 1824; William R. Steuart, 21 Nov. 1824; Frisby Tilghman, 8 Jan. 1825; and Lyde Goodwin, 12 Jan. 1825, ibid. See also Julius Forrest to Gen. James Forrest, 23 Feb. 1823, "Forrest Papers," pp. 275–76.

84. On the occasion of a forthcoming congressional convention, Graham commented: "It would be a painful thought, indeed, that from the want of a good understanding throughout the district, the strength of the National Republicans should be paralyzed or withheld" (*Easton Gazette*, 14 July 1832). See also the *Gazette*'s efforts to organize party meetings and to resolve conflicts and misunderstanding: "Meetings of National Republicans," 7 June 1831; 20 July 1833; 30 Aug. 1834; 16 May 1835; or letters from "A Veteran Whig" and "A Voice of Friends," 20 June 1835; "Attention Patriots," 27 June 1835; 14 Nov. 1835; and 2 April 1836.

85. William Hayward, Jr., wrote to the secretary of state, 7 April 1829, about the Easton *Republican Star*: "In the late contest however the 'Star' followed the course of too many other papers in which the laws were printed 'by authority' of the late administration, . . . and by placing itself under the direction of Mr. Adams and Clay added much to the difficulties under which the friends of Jackson had to labor in this part of the State" (Publishers of the Laws, NA).

86. The Anti-Jackson party activities may be found in the following newspaper reports: Baltimore *Patriot and Mercantile Advertiser*, 21 June 1827, 5 Sept. 1834, 29 July, 24 Aug., 16 Dec. 1835; *Easton Gazette*, 28 July 1827, 14 June, 26 July, 9 Aug. 1828, 15, 29 Aug., 12 Sept. 1829, 21 May, 11 June, 23 July, 20 Aug., 8 Nov. 1831, 4 Aug., 1 Sept., 6, 20 Oct. 1832, 20 July 1833, 6 Sept. 1834, 21 March, 25 July, 8, 22 Aug., 12, 20 Dec. 1835, 2 April, 30 July, 10 Sept. 1836; Easton *Eastern Shore Whig*, 14 June 1831, 18 Aug. 1835; and Baltimore *Commercial Chronicle and Daily Marylander*, 27 Aug. 1833.

87. Baltimore *Republican*, 28 Sept. 1830. In 1832, Robert H. Goldsborough owned 2,382 acres, 62 slaves, valued at $24,196, which placed him as the third wealthiest person in the county. All the wealth figures are from Talbot County, County Commissioners, Tax Ledgers, 1826, 1832, MdHR.

88. For examples of Robert H. Goldsborough's activities see the Baltimore *Patriot*, 21 June 1827; *Easton Gazette*, 28 July 1827, 14 June 1828, 25 July 1835; the Easton *Eastern Shore Whig*, 11 July 1835, identified the *Gazette* as "the acknowledged organ of Senator Goldsborough."

89. See his public letter in the *Cambridge Chronicle*, 24 Sept. 1831. See also the *Easton Gazette*, 12 Sept. 1829, 24 Aug. 1833, 24 Jan. 1835; *Eastern Shore Whig*, 30 Sept., 11 Nov. 1834; Baltimore *Republican*, "The Senator," 9 Jan. 1835; Baltimore *Chronicle*, 27 Aug., 10 Sept. 1833; Baltimore *Patriot*, 14 Sept. 1829.

90. John Leeds Kerr owned 1,930 acres, 34 slaves, valued at $17,200, placing him as the seventh wealthiest person in the county in 1832. For a biographical sketch see Tilghman, comp., *History of Talbot County*, 1:388–408.

91. Governor Martin was credited with having 400 acres valued at $4,986 on the tax ledgers in 1832, the year after his death; for a biographical sketch see ibid., 1:228–31.

92. Col. John Tilghman, tenth wealthiest man on the tax rolls, who represented the county Anti-Jacksonians at a congressional convention in 1831, was the son of James Tilghman, who served on the Talbot County Committee of Safety in 1776. Tench Tilghman, bearer of a famous revolutionary Tilghman name, married the daughter of John Leeds Kerr in 1832 and stood forty-sixth on the county tax rolls that year. He acted as secretary and delegate to party meetings between 1831 and 1836. William H. Tilghman was even more active in the party cause. Martin Goldsborough, whose wealth placed him thirty-seventh on the tax rolls, acted as a delegate to several party meetings. Nicholas Goldsborough, who married a daughter of revolutionary hero Col. Tench Tilghman in 1811 and whose grandfather was a delegate to the Convention of 1774, was the eleventh wealthiest person in the county. He served as secretary and chairman of several early party meetings.

93. For a more elaborate discussion of the scoring system, see Appendix I, Methodological Procedures.

94. Gen. Solomon Dickinson owned 590 acres, 23 slaves, valued at $6,285, which placed him thirty-first on the tax rolls.

95. Col. Edward N. Hambleton owned 1,850 acres, 35 slaves, valued at $18,500, placing him fifth on the tax rolls. His father-in-law, Hugh Sherwood of Huntington, a Federalist community leader in the first party era, stood twenty-sixth on the tax rolls in 1798.

96. "A Democrat," 9 Sept. 1834, Easton *Eastern Shore Whig*; see also in the same issue, "AZ"'s attack on Col. William Hughlett.

97. For the Jackson party activities, see the relevant articles in the following newspapers: Easton *Eastern Shore Whig*, 17 Aug., 14 Sept. 1830, 9, 19 July, 30, 31 Aug., 6, 27 Sept., 4 Oct. 1831, 7 Feb.,3, 17 April, 29 May, 3, 17, 24 July 1832, 2, 9, 16 Sept. 1834, 4, 7 April, 2 May, 14 July, 1, 18, 22 Aug., 8, 19 Sept. 1835, 26 March, 23 April, 28 June, 6, 9 Aug., 6 Sept., 8 Oct. 1836; *Easton Gazette*, 13 Aug. 1831, 6 Oct. 1832, 26 Sept. 1835; Baltimore *Republican*, 30 Aug. 1831, 4, 25 May 1832, 18 Sept. 1833, 20, 21 May, 3 Aug. 1835, 29 April 1836.

98. For a convenient biographical description of Edward Lloyd V, see Tilghman, comp., *History of Talbot County*, 1:184–210. Tilghman would have us believe that Col. Lloyd retired from politics in the late 1820s (1:199), but there is strong evidence that Col. Lloyd was an important figure in the evolving Jackson party; see Dabney S. Carr to Secretary of State, 10 Dec. 1829, Publishers of the Laws, NA; and the election report in the Baltimore *Patriot*, 8 Oct. 1828.

99. Richard Spencer owned 690 acres, 20 slaves, valued at $7,800. For a short biographical statement, see the Easton *Eastern Shore Whig*, 30 Sept. 1834, and the *Biographical Directory of the American Congress, 1774–1961*, p. 1638. For a contemporary view of his political activities, see James P. Heath to John Leeds Kerr, 2 Sept. 1829; Kerr to Heath, 20 Sept. 1829; Jacob C. Wilson to Kerr, 4 Oct. 1831, Bozman-Kerr Papers.

100. Samuel Dickinson, Dr. Dickinson's father, stood seventeenth on the tax rolls in 1798.

101. Richard Frisby to Francis P. Blair, 21 Oct. 1832, Blair-Rives Papers, LC.

102. The Easton *Eastern Shore Whig*, 30 July 1830, hailed the Maysville veto because it sought "to check extravagance, to limit the constitutional power of government, and to protect the people from the oppression and abuse of their agents." See also ibid., 7 March 1835, 5 April 1836.

103. See "At Last," *Easton Gazette*, 14 Dec. 1835. Col. Thomas Emory, state senator from Queen Annes County, was the leading proponent of the omnibus internal improvements project on the Eastern Shore; see his public letters in the *Easton Gazette*, 12 March, 4, 16, 23, 30 April, 7 May 1836.

104. For the meeting, called by the *Easton Gazette*, see the issues for 21, 28 May 1836.

105. Easton *Eastern Shore Whig*, 8 May 1832; see also, regarding the reform issue, 31 Oct., 17, 21 Nov., 29 Dec. 1835, 12, 15, 24 Nov. 1836.

106. For contemporary opinion on this proposal, see Easton *Eastern Shore Whig*, 16 Feb., 16 March 1833; *Easton Gazette*, 16 Feb., 23 March, 13 April 1833, 25 Jan., 15 Feb. 1834. See also James C. Mullikin, "The Separatist Movement and Related Problems, 1776–1850," pp. 453–84.

107. *Easton Gazette*, 14 April 1832; and 7, 28 April 1832, 13 April 1833.

108. Ibid., 1 Oct., 19 Nov. 1836; see also *Niles Weekly Register* 51 (24 Sept. 1836): 52; 51 (1 Oct. 1836): 69–70.

109. Nominations were made by the delegates sent to the lower house and state senate; see letters to the Governor and Council from [Talbot County Delegation], 9 Feb. 1828, 24 Feb. 1834; William Hughlett et al., 15 March, 3 June 1836; Edward N. Hambleton et al., 27 Nov., 27 Dec. 1836, State Papers. For the federal level, see Maryland Congressional Delegation to Henry Clay, 23 March 1826; Samuel Smith to Clay, 10 Feb. 1827, reel 3, Letters of Application and Recommendation during the Administration of John Quincy Adams, NA; Maryland Delegation to Martin Van Buren, n.d., reel 11, Mary-

land Delegation to Secretary of State, 29 Jan. 1833, reel 2, Letters of Application and Recommendation during the Administration of Andrew Jackson, NA. See also George Mitchell, Richard Spencer, and William Carmichael to Secretary of State, Dec. 1829, Publishers of the Laws, NA.

110. For an indication of the dominance of the Anti-Jacksonians in local patronage positions, many of whom were also former Federalists, see the Easton *Eastern Shore Whig*, 28 July, 18 Aug. 1835.

111. For a listing of the federal officeholders in Talbot County during the Jackson era, see the U.S. Department of State, *Register of Officers*, from 1827 through 1835, passim. John D. Green, the first editor of the Easton *Eastern Shore Whig*, retired when he was appointed postmaster of Easton. Edward Mullikin, the second editor of the Jackson paper, was appointed postmaster on Green's death. For the correspondence regarding the publication of the laws, see letters addressed to the secretary of state from Edward Lloyd V, 5 April 1829, John D. Green, 10 April, 22 June 1829, George E. Mitchell et al., Dec. 1829, Publishers of the Laws.

112. See letters to the Governor and Council from: William Loveday, Dec. 1835, Robert H. Goldsborough, 28 Nov. 1835, E. N. Hambleton, 10 Dec. 1835, A. C. Bullitt, 13 Dec. 1835; and letters to the judges to the Court of Appeals from E. Tilghman, 30 Nov. 1835, R. H. Goldsborough, 8 Dec. 1835, T. Tilghman, 8 Dec. 1835, T. R. Lockerman, 12 Dec. 1835, T. C. Nicols, 12 Dec. 1835, State Papers.

113. For Kerr's efforts to secure a judicial appointment, see his letters to R. W. Bowie, 10 June 1834; Gov. James Thomas, 10 June 1834; and two letters dated 30 June 1834 to Kerr from George C. Washington, Bozman-Kerr Papers.

114. For a list of the decisional elite see the Appendix III, Table A3.26.

115. There are essentially two categories here: men of some wealth, such as Robert Banning, Gen. Solomon Dickinson, Col. Edward N. Hambleton, Col. William Hughlett, and Richard Spencer; and men without remarkable wealth, such as Joseph Bruff, Spry Denny, Alexander Graham, Thomas R. Lockerman, and Edward C. Mullikin, who participated actively in leadership positions.

116. The Nat Turner insurrection troubled Maryland slaveowners in 1831; see the reports of the various meetings following that event in the *Easton Gazette*, 29 Oct., 24 Dec. 1831. In July 1831, the Talbot County Colonization Society was organized. Familiar community leaders participated: Col. John Goldsborough was chairman and president, T. R. Lockerman was secretary and a vice-president, Gen. Solomon Dickinson and William Rose, a Jackson party activist and unsuccessful candidate to the state legislature, were also vice-presidents. The twelve managers included three members of the decisional elite, Joseph Bruff, T. R. Lockerman, and Peter Webb, and John Stevens, Jr., whose father belonged to both elites. Nine of the twelve managers, not counting John Stevens, Jr., owned slaves. For the report of the meeting, see ibid., 21 July 1831.

Chapter 3

1. The ethnic composition was derived from the 1790 federal census; see David A. Bohmer, "Voting Behavior during the First American Party System: Maryland, 1796–1816," Ph.D. dissertation, University of Michigan, 1974, p. 96.

2. For examples of the German indentured servant trade, see the Fredericktown *Rights of Man*, 27 July, 10 Aug. 1796.

3. Contemporary evaluations can be useful to flesh out what is suggested in the census. Andrew Shriver, an assimilated member of a politically active family, supported his request for a local German-speaking appointment by observing that in this district "the inhabitants are nine tenths Germans generally in middling circumstances, many of them poor . . . few of them speak English" (Shriver to Arthur Shaaf, 13 April 1799, State Papers, MdHR). Three years later, he wrote his congressman about Frederick County's German population: "They are certainly the most useful class of people in our county but they neglect education too much and are eager to make money *only*. . . . But their want of information is a great evil, it necessarily makes them *dependent* on affairs of more importance on the opinions of others. . . . most of the Old Germans have been brought up under such despotic Govern-

ments and the doctrine of slavish submission and the prejudices of the parent are planted and so strongly rooted in the child that it is next to impossible to remove them" (Shriver to Daniel Heister, 14 March 1802 [MS 2085], Shriver Papers, MdHS).

4. As examples of the decayed state of the Episcopal church in Frederick County, see Proceedings of the Superintendence Committee (Western Shore), 25 Sept. 1788; Rev. Thomas Read, Visitation to the Fifth District, 27 April 1798; John H. Thomas to Rev. James Kemp, 27 Feb. 1814; Thomas to Rev. James Jackson, 28 Nov. 1814, MdDA. See also Rev. Ethan Allen, "All Saints and St. Marks Parish," pp. 22–23, ibid.

5. See the following reports on the growing influence of Methodism from Rev. Joseph J. G. Bend, Report of the Standing Committee, 1791–92; Bend, Visitation Report, 20 June 1796; William Tyler to Rev. W. D. Addison, 27 May 1814; Rev. John Johns to Bp. Kemp, 18 Jan. 1825, ibid.

6. The number of white Methodists in Frederick County was between two and three hundred in the 1790s and between four and seven hundred in the first decade of the nineteenth century. Considering that the white population of the county was 26,478 in 1800, the church did not appear to have had wide support. For Methodist membership statistics, see *Minutes of the Methodist Conferences, 1773 to 1813*, passim; and Thomas J. C. Williams, *History of Frederick County, Maryland*, 1:456–59. There were two Baptist churches in Frederick County, one in Fredericktown and the other in Taneytown, whose membership totaled 65 in 1793; see John Asplund, *The Universal Register of the Baptist Denomination in North America. For the Years 1790 . . . and Part of 1794*, p. 23.

7. For a short treatment of the various Frederick County churches, see Williams, *History of Frederick County*, 1:406–506; and Abdel R. Wentz, *The Lutheran Church of Frederick Maryland, 1738–1938*.

8. [Maryland] Intendant of the Revenue, 1784, *An Account of the Gross and Average Value of the Land*.

9. U.S. Bureau of the Census. *First U.S. Census, 1790*, p. 47; *Fifth U.S. Census, 1830*, pp. 80–83.

10. Joseph Scott maintained that there were about 700 dwellings there in 1795, which would indicate a population of 4,200 (*United States Gazetteer*). Williams reprinted a contemporary description of Fredericktown which I accept as being more accurate (*History of Frederick County*, 1:269–70).

11. Andrew Shriver to Samuel Smith, 20 Oct. 1808 (MS 2085), Shriver Papers.

12. Of the eighteen men appointed as lieutenant colonel or major in 1794 (Annapolis *Maryland Gazette*, 17 June 1794), six served in the Revolution; eight served in government during the 1790s or before, and seven were among the eighty wealthiest men on the 1797 tax rolls.

13. Very little has been written about the Whiskey Rebellion in Maryland. The two county histories give it only cursory attention. Frank Cassell's biography of Samuel Smith, the leader of the relief forces, treats it with an emphasis on his protagonist. Col. Joshua Gist, a revolutionary officer who stood fifty-seventh on the 1797 tax records, is credited by Scharf with single-handedly intimidating a contingent of Whiskey Boys who erected a liberty poll in Westminster (J. Thomas Scharf, *History of Western Maryland*, 2:791). Former Governor Thomas Johnson chaired a meeting concerning the crisis in Fredericktown (ibid., 1:165). The local discontent was revealed by a militia general's response to the governor's call for volunteers: "There appears to be a diversity of sentiment prevailing here among the people respecting the conduct of the insurgents Westward" (Gen. M. Bayley to Governor, 23 Aug. 1794, Adjutant Generals Papers, MdHR, hereafter cited as AG Papers).

14. See in the Fredericktown *Rights of Man*, ironically a Federalist paper despite its title, letters to the editor from "Camillus," 19 Aug., 2 Sept. 1795; and "Atticus," 11 May 1796. In the same paper, see also several public letters from candidates denying membership in any "opposition" party: from George Baer, Jr., 24 Aug. 1796, and from John Tyler, 5 Oct. 1796.

15. J. Kurtz to Abraham Shriver, 20 Oct. 1802 (MS 750.1), Shriver Papers. See also the Fredericktown *Hornet*'s editorial on New York politics, 1 April 1806.

16. For the activities of the reform movement, see the Baltimore *Federal Gazette*

and Baltimore Daily Advertiser, 22 Aug. 1797; Fredericktown *Bartgis's Federal Gazette*, 13 Sept. 1797.

17. Fredericktown *Bartgis's Federal Gazette*, 30 Aug., 13, 20 Sept. 1797.

18. See letters from "Phidon," "A.B.," 30 Aug., "A Dutch Farmer," 20 Sept. 1797, ibid.

19. "Veritas," 30 Aug. 1797, Fredericktown *Rights of Man*. See also "Half-Dutch," 27 Sept. 1797, Fredericktown *Bartgis's Federal Gazette*. The rural position would probably be better documented if more copies of the *Rights of Man* had survived.

20. For the election results, see the Fredericktown *Bartgis's Federal Gazette*, 11 Oct. 1797. Running for reelection in 1799, Henry R. Warfield, a 1797 reformer, promised voters continued support for the district system (ibid., 18 Sept. 1799).

21. See the address of the Federalist convention, *Frederick-Town Herald*, 12 Aug. 1803. See also, in the same paper, "A Voter," 16 July and two editorials, 20 Aug., 8 Oct. 1803, stressing the same theme. The editor had observed, 19 May 1804, "In Virginia, where churches are out of fashion, democracy is most in fashion. In Connecticut, where they have yet more room for their Meeting Houses and Schools and less for whiskey shops and brothels, there is less of democracy and more of federalism." This creeping malaise was ascribed to the corrupting influence of foreigners.

22. Thomas Johnson chaired a Fredericktown meeting to support President Adams in 1798; his brother, Col. James Johnson, chaired a presidential elector meeting in 1800. In 1798, Dr. Philip Thomas worked behind the scenes; in 1800, Richard Potts campaigned actively to implement "Legislative Choice." See Baltimore, *Federal Gazette*, 3, 17 May 1798; Fredericktown *Rights of Man*, (?) June, 5 Nov. 1800; Dr. Philip Thomas to John Eager Howard, 5, 12 Sept. 1798, Bayard Papers, MdHS; Richard Potts to Benjamin Mackall, 7 Oct. 1800, William Potts Papers, DU.

23. As examples of their convention and organization activities, see the following reports: Fredericktown *Bartgis's Republican Gazette*, 11 Feb. 1801; *Frederick-Town Herald*, 21 Aug. 1802, 2 July, 12 Aug. 1803; Fredericktown *Hornet*, "W. E.," 16 Aug., "Candor," 20 Sept., 4 Oct. 1803; Fredericktown *Republican Advocate*, 24 June, 1 July, 5 Aug. 1803, 5 Aug. 1804; Fredericktown *Rights of Man*, 12 Sept. 1798. See also Daniel Clarke, Jr., to Andrew Shriver, 20 Aug. 1802; Andrew Shriver to [Postmaster General], 10 Sept. 1802; Abraham Shriver to Andrew Shriver, 10 Sept. 1802; Lawrence Brengle to Andrew Shriver, 26 June 1803 (MS 2085), Shriver Papers.

24. A fascinating account of electioneering at a militia muster was provided by "A. B.," Fredericktown *Rights of Man*, 5 Sept. 1798; see also, in the same issue, the toasts drunk at the battalion meeting in favor of the Adams administration. Abraham Shriver advised Samuel Smith, 25 May 1809, "The Federalists for the last week or ten days have been continually addressing the people at the different Battalion parades" (Vertical File, MdHS). For Federalist Fourth of July celebrations, see the *Frederick-Town Herald*, 10 July 1802, 7 July 1804. For Federalist barbecues, see Abraham Shriver to Andrew Shriver, 9, 26 Sept. 1803 (MS 2085), Shriver Papers.

25. Col. Key was quoted in a letter from Lt. Col. Robert Cumming to Gov. Ogle, 10 May 1800, AG Papers. Col. Cumming also wrote David Shriver, 1 Nov. 1801: "These Men it appears have become the objects of Mr. Key's vengeance the crime he alleges is a difference in Politics . . . [he] has spread orders to his Captains to order them to leave their own Regt. and to do duty in his, and in the case of refusal to fine them as absentees. The result is that they have been fined and the fines amounting to about 200 dollars put in the hands of the Sheriff for collection. Col. Key declared in my presence that his motive was merely to punish the Petitioners for being of different Politics from himself with much abuse lavished on them at the same time" (MS 2085.3), Shriver Papers. See also "Candour," Baltimore *American and Commercial Advertiser*, 10 June 1800.

26. For background of the establishment of Thompson and the *Frederick-Town Herald* as the new "official" Federalist paper, see John Winter's public letter and the report of the incident, Fredericktown *Bargis's Republican Gazette*, 31 March 1802; *Frederick-Town Herald*, 3 July 1803; and a letter from Dr. John Tyler to Andrew Shriver, 30 March 1802 (MS 750.1), Shriver Papers. Williams reports that in 1798 Dr. John D. Cary edited a

Federalist paper called the *Key*, named in honor of Col. John Ross Key (*History of Frederick County*, 1:269). No copies of this paper have been found.

27. For perceptions of Federalist activities, see Lawrence Brengle to Andrew Shriver, 11 April 1802 (MS 750.1), Shriver Papers, and Robert Wright to Andrew Shriver, 12 April 1802 (MS 2085), ibid.; *Frederick-Town Herald*, 31 July 1802.

28. Harper to John H. Thomas, 10 Sept. 1812, Harper-Pennington Papers, MdHS. As examples of the Federalist spoiling strategy, see Daniel Clarke, Jr., to Andrew Shriver, 7 Oct. 1801, Abraham Shriver to (?), 19 Oct. 1808, Abraham Shriver to Andrew Shriver, 24 March, 10 April 1811, Abraham Shriver to Jacob Shriver, 2 Oct. 1811 (MS 2085), Shriver Papers; Fredericktown *Republican Advocate*, 28 Sept. 1804; Fredericktown *Bartgis's Republican Gazette*, 9 Sept. 1809.

29. If we accept R. G. Harper's judgment as to who were Frederick County's most important Federalists in 1812, stated in his previously cited letter, they would include Dr. Philip Thomas, John Hanson Thomas, George Baer, Jr., Col. John McPherson, Col. John Thomas, and Roger B. Taney—all of them leaders throughout the entire period.

30. By pluralism I mean an acceptance of cultural diversity and a toleration of more than one standard of behavior. The Republican acceptance of pluralism was stated in several sources and in the public prints: "Civis" accepted a diversity of opinion as a sign of strength (Fredericktown *Bartgis's Federal Gazette*, 23, 30 Aug. 1797); despite Federalist attacks on them for being irreligious, Republicans, both publicly ("Puzzled," Fredericktown *Republican Advocate*, 10 Dec. 1802; "Politics," Fredericktown *Hornet*, 13 Sept. 1803; "Republican Farmer," ibid., 15 May 1804; "A Listener," Fredericktown *Bartgis's Republican Gazette*, 11 Feb. 1809) and privately (Daniel Clarke, Jr., to Andrew Shriver, 19 April 1803 [MS 750], Shriver Papers) advocated religion and religious toleration; but their future success in Frederick County was tied to the cultivation of the German community ("Tribute and Praise to the Germans," Fredericktown *Bartgis's Republican Gazette*, 13 Aug. 1802; "Ein deutscher Bauer, an die Deutschen Einwohnen von Friederick County," Fredericktown *Hornet*, 23 Aug. 1803; "Republikanische Versammlung," ibid., 30 Aug. 1803; Fredericktown *Republican Advocate*, 29 June 1804); see also the political correspondence regarding Republican strategy to mobilize the Germans, Daniel Clarke, Jr., to Andrew Shriver, 20 Aug. 1802, 22 Aug. 1803, Abraham Shriver to Andrew Shriver, 21 Sept. 1802 (MS 2085), Shriver Papers. "Barclay" modestly summarized the Republican successes: "The *Republicans* have secured to us the right of Suffrage—released us from unnecessary taxes—preserved freedom of opinion on religious and political subjects—and saved us from war and carnage, by negotiating for and obtaining the cessation of Louisiana" (Fredericktown *Republican Advocate*, 22 July 1803).

31. In the *Frederick-Town Herald*, see, for the first quote, 25 Feb. 1804; and, for the second, "Modern Republicanism," 27 April 1805. See also "The Spirit of the Times," 8 Oct. 1803; "The Dominant Party," 7 Jan. 1807; and "Our Present Administration," 7 March 1807.

32. As examples of Republican organization, see the announcements calling for party meetings in the following newspapers: Baltimore *Federal Gazette and Baltimore Daily Advertiser*, 20 Dec. 1799, 27 Aug. 1801; Fredericktown *Hornet*, 24 June 1806; Fredericktown *Republican Advocate*, "An Old Man," 11 March, 13 April, "Worthy of Emulation," 20 April, 27 July, 10 Aug. 1804, "The Republican Citizens of Middletown District," 14 June, "Libertytown," 9 July 1805. For descriptions of barbecues, see *Frederick-Town Herald*, 24 Sept. 1803; Fredericktown *Hornet*, 20 Sept., 25 Oct. 1803, 9 July 1805; Fredericktown *Republican Advocate*, 8 July, 14, 24 Sept., 7 Oct. 1803; Hagerstown *Maryland Herald and Hagerstown Weekly Advertiser*, 14 Oct. 1808. An unusually good source revealing the intricacies of local political organization is the Shriver Papers. See, for examples of the planning behind campaign tours by candidates, Abraham Shriver to Andrew Shriver, 29 Sept. 1802, and R. Nelson to Andrew Shriver, 30 Sept. 1802 (MS 750.1); for examples of mobilizing local riders to counteract opposition tactics or to rouse voters to attend the polls, Jacob Shriver to Andrew Shriver, 21 Sept. 1802 (MS 750.1), Abraham Shriver to Andrew Shriver, 26 Sept. 1803 (MS 2085), Abraham Shriver to David Shriver, Sr., 1 Oct. 1806 (MS 750), 23 Aug. 1811 (MS 2085); for examples of political debates at battalion

meetings, Abraham Shriver to Andrew Shriver, 27 Aug. 1803 (MS 2085); and for examples of the planning and operation of barbecues, Abraham Shriver to Andrew Shriver, 9, 26 Sept. 1803 (MS 2085), 1 Sept. 1809 (MS 750.1), memorial, fall 1809 (MS 2085).

33. Bartgis established the first press in Frederick County in 1785 and published papers until his death in 1825. See Clarence S. Brigham, *History and Bibliography of American Newspapers, 1690–1820*, 1:258–63; Joseph T. Wheeler, *The Maryland Press, 1777–90*, pp. 57–64; Fredericktown *Bartgis's Republican Gazette*, 11 Feb. 1801; Fredericktown *Hornet*, 7 April 1802.

34. For Abraham Shriver's literary efforts see his letters to Andrew Shriver, 5 Feb., 4 Aug. 1802 (MS 2085), Shriver Papers; for a discussion of Andrew Shriver's role in informing the German community through the Pennsylvania German press see letters to him from William D. Lepper, 21 Nov. 1801 (MS 2085), 2 Sept., 1, 21 Nov. 1802 (MS 750.1), 18 Jan., 7 Sept. 1803 (MS 2085); and from Daniel P. Lange, 26 Aug. 1811 (MS 2085), 19 Sept. 1818 (MS 750); and Andrew Shriver to Stark and Lange, 22 Sept. 1807 (MS 750), ibid.

35. See Abraham Shriver to Andrew Shriver, 10, 16 Sept. 1802 (MS 2085), ibid.

36. See Abraham Shriver to Andrew Shriver, 8 Oct. 1802 (MS 2085), 15 Nov. 1802 (MS 750.1); John B. Colvin to Andrew Shriver, 17 Dec. 1807 (MS 750), ibid.; and Brigham, *History and Bibliography*, 1:265, 2:1394–95. For a discussion of the paper's circulation, see Fredericktown *Republican Advocate*, 2 March 1804.

37. There are no surviving copies of this paper (Brigham, *History and Bibliography*, 2:856–57, 1444). For the use of this press see letters to Andrew Shriver from Abraham Shiver, 31 Jan. 1801, 21 Sept. 1802; Daniel Clarke, Jr., 22 Aug. 1803; and Roger Nelson, 25 Dec. 1808 (MS 2085), Shriver Papers.

38. Besides the organizational activities illustrated above in the Shriver correspondence, the primary source for convention activities was newspapers. See the reports in the following papers: Baltimore *American*, 11 June, 1 Nov. 1800, 19 March, 22 Aug. 1801, 24 Aug., 13 Sept. 1804, 9 Sept. 1805; Baltimore *Telegraphe and Daily Advertiser*, 30 Sept. 1800; Fredericktown *Independent American Volunteer*, 11 May, 7, 21, 28 Sept. 1808; Fredericktown *Bartgis's Republican Gazette*, 18 Feb., 20 May 1801, 13 Aug. 1802; *Frederick-Town Herald*, 17 Sept. 1803; Fredericktown *Hornet*, 6 March 1804, 9 July 1805, 15, 19, 26 July 1806; Fredericktown *Republican Advocate*, 5, 26 Aug. 1803, 17 Feb., 6 July, 10, 17, 31 Aug. 1804, 5, 19 July, 2, 9, 16 Aug. 1805; Hagerstown *Maryland Herald*, 11 Nov. 1808.

39. Andrew Shriver's antipathy is hinted in letters from Abraham: see, for example, Abraham Shriver to Andrew Shriver, 19 Aug. 1811 (MS 2085), 7 June 1813 (MS 750.1), Shriver Papers. Other correspondence illustrated problems of apathy, regional jealousy, and factionalization within the Republican party. See Abraham Shriver to Andrew Shriver, 10 Aug. (MS 750.1), 10 Sept. 1802 (MS 2085), and Lawrence Brengle to Andrew Shriver, 9 May 1805 (MS 750.1), ibid.; Fredericktown *Republican Advocate*, 20 Sept. 1805.

40. For the family history, see Samuel S. Shriver, comp. and ed., *History of the Shriver Family and Their Connections, 1684–1888*. For the Federalist attack on the Shrivers, see *Frederick-Town Herald*, 5 Feb. 1803, 8 Sept. 1804; and for the Republican counterattack, see the Fredericktown *Republican Advocate*, 11 Feb. 1803, and Abraham Shriver to Andrew Shriver, 27 Aug. 1803 (MS 2085), Shriver Papers.

41. Abraham Shriver wrote Andrew Shriver that the nomination had been "brought into existence under Masonic influence" (6 Sept. 1808); he later reported that "the tide against Masonry runs very high—It is proposed by some (with Lawyer Jacob Getzendanner, as he is called, as the head) to have articles of association drawn up to be signed to form an association opposed to Masonry" (4 Oct. 1808 [MS 2085], ibid.).

42. "The reading room of the Republican Library Company in the house of *George Creager* Sr. is provided with fire, candles, newspapers and public documents, for the use of republican citizens without charge or exception" (Fredericktown *Bartgis's Republican Gazette*, 18 Feb. 1809).

43. For an inside description of the creation of the Republican Library Company, see Abraham Shriver's letters to Andrew Shriver, 14 Jan. (MS 2085), Peter Little, 20 March, and Andrew Shriver, 20 March 1809 (MS 750.1), Shriver Papers.

44. See letters to Abraham Shriver from John Schley, 10 Feb., Peter Little, 15 March, Alexander McKim, 21 March, 1 April, George T[risler], 27, 30 March, 2 April, [Gen. Samuel Smith], 31 March, Abraham Shriver to [Alexander McKim], 25 March 1809 (MS 750.1), ibid. See also Abraham Shriver to Samuel Smith, 25 May 1809, Vertical File, MdHS.

45. Four years later (15 March 1813), Abraham Shriver complained to Andrew Shriver of receiving a Republican delegation from Baltimore City "who style themselves the central committee having for their object a similar organization here for Frederick County. Meetings accordingly were had and the object has been effected" ([MS 750], Shriver Papers).

46. A comprehensive study of poll-book data was undertaken by Bohmer in "Voting Behavior"; see especially chaps. 5, 6, and 7.

47. Ibid., Table VII–6, p. 247.

48. See the following newspaper articles and editorials endorsing the construction of roads: Fredericktown *Republican Advocate*, "A Marylander," 26 Oct., 2, 16, 30 Nov., 14 Dec. 1804; 22 March 1805; Fredericktown *Hornet*, 10 Jan., 6 Nov. 1804; for a discussion of improving the Monocacy River, ibid., 17 Jan., 27 March 1804.

49. For the bill, see *Laws of Maryland*, 1798, chap. 34.

50. For comments on the role played by the Levy Court and road management, see Abraham Shriver to [Andrew Shriver], 24 Nov. 1801 (MS 2085), and John Schley to Andrew Shriver, 27 Nov. 1805 (MS 750.1), Shriver Papers.

51. As examples, see the following correspondence from Andrew Shriver (MS 2085 unless otherwise specified) to [State Delegation], 1 Dec. 1800; David Shriver, Sr., 19, 26, 29 Nov. (MS 750), 24 Dec. 1801 (ibid.), 24 Dec. 1805 (ibid.); 28 Nov. 1808; Daniel Clarke, 28 Nov. 1803. See also letters to Andrew Shriver from Roger Nelson, 23 Jan. 1801; David Shriver, Sr., (?) (Vertical File), (MS 2085.3) 18 Dec. 1801, 26 Nov. 1802; Daniel Heister, 10 April 1802 (MS 750.1); Abraham Shriver, 23 Aug. 1803; Thomas Dickson, 6 Dec. 1808; and Isaac Shriver, 20 Nov. 1811 (MS 750).

52. For an identification of the various commissioners authorized to take subscriptions, see the Fredericktown *Bartgis's Republican Gazette*, 21 Feb. 1798, and the Fredericktown *Republican Advocate*, 15 March 1805.

53. Former Congressman George Baer, Jr., and Federalist leader Col. John McPherson, for instance, were elected as directors of the Baltimore and Fredericktown Turnpike Company, Fredericktown *Republican Advocate*, 24 May 1805; *Frederick-Town Herald*, 18 Oct. 1806.

54. As examples, see David Shriver, Sr., et al., to Governor and Council, 1 Dec. 1800, Roger Nelson et al., to Clerk of the Council, 5 July 1803, 20 April 1804, and Abraham Shriver et al., to Governor and Council, [Jan. 1806], State Papers. See also David Shriver, Sr., to Andrew Shriver, 20 Nov. 1801, and Roger Nelson to A. Shriver, 15 Dec. 1802 (MS 2085), Shriver Papers. The only exceptional patronage situation was caused by the death of the register of wills, George Murdock, in 1805. The Republicans rallied behind the nomination of Richard Butler, Murdock's assistant, and he received the appointment without serious opposition. See Patrick Magill to Governor and Council, 5 May 1805, John L. Copley to Governor, 6 May 1805 (Petition), and Richard Butler to Governor and Council, 7 May 1805, State Papers.

55. Andrew Shriver was highly successful in obtaining and protecting his store in Union Mills as a post office. See his correspondence in the Shriver Papers (MS 2085 unless otherwise specified) to George Baer, Jr., 14 Feb. 1797, Postmaster General [May 1802], Roger Nelson, 3 Dec. 1804, Patrick Magruder, 27 July 1807 (MS 750), Samuel Smith, 18 Dec. 1809 (ibid.); and letters to him from Daniel Heister, 1 May 1802, 5 Feb. 1803, Patrick Magruder, 17 Feb. 1806 (MS 750.1), and John B. Colvin, 9 Feb. 1808; and Abraham Shriver to Roger Nelson, 30 Jan. 1807 (MS 750). Earlier, Richard Potts unsuccessfully solicited the appointment as collector of the Port of Baltimore upon the death of O. H. Williams, but he was later able to obtain a judicial appointment; see R. Potts to the President, 17 July 1794, and Charles Carroll of Carrollton to George Washington, 21 July 1794, reel 122, George Washington Papers, LC.

56. The rivlary within the party leadership cadre and the quest for political office are revealed in an intimate exchange of letters between Abraham Shriver and his brother, Andrew, dated (MS 2085 unless otherwise specified); 8 (MS 750.1), 12 Jan., 5 Feb. 1802, 3 Jan. 1803; from Daniel Clarke and Roger Nelson to Andrew Shriver, 8, 12 Jan. 1802; and from Andrew Shriver to Clarke and Nelson, 11 Jan. 1802, Shriver Papers.

57. For the names and characteristics of the decisional elite, see the Appendix III, Table A3.9.

58. Wealth information was taken from the Frederick County, County Commissioners, Tax Ledgers, 1797, MdHR. An unusually helpful source for determining vital statistics and religious information was Jacob M. Holdcraft, *Names in Stone*. For a further discussion of sources and research techniques, see Appendix I, Methodological Procedures.

59. The best description of Fredericktown in the 1830s may be found in Charles Varle, *Complete View of Baltimore*, pp. 124–25.

60. See the petition of the Inhabitants of Westminster, 1817 (MS 750.1), Shriver Papers; also Williams, *History of Frederick County*, 1:526.

61. Wentz, *Lutheran Church*, pp. 171–98; Dieter Cunz, *The Maryland Germans*, pp. 197–283.

62. Abraham Shriver wrote his father, David Shriver, Sr., 12 July 1822: "who the candidates for the Assembly will be seem to be a mystery as yet. The secret meetings in Westminster seems to have turned out so badly as to have deterred their friends elsewhere from proceeding in a like manner. A little further time will no doubt show how the matter is to be—The prejudice against committees appears to be considerable all over the county" ([MS 2085.3], Shriver Papers).

63. For a complete description of this controversy, see Abraham Shriver to Andrew Shriver, 25 March 1821 (MS 750), ibid.

64. See John S. Shriver to Andrew Shriver, 9, 20 March 1822, and Upton Bruce to J. S. Shriver, 22 March 1822 (MS 750), ibid.

65. Andrew Shriver to James Shriver, 8 Feb. 1823 (MS 2085.3), ibid.

66. See the following reports of Anti-Jackson political activity from which leadership roles were scored: Baltimore *Marylander*, 13, 30 Aug. 1828; Baltimore *Patriot and Mercantile Advertiser*, 5, 9, 12 June 1827, 15 Oct. 1832, 8, 20 May, 7, 11 Aug. 1834, 6 Aug., 14, 23, 24 Dec. 1835; Baltimore *Republican and Commercial Advertiser*, 20 July 1835; Cumberland *Weekly Civilian*, 23 July 1833, 23, 30 June 1835; *Frederick-Town Herald*, 19, 26 April, 10, 17, 24, 31 May 1828, 1, 15, 22, 29, 30 Aug., 5, 19, 29 Sept. 1829, 5, 12, 19 June 1830, 14, 28 May, 4, 11, 18 June, 9, 14 July, 6, 13, 27 Aug., 8 Oct. 1831, 28 April, 26 May, 16, 23, 30 June, 14 July, 8 Sept., 27 Oct. 1832, 6, 20 April, 18 May, 22 June, 3, 13, 17, 24, 31 Aug., 7, 14, 21 Sept. 1833, 17, 21 May, 5 July, 2, 23 Aug., 11 Oct. 1834, 12 May 1835; Fredericktown *Political Examiner and Public Advertiser*, 6, 13, 27 May, 3, 10 June, 9 Dec. 1835; Fredericktown *Maryland Weekly Times*, 11 April, 29 Aug. 1833; *Hagerstown Mail*, 13 May 1831; Hagerstown *Torch Light*, 4 June, 6 Aug. 1835.

67. For a complete list of Frederick County Anti-Jackson party leaders, ranked by their activity scores, see Whitman H. Ridgway, "A Social Analysis of Maryland Community Elites, 1827–1836: A Study of the Distribution of Power in Baltimore City, Frederick County, and Talbot County," Ph.D. dissertation, University of Pennsylvania, 1973, Table 3–19, pp. 197–98.

68. Worman, whose precise occupation cannot be determined, owned 420 acres, 5 slaves, valued at $6,500. The wealth figures were found in the Frederick County, County Commissioners, Tax Ledgers, 1835, MdHR.

69. For William Ogden Niles, see the Baltimore *Republican*, 12 Oct. 1830; for Samuel Barnes, see the Baltimore *Patriot*, 1 Jan. 1830, *Frederick-Town Herald*, 3 Jan. 1835, and Scharf, *History of Western Maryland*, 1:530–31. Scharf said that Barnes sold the paper in 1832, when it was sold in 1829 and he moved to Baltimore.

70. For a discussion of representative leaders, see Ridgway, "A Social Analysis," pp. 202–3.

71. Jackson party leadership roles were determined and scored from the following

sources: Baltimore *American*, 22 May 1827; Baltimore *Patriot*, 26 April, 4, 11 May 1827, 20 Aug. 1829; Baltimore *Republican*, 29 June 1829, 4, 25 May, 21 June 1830, 23, 25 May, 30 Aug. 1831, 22 March, 22, 25 May 1832, 29 May, 7, 19 Aug. 1833, 11 April, 25 Aug. 1834, 27 April, 21 May, 19 June, 8 July, 14 Sept. 1835, 22 March 1836; *Frederick-Town Herald*, 19 April, 10, 17, 24 May, 7 June 1828, 3 Oct. 1829, 25 June, 2 July 1831; Fredericktown *Maryland Weekly Times*, 28 June 1832, 22 Aug. 1833; *Hagerstown Mail*, 25 June 1830, 27 May, 1 July 1831, 19 July 1833, 26 Aug. 1836. There are few surviving copies of the major Jackson paper, the Fredericktown *Independent Citizen*, but fortunately coverage in district and state papers provides a wide sample of activities.

72. For a complete list and discussion of individual Jacksonian leaders, see Ridgway, "A Social Analysis," Table 3–16, pp. 186, 187–95; see also Alexander Levin, "Two Jackson Supporters," pp. 221–29.

73. For a short biographical sketch of Francis Thomas, see Scharf, *History of Western Maryland*, 1:403–4.

74. John Nelson's local prominence was reflected in letters regarding a federal appointment in 1829; see, for instance, John Nelson to Gen. Samuel Smith, 20, 28 March 1829, Samuel Smith Papers, LC; Virgil Maxcy to John C. Calhoun, 9 April (pp. 795–98), 7 May 1829 (pp. 800–807), J. Franklin Jameson, ed., *Correspondence of John C. Calhoun*; John C. Calhoun to V. Maxcy, 21 June 1829, Maxcy-Markoe Letterbook, Galloway-Maxcy-Markoe Papers, LC; and Nicholas G. Ridgely to Duff Green, 17 June 1829, 27/123–25, Letters of Application and Recommendation during the Administration of Andrew Jackson, NA. See also Howard R. Marrano, "John Nelson's Mission to the Kingdom of the Two Sicilies, 1831–1832," pp. 149–76.

75. See Abraham Shriver to David Shriver, Sr., 12 June 1829 (MS 2085.3), and John S. Shriver to William Shriver, 17, 27 Sept. 1829 (MS 2085), Shriver Papers.

76. For a comparison between urban versus rural origins of the leaders of both parties, see Ridgway, "A Social Analysis," Table 3–21, p. 204.

77. The Fredericktown *Independent Citizen* was edited by George W. Sharpe between 1828 and 1833; he moved to Ohio in 1834. Dr. Samuel L. McKeehan took over from 1832 until his suicide in 1835; hereafter the paper was edited by Peter H. Brown. All of these men were party organizers during their tenure as editor.

78. See John S. Shriver to Andrew Shriver, 1 March (MS 750), 10 March 1830 (MS 750.1), and Abraham Shriver to Andrew Shriver, 19, 22 June 1830 (ibid.), Shriver Papers.

79. Regarding the formation of this paper, edited by James Maxwell, see Francis Thomas to [?], 27 Sept. 1838, Francis Thomas Papers, DU; Scharf, *History of Western Maryland*, 1:534; Fredericktown *Maryland Weekly Times*, 13 June 1833. Concerning the rivalry between Francis Thomas and John Nelson, Dr. Tyler, and their congressional favorite, James Dixon, see William Tyler to Edward Lloyd V, 19 Sept. 1833, Edward Lloyd Papers, MdHS; *Hagerstown Mail*, 28 Sept., 11 Oct. 1833.

80. See Francis Thomas to Dr. Charles Magill, 7, 12 May, 18 June 1837, Charles Magill Papers, DU.

81. Walter S. Sanderlin, *The Great National Project*, p. 104.

82. Merrick's reputation was indicated by William R. Steuart's comment on the passage of the 1836 bill, "Col. Merrick has renowned himself extremely popular. The citizens intend to give him some token of their regard" (Steuart to James Thomas, 6 June 1836, Gift Collection, James Thomas Papers, MdHR); see letters in the *Hagerstown Mail*, 20 March 1835. Merrick represented the canal company in land purchases in Washington County, as well as acting as a lobbyist; see Merrick to Washington, 25 June 1835, Merrick to Board of Directors, 11 Oct. 1835, Letters Received; John P. Ingle to Merrick, 16 Jan. 1836, Letterbook C, pp. 197–200; Journals and Proceedings of the Directors, ser. E, 29 June 1836, p. 83, Records of the Chesapeake and Ohio Canal Company, NA. For George C. Washington, see his letters to J. P. Ingle, 14, 23 Feb., 1, 11, 13, 19 March 1835, Letters Received; Journals and Proceedings of the Board of Directors, ser. D, pp. 261, 265; Washington to Ingle, 26, 29 May 1836, Letters Received, ibid.

83. For the reports of the internal improvements meetings, see Baltimore *American*,

16, 22, 26 April, 3 May 1836; *Frederick-Town Herald*, 19 Nov. 1831, 29 Nov. 1834; Fredericktown *Reservoir and Public Reflector* (Extra), 26 Aug. 1828; J. Thomas Scharf, *Chronicles of Baltimore*, p. 419.

84. For a list of the internal improvements activists, see Ridgway, "A Social Analysis," pp. 500–501.

85. Outerbridge Horsey, Martin Eichelberger, William M. Beall, Cyrus Mantz, several Shrivers, several Schleys, Richard Potts, Jr., Col. John Thomas, Congressman Francis Thomas, Drs. William and William Bradley Tyler, Washington Van Bibber, and Thomas Contee Worthington.

86. George Baer, George Baltzell, John Baltzell, William M. Beall, Thomas Carlton, George M. Eichelberger, Caspar Mantz, Cyrus Mantz, John McPherson, Jr., Dr. William S. McPherson, Richard Potts, Jr., William Ross, Frederick A. Schley, Henry Schley, John P. Thompson, Dr. William Tyler, and Moses Worman.

87. Former Congressman George Baer and Congressman F. Thomas; state Senator John Nelson; council member T. C. Worthington; members of the House of Delegates Roderick Dorsey, John Kinzer, Dr. William S. McPherson, Joseph M. Palmer, William Schley, and Isaac Shriver.

88. An extreme example of anti-Baltimore sentiment was provided at a Libertytown meeting in 1829; see *Niles Weekly Register* 29 (1 Oct. 1829): 69, Baltimore *Republican*, 2 May 1833, 10, 14, 16 Nov. 1835.

89. For a complete list of reform leaders, see Ridgway, "A Social Analysis," pp. 492–99. For reform sources, see Baltimore *Commercial Chronicle and Daily Marylander*, 22 Dec. 1832, 18 April, 29 May, 3 June, 31 Aug. 1833; Baltimore *Patriot*, 16 Nov., 26 Dec. 1835, 15 Oct. 1836; Baltimore *Republican*, 13 March, 29 Nov., 22 Dec. 1832, 9 Jan., 2 May, 3 June, 31 Aug. 1833, 10, 14, 17, 23 Nov. 1835, 3 Feb., 13, 20 June, 6, 15 Oct., 21 Nov. 1836; Baltimore *Voice of the People*, 19, 26 May, 2 June 1836; *Frederick-Town Herald*, 10, 24 March 1832, 12 Jan., 1 June 1833; Fredericktown *Political Examiner and Public Advertiser*, 20, 23 Dec. 1835; Fredericktown *Maryland Weekly Times*, 4 April, 6 June, 18 July, 8 Aug., 5 Sept., 22 Dec. 1833; *Hagerstown Mail*, 13, 20 Nov. 1835, 24 June, 16 Sept., 7, 14, 21, 28 Oct. 1836.

90. See especially in this regard, Baltimore *Chronicle*, "Reform in Maryland," 23 Nov. 1832; Fredericktown *Political Examiner*, 23 Dec. 1835; *Frederick-Town Herald*, 12 Jan., 1 June, 22 Dec. 1833; Baltimore *Patriot*, 26 Dec. 1835.

91. For Thomas's public role, see *Niles Weekly Register* 51 (24 Sept. 1836): 51, 51 (22 Oct. 1836): 120, 51 (29 Oct. 1836): 135, 51 (3 Dec. 1836): 215; *Hagerstown Mail*, 16 Sept., 7, 14, 21, 28 Oct. 1836. For his own description of his activities, see Francis Thomas to Dr. J. C. Hays, 2 March 1838, Francis Thomas Papers, DU; F. Thomas to [Charles Magill], 7 Oct. 1836, Charles Magill Papers, DU; and David Campbell to Captain William B. Campbell, 2 Oct. 1836, David Campbell Papers, DU.

92. The contest between Thomas and Tyler was graphically described in letters from John W. Pratt to Abraham F. Shriver: "The war between Thomas, Tyler, and Dixon and their friends goes on heavily. Thomas is rallying the Jackson Party" (3 Oct. 1833); and "Thomas and Dixon and their friends are much incensed against each other. . . . Most of the Clay men here are for Thomas and the Jackson men almost to a man" (26 Sept. 1833 [MS 2085.3], Shriver Papers).

93. See the *Frederick-Town Herald*, 10 March 1832; Baltimore *Republican*, 22 Dec. 1832; Baltimore *Chronicle*, 29 May 1833; Fredericktown *Maryland Weekly Times*, 6 June, 8 Aug. 1833.

94. Since only a few issues of the *Independent Citizen* have survived, historians must evaluate it in terms of the responses it generated. See the following in the Anti-Jackson Baltimore *Chronicle*: "Reform," 26 March, 23 April, "Reform in Maryland," 23 Nov. 1832, "Reform," 3 June 1833.

95. *Hagerstown Mail*, 28 Oct. 1836; *Niles Weekly Register* 51 (29 Oct. 1836): 135.

96. Richard Potts, Jr., William O. Niles, Col. John H. McElfresh, former Congressmen Henry R. Warfield, and John Lee.

97. Roderick Dorsey, John Rigney, Henry Nixdorff, Capt. George W. Ent, Peter H. Brown, Madison Nelson, William M. Beall, and Joseph Taney.

98. Washington Van Bibber to Governor Veazey, 7 Nov. 1836, State Papers. See also Gen. Thomas C. Worthington to Gov. Veazey, 24 Sept., 11 Nov. 1836, ibid.; Gen. Worthington to Adjutant General, 5 Dec. 1836, AG Papers.

99. Before visiting the editor of the Fredericktown *Maryland Weekly Times*, John W. Pratt discussed the goals of the proposed new paper: "It will be a County paper—supporting the County interest—resisting Fredericktown control and dictation and exposing when it is necessary the machinizations of its Juntos and laying bare the motives of its master spirits" (Pratt to F. A. Shriver, 24 June 1833 [MS 2085.3], Shriver Papers); regarding the establishment of the *Carrolltonian*, see "Prospectus," Fredericktown *Maryland Weekly Times*, 4 July 1833; unfortunately, only a few issues of this paper have survived.

100. William Cost Johnson described the campaign to F. A. Shriver, 21 Sept. 1832: "The Jackson candidates have been through here giving my opponents their cue. They say that the New County is 'a mere get up' by a few men, etc.—That it will be a Tax to this part of the County and Frederick County will lose her weight, etc.—A Jackson delegate of last session—Brookhart who tried with Ely to defeat the bill last winter has been riding all through the border of this county electioneering against me" ([MS 2085.3], Shriver Papers).

101. *To The Honourable the General Assembly of Maryland The Petition of the Subscribers, Inhabitants of the Upper Part of Baltimore County and the Lower Part of Frederick County, Humbly Submit . . .*; David Shriver, Jr., to David Shriver, Sr., 2 Dec. 1806, Abraham Shriver to D. Shriver, Sr., 5 Dec. 1814 (MS 2085.3), Shriver Papers; Scharf, *History of Western Maryland*, 2:794–96.

102. See Isaac Shriver to [?], 27 Dec. 1832, [Carroll County Meeting], 17 Sept. 1833, John W. Pratt to A. F. Shriver, 3, 10 Oct. 1833, A. F. Shriver to Andrew Shriver, 14 Jan. 1837 (MS 2085.3), Shriver Papers; Baltimore *Republican*, 3 July 1833.

103. Rockville *Maryland Journal and True American*, 14 May 1834; Williams, *History of Frederick County*, 1:215–16.

104. See, for instance, letters to the Governor and Council from Frederick County Delegates, 1828, 7 Feb. 1831, 28 Feb. 1835, 29 March 1836; and Thomas Sappington to Gov. Thomas, 17 May 1835, Sappington to Thomas Culbreth, 17 May 1835, Dr. [William] Willis to Governor, 9 Oct. 1836, State Papers.

105. See correspondence to the Governor and Council from John Baugher et al., 14 May 1836, Lewis Motter, 6, 9 March 1835, 20 May 1836, ibid.

106. See Martin Eichelberger to Robert Annan, 17 May 1835, Isaac Baugher et al., to Annan, 7 Feb. 1835, ibid.; and letters to Jacob Shriver from William P. Farquhar, 29 Jan. 1829, Joshua Motter, 11 Feb. 1829, and John Wampler, 13 Feb. 1829 (MS 2085.3), Shriver Papers.

107. See Thomas C. Worthington's comment appended to letter from Darius Richardson et al. to Governor and Council, 7 Feb. 1831, and Worthington to Gov. Thomas, 1 June, 2 Aug. 1834, State Papers.

108. The Baltimore *Republican*, 17 June 1833, described the political composition of state appointees in Frederick County as being overwhelmingly Anti-Jacksonian.

109. See letters to the secretary of state from Samuel Barnes and George Woodbridge, 5 Feb. 1829, William Tyler, 11 May 1829, John Nelson, 1 June 1829, George Sharpe, 28 Dec. 1829, Roger B. Taney, 22 Jan. 1832, Samuel McKeehan, 17 Nov. 1832, Francis Thomas, 19 Nov. 1832, and Peter H. Brown, 22 Oct. 1835, Miscellaneous Letters Received Regarding Publishers of the Laws, NA.

110. William Tyler et al. to Secretary of State, 1 March 1829, reel 5, Jackson Recommendations; Tyler to Andrew J. Donelson, 16 March 1829, Andrew Jackson Donelson Papers, LC.

111. For examples of the patterns followed under Adams, see letters to the secretary of state from Henry R. Warfield, 19 March 1826, 11 Feb. 1827, reel 8, Thomas C. Worthington, 16 Oct. 1825, reel 8, Letters of Application and Recommendation during the Administration of John Q. Adams, NA.

112. See J. P. Alricks and R. Frisby to Isaac McKim, 7 Feb. 1835, 13/572–75, Jackson Recommendations. For Nicholas Snyder's appointment, see U.S. Senate, *Journal of Executive Proceedings, 1829–1869*, 4:467, 471.

113. For a list of the decisional elite, see Appendix III, Table A3.13.

114. Peter H. Brown, Dr. Samuel L. McKeehan, William Ogden Niles, Neilson Poe, George W. Sharpe, and George Woodbridge.

Chapter 4

1. For the role of merchants, see Frank A. Cassell, *Merchant Congressman in the Young Republic*, and Gary L. Browne, "Baltimore in the Nation, 1789–1861: A Social Economy in Industrial Revolution," Ph.D. dissertation, Wayne State University, 1973, pp. 1–38. For the role of the Germans, see Clarence P. Gould, "The Economic Causes of the Rise of Baltimore," pp. 225–51. For a suggestive interpretation of the dynamic role of the Scotch-Irish Presbyterians in the city's growth, see LeRoy J. Votto, "Social Dynamism in Boom-Town: The Scots-Irish in Baltimore, 1760–1790," Master's thesis, University of Virginia, 1969.

2. William B. Wheeler, "Urban Politics in Nature's Republic: The Development of Political Parties in the Seaport Cities in the Federalist Era," Ph.D. dissertation, University of Virginia, 1967, p. 148.

3. Wheeler elaborated further: "The city was dominated by less than two hundred men, mostly merchants, who were congressmen, state legislators, town commissioners, city councilmen, and the vestrymen and elders of the city's churches" (ibid., p. 147). Unfortunately, he never identifies these men, nor does he specify when, where, or under what conditions they were sucessful community leaders. He presumes that those who held positions of power were in fact powerful.

4. For examples of self-nomination, see the Baltimore *Maryland Journal and Baltimore Advertiser*, 12 Aug. 1791; Baltimore *Eagle of Freedom; or, the Baltimore Town and Fell's Point Gazette*, 26 Oct. 1796; and Baltimore *American and Commercial Advertiser*, 28 Sept. 1801, 14 Sept. 1804. For nominations by others, see the Baltimore *Telegraphe and Daily Advertiser*, "A Voter," 3 Feb., "A Friend of Mankind," 5 Aug., and "A Republican," 8 Aug. 1800; Baltimore *Federal Gazette and Baltimore Daily Advertiser*, "A Voter," 25 Sept. 1797, 30 Sept. 1799, and 27 Sept. 1805; and Baltimore *American*, "An Independent Voter," 13 Sept. 1804. As an example of policy statements, see James Winchester to the Voters of the City and County of Baltimore, Baltimore *Federal Gazette*, 17 Aug., 5 Sept. 1798.

5. Baltimore *Maryland Journal*, 12 Sept. 1794; *Baltimore Daily Intelligencer*, 6 Oct. 1794.

6. Baltimore *Federal Gazette*, 22, 25 Sept. 1798.

7. Ibid., "Publius," 19 Aug., 4 Oct. 1803.

8. Fredericktown *Republican Advocate*, 26 Aug. 1803.

9. A letter from "Fair Play" succinctly stated the Republican goals: "The only thing that can be done now to ascertain public opinion; harmonize the jarring interests; to prevent a minority from ruling the majority, is, a strict attendance on the ward meetings. If this be done, and anything like a fair expression of the public sentiments should be made, I make no doubt but all friends to the principles of republican government; all real democratic republicans, will unite as usual" (Baltimore *American*, 24 Sept. 1804); see also the editorial for 19 Sept. 1804. For the convention planning and results, see ibid., 6, 14, 29 Sept. 1804. For the problem of voter apathy, see ibid., 27 Sept., 10 Oct. 1799, 15 Sept. 1804.

10. On 18 July 1808, the editor of the Baltimore *American* admonished Republicans, "Surely these are times which call for harmony, activity and concert among the friends of liberty, a free government, and national honor and independence"; on 14 April 1809 the Baltimore *Whig* warned, "There are more juntas in Maryland than in Spain, with the same end in view, the establishment of Civil and religious tyranny. If the republicans are not active, the consequences may be fatal." See also Baltimore *American*, 11, 27 Feb. 1808.

11. The Republican newspaper enjoyed exposing Federalist cabals whenever it could,

especially when they included R. G. Harper or Samuel Chase. It reported that a caucus met at Harper's house, where "Justice Chase was the usual head man; Mr. [James] Carroll was also present" (Baltimore *American*, 22 Aug. 1800). See also Col. John O'Donnell to Governor, 8 Aug. 1798, Adjutant Generals Papers, MdHR (hereafter cited as AG Papers).

12. "A Republican Federalist" to the Voters of Baltimore County, Baltimore *Federal Gazette*, 31 Aug. 1803. Another writer observed on caucuses: "Their despotic nature is palpable and abhorrent to every good man" ("Of the Ward Meetings," ibid., 26 Sept. 1804.

13. Ibid., 15 Sept. 1804.

14. See, for example, the following reports in the Baltimore *Federal Gazette*: "Monitor," 13 Aug. 1803; 20 Sept. 1804; "Come to the Polls," 7 Oct, 1805.

15. For an example, see Robert G. Harper to his Constituents, 24 Feb. 1801, Bayard Papers, MdHS.

16. Correspondents used such pseudonyms as Agricola, Amicus, Aristides, as well as some more easily understood, such as Anti-Gallican and Truth.

17. For a short history of this paper, see Clarence S. Brigham, *History and Bibliography of American Newspapers, 1690–1820*, 1:232–34; 2:1508. See also Amanda R. Minick, *A History of Printing in Maryland, 1791–1800*, pp. 43–45.

18. Consider the following letter from Secretary of War James McHenry to Federalist Robert Oliver, 2 Oct. 1799: "Will you be able to buy the Telegraph? If not, may he rely upon a loan to enable him to set out independently and as the sole proprietor of the establishment? Ascertain facts; do not mention my name; but you may consider me as willing to be a lender. If you can induce him to settle, he will be a real acquisition" (James McHenry Papers, LC).

19. The Baltimore *Republican; or, Anti-Democrat* was founded by R. G. Harper and others with a capital of $8,000 in 1802. See David H. Fischer, *The Revolution of American Conservatism*, p. 138. For contemporary comments, see Easton *Republican Star*, 21 Sept. 1802; Baltimore *Federal Gazette*, 1 June 1803; *Frederick-Town Herald*, 11 June 1803; and a letter from Finley, Taylor, & Finley to Andrew Shriver, 20 Aug. 1803 (MS 2085), Shriver Papers, MdHS.

20. For the career of William Pechin, see Brigham, *History and Bibliography*, 1:229, 237–38; 2:1465. See also the prospectuses for the *Eagle of Freedom*, Baltimore *Federal Gazette*, 7 April 1796; and for the *Intelligencer*, Baltimore *Telegraphe*, 4 Sept. 1797.

21. In a political statement, the editor of the new *American* promised: "Honest republicanism, and the support of the Federal Constitution are the only politics that shall be advanced by this paper" (16 May 1799).

22. Brigham, *History and Bibliography*, 1:228. All extant copies of this paper are at the Houghton Library, Harvard University, Cambridge, Mass.

23. Contrast the enthusiasm for the militia in 1798: "The Youth of Our City are forming themselves into Companies for the Defense of their Country—The Spirit of real American Patriotism predominates here and daily gains strength" (T. & S. Hollingsworth to L. Hollingsworth & Sons, 20 May 1798, Hollingsworth Papers, HSPa) with Col. William Lowry's report in 1805: "It is extremely difficult to persuade respectable characters who are generally here men in business to accept situations the duties of which may interfere with their respective employments" (Lowry to N. Pinckney, 5 April 1805, AG Papers). For accounts of the fallen state of the militia, see Baltimore *American*, 6 July 1801; Baltimore *Telegraphe*, 3 May 1802; Baltimore *Democratic-Republican; or, Anti-Aristocrat*, 6 May 1802; and Baltimore *Federal Gazette*, 6 July 1802. Yet, a new foreign threat revitalized the militia: "Since British *insolence* and *outrage*, have become the topic of the day, our men are raving and desirous of being in a state of organization as soon as possible" (Col. Thomas Hillen to Governor, 23 July 1807, AG Papers); "There never was perhaps so great a military spirit displayed in any city as there is in Baltimore at this time" (Col. James Mosher to Governor, 4 Aug. 1807, ibid.).

24. George W. McCreary, *The Ancient and Honorable Mechanical Company of Baltimore*, p. xi.

25. The Maryland Tammany Society is not mentioned in the general history of that organization; see Jerome Mushkat, *Tammany*. One reason might be that, although the society met frequently during 1808–9, very little beyond public notices was written about it in the press. See Baltimore *American*, 21 Jan., 4 Feb., 6 April, 4, 10 May 1808; Baltimore *Whig*, 1, 16, 25, 28 March, 8 April 1809. It was active, however, and its impact may be discerned from a dispute with Frederick County Republicans, who opposed its encroachments. See the following letters (MS 750.1 unless otherwise indicated); Peter Little to Abraham Shriver, 15 March 1809; Shriver to Little, 20 March 1809; Shriver to Andrew Shriver, 20 March 1809; Alexander McKim to Shriver, 21 March 1809; Shriver to McKim, 25 March 1809; George Trisler to Shriver, 27, 30 March 1809; [Samuel Smith] to Shriver, 31 March 1809; [A. McKim] to Shriver, 1 April 1809; and Shriver to Andrew Shriver, 14 Jan. 1809 (MS 2085), Shriver Papers.

26. For Harper's early association with the Washington Benevolent Society, see A. C. Hanson to R. G. Harper, 3 March 1810; [Harper] to [Hanson], 5 March 1810, Robert G. Harper Papers, LC; Catherine Harper to Harper, 5 March 1810; Hanson to Harper, 10, 26 June 1810, Harper-Pennington Papers, MdHS. For an extended treatment of the society, see Fischer, *Revolution of American Conservatism*, pp. 110–28. The Saint George Society was an earlier association of Federalists whose impact is not precisely known. See Baltimore *Federal Gazette*, 24 April 1799; Baltimore *American*, 28 April 1800.

27. See Cassell, *Merchant Congressman*, pp. 1–45, for Smith's precongressional career; also Cassell, "The Structure of Baltimore's Politics in the Age of Jefferson, 1795–1812," pp. 277–96.

28. Smith's community support was described in a postelection letter from George Salmon to James McHenry, 7 Oct. 1798: "Smith's interest among the Mechanic's and militia would surmount all opposition—notwithstanding many of the merchants and people of fortune made every exertion . . . it was astounding the number that would not interest themselves, many of whom receive their living from Government, indeed some of them took a decided part on the other side" (McHenry Papers, LC). See also Jesse Hollingsworth to Levi Hollingsworth & Sons, 22 Aug., 5 Oct. 1798, Hollingsworth Papers. During the campaign, several militia captains dismissed their men in front of Smith's house, which caused a furor among Federalists (Baltimore *Federal Gazette*, 7, 21 Aug. 1798).

29. For a summary of this controversy, see Baltimore *Federal Gazette*, "Observer," 10 Sept. 1798.

30. For a description of the dinner and an insight into its significance, see George Salmon to James McHenry, 31 July 1798, McHenry Papers, LC. The toasts included: "The friends and supporters of the present administration—may their numbers increase, and may their opponents decrease, and be branded, as they deserve, with the contempt of their country" and "Gallatin, Jefferson, Monroe, Tazwell, Mason, Burr, etc. May they obtain the reward of their Jacobean principles, their attachment to the French, and their uniform opposition of all the principal measures of their own government—the universal contempt and destestation of their fellow citizens" (Baltimore *Telegraphe*, 31 July 1798).

31. Howard was trying to prove that Smith had insulted President Adams when he suggested that America should pay the French tribute and avoid war. See the letters to Howard, dated late 1798, from leading Federalists, Bayard Papers, and the Baltimore *Federal Gazette*, 3, 16, 24 Aug. 1798. For Smith's efforts to resist these charges, see his letters to President Adams, 2 Aug. 1798, and to the Voters of the City and County of Baltimore, [7 Sept. 1798], Samuel Smith Papers, LC.

32. The Federalist position was stated succinctly in a toast given at Howard's dinner: "May military commissions only be granted to uniform and tried friends of the federal government" (Baltimore *Telegraphe*, 31 July 1798). In addition, Luther Martin attacked Smith's militia association over his pseudonym, "Anti-Gallican," in the Baltimore *Federal Gazette*, 4, 18 Sept. 1798; see also "A Republican," ibid., 21 Aug. 1798. Some militia officers pledged their support to President Adams during the election polling (Baltimore *Telegraphe*, 2 Oct. 1798), which echoed the sentiments of an earlier subscription for a naval ship (Baltimore *Federal Gazette*, 16 June 1798) and a previous meeting, chaired by Gen.

John Swann, favoring Adams's foreign policy (ibid., 18 April 1798). For a breakdown of the political leanings of specific Baltimore militia companies, see Baltimore *American*, 3 May 1800.

33. For the resolve of the officers of the 27th Militia Regiment to wear uniforms and the American cockade as signs of their patriotism, see Baltimore *Federal Gazette*, 21 June 1798. "Nestor" made the most extreme statement: "The *American* cockade should be esteemed *honorable*, and the *mark* of friendship to this country; the *national*, or *French cockade* should be considered *dishonorable*, and the signal of an enemy; and no one should be permitted to wear it in our streets, unless *French officers*" (ibid., 3 July 1798).

34. A Federalist described Smith's activities: "We have warm work here, Smith being our General Harranging the militia at their Battalion meetings, whilst his riders and attendants lavishly deal out the *Swash*, which at the county meetings has a surprising influence— yet the late discovery of his saving his vessels under French protections, whilst he was in Congress, with some other infamous conduct has lately Turned a current against him which will probably defeat his sanguine hopes" (Thomas Hollingsworth to Levi Hollingsworth, 11 Sept. 1798, Hollingsworth Papers). See also Jesse Hollingsworth to Levi Hollingsworth and Sons, 5 Oct. 1798, and T. & S. Hollingsworth to Levi Hollingsworth and Sons, 9 Oct. 1798, ibid. For Smith's public statements, see Smith to the Voters of the County and City of Balti nore, Baltimore *Telegraphe*, 10 Aug. 1798.

35. See the far from unanimous Federalist evaluation of Winchester as a candidate: James Ash to James McHenry, 24 Aug. 1798, David Stewart to McHenry, 15 Sept. 1798, McHenry Papers, LC; Philip Thomas to John E. Howard, 12 Sept. 1798, Bayard Papers.

36. For Winchester's appointment, see Baltimore *Federal Gazette*, 4 Nov. 1799.

37. Ibid., 8 Oct., 6 Nov. 1798.

38. Under the by-line Sansculottesville, the Philadelphia *Porcupine's Gazette* described the Baltimore election, 8 Oct. 1798: "This night will end our four days election, when Smith, to the infamy of our district, will be chosen by a large majority: a melancholy record of jacobin triumph over the friends of government and its administration. His being a Major General of the Militia, and the lavish distribution, which has been made of money, in every quarter, for the use of the vulgar, has had an influence not to be controlled by reason or justice. . . . In short, the election has been attended with bloodshed and mobs. The peaceable voters have been driven from the hustings. The country parties, against *Smith*, were, as they came in, met by mobs, stoned, brick-batted, and knocked off their horses. In a word, it has been a perfect Paris election, and *Smith* may be looked upon as the Marat of our city." See also ibid., 11, 31 Oct., 5 Nov. 1798. George Salmon wrote James McHenry, 7 Oct. 1798: "Smith's election must have cost him $6,000 at least, no trifle to a man so anxious to make money, he had a dreadful mob that made every thinking person apprehend mischief, his great majority kept them in order" (McHenry Papers, LC).

39. Robert Smith coveted a judicial appointment but refused one when it was offered; see Robert Smith to George Washington, 5 Sept. 1798, reel 123, George Washington Papers, LC; Washington to James McHenry, 31 Aug. 1792, John C. Fitzpatrick, ed., *The Writings of George Washington from the Original Manuscript Sources*, 32: 138. For John H. Purviance, see Samuel Smith to Washington, 8 Aug. 1793, reel 122, Washington Papers; Washington to J. E. Howard, 25 Aug. 1793, Fitzpatrick, ed., *Washington Writings*, 33:66– 67, and Washington to McHenry, 28 Aug. 1793, ibid., 33:72–73. During Jefferson's presidency, Smith still boosted the career of this member of a prominent Federalist family. See John H. Purviance to Samuel Smith, 23 April 1802, reel 9/frame 665, and Smith to [President], 29 April 1802, 9/654, Letters of Application and Recommendation during the Administration of Thomas Jefferson, NA.

40. As examples see letters to Washington from Robert Ballard, 1 Jan. 1789, James Calhoun, 22 June 1789, Samuel Smith, 24 June 1789, and J. E. Howard, 23 July 1789, reel 119, Washington Papers.

41. Washington to J. E. Howard, 19 Nov. 1795, Fitzpatrick, ed., *Washington Writings*, 34:365–66, 30 Nov. 1795, ibid., 34:380.

42. As an early example, see recommendations to Washington favoring Dr. John

Coulter as health officer from Robert Ballard, 28 Dec. 1790, and James McHenry, 6 Jan. 1791, reel 120, Washington Papers. See also Washington to McHenry, 4 Aug. 1798, Fitzpatrick, ed., *Washington Writings*, 36:385.

43. James McHenry favored a judicial appointment for Chase and explained his reasons to Washington: "Among the inducements I feel for presenting his name on this occasion, is his general conduct since the adoption of our government, and the sense I entertain of the part he bore in the revolutionary efforts of a long and trying crisis" (13 June 1795, McHenry Papers, LC). See also Washington to McHenry, 20 Jan. 1796, Fitzpatrick, ed., *Washington Writings*, 34:423–24.

44. James McHenry advised Washington to appoint Martin Eichelberger surveyor because "he is a Dutchman and not without influence among his countrymen . . . [and] I am persuaded it would have a good effect upon his countrymen most of which in this place are highly antifederal" (2 July 1789, reel 120, Washington Papers).

45. Joseph H. Nicholson and Gabriel Christie, who were offered the collectorship; Thomas Rutter, who was appointed U.S. marshal; John Stephen, who was named U.S. district attorney; and Robert Smith, who was appointed Jefferson's secretary of the navy.

46. See letters from Gen. O. H. Williams to the President, 4, 14 July 1789, reel 124; and from McHenry to Washington, 17 April, 24 May 1789, reel 122, 2 July 1789, 6 Jan. 1791, reel 120, Washington Papers. See also Washington to McHenry, 12 Aug. 1792, Fitzpatrick, ed., *Washington Writings*, 32:110–11.

47. See Howard to Washington, 23 July 1789, reel 119, 15 March 1791, reel 123, 10 Aug. 1793, reel 120, Washington Papers; and Washington to Howard, 25 Aug. 1793, Fitzpatrick, ed., *Washington Writings*, 33:66–70; Washington to Charles Carroll of Carrollton, 25 Aug. 1793, ibid., 33:60–61, and Carroll to Washington, 21 July 1794, reel 122, Washington Papers.

48. When the position of surveyor became vacant in 1793, Smith recommended four different individuals for the job. See Smith to Washington, 8 Aug. 1793 (three letters), 9 Aug. 1793, reel 120, Washington Papers.

49. For Williams's appointment, see O. H. Williams to President, 18 April, Williams to Col. Humphreys, 12 May 1789, reel 124, and McHenry to Washington, 24 May 1789, reel 122, ibid.

50. See Richard Potts to President, 17 July 1794, reel 122, Samuel Chase to Washington, 19 July 1794, reel 119, Robert Purviance to Washington, 19 Aug. 1794, reel 122, ibid.; and Washington to Potts, 20 July 1794, Fitzpatrick, ed., *Washington Writings*, 33:436.

51. See Robert Purviance to McHenry, 13 April 1789, and letters to Washington from McHenry, 17 April 1789, 20 July 1794, Purviance, 19 May 1789, J. E. Howard, 25 May 1789, Samuel Smith, 18 July 1794, reel 122, Washington Papers.

52. McHenry to President, 20 April 1791, reel 122, ibid.

53. See John Brice, Jr., to Gen. Smith, 10 Oct. 1806, 1/1062–64, Gabriel Christie to [President], 10 Oct. 1806, 2/186, John Glendy to Jefferson, 10 Oct. 1806, 9/267–68, Daniel Delozier to Secretary of the Treasury, 11 Oct. 1806, 3/190, and Bushrod Washington to Jefferson, 20 Oct. 1806, 9/274, Jefferson Recommendations. See also Robert Smith to Secretary of the Treasury, 14 Oct. 1806, 10/669–70, ibid., where he attacked Delozier and Brice as being Federalists.

54. Samuel Smith to Jefferson, 29 Dec. 1806, 8/35–36, and Smith to [Secretary of the Treasury], 11 Oct. 1806, 1/1066, ibid.

55. Joseph H. Nicholson to President, [Jan. 1807], Joseph H. Nicholson Papers, LC. As an example of the esteem Baltimore Republicans had for Nicholson, see the report of the public meeting after Jefferson's election, Baltimore *American*, 13 March 1801.

56. Gabriel Christie to [Jefferson], 11 Oct. 1806, 2/183–84, 25 Oct. 1806, 2/182, Jefferson Recommendations.

57. McCulloch reported Christie's death to Smith with a politician's sensitivity: "Mr. Christie died yesterday morning and left every place he held on earth to others. His collectorship has become an object of general attention" (2 April 1808, Smith Papers). See also Smith to [Secretary of the Treasury], 4 April 1808, 8/42, Jefferson Recommendations;

and Smith's later reflections on the appointment, Smith to Andrew Jackson, 11 March 1834, Smith Papers.

58. As an example, see Tobias E. Stansbury et al. to [Governor], [ca. Dec. 1807], State Papers, MdHR.

59. See George Salmon to Governor, 3 Jan. 1794, and James Calhoun to Governor and Council, 12 Dec. 1801, ibid.

60. As examples of legislators making recommendations, see David McMechen to J. Wilmer, 7 March 1800, and Cumberland Dugan to Edward Hall, 20 Dec. 1803, ibid.

61. [Anonymous] to Governor, 29 Dec. 1802, ibid.

62. Baltimore *Maryland Journal and the Baltimore Advertiser*, 5, 16 Nov. 1784.

63. Baltimore *Edward's Baltimore Daily Advertiser*, "A.B.," 8 Nov. 1793. See also the broadside "Baltimore Town, Committee Chamber, 2 Dec. 1784."

64. Baltimore *Maryland Journal*, 4 Feb. 1785.

65. Ibid., "A Citizen," 10 March 1786; "A Lover of the Constitution," 7 March 1786.

66. Ibid., "Watchman," 4 Dec. 1787.

67. Ibid., "A Baltimorean," 18 Nov. 1791.

68. *Laws of Maryland*, 1793, Chapter 69, An act to erect Baltimore town, in Baltimore County, into a city, and to incorporate the inhabitants thereof.

69. Baltimore *Edward's Baltimore Daily Advertiser*, 18 Dec. 1793; see also, ibid., "A Citizen to the Baltimore Mechanical Society," 17 Dec. 1793.

70. See Baltimore *Maryland Journal*, "Z," 20 Jan., 3 Feb. 1794; "Moderation," 21 Feb. 1794.

71. Ibid., 13 Jan. 1794.

72. Ibid., 12, 29 Sept. 1794.

73. See letters in the Baltimore *Federal Gazette*: James Calhoun to James Winchester, 22 Dec. 1796; Winchester to Calhoun, 23 Dec. 1796; and Winchester to the Voters of Baltimore town, 30 Dec. 1796. For the role of the oligarchy, see "Aristides" to the People of Baltimore, 30 Jan. 1808, Baltimore *American*.

74. *Laws of Maryland*, 1796, Chapter 68, An Act to erect Baltimore Town, in Baltimore County, into a city and to incorporate the inhabitants thereof.

75. Ibid., 1805, Chapter 108, An Additional supplement to an act, entitled, An Act to erect Baltimore town, in Baltimore County, into a city, and to incorporate the inhabitants thereof.

76. See the Baltimore *Federal Gazette*, "An Old Baltimorean," "A Freeman," "An Citizen," "A Native Baltimorean," 30 Jan. 1808; and the results of the charter vote, 2 Feb. 1808. See also Baltimore *American* for the amendments to the charter, 10 Jan. 1808; for the proreform slate, 27, 29 Jan. 1808; and for letters from "Aristides," "A Native American," "Equity," "Plain Truth," 29 Jan. 1808; "Aristides" II, 30 Jan. 1808; the delegates to the convention, 3 Feb. 1808; and the results of the convention, 9 Feb. 1808. See also Virgil Maxcy to Robert G. Harper, 2 Feb. 1808, Harper-Pennington Papers.

77. Commenting on Baltimore's population growth reflected in the 1800 census, the editor of the Baltimore *Federal Gazette* observed, 30 March 1801: "If we consider that hitherto the wealth of Baltimore has in great measure been drawn from the lands bordering on the Chesapeake and its waters, the back counties of this state, Virginia, and only one or two counties of Pennsylvania, what must be her destinies when the Susquehanna is rendered navigable to the Chesapeake, opening to the enterprise and industry of our citizens a country richer and more inexhaustible than the mines of Peru." See also ibid., 10 Jan. 1804; Baltimore *American*, 6 Nov. 1804.

78. The best work on Baltimore's development is Browne, "Baltimore in the Nation."

79. Baltimore newspapers were sensitive to events in rival towns that might give them an advantage. "Amicus" wrote concerning the proposed improvements on the Potomac that if the work were begun Baltimore would lose "an advantage it will never be able to recover" (Baltimore *Maryland Journal*, 11 July 1783). See also Baltimore *Federal Gazette*, 11 March 1797, 7 April 1798, 15 April 1803, 16 Nov. 1805. For a full account of this competition see James W. Livingood, *The Philadelphia-Baltimore Trade Rivalry, 1780–1830*.

80. The editor of the Baltimore *Federal Gazette* opposed the crosscut canal, 31 Aug. 1796: "There is nothing more threatening, than the scheme to open a communication between the Chesapeake and Delaware Bays. Should that event take place, a very large portion of the Chesapeake trade will forsake its present channel and flow into the port of Philadelphia." See also letters from "Agricola," ibid., 5, 8, 10 March 1796. Individuals from the other sections worked assiduously to obtain the charter: see Levi Hollingsworth, Jr., to L. Hollingsworth & Son, 15 Dec. 1798, Hollingsworth Papers; and George Gale to William Tilghman, 31 March 1803, William Tilghman Papers, HSPa. The directors of the Chesapeake and Delaware Canal Company did not include anyone from Baltimore. George Gale and Tilghman's brother-in-law, William Hemsley, served as directors (Easton *Maryland Herald and Eastern Shore Intelligencer*, 29 March 1803; Baltimore *Federal Gazette*, 9 June 1804).

81. The most convenient analysis of the rise and fall of the "Potowmack" and Chesapeake factions is provided by L. Marx Renzulli, Jr., *Maryland*, pp. 149–59.

82. See the following firsthand reports of the crosscut canal controversy in the Maryland legislature: Levi Hollingsworth, Jr., to Levi Hollingsworth & Son, 29 Nov. 1795; and Hy. Hollingsworth to ibid., 28 Dec. 1795, Hollingsworth Papers.

83. For examples of praise for legislators who had protected the interests of the city, see Baltimore *Federal Gazette*, 31 Jan. 1798, Baltimore *American*, 9 Dec. 1799. For expressions that internal improvements were an important component of a candidate's platform, see Baltimore *Federal Gazette*, 7 July, 25 Sept. 1804; Baltimore *American*, "A Farmer and Planter," 15 July 1804.

84. William Hindman wrote James McHenry from Annapolis to report the passage of the bill, 9 Dec. 1799, McHenry Papers, LC. See also Baltimore *Federal Gazette*, 9 Dec. 1799.

85. For a report of this meeting, see Baltimore *Federal Gazette*, 18 April 1801, and in the same paper exhortations to subscribers, 22 April, 13 May, 1 July 1801. For an earlier comment on the need to improve the Susquehanna, see a letter to the editor, *Baltimore Daily Intelligencer*, 27 April 1798.

86. The deplorable conditions of the roads and the debate generated over the issue of transforming public roads into private companies are illuminated in items in the Baltimore *Federal Gazette*, 20 July, "A Baltimorean," 4 Sept. 1802; 25 June, "A Landholder," 1 July, 17 Aug. 1803; "A Farmer and Planter," 3 July 1804; "Agricola," 20 March, "A Friend to Baltimore," 21 March, "Frederick Turnpike," 22 March 1805.

87. For reports of the meetings, see ibid., 6 July and 2 Aug. 1803.

88. For a list of officers and managers in road companies, see, for the Frederick Turnpike Company, ibid., 14 May 1805; for the Falls Turnpike Road Company, ibid., 2 Oct. 1805; for the Baltimore and Reisterstown Road, ibid., 19 Feb. 1806; and for the Baltimore and York Town Turnpike Road, Baltimore *American*, 18 Jan. 1808.

89. For a report on this meeting, see Baltimore *Federal Gazette*, 21, 30 April, 3 May 1804. For the progress of the subscription, ibid., 2, 8, 9, 10, 12, 18 May 1804.

90. For the results of the annual elections for directors, see ibid., 24 May 1804, 6 May 1805, 8 May 1806. See also *Laws of Maryland*, 1808, Chapter 79, An act to incorporate the President and directors of the Baltimore Water Company. James A. Buchanan and James Mosher were connected to Samuel Smith; Buchanan, Solomon Etting, and John McKim, Jr., were among the most affluent citizens; and Buchanan, William Cooke, Etting, and Mosher served as final officers or directors.

91. See contemporary comments in the Baltimore *Gazette*: "A Considerable Stockholder," 17, 27, 29 Aug., "Polydius," 3 Sept. 1804; and in the Baltimore *American*, where the editors attacked the lack of public spirit shown by Federalist Robert G. Harper, 30 March, 2, 3 April 1800. See also the company advertisement in the Baltimore *Federal Gazette*, 1 June 1805.

92. For the names of the decisional elite, see Appendix III, Table A3.2.

93. Wealth information was taken from the microfilm copy of Baltimore City, Department of the Treasurer, Tax Ledger, 1798?, 1799, 1800, 1803. Slaves were not included in

this tax record. Slaveholding was determined from G. Ronald Teeples, comp., *Maryland*, and Bettie S. Carothers, comp., *Maryland Slave Owners and Superintendents, 1798*, vol. 1. Because slave valuation depended on the age and condition of the individual slave, and my primary interest was in determining who among the elite owned slaves—slaveownership itself is an important social indicator—no effort was made to convert the number of slaves into a dollar value.

94. Occupations were taken from *The New Baltimore Directory and Annual Register for 1800–1801*.

95. For a concise statement of Calhoun's public service during the Revolution, see his letter to George Washington, 22 June 1789, reel 119, Washington Papers. He and Samuel Purviance were active leaders in the Committee of Observation.

96. Archibald Buchanan, James Calhoun, Hercules Courtenay, Isaac Griest, and David McMechen were members of the Baltimore City Committees of Vigilance or Observation, Charles Carroll of Carrollton and Samuel Chase belonged to the Anne Arundel County counterpart, Luther Martin in Somerset County, and John Swann was elected but declined to serve in Frederick County. John E. Howard, James H. McCulloch, Dr. James McHenry, Samuel Smith, and John Stricker were revolutionary officers. James Purviance was the nephew of Samuel Purviance, Jr., the chairman of Baltimore City's Committee of Safety, and James Winchester's father, William, was politically active in Frederick County.

97. Gen. Swann to Gov. Ogle, 6 Dec. 1799, AG papers. Reflecting the same attitude, Lt. Col. John Crooks recommended promotions in the following way: "These gentlemen are men of probity, property, and a very large and Respectable Family Connection, and are friends to the Government and Constitution of the Country and (*American Born*), there is every tie that can attach men to their country" (Crooks to Governor and Council, 10 Aug. 1807, ibid.).

98. My interpretation draws heavily on Browne, "Baltimore in the Nation," esp. pp. 39–206, although I differ in several respects.

99. Of the approximately eighteen major businessmen named by Browne who failed because of such fiscal reversals, only James Calhoun and Samuel Smith were among the decisional elite during the first party era (ibid., p. 147). For the details of Samuel Smith's problems, see Cassell, *Merchant Congressman*, pp. 223–26.

100. See Browne, "Baltimore in the Nation," Table I, p. 464.

101. For a list of the emerging rentier class, the merchants who were ruined, and those who survived, see ibid., pp. 147, 153.

102. Browne identified fifty-four individuals as Baltimore merchants who understood the Industrial Revolution and challenged the old business elite in the 1820s (ibid., note 83, pp. 603–4). With the exception of Alexander Brown, however, Browne does not say what these men did to be so designated. Theoretically, they should have been the backbone of the Anti-Jackson/Whig party, yet only nine belonged to it and another was a Jacksonian congressman.

103. Browne summarizes the 1820 experience elegantly: "The transformation of Baltimore's society from its eighteenth-century aristocratic, mercantilist, and sedentary moorings into its nineteenth-century version—urban, industrial, and democratic—physically began during the 1820s" (ibid., p. 150).

104. Jackson party leadership roles were scored and analyzed on the basis of newspaper reports: Baltimore *American*, 22 May, 19–22, 25, 27 Oct. 1824, 12 Aug. 1831; Baltimore *Patriot and Mercantile Advertiser*, 26 Feb., 2 March, 12, 23 May, 23–24 Nov. 1827, 10 March, 11 June, 1, 16 Aug., 10 Dec. 1828, 8 June, 29 July, 26 Aug. 1829, 8 May 1834; Baltimore *Republican and Commercial Advertiser*, 7–9, 15 April, 5–6 May, 6, 10, 23–24 June, 11, 19, 25, 27 Aug., 7–8 Sept. 1829, 26 July, 3, 8 Sept., 4 Oct. 1830, 9, 29 June, 8, 11–12, 14 July, 11–12 Aug., 6, 20–21, 24, 28 Sept., 25 Oct., 2 Nov. 1831, 6, 16 March, 1, 4, 23, 30 April, 7, 11, 15, 23, 25, 28 May, 20 July, 3, 18, 20 Sept., 18, 22 Oct., 1–2, 12 Nov., 8, 12, 14–15 Dec. 1832, 6 Jan., 6 March, 24 June, 1, 3–4, 10, 19, 22, 24, 31 July, 1, 26–27 Aug., 17 Sept., 3, 7 Oct. 1833, 8 Feb., 8, 13, 19 March, 8, 14, 16, 21, 28 April, 12, 14, 19 May, 13, 16, 18, 21–23, 28 Aug., 6, 8, 10, 17, 23–24 Sept. 1834, 6, 8, 20

Jan., 3 Feb., 6, 19–21 March, 1, 3 April, 9, 15, 21–23, 26, 28 May, 25 June, 10–11, 13, 23–24 July, 1–4, 13 Aug., 6, 8, 10, 12, 14, 17, 19, 21–26, 28, 30 Sept., 1 Oct., 18 Dec. 1835, 23, 30 April, 3, 19–21 May, 1, 13, 15, 20 July, 10, 15, 17, 31 Aug., 12, 14, 17, 30 Sept. 1836.

105. See the Baltimore *Republican*, 16 April 1829, 27 Feb. 1832. For Dabney S. Carr's career, see *Biographical Cyclopaedia of Representative Men of Maryland and the District of Columbia*, pp. 715–16, and Charles Lanman, *Biographical Annals of the Civil Government of the United States during Its First Century*, p. 70. For Samuel Harker, see William A. Miller and Samuel Harker to Secretary of State, 18 Feb. 1820, Miscellaneous Letters Received Regarding Publishers of the Laws, NA.

106. The strain caused by the succession competition between Calhoun and Van Buren was prevalent in the correspondence between Maryland politicians. See John P. Kennedy to Virgil Maxcy, 11 Oct. 1823, Maxcy-Markoe Letterbook, Frederick A. Schley to Maxcy, 25 May 1831, Maxcy Correspondence, Galloway-Maxcy-Markoe Papers, LC; W. H. J. Mitchell to F. P. Blair, 25 June 1831, Blair-Rives Papers, LC; D. S. Carr to F. P. Blair, 4 June 1831, Blair-Lee Papers, PU; Duff Green to R. Geddes, 15 July 1831, Duff Green Papers, UNC; and Richard Frisby to Samuel Smith, 20 Feb., 1 March 1832, Vertical File, MdHS. For local opposition to Martin Van Buren, see Baltimore *Republican*, 24 Aug. 1832, Baltimore *Commercial Chronicle and Daily Marylander*, 22 Aug. 1832.

107. See especially J. Thomas Scharf, *History of Baltimore City and County*, pp. 120–21; Richard P. McCormick, *The Second Party System*, pp. 160–66.

108. The standard biographies of Taney are Walker Lewis, *Without Fear or Favor*, Bernard C. Steiner, *Life of Roger B. Taney*, and Carl B. Swisher, *Roger B. Taney*. For an analysis of Taney's career as secretary of the treasury, see Frank O. Gatell's articles, "Secretary Taney and the Baltimore Pets" and "Spoils of the Bank War." For a different view, see Harry N. Scheiber, "The Pet Banks in Jacksonian Politics and Finance, 1833–1841." For a sense of his local popularity, see Baltimore *Republican*, 29 July 1834.

109. Frank Cassell's biography of Smith, *Merchant Congressman*, emphasizes his national career and suggests that he was not very powerful in local community politics. For a different view, see my article, "McCulloch vs. the Jacksonians."

110. For a short sketch of Isaac McKim see Scharf, *History of Baltimore*, pp. 476–77. There is no indication that he was a particularly active leader in the city party. In fact, when he was renominated for Congress in 1835, he was vacationing in Virginia (McKim to John Nelson et al., Baltimore *Republican*, 20 Aug. 1835), and the opposition press hailed his candidacy by observing that "he travelled through the district on the last occasion with a short speech and a long purse" (ibid., 4 Aug. 1835, quoting the Baltimore *Chronicle*).

111. As examples of their historical reputation, see biographical treatments in Charles H. Bohner, *John Pendleton Kennedy*, John T. Mason, Jr., ed., *Life of John Van Lear McMahon*, and Bernard C. Steiner, *Life of Reverdy Johnson*.

112. For a more complete list of Jackson party activists and leaders, see my dissertation, "A Social Analysis of Maryland Community Elites, 1827–1836: A Study of the Distribution of Power in Baltimore City, Frederick County, and Talbot County," University of Pennsylvania, 1973, pp. 385–98. For a discussion of the scoring method, see Appendix I.

113. Occupations were determined from J. W. Matchett, comp., *Matchett's Baltimore Director*.

114. All wealth information was taken from the Baltimore City, Department of the Treasurer, Tax Ledgers, 1828, 1834. The tax records listed slaves as either "slave" or "slaves," that is, without a numerical statement, so that the extent of slaveholding could not be determined exactly.

115. One indication of Taney's respect for Frick was his letter of introduction to President Jackson, 23 July 1834, Blair-Lee Papers. His direct association with Young was less precise, but it was clear that Young worked with Taney and that he was assimilated into the Treasury Department. See John H. B. Latrobe's entry of a visit to Taney where he met Young and Van Buren, 20 Dec. 1833, John H. B. Latrobe Diaries, MdHS. Young was appointed to the treasury office in Baltimore in 1831 (Baltimore *Republican*, 26 March

1831) and then as chief clerk of the Treasury Department (ibid., 1 Oct. 1833). He was listed as chief clerk drawing $2,000 a year in 1835 (U.S. Department of State, *Register of All Officers and Agents, Civil, Military, and Naval in the Service of the U.S.*, 1835, p. 12).

116. For a more extended treatment, see Chapter 7.

117. Ibid.

118. Dr. Alcock founded the *Reformer* on 14 Jan. 1836, and there are a few issues at the Enoch Pratt Free Library in Baltimore; see Scharf, *History of Baltimore*, p. 161; Baltimore *Patriot*, 14 Jan. 1836; Baltimore *Republican*, 28 Dec. 1836.

119. Steuart announced that he would run as an independent for Congress because he was anti-Van Buren, not anti-Jackson (Baltimore *Gazette*, 5 Oct. 1835). See also Fischer, *Revolution of American Conservatism*, p. 138; Baltimore *Republican*, 20 March 1835.

120. The following were active in the years indicated: Beale Randall, 1827–28; J. J. Graves, 1836; B. C. Howard, 1834–35; R. Lilly, 1834; U. S. Heath, 1828, 1830; J. R. Hayman, 1836; W. Roney, 1835; W. J. Wight, 1830, 1833, 1836; T. L. Murphy, 1832; C. Howard, 1832, 1836; H. McElderry, 1827–28; J. H. Miller, 1832; and G. H. Steuart, 1830.

121. For example: F. J. Dugan, J. Fitch, S. House, J. E. Stansbury, W. J. Wight, S. Ready, J. Hook, P. Storm, J. Bacon, W. G. Read, J. Delcher, C. Southcomb, J. W. Wilmer, H. McKinnell, and A. Miltenberger.

122. See Ridgway, "A Social Analysis," for the sources, which will also specify the losing candidate (pp. 517–19), and Table 7 (pp. 448–51), which identifies all those elected to political positions in Baltimore at this time.

123. The Baltimore City Workingmen's movement is little known. At least two Workingmen's papers were published in the city, the *Mechanics Banner and the Workingmen's Shield* ("Prospectus," Baltimore *Patriot*, 24 Aug. 1833) and the *Workingmen's Newspaper* (Baltimore *Republican*, 25 Feb. 1833), but no issues have survived. The most sympathetic paper was the Baltimore *Gazette*, the least politically inclined daily. For the economic roots of their discontent, see Baltimore *Patriot*, 4 Feb., 27 Nov. 1828; Baltimore *Republican*, 24, 27, 29 July, 2, 12, 16, 19, 21, 24, 27 Aug., 6, 16 Sept., 1 Nov., 23 Dec. 1833, 21, 24 Jan., 14 March, 4 July 1834, 24, 28 April, 8, 9, 19, 23, 26 June, 25 July, 7, 9, 17, 25 Nov., 2 Dec. 1835.

124. For the formation and development of the Workingmen's party, see Baltimore *American*, 10, 12, 18, 20, 21, 25–26 Sept. 1833; Baltimore *Chronicle*, 21 Sept., 4 Nov. 1833; Baltimore *Republican*, 25 Feb., 18, 20–21, 25–28, 30 Sept., 1–4, 7, 19, 30–31 Oct., 4, 18 Nov. 1833. Earlier in 1831, William C. Clayton ran as an independent journeyman for the House of Delegates, but he did not represent a popular movement (Baltimore *American*, 1 Oct. 1831).

125. For the efforts to recommend Judge John McLean, see the Baltimore *Chronicle*, 28–30 Oct. 1833, and the corresponding dates for the Baltimore *Republican*.

126. For an evaluation of the Workingmen's schism, see letters from Benjamin C. Howard to Virgil Maxcy, 9 Nov. 1833, 20 Aug. 1834, Maxcy Correspondence, Galloway-Maxcy-Markoe Papers. See also "Turncoats," Baltimore *Republican*, 25 April 1834.

127. For Anti-Jackson party activities, from which leadership roles were scored, see Annapolis *Maryland Republican*, 14 Oct. 1828; Baltimore *American*, 24–25 Oct. 1824, 6–9, 11, 13, 15–16, 18, 21, 23 June 1827, 10, 12 Aug. 1831, 7 Aug. 1833; Baltimore *Chronicle*, 20 Sept. 1829, 22 March, 30 Aug. 1830, 19 Nov. 1831, 2, 19 Jan., 9, 11 May, 15, 19, 21–22 June, 2 July, 13, 22, 27–29 Sept., 9, 12 Oct. 1832, 31 May, 3, 10, 24 June, 24 Sept. 1834; Baltimore *Freeman's Banner*, 6, 13, 20 Aug., 29 Oct., 5 Nov., 17, 31 Dec. 1831, 21 Jan., 16, 30 June, 7 July, 22 Sept., 13 Oct. 1832, 19 July, 5, 7 Aug. 1833; Baltimore *Marylander*, 15 Dec. 1827, 2–3, 6, 9, 11, 13–14, 16, 23, 27 Feb., 2, 30 July, 12, 17, 20, 24, 27–28 Sept. 1828; Baltimore *Patriot*, 27 April, 5 May, 5–9, 11–13, 15–16, 18, 21, 23, 26 June, 23, 25–26 July, 15 Oct., 15, 19, 22, 24 Dec. 1827, 19, 30 Jan., 8, 11–12, 14, 19, 23, 29 Feb., 3, 7, 12 May, 11, 26 July, 4, 17, 19–20, 22–24, 26–28 Sept., 16, 27 Oct. 1828, 18 March, 4, 8 June, 5, 18, 21 Sept. 1829, 24 Sept., 13–14 Dec. 1831, 16 Aug., 22, 25 Sept., 5, 10–11 Oct. 1832, 6 Feb., 6 March, 19, 21, 23–24 April, 8 May, 14, 18–19,

21, 27, 29–30 Aug., 3–6, 8, 10–13, 15–18, 20, 22–24, 27 Sept., 1–4, 6, 11, 21 Oct. 1834, 1, 6, 10 July, 7 Aug., 9–12, 14–15, 17, 19, 22–26 Sept., 1, 11, 13, 24 Oct., 3, 7, 9, 11, 13, 17, 24 Nov., 3, 7–8, 17, 19, 22–24 Dec. 1835, 31 March, 6, 13–15, 19, 23, 26 July, 1, 30 Aug., 12, 27, 30 Sept., 1, 21, 25, 27–29, 31 Oct., 1–5, 31 Nov. 1836; Baltimore *Republican*, 15 April, 20 May, 9–10 June 1829, 30 July, 28 Aug. 1830, 22 Feb., 12 Aug., 17 Dec. 1831, 12 Jan., 11 May 1832, 7 Aug. 1833, 5 Jan., 11 July, 23–25 Dec. 1835; Rockville *Maryland Journal and True American*, 24, 30 April, 17 Sept. 1834; *Niles Weekly Register* 32 (28 July 1827): 354, 40 (12 March 1831): 28–29, 41 (17 Dec. 1831): 281, 41 (24 Dec. 1831): 301–12.

128. Scharf, *History of Baltimore*, p. 612. See also, regarding Munroe's predilection for Webster, Daniel Webster to Edward Everett, 4 Nov. 1835, Edward Everett Papers, Ms HS; and, regarding the division within Maryland's presidential convention between Harrison and Webster supporters, John M. Steuart to Caleb Cushing, 22 Dec. 1835, Caleb Cushing Papers, LC.

129. "Prospectus," Baltimore *Patriot*, 19 Dec. 1827; Baltimore *Marylander*, 6 Dec. 1828; Baltimore *Chronicle*, 14 Jan. 1829. During the presidential contest of 1832, the printing establishment of Sands and Neilson published an Anti-Jackson campaign paper, the Baltimore *Freeman's Banner*, and in 1836 they introduced the Baltimore *Democratic Whig*.

130. One of the problems of having two party presses in one city was the division of patronage. In 1831 the *Patriot* lost state printing contracts to the *Chronicle*; see Isaac Munroe to Thomas Culbreth, 29 March 1831, Vertical File, MdHS.

131. For Joshua Barney, *Biographical Directory of the American Congress, 1774–1961*, p. 517; for Peter Little, ibid., p. 1224; see also Baltimore *Patriot*, 21 March 1829.

132. For a complete list of Anti-Jackson party activists and leaders, see Ridgway, "A Social Analysis," pp. 399–416. For an explanation of the bank crisis and McCulloch vs. Maryland, see Bray Hammond, *Banks and Politics in America*, pp. 260–72.

133. Neither of Hezekiah Niles's biographers has taken adequate notice of his Baltimore partisan activities; see Norman N. Luxon, *Niles Weekly Register*, and Richard G. Stone, *H. Niles as an Economist*.

134. *Niles Weekly Register* 49 (2 Jan. 1836): 300.

135. For a breakdown of the city's hundred wealthiest individuals, reaggregated from the 1834 tax ledgers, see Appendix III, Table A3.8.

136. *Niles Weekly Register* 31 (30 Dec. 1826): 286.

137. See *Easton Gazette*, 4 July 1835.

138. Fridge held ten lots valued at $6,290; Stapleton had one lot worth $360; and Needham held four lots worth $1,910.

139. See the Baltimore *Republican*, 22 July 1834; *Easton Gazette*, 30 May, 21 Nov. 1835.

140. It is noteworthy that after 1834 the candidates for the lower house from the Anti-Jackson party were not necessarily party leaders. The party apparently made a blatant appeal to the workingmen of the city. Joseph Cushing (1834), Samuel Jones, Jr. (1836), and Samuel Thompson (1836) were not leaders, but were drawn from the ranks of the workingmen.

141. Consider the following editorial: "Where internal improvements have been made, there is wealth and growing prosperity; where they are in progress there is hope and prospective outlay in capital; where they have not yet been commenced there is stagnation or absolute retrogression. Canals and rails are magnets, which attract the two greatest sources of growing prosperity in our country—population and capital" (Baltimore *American*, 2 May 1836).

142. For the various internal improvements meetings, see Baltimore *American*, 6, 8–9, 10 Dec. 1834, 20 Nov., 1 Dec. 1835, 2, 7, 16 April, 3 May 1836; Baltimore *Patriot*, 9 Dec. 1834, 19 Nov. 1835; Baltimore *Republican*, 15 May 1833, 10 Nov., 10 Dec. 1834, 10–11 March, 19–20 Nov., 1 Dec. 1835, 19 Jan. 1836; *Hagerstown Mail*, 11 Dec. 1835; *Niles Weekly Register* 49 (5 Dec. 1835): 237–38.

143. See reports boosting the completion of an internal improvements project advantageous to Baltimore in Baltimore *American*, 18 Sept., 8 Dec. 1834; Baltimore *Chronicle*, 1 March 1832; Baltimore *Republican*, 26 Aug. 1835.

144. Baltimore *American*, 16 Dec. 1834, 16 Nov. 1835.

145. James W. McCulloch's role as a canal company lobbyist is evident in correspondence. McCulloch, aided by J. J. Merrick and David Ridgely, worked with the canal company president, George Corbin Washington, to prod the legislature to enact bills favorable to the canal company. For McCulloch's activities, see Washington to McCulloch, 18 Oct. 1836, Letterbook C; Journals and Proceedings of Directors, ser. E, p. 84 (29 June 1836); David Ridgely to Washington, 4, 22 June 1836, and Charles B. Fiske to Washington, 5 March 1836, Letters Received, Records of the Chesapeake and Ohio Canal Company, NA. Washington observed: "Mr. McCulloch, who is giving us all his aid and influence, is very sanguine, and I candidly confess that I have very strong hopes" (Washington to J. P. Ingle, 23 Feb. 1835, ibid.). McCulloch also served as an intermediary between the canal and the railroad companies; see Philip E. Thomas to Washington, 6 April 1835, and Thomas to McCulloch, 31 May 1835, ibid.

146. His assessed property was for two lots valued at $3,500.

147. The Jackson political leaders were William Krebs and George Winchester; the Anti-Jackson leaders were Reverdy Johnson, Gen. Sheppard C. Leakin, and John V. L. McMahon. The bankers were William Crawford, Jr., Jacob G. Davies, John S. Hollins, Charles Howard, John B. Howell, William Hubbard, and Samuel Jones. The directors of the Baltimore and Ohio Railroad Company, who were also bankers, were John McKim, Jr., and James Swann.

148. William Patterson, Robert Oliver, and Hugh W. Evans.

149. Isaac Munroe, Nathaniel F. Williams, S. C. Leakin, H. Niles, and Solomon Etting.

150. There are suggestions that Congressman Benjamin C. Howard and state Senator C. F. Mayer were also working for internal improvements. See A. J. Donelson to Howard, 4 Dec. 1834, Howard Papers, MdHS. Charles F. Mayer wrote Governor Veazey that he was returning from Washington, where he had been lobbying for internal improvements, and he asked the governor for a confidential meeting (16 July 1836, State Papers).

151. This position was clearly stated in the Baltimore *Chronicle* "Reform" editorials: 26 March, 26–27, 29 Nov., 10, 15, 20 Dec. 1832; see also the comment by the Princess Anne *Village Herald*, 18 Dec. 1832.

152. Baltimore *Chronicle*, 23 Nov. 1832, 7 Jan., 1–2, 30 April, 27 May, 3, 5, 7 June 1833.

153. Ibid., 18 April 1833.

154. In the fall of 1832, the Baltimore *Republican* editorialized: "We are persuaded that the most effectual mode for accomplishing this object is for the Jackson party to take it up as a party measure" (22 Nov. 1832). See also ibid., 14 March, 18 April, 21 Sept., 19 Dec. 1832, 8 April, 4 June 1833, 27–28 Nov., 2, 5, 28 Dec. 1835, and editorials throughout the crisis year of 1836. For an editorial response to the Fredericktown Jackson paper's position, see Baltimore *Chronicle*, 18 April 1833.

155. See Baltimore *Chronicle*, 23 April 1832, 8, 27 May 1833.

156. See Baltimore *Republican*, 9 Jan., 31 Aug. 1833. In 1836 this pattern changed. At the Annapolis reform convention in February 1836, two Baltimore City residents were elected as officers, Philip Laurenson and John J. Graves, and at the June 1836 Baltimore reform convention more Baltimore citizens shared the major offices, in this case James Carroll, Graves, and W. P. Dunnington (ibid., 3 Feb., 20 June 1836). See also ibid., 21 Nov. 1836.

157. As examples, see Baltimore *Chronicle*, 6 March 1832, 1–2 April 1833; Baltimore *Republican*, 9 March 1832, 4, 7, 12 Jan., 9, 14, 22–23 March, 9 April 1833, 11 Jan., 4 Feb. 1834, 23 Jan., 6 April 1836.

158. The Baltimore *Chronicle* stated the Anti-Jackson position, equating reform with potential revolution, as early as 1832: "We are for reform, but not for a revolution. We are parties to a contract by which we must abide, until it can be altered in the mode prescribed

in the instrument itself" (25 April 1832). For an elaboration of the Anti-Jackson position, see Baltimore *Patriot*, 26, 28 Sept., 4 Oct., 9-10 Nov. 1836. The Baltimore *Republican* tried to divest itself of the revolutionary label; see issues of 10, 22 Sept., 15, 24 Oct., 10, 19, 29 Nov. 1836.

159. The cumulative frustration of the reformers was evident in a series of editorials in the Baltimore *Republican* as the 1836 legislative session went on without any interest in passing reform legislation: "The time has arrived when something should be done; we trust the time has arrived when something decisively *will* be done" (7 Jan. 1836); "If the rotten-borough representatives will not move in the matter, the people should themselves move. We have waited long enough" (22 Feb. 1836); by September it favored the dissolution of government if reform should not be achieved (10 Sept. 1836).

160. Leadership roles were determined from the following sources: Baltimore *Chronicle*, 6 April 1832, 2 April, 5 June, 31 Aug. 1833; Baltimore *Freeman's Banner*, 7 April 1832; Baltimore *Patriot*, 1 Dec. 1835, 11 May, 4 June, 27 Sept., 15 Oct., 10 Nov. 1836; Baltimore *Republican*, 5 April, 8, 12 Dec. 1832, 8-11 Jan., 27 March, 4 June, 22, 31 Aug. 1833, 26 Jan., 3 Feb., 12 May, 4, 13, 20 June, 27 Sept., 1, 12, 18, 21 Oct., 21 Nov., 25 Dec. 1836; *Niles Weekly Register* 51 (24 Sept. 1836): 51-52, 51 (1 Oct. 1836): 70-74, 51 (8 Oct. 1836): 95, 51 (3 Dec. 1836): 215.

161. Carroll ranked fifth on the 1834 tax rolls with $16,000 worth of property; the city directory did not list his occupation.

162. For Richard Marley's activities as a Workingmen's leader, see Baltimore *Republican*, 21 Aug., 6 Sept. 1833, 1 Oct. 1836.

163. The Jackson leaders were state Senator U. S. Heath, Jonathan Fitch, William J. Wight, Joseph White, Stephen Waters, and William G. Read. There were also several party activists (B. I. Sanders, James Piper, John Soran, Louis W. Jenkins, Samuel Sterett, and Robert Howard). The Anti-Jacksonians included leaders Samuel Barnes, John M. Steuart, state Senator Charles F. Mayer, Joseph K. Stapleton, William P. Dunnington, and several party activists (Col. John Berry, Maj. Joshua Dryden, and the collector of the port, James H. McCulloch).

164. The positional leaders included Congressman B. C. Howard and former Congressman John Barney, Mayor Jesse Hunt, former state representative C. C. Harper, and former state Senator Reverdy Johnson. The more important Jackson leaders included Joshua Turner, McClintock Young, William H. Cole, J. I. Donaldson, and Beale Randall; the Anti-Jackson leaders were Luke Tiernan, Peter Leary, Gen. Joshua Medtart, and Solomon Etting.

165. Solomon Etting, John Dushane, Solomon Betts, Luke Tiernan, and Robert D. Millholland, who were vice-presidents; Thomas W. Hall, a secretary; and David Stewart, who gave an address. See the Baltimore *Patriot*, 27 Sept. 1836, for a report of the meeting.

166. Brady to McKim, 8 Feb. 1835, 27/224-25; see also Nicholas G. Ridgely to Duff Green, 17 June 1829, 27/123-35, and William Patterson to Samuel Smith, 18 March 1829, 2/420-22, Letters of Application and Recommendation during the Administration of Andrew Jackson, NA. See also my article, "McCulloch vs. the Jacksonians."

167. For Smith's efforts on behalf of Hughes, see Cassell, *Merchant Congressman*, pp. 255-56; for his interest in boosting the career of Dabney S. Carr, see Smith to Henry Clay, 8 March 1825, Petition to President, Feb. 1826, Nathaniel H. Claiborne et al. to Secretary of State, 20 Feb. 1826, 2/76-83, Letters of Application and Recommendation during the Administration of John Q. Adams, NA; Petition to A. Jackson, 20 Feb. 1829, William H. Marriott to Jackson, 27 Feb. 1829, 4/259-65, Jackson Recommendations; Smith to Secretary of the Treasury, 18 March 1829, 21st Congress, Nomination Papers of the U.S. Senate, NA.

168. For the effort to make Barney's dismissal a public issue, see letters from Jackson leaders to Mrs. Barney: Hugh McElderry, April 1829, Roger B. Taney, 18 April 1829, and B. C. Howard, 18 April 1829, as well as William B. Barney to U.S. Senate, 14 Jan. 1830, 21st Congress, Senate Nomination Papers.

169. For Smith's efforts on behalf of McCulloch in 1806, see note 57. In 1834, responding to a hint that he might be appointed collector when he retired from the Senate,

Smith was quick to protect McCulloch because he was old and poor, but also because Smith "had the pleasure of procuring for him his present office which he conducted to the entire satisfaction of the merchants and I believe the Treasury department" (Smith to Andrew Jackson, 11 March 1834, Smith Papers). For Smith's interest in Nathaniel Williams, the U.S. attorney, see Smith to Williams, Oct. 1820, ibid.; and John Stricker to James Monroe, (ca. 1824), 19/139–41, Letters of Application and Recommendation during the Administration of James Monroe, NA.

170. See his file, reel 3/635–78, but especially Elias Brown to the President, 17 March 1829, 3/656–58, Jackson Recommendations.

171. In contrast to the formal letter he wrote for Buchanan cited above, Smith's letter on behalf of Harper noted that Charles Carroll of Carrollton would increase Harper's allowance to $2,000 per year if he were appointed; see Martin Van Buren to Smith, 26 May 1829, Smith Papers, and Smith to Van Buren, 28, 29 May 1829, 10/469–73, Jackson Recommendations. See also Robert Oliver to President, 10 Oct. 1831, 10/477–80, ibid.

172. Baltimore *Republican*, 11 March 1835. The Anti-Jacksonians were quick to criticize the new administration's patronage policies; see reports and editorials in the Baltimore *Chronicle*, 29 May 1833, Baltimore *Freeman's Banner*, 13 Oct. 1832, Baltimore *Marylander*, 11 Oct. 1828, Baltimore *Patriot*, 7, 14–15, 23 April 1829, 9 Feb. 1830, and Washington *National Intelligencer*, 27 Sept. 1832, 26 June, 11 July 1834. The Jackson press was more tolerant of the political dimension of patronage and attacked their opponent's hypocrisy for charging the Jacksonians with being proscriptive when they had followed a more partisan policy for years in Maryland; see Baltimore *Republican*, 14 April, 11 Aug. 1829, 20–21, 30 Jan. 1830, 14 Sept. 1831, 1 Jan., 7, 11, 13 March, 22 April, 29 June, 3 July, 8, 20, 28 Oct. 1835.

173. Finley worked hard for reappointment, but he clearly was vulnerable. One of his supporters tried to explain the situation away: "The fact is, his son is a forward, impudent young man and the father has been exceptionally mortified by the course he took and did all in his power to prevent it" (I. D. Maulsby to Secretary of State, 20 Dec. 1834, 8/135–36, Jackson Recommendations).

174. Jonathan Fitch's nomination was secretive and unexpected. The Fredericktown *Herald* articulated the Anti-Jacksonian opposition best, 7 Feb. 1835: "Fitch is a furious partisan and presided at a public meeting. . . . If, after such vile slanders, the senate had confirmed the nomination of Fitch, they would have furnished [at] once evidence that they deserved the ubiquity that has been heaped upon them." Jacksonians themselves only mildly supported his nomination; see Louis W. Jenkins and George R. Mosher to McClintock Young, 28 Jan. 1835, 13/585–91, Jackson Recommendations. Fitch's efforts to redeem himself before the Senate were as unsuccessful as Barney's had been; see the Fitch file, 23d Congress, Senate Nomination Papers. His rejection, however, became a political issue and was used by the Jackson party press; see Baltimore *Republican*, 5, 9 Feb. 1835.

175. See the various letters for John W. Wilmer, 27/209–26, and Philip Laurenson, 13/568–97, Jackson Recommendations. Both men were party leaders.

176. In an effort to protect his own position by showing his nonpartisanship while in office, D. S. Carr wrote to Senator John Leeds Kerr that the collectorship "was an office of the most patronage of any in the gift of the Government in Baltimore and the efforts of the politicians of my party were continued, throughout General Jackson's administration, to oust him. I exerted myself, in opposition to them and incurred their bitter displeasure, for what was believed to be owing to my exertions made directly and through my old uncle General Smith" (March 1842, 27th Congress, Senate Nomination Papers).

177. Upon McCulloch's death, Carr tried to obtain administration support for his own appointment; see Carr to F. P. Blair, 12 Nov. 1836, Blair-Lee Papers, and especially the Carr file in Box 96, Collectors of the Customs: Applications, Maryland, Baltimore, NA. Throughout his service as naval officer he had provided political advice for the administration, but he had always avoided public activities; see his letters to President, 19 March 1829, 3/662–64, Secretary of State, 10 June 1829, 11/657–58, Jackson Recommendations; to F. P. Blair, 4 June 1831, 24 Nov. 1835, Blair-Lee Papers; and to John L. Kerr, 17 March 1842, 27th Congress, Senate Nomination Papers.

178. Once in office, Frick requested authorization to remove some of his staff because "the incumbents are far advanced in life, and have now become incapable of personal attention to the duties required of them by law" (Frick to Secretary of the Treasury, 15 June 1838, Letters Received from Collectors of the Customs, NA).

179. There are many letters scattered throughout the Adams and Jackson Recommendation series from various Baltimore congressmen; see Ridgway, "A Social Analysis," note 80, pp. 252–53. See also, regarding Congressman Benjamin Howard's efforts to influence patronage, Howard to Jackson, 22 March 1829, and Jackson to Howard, 23 March 1829, Howard Papers; Howard to Jonathan Meredith, 21 April 1830, Jonathan Meredith Papers, LC; and V. Macxy to John C. Calhoun, 7 May 1829, J. Franklin Jameson, ed., *Correspondence of John C. Calhoun*, p. 804. Roger B. Taney also gave political advice regarding patronage matters. See his letters to President, 22 May 1829, 11/21–22, and Van Buren, 6 Nov. 1830, 12/213–15, U. S. Heath to Taney, 9 June 1833, 2/215–17, Jackson Recommendations; to Secretary of State, 22 Jan. 1832, Publishers of the Laws, NA; and to Van Buren, 15 March 1836, Papers of Martin Van Buren, LC. After his appointment to the Supreme Court, he tried to abstain from patronage matters; see Taney to Benjamin F. Butler, 28 Oct. 1836, Benjamin F. Butler Papers, PU.

180. The Baltimore City state senators were Charles F. Mayer and John B. Morris, and the members of the Executive Council were William R. Steuart, Samuel Mass, and Nathaniel F. Williams. Hugh McElderry was a Jacksonian member, and Luke Tiernan twice declined appointment to that body. As examples of how the urban system worked, see letters to the executive in 1836 from Robert Neilson and Samuel Sands, 14 Jan., Thomas W. Bond, 29 Jan., Lewis Kemp, 18 Feb., Hugh W. Evans, 23 Feb., Luke Tiernan, 23 Feb., William Gwynn, 3 March, Thomas H. Carroll, 8 March, Charles F. Mayer, 27 July; and Lewis Kemp to C. F. Mayer, 18 Feb. 1836, State Papers.

181. A frustrated aspirant for political preference described how the system worked when the Jacksonians held power: "I got down in the stage [to Annapolis] on Friday at two pm but understood in a couple of hours after my arrival that our Delegates and McElderry had made up their lists for Baltimore appointments the preceding night and that the Council met according to this arrangement and they were made" (William T. Steiger to Abraham F. Shriver, 8 Feb. 1830 [MS 2085.3], Shriver Papers). See also John S. Shriver to William Shriver, 15 Feb. 1830 (MS 750), ibid.

182. For a list of the Baltimore decisional elite for the second party era, see Appendix III, Table A3.6.

183. The following were members of the decisional elite in both party periods: Solomon Etting, John Hillen, John McKim, Jr., William Patterson, Samuel Smith, and Luke Tiernan.

184. The following were sons of members of the first party decisional elite: William Frick, John S. Hollins, Benjamin C. Howard, Charles Howard, Hugh McElderry, Isaac McKim, Robert Purviance, and George Winchester. The following married into elite families: Hugh W. Evans, John P. Kennedy, James W. McCulloch, William H. Marriott, John B. Morris, and William G. Read.

Chapter 5

1. The concept of strategic elites in a modern context has been developed nicely by Suzanne I. Keller, *Beyond the Ruling Class*. In previous papers and articles I referred to the propertied elite as the traditional elite. Unfortunately, "traditional" is a value-laden word that resulted in unnecessary confusion. Therefore, I am substituting "propertied" as a more neutral description of this elite.

2. For a complete list of the positional elite by county and time period, see Appendix III, Tables A3.3, 7, 10, 14, 16, 19, 23, and 27.

3. A good example of such imperfections is provided by Solomon Betts. In the 1834 Baltimore City tax ledgers he was credited with owning $5,270 in property, placing him as the seventy-eighth wealthiest person on the list. Yet Roswell L. Colt wrote Nicholas Biddle in the next year observing that Betts was worth $150,000 (Colt to Biddle, 20 Nov. 1835, reel 21, Nicolas Biddle Papers, LC). Therefore I maintain that tax records do not permit a

totally accurate assessment of a man's real wealth, but that such deflation is probably
constant and that they do indicate *relative* positions. For another view of evaluating wealth
from tax records see Edward Pessen, *Riches, Class, and Power Before the Civil War*, pp.
11–26. See also my review of this influential book, "Measuring Wealth and Power in Ante-
Bellum America," pp. 75–78.

4. See the tax laws, which describe and update the general taxation procedures: *Laws
of Maryland*, 1785, Chap. 53, 1812, Chap. 191, 1821, Chap. 252, 1831, Chap. 118, and
1834, Chap. 22. These laws were updated and consolidated by 1841, Chap. 23.

5. For a complete list of the propertied elite by county and time period, see Appendix
III, Tables A3.4, 8, 11, 15, 17, 20, 24, and 28.

6. For instance, William Patterson, listed as the individual with the most property in
the 1800 and in the 1834 city tax rolls, was identified as holding 1,200 shares of Bank of
the United States stock. If we assume that Biddle's "friends of the bank," whom he wrote
in 1832 soliciting support for the recharter of the Second Bank of the United States, were
also stockholders, this impression is strengthened; see his letters, all dated 16 Jan. 1832, to
William Patterson, George Hoffman, Robert Oliver, Robert Gilmor, and John McKim, Jr.,
reel 44, Biddle Papers. All of these men were among the hundred wealthiest men on the
1834 tax rolls; of these hundred, 51 percent also served as bank directors or officers.

7. For a complete list of the commercial elite by county and time period, see the
Appendix III, Tables A3.1, 5, 12, 21, and 25.

8. For a discussion of the difficulties of occupational classifications, see Theodore
Hershberg et al., "Occupation and Ethnicity in Five Nineteenth Century Cities," pp. 174–
216.

9. Major William Somerville, second on the tax list with £10,753 and 125 slaves, was
connected to other locally important families, the Hebbs and the Platers, through marital
ties; Major William Thomas, Jr., tenth on the tax list with £3,530 and 52 slaves, was a state
legislator and the dynamic element in the county Jeffersonian party. Uriah Forrest, a
former county delegate to the state legislature who moved to Montgomery County and
represented it in Congress in the 1790s, was a director of the Georgetown Bank of
Columbia in 1802. Although technically not a member of the St. Marys county elite
because of his residence, Forrest epitomizes the identical recruitment pattern.

10. Col. William Hughlett, a member of Talbot County's commercial, positional, and
propertied elites during the second party era also belonged to Baltimore City's commercial
elite in the 1830s. Such reliance on the very wealthy inhibited opportunities for new men
to enter the elite structure.

11. In St. Marys and Talbot counties the men who held the most prominent federal
and state offices in the positional elite in both party periods were members of the rural
oligarchy.

12. Information for nativity and vital statistics concerning St. Marys and Talbot counties is sketchy at best. For St. Marys County, birthplace for twenty-nine persons could be
determined, and all were native-born; for Talbot County, birthplace for sixty-five individuals could be determined, and all but two were born in Maryland. Their average age is
specified below:

	1790s				1830s			
	One Elite	*Two Elites*	*Three Elites*	*Four Elites*	*One Elite*	*Two Elites*	*Three Elites*	*Four Elites*
St. Marys	38	45	37		51	41	33	
(N)	(5)	(5)	(1)		(8)	(11)	(3)	
Talbot	44	45	49		49	43	43	56
(N)	(16)	(9)	(8)		(14)	(16)	(5)	(2)

13. The religious variable was equally elusive for residents of both counties. Religion could be ascribed to twenty-nine individuals in St. Marys County: most were Episcopalians, the rest were Catholics. The Talbot County data are presented below:

	1790s				1830s			
	One Elite	Two Elites	Three Elites	Four Elites	One Elite	Two Elites	Three Elites	Four Elites
N	35	13	7	1	29	15	6	1
Catholic (percent)	3							
Episcopalian (percent)	91	92	100	100	72	40	100	100
Methodist (percent)	3	8			24	60		
Quaker (percent)	3				4			

14. The following table presents religious statistics for the various Frederick County elites.

	1790s				1830s			
	One Elite	Two Elites	Three Elites	Four Elites	One Elite	Two Elites	Three Elites	Four Elites
N	55	15	9		7	11	6	2
Baptist (percent)	2							
Catholic (percent)	7				14			
Episcopalian (percent)	33	60	78		29	18	83	
Evan. Reform (percent)	15	27	11		29	18	17	
Lutheran (percent)	22					27		
Methodist (percent)	5	7			14	27		100
Presbyterian (percent)	11	7	11			9		
Quaker	5				14			

15. The average age and nativity for Frederick County leaders are as follows:

	1790s				1830s			
	One Elite	Two Elites	Three Elites	Four Elites	One Elite	Two Elites	Three Elites	Four Elites
Age	47	47	49		49	44	48	48
(N)	(37)	(19)	(10)		(37)	(27)	(10)	(3)
Nativity:								
Maryland (percent)	80	75	88		81	92	100	
U.S. (percent)		25	12		14			100
Foreign (percent)	20				5	8		
(N)	(5)	(8)	(8)		(21)	(14)	(7)	(1)

16. The following table displays the liturgical and pietistic religious categories for Baltimore City elites at both time periods.

	1790s				1830s			
	One Elite	Two Elites	Three Elites	Four Elites	One Elite	Two Elites	Three Elites	Four Elites
Liturgical (percent)	50	48	45	25	45	55	45	100
Pietistic (percent)	50	52	55	75	55	45	55	
(N)	(88)	(54)	(18)	(8)	(161)	(60)	(11)	(1)

Chapter 6

1. "An Observer," Easton *Eastern Shore Whig and People's Advocate*, 15 July 1834.

2. Oswald Tilghman, comp., *History of Talbot County, Maryland, 1661–1861*, 1:176–83; James Haw, "Politics in Revolutionary Maryland, 1753–1788," Ph.D. dissertation, University of Virginia, 1972, esp. pp. 122–75.

3. For the Lloyd genealogy, see the Edward Lloyd Papers, MdHS; Tilghman, comp., *History of Talbot County*, 1:207.

4. Besides the information presented in Chapter 2 regarding the Lloyds' party activities, see also the humorous Federalist parody of a Republican caucus, Easton *Maryland Herald and Eastern Shore Intelligencer*, 31 Aug., 14, 21 Sept. 1802, which referred to Edward Lloyd V as "Lord Cock-de-doodle-do" and lampooned his political ally, Jacob Gibson.

5. For more information on the Goldsborough family, see Tilghman, comp., *History of Talbot County*, 1:408–14; for his comments on religion, see his charges to the Grand Jury, 13 Sept. 1784, April, 12 Sept. 1786, 1788, April 1791, MdDA.

6. Tilghman, comp., *History of Talbot County*, 2:22–29.

7. Robert Lloyd Nichols stood third on the 1800 tax rolls. He was appointed a major in 1775 and in 1794 when the militia was reorganized. In 1789 he entered into a partnership with David Kerr and Samuel Chamberlaine to open a store in Easton.

8. For a background on the Johnson family, see Genealogy, James Johnson Papers, MdHS; Thomas J. C. Williams, *History of Frederick County, Maryland*, 1:101–10; J. Thomas Scharf, *History of Western Maryland*, 1:629; Frank White, Jr., *The Governors of Maryland, 1777–1970*, pp. 3–9; *Biographical Directory of the American Congress, 1774–1961*, p. 1130 (hereafter cited as *BDAC*).

9. Thomas Johnson's four sons were Thomas Johnson (1732–1819), an attorney, who served in the revolutionary Council of Safety (1775), the Continental Congress (1774–77), as a brigadier general of the Flying Camp (1776–77), governor of Maryland (1777–79), the House of Delegates (1781, 1782, 1786, 1787), delegate to the constitutional ratification convention (1788), state judge (1790–91), and on the U.S. Supreme Court (1791–93). Col. James Johnson (1736–1809) built the Catoctin Furnace with his brothers Baker and Roger Johnson and served as a militia officer, justice of the peace, and on the Levy Court (1800–1801). Col. Baker Johnson (1749–1811), also an attorney, helped to build the Catoctin Furnace, was a delegate to the Constitutional Convention (1775), led a regiment during the war (1776–80), and served as a judge on the Orphans Court (1798–1800). Roger Johnson (1749–1831), known as the ironmaster of Bloomsbury Forge, voted as a Federalist, but did not emerge as a political leader.

10. See Carey Howard, "John Eager Howard," pp. 300–317; see also J. E. Howard to Vestry, 15 March 1805, MdDA.

11. His sons were John Eager Howard II; George Howard (1789–1846), who became governor; Benjamin Chew Howard (1791–1872), a Jacksonian congressman; Dr. William Howard (1793–1834); and Charles Howard (1802–69), who would become the president of the Susquehanna Railroad Company.

12. For a sketch of George Howard, see White, *Governors of Maryland*, pp. 101–7.

13. For a sketch of Benjamin Chew Howard, see *BDAC*, p. 1081.

14. For a sketch of Charles Carroll of Carrollton, see ibid., p. 666; for an analysis of his revolutionary era career, see Ronald Hoffman, *A Spirit of Dissension*, esp. Chap. 8.

15. For the Carroll genealogy, see *Anywhere So Long As There Be Freedom*, Charts 1–3.

16. For a sketch of Robert Goodloe Harper, see David H. Fischer, *The Revolution of American Conservatism*, pp. 36–38; *BDAC*, p. 1010.

17. For Charles Carroll Harper, see Baltimore *American and Commercial Advertiser*, 5 March 1827, Baltimore *Republican and Commercial Advertiser*, 25 April 1834; Samuel Smith to Martin Van Buren, 28, 29 May 1829, reel 10/ frames 469–73, and Robert Oliver to Andrew Jackson, 18 Oct. 1831, 10/447–80, Letters of Application and Recommendation during the Administration of Andrew Jackson, NA.

18. The Somervilles, the Keys, and the Forrests.

19. For a sketch of Gov. George Plater II (1735–92), see White, *Governors of Maryland*, pp. 28–31; for his son, Thomas Plater (1769–1830), see *BDAC*, p. 1463; another son, George Plater III (1766–1802), married the daughter of William Somerville and they had two children, George Plater IV, who wasted his patrimony in his youth and moved to Charles County, and Elizabeth Plater, who married her cousin, John Rousby Plater II; John Rousby Plater (1767–1831) had two children, John Rousby Plater II (d. 1825) and Elizabeth Ann Plater, both of whom predeceased him; a daughter, Rebecca, married Gen. Uriah Forrest (1756–1805), a politician from a prominent St. Marys family who moved to Georgetown (see *BDAC*, p. 905).

20. For a short sketch of Key, see Williams, *History of Frederick County*, 1:314, Scharf, *History of Western Maryland*, 2:898. Col. Key's brother, Philip Barton Key, fought as a British officer during the American Revolution and returned following the war to become an attorney and an important Federalist congressman from southern Maryland; see Williams, *History of Frederick County*, 1:130–31, *BDAC*, pp. 1162–63.

21. For his activities, see Fredericktown *Rights of Man*, 5 Sept. 1798, and Lt. Col. Robert Cumming to Gov. Ogle, 10 May 1800, Adjutant Generals Papers, MdHR (hereafter cited as AG Papers).

22. For the career of Francis Scott Key see Edward S. Delaplaine, *Francis Scott Key*.

23. John Leeds Bozman, his brother-in-law, was the twelfth wealthiest person in the county in 1800. He was a well-educated and a prominent attorney; see Tilghman, comp., *History of Talbot County*, 1:375–88.

24. Ibid., 1:388–408.

25. Ibid., 1:571; *BDAC*, p. 924.

26. Tilghman, comp., *History of Talbot County*, 1:414–23; see also the patronage section of Chapter 2 referring to George S. Leigh.

27. Williams, *History of Frederick County*, 1:180.

28. The sons of William Thomas (1758–1813) were Dr. James Thomas (1785–1836); Richard Thomas (d. 1849); Dr. William Thomas III (1793–1849); and George Thomas.

29. The standard history of the Maryland bar, Conway W. Sams and E. S. Riley, *The Bench and Bar of Maryland*, does not examine this aspect of legal training. Robert Goodloe Harper's Baltimore office is a good example of how political matters were closely linked to legal concerns; see Virgil Maxcy to Harper, 2 Feb. 1808, Harper-Pennington Papers, MdHS; and Maxcy to Harper, 22 May 1820, Robert Goodloe Harper Papers, NYPL.

30. The most recent biography on Taney is Walker Lewis, *Without Fear or Favor*.

31. Taney's financial concerns in Baltimore were handled in his absence by David M. Perine, the long-term register of wills for the county; these letters are in the Howard Papers, MdHS. Taney was connected to the following attorneys: McClintock Young, F. S. Key, and William M. Beall. See also Alexander Levin, "Two Jackson Supporters," pp. 221–29.

32. For instance, John Nelson, William H. Marriott, William Schley, and Reverdy Johnson.

33. For a general treatment of McMahon, see John T. Mason, Jr., ed., *Life of John Van Lear McMahon*; for his activities as a Jacksonian orator, see Allan Nevins, ed., *The Diary of John Quincy Adams*, p. 384; and Chapter 4.

34. For his potential ability to disrupt and divide the Jackson party by taking former Calhoun supporters into the opposition, see the following correspondence: Duff Green to McMahon, 6 Aug. 1831, 30 Aug., 8 Oct. 1832; Green to John Glenn, 27 Aug., 26 Sept. 1832; and Green to John C. Calhoun, 31 Aug. 1832, Duff Green Papers, UNC. See also Baltimore *Republican*, 25 April 1834.

35. William George Read married into the Howard family; John Pendleton Kennedy and John Nelson married daughters of Col. Thomas Tenant.

36. Dr. Philip Thomas of Frederick County; Dr. James Thomas of St. Marys County; and Drs. John, William, and William B. Tyler of Frederick County. Short sketches of prominent physicians were found in Eugene F. Cordell, *Medical Annals of Maryland 1799-1899*, and John R. Queenan, *Medical Annals of Baltimore*.

37. Dr. Edward J. Alcock was the founder and editor of the *Jefferson Reformer and Baltimore Daily Advertiser*; Dr. Samuel L. McKeehan edited the Fredericktown *Republican Citizen*; and John Winter, who practiced medicine without a degree in the late eighteenth century, edited the Fredericktown *Rights of Man*.

38. For Dabney S. Carr's appointment, see Chapter 4; note also that two successive editors of the Easton *Eastern Shore Whig and People's Advocate*, John D. Green and Edward C. Mullikin, retired upon their appointment as postmaster of Easton. The former postmaster, Thomas Perrin Smith, continued to edit his paper while he served the government.

39. For Colvin's career, see Easton *Republican Star*, 21 Dec. 1802, and Baltimore *Telegraphe and Daily Advertiser*, 25 Feb. 1802; for his appointment as editor of the Republican paper in Fredericktown, see Abraham Shriver to Andrew Shriver, 8, 21 Oct., 15 Nov. 1802 (MS 2085), and Colvin to Andrew Shriver, 17 Dec. 1807 (MS 750), Shriver Papers, MdHS.

40. James McHenry wrote George Washington favoring an appointment for Robert Purviance because "he has met with severe misfortunes. . . . In a few months him and his family, from being one of the most opulent in this town, will be one of the most distressed" (17 April 1789, reel 122, George Washington Papers, LC). See, in the same collection, Samuel Smith to Washington, 8 Aug. 1793, reel 122; and Washington to John E. Howard, 25 Aug. 1793, 33:66-67, Washington to James McHenry, 28 Aug. 1793, 33:72-73, John C. Fitzpatrick, ed., *The Writings of George Washington from the Original Manuscript Sources, 1745-1799*.

41. Other Baltimore merchant families, such as the Hollingsworths and the Purviances in the first party era and the McKims in the first and second party periods, would be just as appropriate. For Smith's career, see Frank A. Cassell, *Merchant Congressman in the Young Republic*.

42. Baltimore *Republican; or, Anti-Democrat*, 25 Oct. 1802. In the same vein, consider the advice from William Smith to his grandson, William Elie Williams, suggesting the desirability of courting Samuel Smith's daughter, for "she is said to be amiable [and] he will give $100,000" (Smith to Williams, 20 Dec. 1808, Otho Holland Williams Papers, MdHS).

43. For a short treatment of his life, see Bernard C. Steiner, "General John Spear Smith," pp. 213-20.

44. Other merchant families might include those of Solomon Etting and Jacob Cohen; see Aaron Baroway, "Solomon Etting," pp. 56-57; "The Cohens of Maryland," pp. 357-76, pp. 54-77.

45. See Stuart W. Bruchey, *Robert Oliver*. Mrs. Oliver's niece married Nicholas Biddle in 1811. His two sons, Charles and Thomas Oliver, were not active in local political affairs.

46. As an indication of Oliver's covert activity, see James McHenry to Oliver, 2 Oct. 1799, James McHenry Papers, LC.

47. See, as examples of Colt's economic activities, the following letters: Nicholas Biddle to Colt, 6 May 1831, reel 43, and Roswell L. Colt to Biddle, 30 Sept., 22 Nov. 1834, reel 19, 23 March 1835, reel 20, Nicholas Biddle Papers, LC; and Colt to Jonathan Meredith, 29 June 1831, Jonathan Meredith Papers, LC.

48. On 12 Feb. 1835, Philip Hone wrote in his diary: "It is somewhat remarkable that

the three men who held the most distinguished place in the community of merchants which imparted wealth, splendor, and character to Baltimore have all died within about a year, leaving good names and large fortunes to their children. Alexander Brown, Robert Oliver, and William Patterson might at one time have been considered the royal merchants of America, as the Medici of old were of Italy" (Allan Nevins, ed., *The Diary of Philip Hone, 1828–1851*, p. 148). Oliver's status is also revealed in his correspondence: Oliver to President, 18 Oct. 1831, reel 10, Oliver to Secretary of State, 20 Dec. 1834, reel 8, Jackson Recommendations; N. Biddle to Oliver, 16 Jan. 1832, reel 44, Oliver to Biddle, 26 Nov. 1834, reel 19, Biddle Papers.

49. Patterson's sons, John, Edward, Henry, and Joseph W. Patterson, belonged to the propertied or commercial elites in the second party era.

50. Philip Laurenson's status in the local Jackson party was indicated in various letters of recommendation for a federal patronage positon; see the correspondence on reel 13/569–88 from local political leaders in the Jackson Recommendations.

51. Writing in his diary, 2 Oct. 1826, Lyde Goodwin observed: "Col. Small is a house Carpenter of very industrious habits, and well disposed to do his duty. He is deficient in education, but understands thoroughly the wants, and [the needs] of the city. He is not, it is true, the best man that could [have] been selected, but, any change is for the better and [should he] fail to give satisfaction it will be an easy matter to remove him at the expiration of his term" (Lyde Goodwin Diary, 2 Oct. 1826, Lloyd Papers).

52. Vansant's official biography, *BDAC*, p. 1749, neglects to indicate that he served the state legislature in 1833; see also Vansant to Benjamin Chew Howard, 7, 18, 19 March 1839, Howard Papers.

53. See Samuel S. Shriver, comp. and ed., *History of the Shriver Family and Their Connections, 1684–1888.*

54. For the division within the Frederick County Jeffersonians, which was manifested in a public dispute between Samuel Barnes, the editor of the party paper, and Abraham Shriver, a major party leader, see Abraham Shriver to Andrew Shriver, 25 March 1821 (MS 750), Shriver Papers. Abraham Shriver had earlier been instrumental in obtaining the editorship for Barnes (Abraham Shriver to Andrew Shriver, 11 July 1813 [MS 750.1], ibid.).

55. John Schley (1767–1835) served as the clerk of the County Court from 1815 until his death in 1835. He had several sons who were community leaders in the second party era: David Schley (1797–1852) belonged to the positional and commercial elites and edited the Fredericktown *Examiner*; Edward Schley (1804–?) belonged to the propertied elite; Henry Schley (1793–?) belonged to the commercial and propertied elites; William Schley (1799–1872) was an attorney, who belonged to the decisional and positional elites and moved to Baltimore City in 1837.

Chapter 7

1. For a thought-provoking analysis of Tocqueville's insights, see Robert A. Nisbet, *The Sociological Tradition*, pp. 120–32.

2. George W. Pierson best described the method used by Tocqueville and Beaumont: "They began with a number of observed phenomena. From these, by inductive reasoning, they inferred a general principle governing American society. The general law ascertained, they began to deduce from it all its consequences for similarly organized societies" (*Tocqueville in America*, p. 52; see also pp. 457–68).

3. According to Tocqueville, "It was the law of inheritance which caused the final advance of equality"; and "The wealthy class in the United States are almost entirely outside politics and that wealth, so far as being an advantage there, is a real cause of disfavor and an obstacle to gaining power" (Alexis de Tocqueville, *Democracy in America*, pp. 51, 179).

4. Pierson, *Tocqueville in America*, p. 111.

5. See Chilton Williamson, *American Suffrage*.

6. The most sensitive treatment of the social dimensions of egalitarianism and its implications is in Lee Benson, *The Concept of Jacksonian Democracy*, esp. pp. 336–38.

7. See Edward Pessen, *Riches, Class, and Power before the Civil War*.

8. John H. B. Latrobe to Tocqueville, 30 Oct. 1831, Pierson, *Tocqueville in America*, p. 316.

9. This trend is unnoticed in two of the major treatments of the second party system. See James S. Chase, *Emergence of the Presidential Nominating Convention, 1789–1832*, and Richard P. McCormick, *The Second American Party System*.

10. See especially Pessen, *Riches, Class, and Power*, pp. 281–301; Robert Doherty, *Society and Power*, pp. 82–102. This position is also implicit in the two books by Ralph A. Wooster, *The People in Power* and *Politicians, Planters, and Plain Folk*, and in Robert E. Leipheimer, "Maryland Political Leadership, 1789–1860," Master's thesis, University of Maryland, 1969.

11. The limitations of this approach are elaborated in Whitman H. Ridgway, "Measuring Wealth and Power in Ante-Bellum America," but especially in Lee Benson et al., "Propositions on Economic Strata and Groups, Social Classes, Ruling Classes," paper presented at the Social Science Historical Association convention, Philadelphia, 30 Oct. 1976.

Appendix I

1. Several excellent review articles analyze the state of elite analysis. See especially Lee Benson, "Political Power and Political Elites," pp. 281–309; William A. Welsh, "Methodological Problems in the Study of Political Leadership in Latin America," pp. 3–34; and Carl Beck and James M. Malloy, "Political Elites."

2. The literature on community power is conveniently described in several guides: Willis D. Hawley and James H. Svara, *The Study of Community Power*; Claire W. Gilbert, *Community Power Structure*; and Carl Beck and J. Thomas McKechnie, comps., *Political Elites*.

3. Robert V. Presthus, *Men at the Top*; Chap. 1, but especially p. 9; Robert A. Dahl, *Who Governs?* pp. 89–103.

4. Benson, "Political Power and Political Elites," p. 286.

5. For his complete definition, see ibid., pp. 286–87.

6. Dahl's clearest statement appeared in his essay, "A Critique of the Ruling Elite Model," pp. 463–64; see also Nelson W. Polsby, *Community Power and Political Theory*, pp. 3–5; and Raymond E. Wolfinger, *The Politics of Progress*, pp. 7–12.

7. Presthus, *Men at the Top*, p. 5.

8. Charles Kadushin, "Power, Influence and Social Circles," p. 686.

9. Benson, "Political Power and Political Elites," p. 288.

10. Benson defines a political elite as follows: "In any political system, the political elite consists of those individuals who may or may not hold government office but who do hold relatively much greater political power than other individuals" (ibid., p. 289). Andrew McFarland defined a leader "as one who has unusual *influence*. Influence may be viewed as one's capacity to make people behave differently than they would have otherwise. A leader may also be defined as one who has unusual *power*. Here we view 'power' as a person's capacity to make others do something that they would not do otherwise and that the person specifically wants or intends" (*Power and Leadership in Pluralist Systems*, p. 154).

11. A good collection of responses to this work is provided by G. William Domhoff and Hoyt B. Ballard, comps., *C. Wright Mills and the Power Elite*. For a discussion of the positional method, see Terry N. Clark, ed., *Community Structure and Decision Making*, pp. 73–74; Marvin Olson, ed., *Power in Societies*, Chap. 5; and Linton C. Freeman et al., "Locating Leaders in Local Communities," pp. 791–98.

12. See especially Talcott Parsons, "The Distribution of Power in American Society," pp. 60–87; and Daniel Bell, "The *Power Elite* Reconsidered," pp. 189–225.

13. See Ralph A. Wooster, *The People in Power* and *Politicians, Planters and Plain Folk*.

14. Peter H. Rossi suggested another dimension of the positional approach: "The pattern taken by the power structure of a community is a function of the kind of political life to be found therein" ("Power and Community Structure," in Clark, ed., *Community Structure*, p. 132).

15. Floyd Hunter, *Community Power Structure*. For comments on Hunter's approach, see Clark, ed., *Community Structure*, pp. 74–78; Polsby, *Community Power*, pp. 45–56.

16. Hunter presents his methodology in *Community Power Structure*, pp. 11–12, 256–57.

17. Presthus, *Men at the Top*, p. 57.

18. Hunter, *Community Power Structure*, p. 11. Hunter also defined power as "a word that will be used to describe the acts of men going about the business of moving other men to act in relation to themselves or in relation to organic or inorganic things" (ibid., p. 2).

19. Ibid., p. 61.

20. See William V. D'Antonio et al., "Institutional and Occupational Representations in Eleven Community Influence Systems," pp. 319–32; D'Antonio and E. C. Erickson, "The Reputational Technique as a Measure of Community Power," pp. 362–76; Charles M. Bonjean, "Community Leadership," pp. 672–81; Lawrence J. R. Hershon, "In the Footsteps of Community Power," pp. 817–30.

21. William A. Gamson, "Reputation and Resources in Community Politics," p. 131.

22. Ibid., p. 124.

23. Another study that recommends testable refinements is M. Herbert Danzger, "Community Power Structure," pp. 707–17.

24. Raymond E. Wolfinger, "Reputation and Reality in the Study of Community Leadership," pp. 636–38; Polsby, *Community Power*, pp. 48–49.

25. Raymond E. Wolfinger, "A Plea for a Decent Burial," p. 844.

26. Wolfinger, "Reputation and Reality," pp. 642–43.

27. Polsby, *Community Power*, p. 48.

28. Wolfinger observes: "The reputational method, then, does not do what it is supposed to do: the ranking of leaders is not a valid representation of the distribution of political power in a given community" ("Reputation and Reality," p. 642).

29. Polsby, *Community Power*, p. 51.

30. Polsby, "Community Power," p. 839.

31. Polsby commented: "All of these issues were either trivial or clearly of predominant concern to businessmen, or both. Furthermore, they seem to have been issues on which Hunter's 'power elite' met with relative success, in contrast to other issues Hunter lists, of much wider concern to the community, where the 'power elite' was either split wide open or unified but ineffective" (Polsby, *Community Power*, p. 54).

32. Wolfinger, "Plea for a Decent Burial," p. 841.

33. Howard J. Ehrlich, "The Reputational Approach to the Study of Community Power," p. 927; William V. D'Antonio, H. J. Ehrlich, and E. C. Erickson, "Further Notes on the Study of Community Power," pp. 848–53; Clark, ed., *Community Structure*, p. 77; Gamson, "Reputation and Resources," pp. 130–31; Danzger, "Community Power Structure," pp. 707–17.

34. Polsby, *Community Power*, p. 113.

35. "But if, even in America, with its universal creed of democracy and equality, there are great inequalities in the conditions of different citizens, must there not also be great inequalities in the capacities of different citizens to influence the decisions of their various governments? And if, because they are unequal in other conditions, citizens of a democracy are unequal in power to control their government, then who in fact does govern? How does a 'democratic' system work amid inequality of resources?" (Dahl, *Who Governs?* p. 3).

36. Dahl, "A Critique of the Ruling Elite Model," p. 466.

37. Dahl, *Who Governs?* pp. 333–34. Polsby, reacting to criticism of issue selection, makes the general criteria more explicit in *Community Power*, pp. 95–96.

38. Polsby, *Community Power*, p. 95; Dahl, *Who Governs?* pp. 102–3.

39. Peter Bachrach and Morton S. Baratz commented on this problem in important articles, "Decisions and Nondecisions," and "Two Faces of Power," which are reprinted in their book, *Power and Poverty*. See also Raymond E. Wolfinger, "Nondecisions and the Study of Local Politics," pp. 1063–80; Frederick W. Frey, "Comment," pp. 1081–1101; Wolfinger, "Rejoinder," pp. 1102–4.

40. D'Antonio et al., "Further Notes," p. 853; McFarland, *Power and Leadership*, p. 226; Richard M. Merelman, "On the Neo-Elitist Critique of Community Power," pp. 451–60.

41. See the introduction in Baltzell, *Philadelphia Gentlemen*, pp. 3–14.

42. Polsby, *Community Power*, pp. 14–24.

43. Ibid., pp. 24–30, 42–44.

44. Baltzell, *Philadelphia Gentlemen*, pp. 131, 364–83.

45. For a discussion of this approach, see Benson, "Political Power and Political Elites," pp. 297–98; and Charles Kadushin, "Power, Influence and Social Circles."

46. John T. Walton, "Substance and Artifact," p. 438.

47. Freeman et al., "Locating Leaders in Local Communities," p. 798; see also Linton C. Freeman et al., *Patterns of Local Community Leadership*.

48. See Presthus, *Men at the Top*, pp. 53–54, 74, 89, 137–38, 159; for another example, see John T. Walton, "Development Decision Making," pp. 828–51.

49. See esp. Hunter, *Community Power Structure*, p. 255; Dahl, *Who Governs?* p. 334.

50. A contemporary study tried to use newspapers as a reputational source from which leaders were ranked; see Howard J. Ehrlich and Mary L. Bauer, "Newspaper Citation and Reputation for Community Leadership," pp. 411–15.

51. Most manuscript collections contain only incoming letters; letters sent are to be found most often in the collections of the recipients. One is delighted to discover a letter containing the admonishment "burn this," but must wonder how many letters from that individual were actually burned. Furthermore, there is evidence that some people wrote letters "for the record" that then were deposited in their collections. Such material must be used judiciously and with caution.

52. Polsby suggested that decisions be ranked by: (1) how many people are affected by outcomes; (2) how many different kinds of community resources are distributed by outcomes; (3) how much in amount of resources are distributed by outcomes; (4) how drastically present resource distributions are altered by outcomes (*Community Power*, p. 96). My evaluation is grounded on a content analysis of selected newspapers in the 1830s; see my dissertation, "A Social Analysis of Maryland Community Elites, 1827–1836: A Study of the Distribution of Power in Baltimore City, Frederick County, and Talbot County," University of Pennsylvania, 1973, pp. 79–93. Based upon my evaluation of the importance of these issues in an earlier time, supported by my impressions after researching widely in period newspapers, I feel that these were the major issues.

53. The power literature contains few examples of numerical scoring. Robert Presthus, who developed one for his study, observed: "In making these assignments, we depended primarily upon our *Verstehen* as to the nature and importance of each leader's role in a given issue" (*Men at the Top*, p. 189).

54. In Baltimore City, nomination conventions were called by the central committees of the party or by the party newspaper. For the Jackson party, see Baltimore *Republican and Commercial Advertiser*, 28 March, 11 Aug. 1829, 3 Sept. 1830, 21 June, 25 Oct. 1831, 3 Sept., 8 Dec. 1832, 28 Apr., 13 Aug. 1834. For the Anti-Jackson party, see Baltimore *Patriot and Mercantile Advertiser*, 28 June 1828, 14 Aug. 1834, 11 Sept., 24 Nov., 3 Dec. 1835; Baltimore *Commercial Chronicle and Daily Marylander*, 30 Aug. 1830, 15 June 1832, 19 July 1833. See also Central Committee, National Republican Party (Baltimore) to James Moores, 24 Aug. 1832, encouraging circulation of the campaign paper, Moores Correspondence, Harford County Papers, MdHS. In the rural areas, many of which lacked central committees, the newspapers fulfilled this function.

55. Editors were scored five points for each year of activity; local central committee members, three points; city-district central committee members, eight points; secretary of the central committee, nine points; and chairman of the central committee, ten points.

56. For a development of the concept of strategic elites and a clear examination of their role in a modern context, see Suzanne I. Keller, *Beyond the Ruling Class*.

57. As examples of such studies, see E. Daniel Potts, "The Progressive Profile in Iowa," pp. 257–68; William T. Kerr, Jr., "The Progressives of Washington, 1910–1912,"

pp. 16–27; Heinz Eulau and David Koff, "Occupational Mobility and Political Career," pp. 507–21; and Lester G. Seligman, "Political Change," pp. 177–87.

58. Herbert Jacob, "Initial Recruitment of Elected Officials in the U.S.," p. 706.

59. Lawrence Stone, "Prosopography," p. 46.

60. Lewis J. Edinger and Donald D. Searing observe: "By and large, applications of the social background approach have left unanswered the question of how and to what extent data of this nature actually can be used to forecast attitudinal distributions. Which social background variables best predict which attitude under what condition" ("Social Background in Elite Analysis," p. 431). See also William J. Hanna, "Political Recruitment and Participation," pp. 407–20.

61. See American Council of Learned Societies, "Report of Committee on Linguistic and National Stocks in the Population of the United States," and David A. Bohmer's Frederick County test data on file at the Maryland Hall of Records.

62. During the first party era, some of the tax records gave valuations in Maryland pounds. For the sake of comparability, all such data were converted to dollars.

63. These data are conveniently found in G. Ronald Teeples, comp., *Maryland*, and Bettie S. Carothers, comp., *Maryland Slave Owners and Superintendents, 1798*.

64. For the code book, see Ridgway, "A Social Analysis," pp. 378–83.

Bibliography

PRIMARY SOURCES

Collections of Personal and Political Papers

Annapolis, Maryland
  Maryland Hall of Records
    Adjutant Generals Papers
    Frederick County. County Commissioners. Tax Ledgers, 1797, 1835
    Gift Collection. James Thomas Papers
    Minutes of the Executive Council, 1790–1810, 1826–36
    St. Marys County. County Commissioners. Tax Ledgers, 1800, 1831
    State Papers, 1788–1837
    Talbot County. County Commissioners. Tax Ledgers, 1798, 1826, 1832
Baltimore, Maryland
  Baltimore City Hall, Records Management Office, Department of the Treasurer
    Tax Ledgers, 1798?, 1799, 1800, 1803, 1828, 1834
  Maryland Historical Society
    Bayard Papers (MS 109)
    Dielman-Hayward File
    Harper-Pennington Papers (MS 431)
    Howard Papers (MS 469)
    James Johnson Papers (MS 1604)
    John H. B. Latrobe Diaries (MS 1677)
    John Leigh Papers (MS 1755)
    Edward Lloyd Papers (MS 2001)
    McHenry Family Papers (MS 647)
    Maryland Diocesan Archives of the Protestant Episcopal Church
    Moores Correspondence, Harford County Historical Society Papers (MS 2000)
    Potts Papers (MS 1392)
    Shriver Papers (MSS 750, 750.1, 2085, 2085.3)
    Vertical File
    Otho Holland Williams Papers (MS 908)
Boston, Massachusetts
  Massachusetts Historical Society
    Edward Everett Papers
Chapel Hill, North Carolina
  University of North Carolina
    Duff Green Papers, Southern Historical Collection

Durham, North Carolina
  Perkins Library, Duke University
    David Campbell Papers
    Charles Magill Papers
    William Potts Papers
    Francis Thomas Papers
    William Tilghman Papers
New York, New York
  New York Historical Society
    Rufus King Papers
    Miscellaneous Manuscripts
  New York Public Library
    Robert Goodloe Harper Papers
Philadelphia, Pennsylvania
  Historical Society of Pennsylvania
    Gratz Collection
    Hollingsworth Papers
    Society Collection
    William Tilghman Papers
Princeton, New Jersey
  Firestone Library, Princeton University
    Blair-Lee Papers
    Benjamin F. Butler Papers
Washington, D.C.
  Manuscript Division, Library of Congress
    Nicholas Biddle Papers
    Blair-Rives Papers
    Bozman-Kerr Papers
    Caleb Cushing Papers
    William Darlington Papers
    Andrew Jackson Donelson Papers
    Galloway-Maxcy-Markoe Papers
    Robert G. Harper Papers
    James McHenry Papers
    Jonathan Meredith Papers
    Joseph H. Nicholson Papers
    William C. Rives Family Papers
    Samuel Smith Papers
    Martin Van Buren Papers
    George Washington Papers
  National Archives and Records Service
    Records of the Legislative Branch, Records of the U.S. Senate, Record
      Group 46
      Nomination Papers of the U.S. Senate, 1789–1901
    Records of the Executive Branch, Records of the Department of State,
      Record Group 59

Letters of Application and Recommendation during the Administration of John Q. Adams, 1825–29, National Archives Microfilm Publication M-531

Letters of Application and Recommendation during the Administration of Andrew Jackson, 1829–37, National Archives Microfilm Publication M-639

Letters of Application and Recommendation during the Administration of Thomas Jefferson, 1801–9, National Archives Microfilm Publication M-418

Letters of Application and Recommendation during the Administration of James Monroe, 1817–25, National Archives Microfilm Publication M-439

Miscellaneous Correspondence, Miscellaneous Letters Received Regarding Publishers of the Laws, 1789–1875

Records of the Executive Branch, Records of the Department of the Treasury, Record Group 56

Collectors of the Customs: Applications, Maryland, Baltimore

Letters Received from Collectors of the Customs, 1833–69, National Archives Microfilm Publication M-174

Records of the Executive Branch, Records of the Department of the Interior, National Park Service, Record Group 48

Records of the Chesapeake and Ohio Canal Company

Religious Manuscript Materials

Annapolis, Maryland

Maryland Hall of Records

All Saints Parish, Frederick County. Register

————. Vestry Records, vol. 1 (1807–53)

Methodist Records (Film No. 411), containing: East Baltimore Station, 3, Church Register , 1829–36

E. B. Station, 2 (Fells Point), Church Register, 1818–28

E. B. Station, 1, Church Register, 1800–1818

Ebenezer Baptist Church, 1821

Reinicke, E. W., trans. Index of Births and Baptisms, in the Evangelical Reformed Church in Frederick, Maryland, 1746–1951

Zahn, C. T., trans. First Record Book for the Reformed Congregation of St. Benjamin's, or Kreider's Church at Pipe Creek (Frederick County), Md.

Baltimore, Maryland

Maryland Historical Society

Associate Reformed Congregation, Baltimore: Register, 1812–65

Church of the Ascension, Baltimore: Register

English Lutheran Church, Baltimore: Register

Evangelical Lutheran Church, Fredericktown: Vital Records, 1742–1807, 1810–50

First Christian Church of Baltimore: Records, 1810–92 .

First Evangelical Lutheran Church, Baltimore: Records, 1823
German Evangelical Reformed Church (Old Otterbein), Baltimore: Records, 1798–1850
German Reformed Church, First, Baltimore: Records
Methodist Episcopal Church, First, Baltimore: Records
————, Light Street, Baltimore: Burial Records
New Jerusalem (Swedenborgen) Church, Baltimore: Register, 1793–1862
Presbyterian Church, Faith, Baltimore: Inscriptions, Tombstones
————, First, Baltimore: Records, 1767–1879
————, Second, Baltimore: Records
————, Baltimore, Westminster Cemetery: Records
Protestant Episcopal Church: Maryland Diocesan Archives
————, Christ's Church Parish, Baltimore: Register of Marriage, Baptism, and Burials, 1828–71
————, St. Paul's, Baltimore: Records
————, St. Peter's, Baltimore: Register, 1803–95
————, Trinity, Baltimore: Records
Roman Catholic Church, Baltimore: Burial Records, 3 vols. and Index
Unitarian Church (Independent Church of Baltimore), First, Baltimore: Records

Published Public Documents

Federal

U.S. Bureau of the Census. *First Census of the U.S., 1790*. Philadelphia: Childs and Swain, 1791.
————. *Second Census of the U.S., 1800*. Washington, D.C.: William Duane, 1801.
————. *Third Census of the U.S., 1810*. Washington, D.C.: n.p., 1811.
————. *Fourth Census of the U.S., 1820*. Washington, D.C.: Gales and Seaton, 1821.
————. *Fifth Census of the U.S., 1830: Compendium*. Washington, D.C.: Duff Green, 1832.
————. *Sixth Census of the U.S., 1840: Compendium of Enumeration*. Washington, D.C.: Thomas Allen, 1841.
————. *Seventh Census of the U.S., 1850: Statistical View*. James D. B. DeBow, comp. Washington, D.C.: Beverly Tucker, 1851.
————. *Historical Statistics of the U.S., Colonial Times to 1970*. 2 vols. Washington, D.C.: U.S. Government Printing Office, 1975.
U.S. Senate. *Journal of Executive Proceedings, 1829–69*. 20 vols. Washington, D.C.: U.S. Government Printing Office, 1884–1901.

State

Archives of Maryland. 72 vols. Baltimore: Maryland Historical Society, 1883–1972.
Intendant of the Revenue, 1784. *An Account of the Gross and Average Value of the Land*. Annapolis: n.p., 1784.

Journal and Proceedings of the House of Delegates. Annapolis: 1790–1837.
Journal and Proceedings of the Senate. Annapolis, 1790–1837.
Laws of Maryland. Annapolis, 1793–1841.

Local
   Ordinances of the Mayor and City Council of Baltimore. Annual Reports. Baltimore, 1820–36.

Newspapers

District of Columbia, Washington
   Globe. 1832.
   National Intelligencer. 1827–35.
   National Journal. 1827–30.
Maryland
   Annapolis, Anne Arundel County
      Carrolltonian. 1827–29.
      Maryland Gazette. 1794–1836.
      Maryland Republican. 1823–39.
   Baltimore City, Baltimore County
      American and Commercial Advertiser. 1799–1810, 1823–37.
      American Patriot and Fells Point Advertiser. 1803.
      Baltimore Daily Intelligencer. 1794.
      Baltimore Daily Repository. 1792–93.
      Commercial Chronicle and Daily Marylander. 1829–33.
      Democratic-Republican; or Anti-Aristocrat. 1802.
      Eagle of Freedom; or, the Baltimore Town and Fell's Point Gazette. 1796.
      Edward's Baltimore Daily Advertiser. 1793.
      Federal Gazette and Baltimore Daily Advertiser. 1796–1810, 1827–35.
      Federal Intelligencer. 1798–99.
      Fells Point Telegraphe. 1795.
      Freeman's Banner. 1831–32.
      Jefferson Reformer and Baltimore Daily Advertiser. 1836.
      Maryland Journal and the Baltimore Advertiser. 1783–94.
      Marylander. 1827–29.
      Niles Weekly Register. 1820–36.
      Patriot and Mercantile Advertiser. 1823–36.
      Republican and Commercial Advertiser. 1827–36.
      Republican; or, Anti-Democrat. 1802.
      Telegraphe and Daily Advertiser. 1795–1805.
      Voice of the People. 1836.
      Whig. 1807–9.
   Bel Air, Harford County
      Bond of Union and Harford County Advertiser. 1823, 1828–29.
      Independent Citizen. 1828–35.
   Cambridge, Dorchester County
      Cambridge Chronicle. 1826–36.

396   Bibliography

Dorchester Aurora. 1835–36.
Cecil, Cecil County
   Cecil Gazette and Farmers' and Mechanics' Advertiser. 1835.
   Cecil Whig and Port Deposit Courier. 1835.
Centreville, Queen Annes County
   Centreville Times and Eastern Shore Advertiser. 1828–34.
Chestertown, Kent County
   Chestertown Telegraph. 1828–29.
   Kent Bugle. 1834–35.
Cumberland, Allegany County
   Maryland Advocate. 1823–31, 1833–35.
   Weekly Civilian. 1828–36.
Easton, Talbot County
   Eastern Shore Whig and People's Advocate. 1830–36.
   Easton Gazette. 1826–36.
   Maryland Herald and Eastern Shore Intelligencer. 1795–1804
   Republican Star. 1802–6, 1823–26, 1828.
Elkton, Cecil County
   Elkton Press. 1824, 1827, 1828–29.
Fredericktown, Frederick County
   Anti-Jacksonian. 1828
   Bartgis's Federal Gazette. 1796–1801.
   Bartgis's Republican Gazette. 1801–9, 1823–24.
   Frederick-Town Herald. 1802–7, 1824, 1831–35.
   Hornet. 1803–6.
   Independent American Volunteer. 1808.
   Maryland Weekly Times. 1832–34.
   Political Examiner and Public Advertiser. 1823–26, 1828–29, 1835–36.
   Political Intelligencer or Republican Gazette. 1824–25.
   Republican Advocate. 1802–5, 1807–8.
   Reservoir and Public Reflector. 1823–24, 1828.
   Rights of Man. 1795–1800.
Hagerstown, Washington County
   Courier and Enquirer. 1834–35.
   Farmer's Register and Maryland Herald. 1828.
   Hagerstown Mail. 1830–35.
   Maryland Herald and Hagerstown Weekly Advertiser. 1808.
   Our Country. 1828.
   Torch Light and Public Advertiser. 1823–24, 1827, 1828–35.
Princess Anne, Somerset County
   People's Press. 1836.
   Somerset Iris and Messenger of Truth. 1828–29.
   Village Herald. 1827–36.
Rockville, Montgomery County
   Maryland Journal and True American. 1825–26, 1828, 1830–34.
   True American and Farmer's Register. 1824.

Snow Hill, Worcester County
   Borderer, 1834–35.
   Snow Hill Messenger. 1828, 1830–33.
Williamsport, Washington County
   Republican Banner. 1830–31, 1836.

Pennsylvania
Philadelphia
   Porcupine's Gazette. 1798–99.

Directories, Registers, and Finding Aids

Baltimore: Past and Present, with Biographical Sketches of Its Representative Men: Baltimore: Richardson and Bennett, 1871.

Biographical Cyclopaedia of Representative Men of Maryland and the District of Columbia. Baltimore: National Biographical Publishing Co., 1879.

Biographical Directory of the American Congress, 1774–1961. Washington, D.C.: U.S. Government Printing Office, 1961.

Boyle, Esmeralda. *Biographical Sketches of Distinguished Marylanders*. Baltimore: Kelly, Piet, and Co., 1877.

Brigham, Clarence S. *History and Bibliography of American Newspapers, 1690–1820*. 2 vols. Worcester, Mass.: American Antiquarian Society, 1947.

Cordell, Eugene F. *Medical Annals of Maryland, 1799–1899*. Baltimore: n.p., 1903.

Coyle, Wilbur F. *The Mayors of Baltimore*. Baltimore: n.p., 1919.

Hofstetter, Eleanore O., and Eustis, Marcella S., comps. *Newspapers in Maryland Libraries: A Union List*. Baltimore: Division of Library Development Services, Maryland State Department of Education, 1977.

Hughes, Jeremiah, comp. *The Maryland Pocket Annual*. Annapolis: J. Hughes, 1833–40.

Johnson, Allen, and Malone, Dumas, eds. *Dictionary of American Biography*. 22 vols. New York: Charles Scribners Sons, 1928–58.

Lanman, Charles. *Biographical Annals of the Civil Government of the United States during Its First Century*. Washington, D.C.: James Anglim, 1876.

Matchett, J. W., comp. *Matchett's Baltimore Director*. Baltimore: J. W. Matchett, 1824–37.

Minick, Amanda R. *A History of Printing in Maryland, 1791–1800*. Baltimore: Enoch Pratt Free Library, 1949.

National Cyclopaedia of American Biography. 50 vols. New York: J. T. White and Co., 1893–1968.

The New Baltimore Directory and Annual Register for 1800–1801. Baltimore: Warner and Hanna, 1801.

Passano, Eleanor P. *An Index to the Source Records of Maryland: Genealogical, Biographical, Historical*. 1940; repr. Baltimore: Genealogical Publishing Co., 1967.

Pedley, Avril J. M. *The Manuscript Collections of the Maryland Historical Society*. Baltimore: Maryland Historical Society, 1968.

Portrait and Biographical Record of the Sixth Congressional District, Maryland, Containing Portraits and Biographies of Many Well Known Citizens Past and Present. New York: Chapman Publishing Co., 1898.

Queenan, John R. *Medical Annals of Baltimore.* Baltimore: Isaac Friedenwald, 1884.

Radoff, Morris, et al. *The County Courthouses and Records of Maryland.* Publication No. 13. Pt. 1: *The Courthouses*; pt. 2: *The Records.* Annapolis: Hall of Records Commission, 1960, 1963.

Sams, Conway W., and Riley, E. S. *The Bench and Bar of Maryland: A History 1634–1901.* 2 vols. Chicago: Lewis Publishing Co., 1901.

Scott, Joseph. *United States Gazetteer.* Philadelphia: F. R. Baily, 1795.

U.S. Department of State. *Register of All Officers and Agents, Civil, Military, and Naval in the Service of the U.S.* Washington, D.C., 1824–37.

U.S. Department of the Treasury. *Message from the President of the U.S., Transmitting a Roll of Persons Having Office or Employment under the U.S.* Washington, D.C.: William Duane, 1802.

Varle, Charles. *Complete View of Baltimore.* Baltimore: Samuel Young, 1833.

West, Elizabeth H., ed. *Calendar of the Martin Van Buren Papers.* Washington, D.C.: U.S. Government Printing Office, 1910.

Wheeler, Joseph T. *The Maryland Press, 1777–90.* Baltimore: Maryland Historical Society, 1931.

White, Frank, Jr. *The Governors of Maryland, 1777–1970.* Publication No. 15. Annapolis: Hall of Records Commission, 1970.

Published Correspondence and Autobiographies

[Allison, Patrick] "Vindex." *Candid Animadversions . . .* Baltimore: Hays and Killen, 1783.

"Autobiography of John Nelson." *Maryland Historical Magazine* 51 (March 1956): 56–57.

"Baltimore Town, Committee Chamber, 2 Dec. 1784." Broadside.

Fitzpatrick, John C., ed. *The Writings of George Washington from the Original Manuscript Sources, 1745–1799.* 39 vols. 1940; repr. Westport, Conn.: Greenwood Press, 1970.

"The James Forrest Papers." *Chronicles of St. Marys* 16 (1968): 243–49; 17 (1969): 255–60, 271–79, 295–300, 315–24.

Gibbs, George. *Memoirs of the Administrations of George Washington and John Adams Edited from the Papers of Oliver Wolcott.* 2 vols. New York: William Van Norden, 1846.

Gilmor, Robert, Jr. "The Diary of Robert Gilmor." *Maryland Historical Magazine* 17 (Sept. 1922): 231–68; (Dec. 1922): 319–47.

Gough, Peter. *A Refutation . . .* Baltimore: William Woddy, 1828.

[Harper, Robert Goodloe] "Bystander." *Bystander: Or a Series of Letters.* Baltimore: Yundt and Brown, 1800.

Harrison, Samuel A., ed. "Memoirs of the Hon. William Hindman." Maryland Historical Society, *Fund Publications*, no. 14, pp. 5–59. Baltimore: n.p., 1880.

To the Honorable the General Assembly of Maryland The Petition of the Subscribers, Inhabitants of the Upper Part of Baltimore County and the Lower Part of Frederick County, Hereby Submit . . . Annapolis: Frederick Green, 1785.

Jameson, J. Franklin, ed. *Correspondence of John C. Calhoun.* American Historical Association, *Annual Report*, 1899. Washington, D.C.: U.S. Government Printing Office, 1900.

King, Charles R., ed. *Life and Correspondence of Rufus King.* 5 vols. New York: G. P. Putnam's Sons, 1884–1900.

Latrobe, John H. B. "Reminiscences of Baltimore in 1824." *Maryland Historical Magazine* 1 (June 1906): 113–24.

Lloyd, James. *Address of General James Lloyd to the Citizens of Kent and Queen Annes Counties, in Answer to the Late Calumnious Charge Made against him by Robert Wright.* Annapolis: Frederick Green, 1794.

Minutes of the Methodist Conferences, 1773 to 1813. New York: John C. Totten, 1813.

Morison, Samuel E. *Life and Letters of Harrison Gray Otis, 1765–1848.* 2 vols. New York: Houghton Mifflin Co., 1913.

Nevins, Allan. ed. *The Diary of John Quincy Adams, 1794–1845.* 1928; repr. New York: Frederick Ungar Publishing Co., 1969.

_____. *The Diary of Philip Hone, 1828–1851.* 1927; repr. New York: Kraus Reprint Co., 1969.

Papenfuse, Edward C. "An Undelivered Defense of a Winning Cause: Charles Carroll of Carrollton's 'Remarks on the Proposed Federal Constitution.'" *Maryland Historical Magazine* 71 (Summer 1976): 220–51.

Rowland, Kate Mason. *The Life of Charles Carroll of Carrollton, 1737–1832, His Correspondence and Public Papers.* 2 vols. New York: G. P. Putnam's Sons, 1898.

Smith, Reverend William. *An Address to the Members of the Protestant Episcopal Church of Maryland . . .* Baltimore: Goddard, 1784.

Steiner, Bernard C. *Life and Correspondence of James McHenry.* Cleveland: Burrows Brothers Co., 1907.

"Two Letters of Charles Carroll of Carrollton." *Pennsylvania Magazine of History and Biography* 28 (1904): 216–17.

Washburn, Charles G., ed. "Letters of Thomas Boylston Adams." American Antiquarian Society *Proceedings*, n.s., 27 (1917): 83–176.

SECONDARY SOURCES

Methodology

Agger, Robert, et al. *The Rulers and the Ruled: Political Power and Impotence in American Communities.* New York: John Wiley and Sons, 1964.

Anton, Thomas J. "Power, Pluralism and Local Politics." *Administrative Science Quarterly* 7 (March 1963): 425–57.

_____. "Rejoinder." *Administrative Science Quarterly* 8 (Sept. 1963): 257–68.

Bachrach, Peter, and Baratz, Morton S. "Decisions and Nondecisions: An

Analytical Framework." *American Political Science Review* 57 (Sept. 1963): 632–42.

———. *Power and Poverty: Theory and Practice*. New York: Oxford University Press, 1970.

———. "Two Faces of Power." *American Political Science Review* 56 (Dec. 1962): 947–52.

Baltzell, E. Digby. *Philadelphia Gentlemen*. 1958; repr. New York: Free Press, 1966.

Beck, Carl, and Malloy, James M. "Political Elites: A Mode of Analysis." *Occasional Paper*. Pittsburgh: Archive on Political Elites in Eastern Europe, 1966.

Beck, Carl, and McKechnie, J. Thomas, comps. *Political Elites: A Select Computerized Bibliography*. Cambridge, Mass.: M.I.T. Press, 1968.

Bell, Daniel. "The *Power Elite* Reconsidered." In *C. Wright Mills and the Power Elite*, compiled by G. William Domhoff and Hoyt B. Ballard, pp. 189–225. Boston: Beacon Press, 1968.

Bell, Roderick; Edwards, David V.; and Wagner, R. Harrison, eds. *Political Power: A Reader in Theory and Research*. New York: Free Press, 1969.

Benson, Lee. *The Concept of Jacksonian Democracy: New York as a Test Case*. Princeton: Princeton University Press, 1961.

———. "Group Cohesion and Social and Ideological Conflict: A Critique of Some Marxian and Tocquevillian Theories." *American Behavioral Scientist* 16 (May–June 1973): 741–67.

———. "Political Power and Political Elites." In *American Political Behavior: Historical Essays and Readings*, edited by Lee Benson, Allan G. Bogue, J. Rogers Hollingsworth, Thomas J. Pressly, and Joel H. Silbey, pp. 281–309. New York: Harper and Row, 1974.

———. *Toward the Scientific Study of History: Selected Essays*. Philadelphia: J. B. Lippincott Co., 1972.

———; Gough, Robert; Harkavy, Ira; Levine, Marc; and Remington, Brodie. "Propositions on Economic Strata and Groups, Social Classes, Ruling Classes: A Strategic Natural Experiment, Philadelphia Economic and Prestige Elites, 1775–1860." Paper presented on 30 Oct. 1976 at the Philadelphia meeting of the Social Science History Association.

Blalock, Hubert M., Jr. *Social Statistics*. 2d ed. New York: McGraw Hill, 1972.

Bonjean, Charles M. "Community Leadership: A Case Study and Conceptual Refinement." *American Journal of Sociology* 68 (May 1963): 672–81.

Clark, Terry N., ed. *Community Structure and Decision Making: Comparative Analyses*. San Francisco: Chandler, 1968.

Dahl, Robert A. "The Concept of Power." In *Political Power: A Reader in Theory and Research*, edited by Roderick Bell et al., pp. 36–41. New York: Free Press, 1969.

———. "A Critique of the Ruling Elite Model." *American Political Science Quarterly* 52 (June 1958): 463–69.

———. "Further Reflections on 'The Elitist Theory of Democracy.'" *American Political Science Review* 60 (June 1966): 296–305.

————. "Letter to the Editor." *Administrative Science Quarterly* 8 (Sept. 1963): 250–56.

————. *Polyarchy: Participation and Opposition*. New Haven: Yale University Press, 1971.

————. *Who Governs? Democracy and Power in an American City*. New Haven: Yale University Press, 1961.

D'Antonio, William V.; Ehrlich, H. J.; and Erickson, E. C. "Further Notes on the Study of Community Power." *American Sociological Review* 27 (Dec. 1962): 848–53.

————, and Erickson, E. C. "The Reputational Technique as a Measure of Community Power: An Evaluation Based on Comparative and Longitudinal Studies." *American Sociological Review* 27 (June 1962): 362–76.

————; Form, William H.; Loomis, Charles P.; and Erickson, Eugene C. "Institutional and Occupational Representations in Eleven Community Influence Systems." In Clark, ed., *Community Structure and Decision Making*, pp. 319–32.

Danzger, M. Herbert. "Community Power Structure: Problems and Continuities." *American Sociological Review* 29 (Oct. 1964): 707–17.

Domhoff, G. William, and Ballard, Hoyt B., comps. *C. Wright Mills and the Power Elite*. Boston: Beacon Press, 1968.

Edinger, Lewis J., and Searing, Donald D. "Social Background in Elite Analysis: A Methodological Inquiry." *American Political Science Review* 61 (June 1967): 428–45.

Ehrlich, Howard J. "The Reputational Approach to the Study of Community Power." *American Sociological Review* 26 (Dec. 1961): 926–27.

————, and Bauer, Mary L. "Newspaper Citation and Reputation for Community Leadership." *American Sociological Review* 30 (June 1965): 411–15.

Eulau, Heinz, and Koff, David. "Occupational Mobility and Political Career." *Western Political Quarterly* 15 (Sept. 1962): 507–21.

Flinn, Thomas A., and Wirt, Frederick M. "Local Party Leaders: Groups of Like Minded Men." *Midwest Journal of Political Science* 9 (Feb. 1965): 77–98.

Freeman, Linton C. *Patterns of Local Community Leadership*. New York: Bobbs-Merrill, 1968.

————; Fararo, Thomas J.; Bloomberg, Warner, Jr.; and Sunshine, Morris, C. "Locating Leaders in Local Communities: A Comparison of Some Alternative Approaches." *American Sociological Review* 28 (Oct. 1963): 791–98.

Frey, Frederick W. "Comment." *American Political Science Review* 65 (Dec. 1971): 1081–1101.

Gamson, William A. "Reputation and Resources in Community Politics." *American Journal of Sociology* 72 (Sept. 1966): 121–31.

Gilbert, Claire W. *Community Power Structure*. University of Florida Social Science Monograph, no. 45. Gainesville: University of Florida Press, 1972.

Hanna, William J. "Political Recruitment and Participation: Some Suggested Areas for Research." *Psychoanalytic Review* 52 (Winter 1965–66): 407–20.

Hawley, Willis D., and Svara, James H. *The Study of Community Power: A Bibliographic Review*. Santa Barbara, Calif.: ABC-CLIO, 1972.

Hawley, Willis D., and Wirt, Frederick M., eds. *The Search for Community Power*. Englewood Cliffs, N.J.: Prentice Hall, 1968.

Hershon, Lawrence J. R. "In the Footsteps of Community Power." *American Political Science Review* 55 (Dec. 1961): 817–30.

Hunter, Floyd. *Community Power Structure: A Study of Decision Makers*. 1953; repr. New York: Anchor Books, 1961.

Jacob, Herbert. "Initial Recruitment of Elected Officials in the U.S.: A Model." *Journal of Politics* 24 (Nov. 1962): 703–16.

Kadushin, Charles. "Power, Influence and Social Circles: A New Methodology for Studying Opinion Makers." *American Sociological Review* 33 (Oct. 1968): 685–99.

Keller, Suzanne I. *Beyond the Ruling Class: Strategic Elites in Modern Society*. New York: Random House, 1963.

Kerr, William T., Jr. "The Progressives of Washington, 1910–1912." *Pacific Northwest Quarterly* 55 (Jan. 1964): 16–27.

Kornhauser, William. "'Power Elite' or 'Veto Groups'?" In Bell et al., eds., *Political Power: A Reader in Theory and Research*. New York: Free Press, 1969, pp. 42–52; Marvin Olson, ed., *Power in Societies*. New York: Macmillan, 1970, pp. 282–94.

McFarland, Andrew S. *Power and Leadership in Pluralistic Systems*. Stanford: Stanford University Press, 1969.

Marvick, Dwaine, ed. *Political Decisionmakers*. New York: Free Press, 1961.

Merelman, Richard M. "On the Neo-Elitist Critique of Community Power." *American Political Science Review* 62 (June 1968): 451–60.

Miller, Delbert C. "Democracy and Decision Making in the Community Power Structure." In *Power and Democracy in America*, edited by William V. D'Antonio and Howard J. Ehrlich, pp. 25–72. Notre Dame: University of Notre Dame Press, 1961.

Mills, C. Wright. *The Power Elite*. New York: Oxford University Press, 1956.

Olson, Marvin, ed. *Power in Societies*. New York: Macmillan, 1970.

Parsons, Talcott. "The Distribution of Power in American Society." In *C. Wright Mills and the Power Elite*, compiled by G. William Domhoff and Hoyt B. Ballard, pp. 60–87. Boston: Beacon Press, 1968.

Perry, Geraint. *Political Elites*. New York: F. A. Praeger, 1969.

Polsby, Nelson W. *Community Power and Political Theory*. New Haven: Yale University Press, 1963.

———. "Community Power: Some Reflections on the Recent Literature." *American Sociological Review* 27 (Dec. 1962): 838–41.

———. "How to Study Community Power: The Pluralistic Alternative." *Journal of Politics* 22 (Aug. 1960): 474–84.

———. "Three Problems in the Analysis of Community Power." *American Sociological Review* 24 (Dec. 1959): 796–803.

Potts, E. Daniel. "The Progressive Profile in Iowa." *Mid-America* 47 (Oct. 1965): 257–68.

Presthus, Robert V. *Men at the Top: A Study in Community Power*. New York: Oxford University Press, 1964.

Rossi, Peter H. "Power and Community Structure." In Terry Clark, ed., *Community Structure and Decision Making: Comparative Analysis*, pp. 129–38. San Francisco: Chandler, 1968.

Schulze, Robert O. "The Role of Economic Determinants in Community Power." *American Sociological Review* 23 (Feb. 1958): 3–9.

Seligman, Lester G. "Elite Recruitment and Political Development." *Journal of Politics* 26 (Aug. 1964): 612–26.

————. "Political Change: Legislative Elites and Parties in Oregon." *Western Political Quarterly* 17 (June 1964): 177–87.

Sorauf, Frank J. *Party Politics in America*. Boston: Little Brown and Co., 1968.

Stone, Lawrence. "Prosopography." *Daedalus* 100 (Winter 1971): 46–79.

Walker, Jack L. "A Critique of the Elitist Theory of Democracy." *American Political Science Review* 60 (June 1966): 285–95.

Walton, John T. "Development Decision Making: A Comparative Study in Latin America." *American Journal of Sociology* 75 (March 1970): 828–51.

————. "Substance and Artifact: The Current Status of Research on Community Power Structure." *American Journal of Sociology* 71 (Jan. 1966): 430–38.

Welsh, William A. "Methodological Problems in the Study of Political Leadership in Latin America." *Latin American Research Review* 5 (Fall 1970): 3–34.

Wolfinger, Raymond E. "Nondecisions and the Study of Local Politics." *American Political Science Review* 65 (Dec. 1971): 1063–80.

————. "A Plea for a Decent Burial." *American Sociological Review* 27 (Dec. 1962): 841–47.

————. *The Politics of Progress*. Englewood Cliffs, N.J.: Prentice Hall, 1974.

————. "Rejoinder." *American Political Science Review* 65 (Dec. 1971): 1102–4.

————. "Reputation and Reality in the Study of Community Power." *American Sociological Review* 25 (Oct. 1960): 636–44.

Biography and Genealogy

Anywhere So Long As There Be Freedom: Charles Carroll of Carrollton, His Family and His Maryland. Baltimore: Baltimore Museum of Art, 1975.

Baroway, Aaron. "The Cohens of Maryland." *Maryland Historical Magazine* 18 (Dec. 1923): 357–76; 19 (March 1924): 54–77.

————. "Solomon Etting." *Maryland Historical Magazine* 15 (March 1920): 1–20.

Bohner, Charles H. *John Pendleton Kennedy: Gentleman from Baltimore*. Baltimore: The Johns Hopkins Press, 1961.

Bruchey, Stuart W. *Robert Oliver: Merchant of Baltimore, 1783–1819*. Baltimore: The Johns Hopkins Press, 1956.

Cassell, Frank A. *Merchant Congressman in the Young Republic: Samuel Smith of Maryland, 1752–1839*. Madison: University of Wisconsin Press, 1971.

Delaplaine, Edward S. *Francis Scott Key: Life and Times*. Brooklyn, N.Y.: Biography Press, 1917.

Holdcraft, Jacob M. *Names in Stone*. 2 vols. Ann Arbor: n.p., 1966.

Howard, Carey. "John Eager Howard: Patriot and Public Servant." *Maryland Historical Magazine* 62 (Sept. 1967): 300–317.

Johnston, Christopher. "Key Family." *Maryland Historical Magazine* 5 (June 1910): 194–200.

———. "Lloyd Family." *Maryland Historical Magazine* 7 (Dec. 1912): 420–30.

Lewis, Walker. *Without Fear or Favor: Biography of Roger B. Taney*. Boston: Houghton Mifflin, 1965.

Maryland Daughters of the American Revolution. "St. Paul's Episcopal Church Graveyard." *Maryland Genealogical Records Commission* 34 (1961–64).

Mason, John T., Jr., ed. *Life of John Van Lear McMahon*. Baltimore: E. C. Didier, 1879.

"The Plater Family." *Maryland Historical Magazine* 2 (Dec. 1907): 370–72.

Shriver, Samuel S., comp. and ed. *History of the Shriver Family and Their Connections, 1684–1888*. Baltimore: Guggenheimer, Weil, and Co., 1888.

Silverson, Katherine T. *Taney and Allied Families: A Genealogical Study with Biographical Notes*. New York: American Historical Society, 1935.

Steiner, Bernard C. "General John Spear Smith." *Maryland Historical Magazine* 19 (Sept. 1924): 213–20.

———. *Life of Reverdy Johnson*. Baltimore: Norman, Remington Co., 1935.

———. *Life of Roger B. Taney*. Baltimore: Williams and Wilkins Co., 1922.

Stone, Richard G. *H. Niles as an Economist*. Johns Hopkins University Studies in Historical and Political Science, no. 51. Baltimore: The Johns Hopkins Press, 1933.

Swisher, Carl B. *Roger B. Taney*. New York: Macmillan Co., 1935.

Williams, Stephen W. *The Genealogy and History of the Family of Williams*. Greenfield: Merriam and Merrick, 1847.

Historical Works

Allen, Ethan. *Historical Sketches of St. Paul's Parish*. 2 vols. n.p.: n.p., 1855.

American Council of Learned Societies. "Report of the Committee on Linguistic and National Stocks in the Population of the United States." In *Annual Report of the American Historical Association for the Year 1931*, vol. 4. Washington, D.C.: U.S. Government Printing Office, 1931.

Asplund, John. *The Universal Register of the Baptist Denomination in North America. For the Years, 1790, 1791, 1792, 1793, and Part of 1794*. n.p.: John W. Folsom, 1794.

———. *The Universal Annual Register of the Baptist Denomination in North America for the Year, 1794 and 1795*. Hanover, N.H.: Dunham and True, 1796.

Barker, Charles A. *The Background of the Revolution in Maryland*. New Haven: Yale University Press, 1940.

Brief Outline of the Rise, Progress, and Failure of the Nineteen Van Buren Electors of the Senate of Maryland. Baltimore: Sands and Neilson, 1837.

Carothers, Bettie S., comp. *Maryland Slave Owners and Superintendents, 1798*. 2 vols. n.p.:n.p., 1974.

Carroll, Kenneth. *Quakerism on the Eastern Shore*. Baltimore: Maryland Historical Society, 1970.

Cassell, Frank A. "General Samuel Smith and the Election of 1800." *Maryland Historical Magazine* 63 (Dec. 1968): 341–59.

———. "The Structure of Baltimore's Politics in the Age of Jefferson, 1795–1812." In *Law, Society, and Politics in Early Maryland*, edited by Aubrey C. Land, Lois G. Carr, and Edward C. Papenfuse, pp. 277–96. Baltimore: Johns Hopkins University Press, 1977.

Chase, James S. *Emergence of the Presidential Nominating Convention, 1789–1832*. Urbana: University of Illinois Press, 1973.

Crowl, Philip A. *Maryland during and after the Revolution*. Baltimore: The Johns Hopkins Press, 1943.

Cunz, Dieter. *The Maryland Germans*. Princeton: Princeton University Press, 1948.

Doherty, Robert. *Society and Power: Five New England Towns, 1800–1860*. Amherst: University of Massachusetts Press, 1977.

[Duke, William]. *Observations of the Present State of Religion in Maryland*. Baltimore: Adams, 1795.

Easton District. *History of the Methodist Episcopal Church*. Easton: n.p., 1883.

Fischer, David H. *The Revolution of American Conservatism: The Federalist Party in the Era of Jeffersonian Democracy*. 1965; repr. New York: Harper and Row, 1969.

Formisano, Ronald P. "Deferential-Participant Politics: The Early Republic's Political Culture, 1789–1840." *American Political Science Review* 68 (June 1974): 473–87.

———. "Political Character, Antipartyism, and the Second Party System." *American Quarterly* 21 (Winter 1969): 683–709.

———. "Toward a Reorientation of Jacksonian Politics: A Review of the Literature, 1959–1975." *Journal of American History* 63 (June 1976): 42–65.

Gatell, Frank O. "Secretary Taney and the Baltimore Pets: A Study in Banking and Politics." *Business History Review* 35 (Summer 1965) 205–27.

———. "Spoils of the Bank War: Political Bias in the Selection of Pet Banks." *American Historical Review* 70 (Oct. 1965): 35–58.

Gould, Clarence P. "The Economic Causes of the Rise of Baltimore." In *Essays in Colonial History Presented to Charles McLean Andrews by His Students*, pp. 225–51. New Haven: Yale University Press, 1931.

Grimsted, David. "Democratic Rioting: A Case Study of the Baltimore Bank Mob of 1835." In *Insights and Parallels*, edited by William O. Neill, pp. 125–92. Minneapolis: Burgess Publishing Co., 1973.

———. "Rioting in Its Jacksonian Setting." *American Historical Review* 77 (April 1972): 361–97.

Hagensick, A. Clarke. "Revolution or Reform in 1836: Maryland's Preface to the Dorr Rebellion." *Maryland Historical Magazine* 57 (Dec. 1962): 346–66.

Haller, Mark H. "The Rise of the Jackson Party in Maryland, 1820–29." *Journal of Southern History* 28 (Aug. 1962): 307–26.

Hammond, Bray. *Banks and Politics in America: From the Revolution to the Civil War*. Princeton: Princeton University Press, 1967.

Hanna, Hugh S. *A Financial History of Maryland*. Johns Hopkins University Studies in Historical and Political Science, No. 25. Baltimore: Johns Hopkins Press, 1907.

Harry, James W. *The Maryland Constitution of 1851*. Johns Hopkins Studies in

Historical and Political Science, Ser. 21, Nos. 7–8. Baltimore: Johns Hopkins Press, 1902.

Hershberg, Theodore; Katz, Michael; Blumin, Stuart; Glasco, Lawrence; and Griffen, Clyde. "Occupation and Ethnicity in Five Nineteenth Century Cities: A Collaborative Inquiry." *Historical Methods Newsletter* 7 (June 1973): 174–216.

Hoffman, Ronald. *A Spirit of Dissension: Economics, Politics, and the Revolution in Maryland.* Baltimore: Johns Hopkins University Press, 1973.

Hofstader, Richard. *The Idea of a Party System.* Berkeley: University of California Press, 1972.

Holdcraft, Paul E. *The Old Otterbein Church Story.* New York: n.p., [1959].

Knights, Peter. *The Plain People of Boston.* New York: Oxford University Press, 1972.

Land, Aubrey C.; Carr, Lois G.; and Papenfuse, Edward C., eds. *Law, Society, and Politics in Early Maryland.* Baltimore: Johns Hopkins University Press, 1977.

Lee, Jesse. *A Short History of the Methodists in the U.S.A., 1776 . . . 1809.* Baltimore: Magill and Clime, 1810.

Levin, Alexander. "Two Jackson Supporters: Roger B. Taney and William Murdock Beall of Frederick." *Maryland Historical Magazine* 55 (Sept. 1960): 221–29.

Link, Eugene P. *Democratic-Republican Societies, 1790–1800.* New York: Columbia University Press, 1942.

Livermore, Shaw. *The Twilight of Federalism: The Disintegration of the Federalist Party, 1815–1830.* Princeton: Princeton University Press, 1962.

Livingood, James W. *The Philadelphia-Baltimore Trade Rivalry, 1780–1830.* Harrisburg: Pennsylvania Historical and Museum Commission, 1947.

Luxon, Norman N. *Niles Weekly Register: Magazine of the Nineteenth Century.* Baton Rouge: University of Louisiana Press, 1947.

McCormick, Richard P. *The Second American Party System: Party Formation in the Jacksonian Era.* Chapel Hill: University of North Carolina Press, 1966.

McCreary, George W. *The Ancient and Honorable Mechanical Company of Baltimore.* Baltimore: Kohn and Pollock, 1901.

Marrano, Howard R. "John Nelson's Mission to the Kingdom of the Two Sicilies, 1831–1832." *Maryland Historical Magazine* 44 (Sept. 1949): 149–76.

Mullikin, James C. "The Separatist Movement and Related Problems, 1776–1850." In *The Eastern Shore of Maryland and Virginia,* edited by Charles B. Clark, 3 vols., 1:453–84. New York: Lewis Historical Publications Co., 1950.

Mushkat, Jerome. *Tammany: The Evolution of a Political Machine.* Syracuse: Syracuse University Press, 1971.

Nisbet, Robert A. *The Sociological Tradition.* New York: Basic Books, Inc., 1966.

Persons, Stow. *The Decline of American Gentility.* New York: Columbia University Press, 1973.

Pessen, Edward. *Riches, Class, and Power before the Civil War.* Lexington, Mass.: D. C. Heath, 1973.

Pierson, George W. *Tocqueville in America.* 1938; repr. Gloucester, Mass.: Peter Smith, 1969.

Prince, Carl E. *The Federalists and the Origins of the U.S. Civil Service*. New York: New York University Press, 1977.

Reizenstein, Milton. *The Economic History of the Baltimore and Ohio Railroad, 1827–1853*. Johns Hopkins University Studies in Historical and Political Science, No. 15. Baltimore: Johns Hopkins Press, 1897.

Renzulli, L. Marx, Jr. *Maryland: The Federalist Years*. Rutherford, N.J.: Fairleigh Dickinson Press, 1972.

Ridgway, Whitman H. "McCulloch vs. the Jacksonians: Patronage and Politics in Maryland." *Maryland Historical Magazine* 70 (Winter 1975): 350–62.

_____. "Measuring Wealth and Power in Ante-Bellum America: A Review Essay." *Historical Methods Newsletter* 8 (March 1975): 75–78.

Rightmeyer, Nelson W. *Maryland's Established Church*. Lebanon, Pa.: Sowers Printing Co., 1956.

Risjord, Norman K. *The Old Republicans: Southern Conservatism in the Age of Jefferson*. New York: Columbia University Press, 1965.

Rose, Lisle A. *Prologue to Democracy: The Federalists in the South, 1789–1800*. Lexington: University of Kentucky Press, 1968.

Rothman, David J. *The Discovery of the Asylum: Social Order and Disorder in the New Republic*. Boston: Little, Brown and Co., 1971.

Sanderlin, Walter S. *The Great National Project: A History of the Chesapeake and Ohio Canal*. Baltimore: The Johns Hopkins Press, 1946.

Sapio, Victor. "Maryland's Federalist Revival, 1808–1812." *Maryland Historical Magazine* 64 (Spring 1969): 1–17.

Scharf, J. Thomas. *Chronicles of Baltimore*. Baltimore: Turnbull Brothers, 1874.

_____. *History of Baltimore City and County*. Philadelphia: Louis H. Everts, 1881.

_____. *History of Maryland*. 3 vols. Baltimore: John B. Piet, 1879.

_____. *History of Western Maryland*. 2 vols. Philadelphia: Louis H. Everts, 1882.

Scheiber, Harry N. "The Pet Banks in Jacksonian Politics and Finance, 1833–1841." *Journal of Economic History* 23 (June 1963): 196–214.

Skaggs, David C. *Roots of Maryland Democracy, 1753–1776*. Westport, Conn.: Greenwood, 1970.

Smith, Wilbur Wayne. "Jacksonian Democracy on the Chesapeake: Political Institutions." *Maryland Historical Magazine* 62 (Dec. 1967): 381–93.

_____. "Jacksonian Democracy on the Chesapeake: Class, Kinship, and Politics." *Maryland Historical Magazine* 63 (March 1968): 55–67.

Steiner, Bernard C. "The Electoral College for the Senate of Maryland and the Nineteen Van Buren Electors." American Historical Association, *Annual Report* 1895, pp. 129–67. Washington, D.C.: U.S. Government Printing Office, 1896.

Teeples, G. Ronald, comp. *Maryland: 1800 Census*. Provo, Utah: Accelerated Indexing Systems, 1973.

Tilghman, Oswald, comp. *History of Talbot County, Maryland, 1661–1861*. 2 vols. Baltimore: Williams and Wilkins Co., 1915.

Tocqueville, Alexis de. *Democracy in America*. Edited by J. P. Mayer; translated by George Lawrence. 1966; repr. Garden City, N.Y.: Doubleday and Co., 1969.

Ward, George W. *Early Development of the Chesapeake and Ohio Canal*. Johns Hopkins University Studies in Historical and Political Science, No. 17. Baltimore: Johns Hopkins Press, 1900.

Wentz, Abdel R. *The Lutheran Church of Frederick Maryland, 1738–1938*. Harrisburg, Pa.: Evangelical Press, 1938.

Wheeler, William B. "The Baltimore Jeffersonians, 1788–1800: A Profile of Intra-Factional Conflict." *Maryland Historical Magazine* 66 (Summer 1971): 153–68.

Williams, Thomas J. C. *History of Frederick County, Maryland*. 2 vols. 1910; repr. Baltimore: Regional Publishing Co., 1967.

Williamson, Chilton. *American Suffrage: From Property to Democracy, 1760–1860*. Princeton: Princeton University Press, 1960.

Wood, Gordon. *The Creation of the American Republic, 1776–1787*. 1969; repr. New York: W. W. Norton and Co., 1972.

Wooster, Ralph A. *The People in Power: Courthouse and Statehouse in the Lower South, 1850–60*. Knoxville: University of Tennessee Press, 1969.

_____. *Politicians, Planters, and Plain Folk: Courthouse and Statehouse in the Upper South, 1850–60*. Knoxville: University of Tennessee Press, 1975.

Theses and Dissertations

Bohmer, David A. "Voting Behavior during the First American Party System: Maryland, 1796–1816." Ph.D. dissertation, University of Michigan, 1974.

Brown, Dorothy. "Party Battles and Beginnings in Maryland." Ph.D. dissertation, Georgetown University, 1962.

Browne, Gary L. "Baltimore in the Nation, 1789–1861: A Social Economy in Industrial Revolution." Ph.D. dissertation, Wayne State University, 1973.

Clark, Dennis R. "Baltimore, 1729–1829: The Genesis of a Community." Ph.D. dissertation, Catholic University of America, 1976.

Clemens, Paul. "From Tobacco to Grain: Economic Development on Maryland's Eastern Shore, 1660–1774." Ph.D. dissertation, University of Wisconsin, 1974.

Gilbert, Claire W. "Community Power Structure: A Study in the Sociology of Knowledge." Ph.D. dissertation, Northwestern University, 1966.

Haller, Mark H. "The Rise of the Jackson Party in Maryland, 1820–1830." Master's thesis, University of Maryland, 1953.

Haw, James. "Politics in Revolutionary Maryland, 1753–1788." Ph.D. dissertation, University of Virginia, 1972.

Kutolowski, Kathleen S. "The Social Composition of Political Leadership: Genesee County, New York, 1821–60." Ph.D. dissertation, University of Rochester, 1973.

Leipheimer, Robert E. "Maryland Political Leadership, 1789–1860." Master's thesis, University of Maryland, 1969

Ranneberger, Michael E. "Samuel Chase: Federalist." Master's thesis, University of Virginia, 1973.

Ridgway, Whitman H. "A Social Analysis of Maryland Community Elites, 1827–

1836: A Study of the Distribution of Power in Baltimore City, Frederick County, and Talbot County." Ph.D. dissertation, University of Pennsylvania, 1973.

Smith, Wilbur Wayne. "The Whig Party in Maryland, 1826–1856." Ph.D. dissertation, University of Maryland, 1967.

Verstandig, Lee L. "The Emergence of the Two-Party System in Maryland, 1787–1796." Ph.D. dissertation, Brown University, 1970.

Votto, LeRoy J. "Social Dynamism in Boom-Town: The Scots-Irish in Baltimore, 1760–1790." Master's thesis, University of Virginia, 1969.

Wheeler, William B. "Urban Politics in Nature's Republic: The Development of Political Parties in the Seaport Cities in the Federalist Era." Ph.D. dissertation, University of Virginia, 1967.

Index

411